Homophones and Homographs
FOURTH EDITION

Homophones and Homographs

An American Dictionary

FOURTH EDITION

Compiled by

James B. Hobbs

McFarland & Company, Inc., Publishers
Jefferson, North Carolina, and London

Library of Congress Cataloguing-in-Publication Data

Hobbs, James B., 1930–
Homophones and homographs : an American dictionary /
compiled by James B. Hobbs.—4th ed.
p.   cm.
Includes bibliographical references.

ISBN-13: 978-0-7864-2488-7
ISBN-10: 0-7864-2488-5 (illustrated case binding : 50# alkaline paper)

1. English language—United States—Homonyms—Dictionaries.
2. Americanisms—Dictionaries. I. Title.
PE2833.H63 2006   423'.1—dc22   2006006090

British Library cataloguing data are available

Manufactured in the United States of America

*McFarland & Company, Inc., Publishers
Box 611, Jefferson, North Carolina 28640
www.mcfarlandpub.com*

Table of Contents

Preface

This fourth edition represents a 24-year work-in-progress that originated with a 7-year-old youngster bringing home in the spring of 1982 his class assignment to generate the most homophones possible, like **rain, reign, rein,** within a week. The short-term downer was that his second-place 279 words fell 77 short of the victor's list. The longer term benefit is that his effort jump-started the process that has resulted in 9040 homophones furnished below, plus a bonus of 2133 homographs (like **tear, number, minute**).

This compiler examined each of the 219 sources noted in the bibliography, and solved countless *New York Times* and *Wall Street Journal* crossword puzzles, to glean what comprises this volume. Warranting special mention are two treasure houses of bona fide, or near-, homophones and homographs: John H. Bechtel's 1904 compilation, and Russell H. Goddard's 1999 assemblage and idiosyncratic insights toward researching these phenomena. Probably in excess of four million entries have been reviewed since 1982. Still sources undoubtedly remain unexamined; and I keep pencil and note pad aside the bedstead to jot down thoughts to verify or discard come daybreak.

Although intended to be the most complete and accurate dictionary of this type currently available, I make no claim that it is "the last word." Several homophone and homograph candidates have almost certainly been overlooked during the eyestrain and physical exertion required in examining 13-pound unabridged reference works and their thinner kin. My current best estimate of when this project in American English *may* approach closure is about 11,000 homophones and 3000 homographs. We shall see.

Plaudits and grateful acknowledgment are offered to several individuals who assisted in bringing these four editions to fruition during these 24 years. David C. Weisman, who brought home that second grade assignment, is now a well established neurologist and married with two splendid daughters. Melody, his mother, in addition to suggesting early on that homographs be included in this dictionary, kept safe work-in-process and manuscripts at critical junctures. Peg, my wife, furnished several homophones and homographs associated with her fibre-art creativity, such as **couch, ruffer, sliver, sley,** and **weave.** Her endurance and tolerance were frequently tested while her spouse's nose was ensconced in one or more reference works. Her frequent remark: "The process resembled watching grass grow and flies flit."

Among colleagues at Lehigh University who supplied helpful suggestions and valuable assistance were the late Frank S. Hook, professor emeritus of English, who was well known for his stimulating course entitled simply "Words"; the late David M. Greene, also professor emeritus of English; the late John A. Van Erde, professor emeritus of modern languages and literature; the late R. Allen Moran, associate professor of economics; Eli Schwartz, Charles W. MacFarlane professor emeritus of theoretical economics, and Robert J. Thornton, Charles W. MacFarlane professor of economics, both of whom enjoy backgrounds in etymology and classical languages; Max D. Snider, professor emeritus of marketing and associate dean emeritus of the college of business and economics; Marie-Sophie Armstrong and Mary A. Nichols, both associate professors of modern languages and literature; Herbert Rubenstein, professor emeritus of psycholinguistics; and Albert (Tommy) Wilansky, university distinguished professor emeritus of mathematics, who furnished several bona fide homophones and homographs, including **brother** (male sibling and soup maker) and **mother** (female parent and collector of moths) which make appearances in this edition.

Those also at Lehigh include William F. Finke and Pat Ward, who rendered detective assistance over these many years in securing numerous references and hard-to-obtain texts through interlibrary loan; Robert Kendi, Revelly Paul, Judith Moran, Sharon Ruhf, Janice Schaeffer, Rene Hollinger, and Diane Oechsle, each of whom provided patient aid and comfort at crucial points in manipulating computer programs, word-processing technicalities, and locating several rich repositories of literature relevant to this endeavor.

Elsewhere in the world are contributors to this labor of love: John D. Hitchcock of Laramie, Wyoming; Felicia Lamport of Cambridge, Massachusetts; Sybil P. Parker at the McGraw-Hill Book Company; John L. Turner of Scotts Valley, California; Richard A. Schaphorst of Jenkintown, Pennsylvania; Jule Shipman of Doylestown, Pennsylvania: and Doug Fink, a compiler of numerous homphones. The late Russell H. Godard of Corvallis, Oregon, made a unique contribution with his eagle-eye for detail, fantastic memory recall, and idiosyncratic approaches to the collection of homophones and homographs. Drs. William Davis of Newark, Delaware, and Bevan J. Clarke, professor of accountancy and management information systems at the University of Canterbury in Christchurch, New Zealand, both evince insatiable and contagious curiosity in a variety of intellectual endeavors.

Finally, I extend thanks to each author and editor cited in the annotated bibliography that appears at the end of this dictionary. Their contributions confirm the research adage: "We can rise higher only atop the shoulders of predecessors." And the offer still stands of awarding $1 for each bona fide homophone or homograph furnished to this compiler that does not appear in these pages.

J. B. H.
Bethlehem, Pennsylvania

Overview of Homophones and Homographs

This brief orientation addresses several aspects of homophones and homographs to provide context and perspective for these phenomena: definitions; the "Conflict of Homophones" controversy; criteria for including and excluding words in this volume; notational devices and phonetic symbols used hereafter; and the organization of the dictionary. Some final thoughts precede the detailed listing of words.

Definitions

This dictionary focuses on American homophones and homographs, and is based on pronunciations that prevail in most areas of the United States. Briefly and precisely, a **homophone** is a word that is pronounced the same as another (a "sound-alike" or an aural/oral echo) but which differs in spelling *and* meaning, such as **cite, sight,** and **site.** A **homograph**, on the other hand, is a word that is spelled the same as another (a "look-alike" or visual echo) but which differs in sound *and* meaning, such as **tear** (to separate or pull apart) and **tear** (a secretion from the eye). The relationship and significance of these two classes of words in the English language may be more clearly understood by referring to the diagram on the following page, which divides all English words into eight categories according to the three characteristics of sound (or pronunciation), spelling, and meaning. The third group, **homonym,** is a word that has the same sound *and* spelling but has more than one meaning, such as **set,** which may possess the largest number of different meanings of any English word.

The sharp distinction between the first three categories in the diagram is adopted in this dictionary because the definitions for those terms in *Webster's Third New International Dictionary of the English Language Unabridged* (which nevertheless is a key reference work for this particular dictionary) are ambiguous and overlapping:

Category	A word with the same/similar (+) or different (-) following characteristic as another:			Comment or example
	Sound	Spelling	Meaning	
1. **Homonym**	+	+	-	A huge number of words comprise this category, such as **plane**: a tool for smoothing, a type of tree, to skim across water, or to soar in air
2. **Homophone** ("sound-alike" or aural/oral echo)	+	-	-	A considerable number of words (over 9000 in this dictionary) make up this category, such as **right, rite, wright** and **write**
3. **Homograph** ("look-alike" or visual echo)	-	+	-	Many words (over 2100 in this dictionary) comprise this category, such as **bass** (a fish) and **bass** (a low voice)
4. **Synonym**	-	-	+	A large number of words fall into this category such as **pig, hog** and **swine** or **serpent** and **snake**
5. **Heterograph** (not a universal definition)	+	-	+	Very few words are in this category, such as **comptroller/controller, czar/tsar, drachm/dram,** and **china/quina**
6. **Heterophone** (not a universal definition)	-	+	+	Many words have alternate pronunciations, such as **either, garage,** and **potato***
7. **No formal designation**	-	-	-	A vast number of words fall into this category, each of which is unique with respect to sound, spelling, and meaning
8. **No formal designation**	+	+	+	This category is probably empty, since no two words could have all three characteristics in common yet be considered distinct words

*either—ˈēthər or ˈithər
garage—gəˈrazh or gəˈräj or ˈga räzh or ˈgarij
potato—pəˈtādō or pəˈtädō

Homonym: One of two or more words spelled and pronounced alike, but different in meaning. A homophone or homograph.

Homophone: One of two or more words pronounced alike but different in meaning or derivation or spelling. Also called homonym.

Homograph: One of two or more words spelled alike but differing in derivation or meaning or pronunciation. Also called homonym.

In short, these three *Webster's Third Unabridged* definitions confuse because they lack clarity.

Each of these three word categories should be sharply distinguished as shown in the diagram, and will be considered as such throughout this dictionary. (Please note that the two "no formal designation" categories at the bottom of the diagram are included merely to present all eight possibilities that arise because of the three characteristics—sound, spelling, and meaning.)

The "Conflict of Homophones" Controversy

Many languages are blessed or burdened, depending on one's viewpoint, with homophones and homographs. The world champion for number of homophones is probably Chinese, partially as a result of its subtle voice inflections, facial gestures, and other almost imperceptible nuances. But the English language has more than many others, for several reasons. First, English has borrowed liberally from other languages. For example, each of **air**, **err**, and **heir** stems from Middle English, Old French, and Latin. Second, the English and Americans have a penchant for shortening words, which itself creates numerous homophones, such as **plane** (from airplane) which is homophonous with **plain**, or **ads** (from advertisements) which is homophonous with **adds** and **adz(e)**. Third, some homophones are created by converting proper names to specific things, like (James) **Joule** which is homophonous with **jewel**. Fourth, the prevalence of acronyms in America and elsewhere generates numerous homophones, such as **WAACS** (Women's Army Auxiliary Corps), homophonic with **whacks** and **wax**. Finally, sound changes occur through a process known as assimilation, by which the "d" in **chased** approaches the "t" in **chaste**, or the distinction between **ladder** and **latter** becomes almost imperceptible in normal conversation. This last phenomenon frequently results in the creation of puns or double entendres. For example: "The seriously chased are seldom chaste for long" or its equally valid reversal, "The seriously chaste are seldom chased for long."

Several linguistic and language scholars have addressed a more sophisticated question: Do homophones, whether in English or any language, tend to self-destruct because of their apparent tendency to create confusion and ambiguity? Jules Gilliéron advanced a doctrine between 1902 and 1921 which stated that two words of different origin that become homophones by regular sound-changes may, because of ambiguity and confusion, interfere with each other to such an extent that one is ultimately driven from the vocabulary of a particular dialect. This doctrine or hypothesis is referred to as the "Conflict of Homophones."

Professor Robert Menner of Yale University addressed this concept in 1936, arguing that if a word that had become homophonous with another were lost, the loss should not be attributed solely to homophonic conflict without observing two rules of caution. First, two homophones are unlikely to interfere unless they belong to the same part of speech. A verb is unlikely to conflict with a noun, or a noun with an adjective. Second, the words must fall within the same sphere of ideas and be likely to appear in similar contexts. If these two conditions are fulfilled, Menner asserted, it is possible that a combination of like sounds representing two different words could become ambiguous, and the resultant confusion so marked as to lead to the elimination of one of the words. But Menner stated further that even if a homophone were lost due to these circumstances, it would be difficult to prove that homophony was the sole determinant. Other and more usual causes of obsolescence, such as changes in popularity, style, or frequency of use, must first be ruled out—a process that is difficult because such changes are often obscure and elusive.

Julian Franklyn (see his citation in the annotated bibliography) stressed the point in 1966 that homophony tends to be local in time as well as in space. "Homophones of 1764 are not quite the same as those of 1964; and homophones north of Trent differ from those recognized south of that select boundary." In short, **aunt** and **ant** may be homophonous for some, while others would insist that **aunt** must properly rhyme with **font** or **taunt**, but never with the insect.

Professor Edna Rees Williams of Smith College reinforced many of these key points in her 1936 doctoral dissertation (with Professor Menner chairing her dissertation committee). Dr. Williams argued that words become subject to mutual confusion and conflict due to homophony only when the words concerned (a) are alike in sound, (b) are in common use in the same social and intellectual circles, and (c) perform the same syntactical functions in the language within a common sphere of ideas. She observed that the conflict of homophones is only one of many alleged causes of word loss, and one of the least frequent relative to the vast number lost in English. Seldom, she summarized, are circumstances so simple and obvious that we may say without debate that the loss of a word had a single cause. The most that can be said is that homophony may have been one contributing factor, or perhaps in some cases almost certainly the main factor, that led to the unpopularity of certain terms and the disappearance of others.

Criteria for Including and Excluding Words

This lexicographer believes it is ill-advised to limit oneself to a single reference work in searching for and verifying definitions, phonetics, and spellings for homophones and homographs. Our language is far too complex, subtle, and nuanced to regard one particular group of professionals, however competent they may be, as having the sole touchstone for credibility and insight. Those of different persuasion are cautioned to not read far beyond this sentence lest their preconceptions be challenged or horizons extended.

Three dictionaries served as principal authorities for entries contained in this dictionary: *The Random House Dictionary of the English Language,* 2nd edition unabridged, 1987; *Webster's New International Dictionary of the English Language*, 2nd edition unabridged, 1949; and *Webster's Third New International Dictionary of the English Language Unabridged*, 1981. *Webster's Third* played the central role with respect to spelling, pronunciation, phonetics, and definitions. In particular cases, other dictionaries cited in the annotated bibliography were consulted to arbitrate differences and disparities, particularly the 20-volume *The Oxford English Dictionary*, 2nd edition.

With respect to **homophones**, at least one pronunciation had to be common to two or more homophonic candidates for them to be included in this dictionary as bona fide homophones. With respect to **homographs**, on the other hand, at least one pronunciation of homographic candidates had to be dissimilar for words to be listed as bona fide homographs. In general, r's were not "dropped" (as is prevalent in New England) to create homophones or homographs, such as dropping the r from **car** to make it homophonic with **caw.** Nor were r's added, such as **idea(r)** to create a homophone or homograph. Neither were h's dropped to make words homophonic or homographic, such as dropping the "h" from **heady** or **hitch** to make them homophonic with **eddy** or **itch,** respectively.

Words that are deemed near-but-unacceptable homophones and homographs are those whose meanings are similar, closely related, or stem from the same basic word-root, but differ primarily in grammatical usage, such as **absence/absents** or **abuse** (the noun)/**abuse** (the verb). These are classified hereafter as **GROUP I** homophones or homographs. Near-but-unacceptable homophones with close but perceptible different pronunciations are classified as **GROUP II**, such as **loose** ('lüs) and **lose** ('lüz). A few homophones, such as **mystic** and **mystique**, are near-but-unacceptable because they fall into both **GROUP I** and **II**.

Even the casual reader will observe that an exhaustive listing of all meanings and nuances of a particular homophone or homograph is not included in that word's definition due to lack of space. Not included, for example, are the more than 114 different definitions for **set** depending on whether it is used as a transitive or intransitive verb, noun, or adjective. Nor are suffixes added to homophones merely to lengthen listings, such as **sew** (then **sewed, sewing, sews**) or **sow** (then **sowed, sowing, sows**).

In general, the following words are excluded from this dictionary: obsolete, archaic, and rarely used words; words associated primarily with regional dialects, especially those restricted to England, Scotland, and small regions of the United States; most colloquialisms, although several slang expressions are included; proper names, such as **Claude** (homophonic with **clawed**), **Jim (gym),** and **Mary (merry)**; and most units of foreign money, weight, and measurement, except such familiar ones as the former English **shilling**, French **franc,** and Italian **lira.** On the other hand, several countries, provinces, major cities, nationalities, and racial groups are included—the rationale being that recognition of distinctive regions and peoples of Earth might help broaden a sometimes parochial or provincial American perspective. On rare occasion, foreign terms that are generally widespread and readily understood in this country, such as the French **oui** or the Spanish **sí** for "yes," are included.

Some readers may take exception to two other decisions this compiler has made for inclusion in this dictionary: considering a hyphenated word as a different spelling from its unhyphenated relative, such as the homophones **recoil/re-coil**; and treating capitalized and lower-case words, such as the homographs **Ara/ara,** as two separate entries. Critical readers are invited to respectfully disagree.

Notational Devices and Phonetic Symbols

Homophones and homographs are arranged alphabetically within their respective categories. All homophones are cross-referenced in alphabetical order, but the definition of each is given only once, where it first appears. For example, **abeyance** and **obeyance** are grouped together and defined at their original appearance in the A section. **Obeyance** then reappears without definition after **obe** in the O section, with parenthetical reference to "see **abeyance**."

An <u>underlined word</u> is both homophone and homograph.

Recall that Group I homophones and homographs (which follow bona fide homophone and homograph entries) are near-but-unacceptable homophones and homographs whose meanings are closely related, similar, or stem from the same basic word root, and differ primarily in grammatical usage. Group II homophones are also near-but-unacceptable homophones because of close but perceptibly different pronunciations. Some homophones are both Group I and II.

The following pronunciation symbols and notations are adapted from *Webster's Third New International Dictionary of the English Language Unabridged* and used throughout this dictionary. (Because of their complexity, formidableness, and general unfamiliarity, symbols and notational devices of the International Phonetic Alphabet were not adopted.)

a	…	cat
à	…	cart, as pronounced by "r-droppers"
ä	…	cot
ā	…	fade
ar	…	care
aú	…	**out**
e	…	bed
ē	…	feed
i	…	silver or ear
ī	…	side
ŋ	…	sing
ȯ	…	saw
ȯi	…	oil
ȯ(ə)r	…	**orb**
ō	…	tone
th	…	ether
<u>th</u>	…	either

ə	...	c**u**rb, Americ**a**, or immediately preceding l, m, n, and ŋ, p, or s—as in kitten
ə̇	...	unstressed variant, as in hab**i**t
u̇	...	w**oo**d
ü	...	t**oo**l
œ	...	French **ue**
yu̇	...	c**u**rable
yü	...	f**ew**
ⁿ	...	the preceding vowel is pronounced with the nasal passages open, as in French vi**n** bla**n**c
'	...	the mark preceding a syllable with the primary (stronger) stress, as in **'book** keeper
ˌ	...	the mark preceding a syllable with the secondary (weaker) stress, as in 'bookˌ**keeper**
:	...	the mark preceding a syllable whose stress can vary between primary and secondary
ǀ	...	indicates the placement of a variant pronunciation, such as **quart**, 'kwȯrǀt or 'kwȯrtǀ
•	...	the mark of syllable division that is inserted in a sequence of sounds which can have more than one syllable division, such as **nitrite**, 'nī•trīt or 'nīt•rīt

Diacritics are used at appropriate points throughout this volume to assist pronunciation. Some linguists might say these marks are an integral part of the spelling, so that, for example, **charge** and **chargé** are two distinct spellings rather than variant pronunciations of the same spelling. The reader may elect to allow or disallow "diacriticized" words bearing the following accent marks as bona fide homographs:

acute—á—the vowel is pronounced with a rise in pitch
cedilla—ç—placed under a letter to indicate a sound different from its normal usage
circumflex—â—the vowel is pronounced with a rising-then-falling tone
grave—à—the vowel is pronounced with a fall in pitch
macron—ā—the vowel is pronounced with a "long" sound
tilde—ñ—in Spanish, to indicate the sound **n**ʸ
umlaut—ü—partial assimilation with a succeeding sound

Organization of the Dictionary

Alphabetized homophones are presented first, on pages 14 through 292, followed by alphabetized homographs, beginning on page 294. The table on page 10 summarizes the number of homophones and homographs listed under the respective letters of the alphabet. For example, a total of 440 homophones begin with **a**, of which 63 are one-syllable, and so on; 176 homographs begin with **a**. The rightmost column indicates the number of words that are both homophonic and homographic.

| | Total words | Homophones | | | | Homographs | Homophones* *and* Homographs* |
		1-syllable words	2-syllable words	3-syllable words	4–6 syllable words		
A	441	63	182	134	62	176	14
B	715	343	335	31	6	146	36
C	1113	330	559	166	58	278	43
D	383	147	189	35	12	80	16
E	169	36	65	54	14	49	5
F	354	178	139	36	1	57	13
G	376	192	166	16	2	78	16
H	297	139	136	16	6	66	9
I	133	16	47	47	23	32	—
J	92	55	33	2	2	29	—
K	232	101	116	14	1	27	4
L	375	166	175	28	6	99	23
M	512	178	253	67	14	178	34
N	174	74	87	11	2	37	10
O	153	38	56	49	10	30	6
P	796	276	370	106	44	201	35
Q	71	34	35	2	—	8	3
R	485	181	236	68	—	121	25
S	891	388	409	70	24	192	39
T	558	231	264	47	16	143	30
U	195	11	99	69	16	46	—
V	95	27	49	11	8	30	5
W	351	227	114	8	2	18	6
X	14	3	8	3	—	—	—
Y	47	33	14	—	—	8	—
Z	18	7	8	3	—	4	—
Total	9040	3474	4144	1093	329	2133	372

*These words are also included in their respective categories at the left.

An appendix beginning on page 351 lists the following notable word groupings:

- Homophones—five or more 1-syllable words, the largest number being three 8-word groupings: **cees, c's, psis, seas, sees, seize, sis, Szis; lais, lase, lays, laze, leas, leis, les, leys,** and **raise, rase, rays, raze, rehs, reis, res, reys**

    —four or more 2-syllable words, the largest number being the 7-word grouping **Male, Mali, Mal(l)ie, maulie, molle, molly, moly**

    —three or more 3-syllable words, the largest number being one unarguable 5-word grouping: **manacan, manakin, manikin, mannequin, mannikin**

    —all 4-, 5-, and 6-syllable words, including one unarguable triplet: **androgenous, androgynous, androgynus.** Two pairs of 6-syllable homophones are **synechological, synecological,** and **uncomplementary, uncomplimentary**
- Homographs—three or more words each with a different pronunciation, the largest being three 4-word groupings: **papa, pate,** and **Rabat/rabat**
- All words that are both homophonic and homographic

The final section is the annotated bibliography reflecting 219 references that were consulted in compiling this edition of the dictionary.

Some Final Thoughts

So, why this fascination with such oddities as homophones and homographs? First and very simply, they are interesting, fun, and often lead to humorous insights into the language. Shakespeare's works are replete with punnery. Second and perhaps more important, examination of them and "why they are and have come to be" provides many clues for understanding the frequent observation that English is extremely difficult to learn for persons born and raised in another language and culture. For example, in Spanish, which is almost totally phonetic, an **a, e, i, o,** or **u** is almost always pronounced the same wherever it appears, *viz.,* ä, ā, ē, ō, ü, respectively. Not so in English, where an **a** is pronounced differently in cat, cart, caught, awesome, banana, and care. Third, detailed examination of homophones and homographs provides a valuable tool for obtaining a richer, deeper perspective with which to attack and comprehend the structure of any language—foreign or domestic—at its most fundamental level, *viz.,* phonetics.

For the statistically minded, the following comparative summary indicates the evolution of this dictionary with respect to number of homophones and homographs, ratio of homophones to homographs, and bibliographic sources:

Edition	Homophones	Homographs	Ratio of Homophones to Homographs	Bibliographic sources
1st	3625	602	6.0:1	42
2nd	7149	1469	4.9:1	97
3rd	7870	1554	5.1:1	131
4th	9040	2133	4.2:1	219

The tome appears to have grown in size and complexity.

When will the task of locating all homophones and homographs in English (or for that matter any language) be complete? First and foremost, the language must cease evolving—which is quite unlikely. Language undergoes continual change, with new words arriving, old ones departing, and some lying dormant pending revival or burial. Pronunciations and meanings often shift, sometimes almost imperceptibly. Second, to thoroughly capture and evaluate all homophones and homographs in English, one would need to phoneticize every word, including all alternate pronunciations and suffixes. Then one would have to enter that vast accumulation into a computer database, identify each possible phonetic combination, and finally match up all words whose phonetics are identical. An added requirement: maintain that compilation as long as the language exists. An awesome and probably unfathomable task!

Homophones

A

a an indefinite article
ay an expression of sorrow or regret
eh an expression of inquiry or slight surprise

a an indefinite article
ugh an expression of disgust or horror; the sound of a cough or grunt

a(a)h an expression of delight, relief, regret, or contempt
I a personal pronoun

aal Indian mulberry, an East Indian shrub or small tree with axillary heads of flowers and pulpy fruit
all the entire amount
awl a pointed tool

Ab in Egyptian religion, the spirit of the physical heart and the seat of the will and intentions
abb coarse wool from the inferior parts of a fleece

aba A loose sleeveless Arabian garment
Abba an honorific title given to the Deity, bishops, partriarchs, and Jewish scholars

abaisse a thin undercrust of pastry
abase to lower or reduce in rank or esteem

abb (see **Ab**)

Abba (see **aba**)

abele a white poplar tree
able possessing resources needed to accomplish an objective

abeyance temporary inactivity or suppression
obeyance an act or custom of obeying

able (see **abele**)

absence lack of contact between blades, in fencing
absents keeps away

absinthin a bitter white crystalline compound constituting the active ingredient of wormwood
absinthine a moderate yellow green color

absorbance the measurable capacity of a substance to absorb radiation
absorbents liquids used in separating gases or volatile substances in gas manufacture and petroleum refining

Acacian relating to a schism occurring A.D. 484–519 between Eastern and Western Christian churches
acaciin a crystalline glycoside found in the leaves of a common North American locust tree

Acadian a native or inhabitant of Acadia; a French colony consisting principally of what is now Nova Scotia; a Louisianian descended from French-speaking immigrants from Acadia
Akkadian a Semitic inhabitant of Mesopotamia before 2000 B.C.

acanthin the substance, consisting of strontium sulphate, forming the internal skeleton of radiolarians
acanthine a basic compound obtained from the livers and embryos of the spiny dogfish; resembling the leaves of an acanthus plant

acanthous bristling, sharp, or thorny
Acanthus a genus of prickly herbs of the Mediterranean

Acarus a genus of arachnids including a number of small mites
Acorus a genus of rushlike herbs with the flowers in a close spadix

accede to express approval or give consent
exceed to surpass, excel, or outdo

accept to take without protest
except to omit something

accepter a person who takes without protest

acceptor a substance or particle capable of combining with another substance or particle; a circuit that combines inductance and capacitance in series so as to resonate to a given impressed frequency

access a way to approach or reach
excess an amount exceeding the usual or normal

accidence a part of grammar that deals with inflections
accidens any fortuitous or nonessential property, fact, or circumstance
accidents sudden events that occur without intent

acclamation a loud eager expression of approval, praise, or assent
acclimation a physiological adjustment to a change in the environment

accouter to equip or fit out
acuter a sharper point or angle

ace a playing card ranking highest in its suit; a person who excels at something
Ais a people in the Indian river valley, Florida
ase an enzyme

acephalous having the style issuing from the base instead of from the apex of the ovary
acephalus a headless fetal monster

Aceria a large genus of eriophyid mites including several parasites of economic plants
Assyria an ancient empire of western Asia

acetic related to acetic acid or vinegar
ascetic extremely strict in religious exercises
Ossetic relating to or characteristic of the Ossets, a tall Aryan people of central Caucasus

acher a person who suffers a dull persistent and throbbing pain

acre a unit of measure in the U.S. and England equal to 43,560 square feet or 160 square rods

Achillean like Achilles in strength, invincibility, moodiness, or resentful wrath
achilleine a brownish red bitter alkaloid

achy afflicted with aches
aikie to lay claim to something; to demand equal division of something found

acidic sharp or biting to the taste; sour; tart
ascitic pertaining to or affected with a collection of serous fluid in the peritoneal cavity

Acorus (see **Acarus**)

acouchi a resin similar in nature to elemi and obtained from various South American trees
acouchy a small species of agouti

acre (see **acher**)

acrogenous increasing by growth from the summit or apex
acrogynous having the archegonia at the apex of the stem and involving the apical cells in their formation

acron the unsegmented part of the body in front of a segmented animal's mouth
Akron a city in northeastern Ohio

actin a protein of muscle
actine a star-shaped spicule, as of a sponge
acton a jacket plated with steel

acts performs
ax(e) a cutting tool

acuter (see **accouter**)

Adam the unregenerate nature of man; a style of furniture designed in the late 18th century
atom a minute particle of matter

adder a snake
attar a perfume obtained from flowers

addition a result of increasing or augmenting

edition a form in which a literary work is published

addle to throw into confusion or disorder

attle in mining, waste rock

adds joins or unites

ads notices to attract attention to a product or business

adz(e) a cutting tool

Adelea a large genus of protozoans that are parasitic on arthropods

Adelia a genus of tropical American shrubs with toothed leaves

adeps animal fats, such as the purified internal abdominal fats of a hog

adepts high skilled or well-trained individuals; experts

ades sweetened drinks

aides assistants

AIDS acquired immunodeficiency syndrome (an acronym)

aids helps

adherence steady or faithful attachment; continued observance

adherents persons who adhere to or follow; persons 14 years or older who are listed on the records of the Salvation Army but have not yet become soldiers

adieu an expression of farewell

ado bustling about

adjutant a staff officer acting as a general and administrative assistant to the commanding officer

agitant a person who is active in or furthering a course of action

ado (see **adieu**)

Adoptian relating to the doctrine that Jesus became the son of God by exaltation to a status that was not by his birth

adoption the taking of an outsider into a family, clan, or tribal group

ads (see **adds**)

adventuress a woman who schemes to win social position or wealth by unscrupulous or questionable means

adventurous inclined to engage in exciting or very unusual experiences

adz(e) (see **adds**)

aerial related to the air

areal relating to an area or an extent of space

ariel a small Australian flying marsupial; an Arabian gazelle

aerie a high eagle's or hawk's nest

aery having an aerial quality

airy resembling or related to air; having an affected manner

arrhae monies paid as earnest or a pledge

arrie any of several guillemots of the genus *Mura*

Eire the republic of Ireland

aerie a high eagle's or hawk's nest

eerie weird

Eire the republic of Ireland

Erie an Iroquoian people of northern Ohio, northwestern Pennsylvania, and western New York; a city in northwestern Pennsylvania; the next smallest of the five Great Lakes

aero of or relating to aircraft or aeronautics; designed for aerial use

arrow a missile weapon shot from a bow

aerose brassy

erose having the margin irregularly notched, as if gnawed

aery (see **aerie**)

aes in Roman antiquity, anything made of bronze or copper

ease relaxation; naturalness

Aeta A Negrito people inhabiting the central and southern Zambales mountains in the Philippines

eta the 7th letter of the Greek alphabet

affect to influence or make an impression on

effect a resultant condition

affecter one who strives after or pretends to something

effector a bodily organ that becomes active in respose to stimulation

affective relating to feelings or emotions
effective productive of results; efficient

affiance solemnly promise to marry
affiants those that swear to an affidavit

affirmance a decision by a person to deal with an unauthorized act as though authorized
affirmants persons who state positively or with confidence

affluence an abundance of property
affluents tributary streams

affusion the act of pouring a liquid upon, as in baptism
effusion unrestrained expression of feeling

afterward at a later or succeeding time
afterword the final part that serves to complete the design of a nondramatic literary work

Agamae a class or subkingdom embracing all plants reproducing by means of spores rather than flowers or seeds
agamy the absence, nonregulation, or nonrecognition of marriage

agaricin an impure form of the active principle of the dried fruit body of a mushroom
agaricine a crystalline or syrupy liquid base widely distributed among animal and plant products

agitant (see **adjutant**)

ah an expression of delight, relief, regret, or contempt
aw an expression of mild incredulity or disgust
awe reverence or wonder with a touch of fear

Aht a Wakashan people of Vancouver Island and the Cape Flattery region in northwestern Washington

aught zero or a cipher (also **ault**)

ai a three-toed sloth; an expression of grief, despair, or anguish
ay an expression of sorrow, regret, or surprise
aye an affirmative vote
eye an organ of sight
I a personal pronoun
i a unit vector parallel to the x-axis, in mathematics

aides (see **ades**)

AIDS and **aids** (see **ades**)

aiel a writ by which an heir enters a grandfather's estate and dispossesses a third party who attempts to gain possession
ail to affect with pain or discomfort
ale a beverage

aikie (see **achy**)

ail (see **aiel**)

air the atmosphere
are 100 square meters
e'er a contraction of ever
ere before
err make a mistake
eyre a journey
heir an inheritor

airable capable of being aired
arable fit for tillage and crop production

aire a person in early Irish society ranking between a common freeman and the king
Ara a genus of macaws containing the blue and yellow and the military macaws
ara a Polynesian screw pine called the textile screw pine
arrah any expession of surprise of excitement
arrha money paid as earnest or a pledge
Eire of or from the Republic of Ireland

airer a network or organization that broadcasts or transmits by radio or television
error a mistake, blunder, slip, or lapse

airless lacking air or movement of air
heirless having no inheritor

airship a lighter-than-air aircraft with propelling and directional control systems
heirship the right of inheritance

airy (see **aerie**)

Ais (see **ace**)

aisle a passage between seats
I'll a contraction of I will or I shall
isle a small island

Aissor a people in parts of Asiatic Turkey and Persia calling themselves Syrians
icer a worker who covers food with ice before shipment; a worker who mixes icing or ices baked goods

ait a little island
ate consumed food
eight a number between seven and nine

Aka a hill tribe north of Assam
aka any of several species of New Zealand woody vines
Akha the most southerly group of Lolo-speaking Tibeto-Burman people forming a large part of the hill tribes of Shan State, Myanmar; a Pygmy people of the Vele basin in the Belgian Congo

Akhs the spirits of deceased persons conceived as gloriously transferred so as to reflect the deeds of the persons in life
ox an adult castrated male bovine

Akkadian (see **Acadian**)

Akron (see **acron**)

Alascan a foreign Protestant in England during the reign of Edward VI
Alaskan relating to or characteristic of the state of Alaska

albumen egg white
albumin a large class of simple proteins

alcanna a color varying from reddish brown to strong brown

Alkanna a genus of herbs native to southern Europe
alkanna an Old World tropical shrub or small tree

alcatras a large water bird, such as the pelican or frigate bird
Alcatraz the island in San Francisco Bay, California formerly a highsecurity prison

ale (see **aiel**)

Alectrion the type genus of Nassariidae comprising various typical basket shells
Alectryon a monotypic genus of New Zealand trees with alternate compound leaves and showy paniculate flowers

aleph the first letter of the Hebrew alphabet
alif the first letter of the Arabic alphabet

alfa either of two Spanish and Algerian grasses of which cordage, shoes, baskets, and paper are made
alpha the first letter of the Greek alphabet; the first in a sequence

alfonsin any of several (usually bright red) fishes of the genus Beryx
alphonsin a surgical instrument having three elastic branches (a 3-armed forceps) for extracting bullets from the body
Alphonsine relating to the set of astronomical tables prepared in 1252 by the order of Alfonso X

alif (see **aleph**)

alison a plant of the genus Alyssum
allicin a liquid compound with a garlic odor and antibacterial properties

Alkanna and **alkanna** (see **alcanna**)

alkenyl any univalent aliphatic hydrocarbon radical derived from an alkene by removal of one hydrogen atom
alkynyl a univalent aliphatic hydrocarbon radical containing a triple bond

alkide a binary compound of an alkyl, especially with a metal

alkyd any of a large group of thermoplastic or thermosetting synthetic resins that are essentially polyesters

alkynyl (see **alkenyl**)

all (see **aal**)

allay to reduce in intensity
allée a formal avenue or mall

allegation something asserted
alligation the action of attaching or the state of being attached; a process for the solution of problems concerning the mixing of ingredients that differ in price or quality

allegator a person who asserts, affirms, or states without proof
Alligator the genus of Crocodylidae comprising the American and Chinese alligators
alligator either of two crocodilians; a machine with strong jaws, one of which opens like a movable jaw of an alligator

allergen a substance that induces an exaggerated or pathological reaction marked by sneezing, rash, etc.
allergin a substance in the blood of persons with syphilis that is sometimes held to be an antibody

allicin (see **alison**)

alligation (see **allegation**)

Alligator and **alligator** (see **allegator**)

allision the running of one ship upon another ship that is stationary
elision the act of dropping out or omitting something
Elysian sweetly blissful

alliterate characterized by the repetition, usually initially, of a sound that is usually a consonant in two or more adjacent words or syllables
illiterate showing a lack of familiarity with language and literature; having little or no education

allo isomeric or closely related
<u>aloe</u> a pale green color

allowed permitted
aloud audible

alluded referred to indirectly
eluded evaded
eluted removed from an absorbment by means of a solvent; washed out or extracted
illuded deceived

allusion an indirect reference
elusion an evasion
illusion a misleading image

aloe (see **allo**)

aloud (see **allowed**)

alpha (see **alfa**)

alphonsin (see **alfonsin**)

Alphonsine (see **alfonsin**)

altar a place of worship or sacrifice
alter to become different or cause to become different

alumen alum; either of two colorless or white isomorphous crystalline double sulfates of aluminum having a sweetish-sourish astringent taste
illumine illuminate

aluminate to treat or combine with alum or alumina
illuminate to give physical light to

am the present first person singular of be
em a unit of measure in printing
'em them (by assimilation or contraction)

ama a Japanese woman diver who works usually without diving gear; a vessel for eucharistic wine
amah a female servant typically Chinese, especially a nurse
amma an abbess or spiritual mother

amaretto an almond-flavored liqueur
amoretto a naked usually infantile figure representing the god of love and often holding a bow and arrow

amatol an explosive consisting of ammonium nitrate and TNT

Amytal a crystalline compound used as a sedative and hypnotic

amba a table-mountain formation with nearly perpendicular sides
anba a title given to bishops or patriarchs in the Coptic church

Ambassadeur a bearded iris with maroon and bronze flowers
ambassador an official representative of a sovereign or state

ambrosin a Milanese gold or silver coin of the late 13th and early 14th centuries bearing the likeness of St. Ambrose
ambrosine a resinous hydrocarbon mineral that is a variety of amber

ameen a minor official of the judicial and revenue departments in India
amine a compound containing one or more halogen atoms
ammine a molecule of ammonia

amend to reform oneself or become better
amende a fine, penalty, or reparation; a full apoplogy
emend to correct a literary work

amerce to punish by a monetary penalty
immerse to dip into liquid

America of or from North, Central, or South America; of or from the United States
Amerika the fascist or racist aspect of American society

amidin a soluble matter of starch
amidine any of a group of compounds containing the CN_2H_3 group

amine (see **ameen**)

amma (see **ama**)

ammine (see **ameen**)

Ammanite an Amish Mennonite
Ammonite a member of a people who in Old Testament times lived east of the Jordan between the Jabbok and the Arnon rivers

ammonite any of numerous fossil shells of cephalopods of the order Ammonoidea, some being over three feet in diameter

amoretto (see **amaretto**)

amorous strongly moved by love; manifesting love
Amyris a genus of tropical American trees and shrubs with compound leaves and white flowers

amorphous without definite form or shape
amorphus a fetus with head, heart, or limbs

amotion removal of a specified object or person from a place or position
emotion feeling or an expression of feeling

amphibalus a vestment resembling the chasuble worn by the Gallician clergy prior to the 9th century
amphibolus capable of two meanings

amphibian having or combining two lives, positions, or qualities
amphibion an aircraft that can take off from and land on either water or land

amphibolus (see **amphilabus**)

ample more than adequate
ampul a small bulbous glass vessel

amtrac an amphibian flat-bottomed vehicle that moves or tracks over land and which can be propelled through water
Amtrak the government-subsidized public intercity passenger railroad system in the U.S.

amygdalin a white crystalline glucoside that occurs in the kernels of the bitter almond
amygdaline pertaining to a tonsil

Amyris (see **amorous**)

Amytal (see **amatol**)

an indefinite article used before words with an initial vowel sound
and along with or together with

an an indefinite article
en a unit of measure in printing

analyst a person who weighs or studies to arrive at an answer
annalist a writer of annals

ananym a pseudonym consisting of the real name written backward
anonym an idea that has no exact term to express it

anba (see **amba**)

anchor a device to hold an object in place
anker a U.S. unit of measure equal to ten gallons

anchored secured firmly
ancred a cross with each arm divided into two recurving points

anchorite a person who lives in seclusion, usually for religious reasons
ankerite a variety of dolomite containing considerable iron

ancred (see **anchored**)

and (see **an**)

and a conjunction, meaning also or in addition
end a cessation or terminus

androgenous pertaining to the production of or tending to produce male offspring
androgynous in astronomy, sometimes hot and sometimes cold with respect to planets
androgynus an individual possessing characteristics of both sexes

ands conjunctions, meaning also or in addition
ends terminations; leftover scraps
ens a thing's being or essence; in typesetting, en quads

angelin a cabbage tree
angeline a white crystalline alkaloid found in the bark of a South American tree

anger a strong feeling of displeasure and usually of antagonism
angor extreme distress or mental anguish, usually of a physical origin

anil a West Indian shrub, one of the sources of indigo
anile old-womanish; infirm

anils Schiff bases derived from aromatic amines
annals historical records

animas souls or lives
animus intention or objective

anker (see **anchor**)

ankerite (see **anchorite**)

annalist (see **analyst**)

annals (see **anils**)

annunciate to announce
enunciate to utter articulate sounds

anonym (see **ananym**)

ansae parts of a celestial body having the appearance of handles; structures resembling loops
antsy eager, impatient, or restless

Anser a genus of birds comprising geese
answer a reply

ant an insect
aunt a sister of either of one's parents

antae piers produced by thickening a wall at its termination
ante a poker stake; before
anti one who is opposed
auntie an aunt, often used endearingly

antecedence an apparent motion of a planet toward the west; retrogradation
antecedents significant events, principles, or activities of one's earlier life; predecessors in a series

antetype an earlier type or prototype

antitype an opposite type, such as a symetrically reversed appendage

anti (see **antae**)

antitype (see **antetype**)

antsy (see **ansae**)

Aor one of a group of related peoples inhabiting the Naga hills in eastern Assam along the Myanmar frontier

hour a time measurement equal to 60 minutes or 1/24 of a day

our belonging or related to us

Aoul a member of any of several small peoples living in the malarial swampy lowland districts of Nepal

aoul an Abyssian gazelle

aul a Central Asiatic tent made of felt or skin fastened over a circular wooden framework

owl a nocturnal bird of prey

apatite a group of calcium phosphate minerals containing other elements

appetite a natural desire

apian relating to bees

apiin a crystalline glycoside obtained from parsley

Apis a type genus of *Apidae* includibng brownish social bees

Apus a genus of birds containing the typical Old World swifts

apus a crustacean of the genus *Triops*, containing forms which are destructive pests of young rice

aplanatism freedom from spherical aberration

aplanetism the state of producing non-motile asexual spores

apophasis denial of one's intention to speak of a subject that is simultaneously named or insinuated

apophysis a swelling, such as a process of a bone or the cone scale of certain conifers

aport toward the left side

apport the production or motion of an object by a spiritualist medium without physical activity or contact

apothegm a terse aphorism

apothem a perpendicular from the center to one of the sides of a regular polygon

Appalachian of or relating to a system of mountains in the eastern U.S. or to the region where they are found

appellation a name or title by which a person, thing, or clan is called or known

appetite (see **apatite**)

apport (see **aport**)

appose to place side by side

oppose to act against or provide resistance to

appositive being a grammatical construction of two nouns or noun equivalents

oppositive functioning in the expression of contrariety

appressed pressed close

oppressed weighed down

Apus and **apus** (see **Apis**)

aquation the replacement of a coordinated atom by water molecules

equation a statement of equality between two mathematical expressions

Ara and **ara** (see **aire**)

Arabi a breed of sheep

Araby Arabian

arable (see **airable**)

Araby (see **Arabi**)

araneous covered with or composed of soft loose hairs or fibers

Araneus a genus of orb-weaving spiders

Arau a Papuan people of western New Guinea

arrau a large turtle found in the Amazon river and valued for its edible eggs and as a source of oil

arcs portions of a curved line
arks boats or ships
arx a citadel, in Roman antiquity

are (see **air**)

are exist, the present 2nd singular and present plural of be
our belonging or related to us

area the extent of space
aria a melody or tune
eria the Assam silkworm which feeds on the castor-oil plant

areal (see **aerial**)

arear to the rear
arrear behind in discharging one's obligations

arête a sharp crested ridge in rugged mountains
arret a judgment, decision, or decree of a court or sovereign

argal therefore, used chiefly to imply that the reasoning is specious or absurd; a grayish or reddish crystal line crust deposited in wine casks during aging; dry cattle or camel dung used for fuel
argel either of two related African plants whose leaves have been used to adulterate senna
argil potter's clay

Argas a genus of ticks including the cosmopolitan chicken tick
Argus a vigilant guardian
argus any of several large brilliantly patterned East Indian pheasants; any of several butterflies

argee cheap, inferior whiskey
Argie an Argentinian

argel (see **argal**)

Argie (see **argee**)

argil (see **argal**)

argon a colorless odorless inert gaseous element
Argonne a wooded region in northeast

France noted for battles in World Wars I and II

Argus and **argus** (see **Argas**)

aria (see **area**)

Arianism a theological movement initiated by Arius in opposition to Sabellianism that won strong support during the 4th century A.D. chiefly in the Eastern churches
Aryanism the doctrine popularized by Nazism that Aryan peoples possess superior capacities

ariel (see **aerial**)

aril a covering of certain seeds
arrhal earnest or pledge money
aryl a univalent radical (as phenyl) derived from an aromatic hydrocarbon

Arion a genus of slugs including a common European black slug
orion Holland blue or a dark blue color

Arkansas a state in the south central U.S.
arkansaw to kill in an unsportsman like manner; to cheat or take advantage of

Arkie a native of Arkansas; a rustic or insignificant person
arky old-fashioned or out of style

arks (see **arcs**)

arky (see **Arkie**)

armer a person or device that arms a weapon
armoire a usually large and ornate cupboard or wardrobe
armor defensive covering for the body

aroar roaring or bellowing
aurore an hydrangea pink color

arrah (see **aire**)

arrant notoriously bad or shameless
errant quixotically adventurous; aimlessly moving about

arras a wall hanging or hanging screen of tapestry

arris the sharp edge formed by the meeting of two surfaces
heiress a female heir to property

arrau (see **Arau**)

array to set in order; a regular grouping or arrangement
arret a judgment of a court or sovereign

arrear (see **arear**)

arret (see **array** and **arête**)

arrha (see **aire**)

arrhae (see **aerie**)

arrhal (see **aril**)

arrie (see **aerie**)

arris (see **arras**)

arrosive of the nature of gnawing
erosive tending to erode or affecting erosion

arrow (see **aero**)

arusa a small shrub found in India with leaves yielding a yellow dye
arusha an Indian shrub yielding a flaxlike fiber

arx (see **arcs**)

Aryanism (see **Arianism**)

aryl (see **aril**)

As a chief god of pagan Scandinavia
as a bronze coin of the ancient Roman republic
ass a beast of burden; a simpleminded fool
asse a fox of southern Africa

asale for or on sale
assail to attack with violence or vehemence

ascendants ancestors or persons that precede in genealogical succession
ascendence leadership or domination

ascent rising
assent concurrence

ascetic (see **acetic**)

ascian an inhabitant of the torrid zone where the sun is vertical at noon for a few days each year such that no shadow is cast
ashen deadly pale or pallid in color

ascitic (see **acidic**)

ase (see **ace**)

ashen (see **ascian**)

askar a native infantryman in an Arabic-speaking country
asker one who poses or asks questions

asperate to make rough, harsh, or uneven
aspirate to pronounce with an h-sound as the initial element; to draw or withdraw by suction

aspire seek to attain or accomplish something
espier a person who observes or looks about closely

ass (see **As**)

assail (see **asale**)

assay to judge the worth of
essay a short literary composition

asse (see **As**)

assemblé a ballet movement
assemblée a social gathering

assent (see **ascent**)

Assyria (see **Aceria**)

Aster a large genus of chiefly fallblooming leafy-stemmed herbaceous plants native to temperate regions
aster any plant of the genus Aster
Astur a genus consisting of goshawks
astur a goshawk

astray into a wrong or mistaken way of thinking or acting; off the correct route
estray something that has wandered or gone out of its normal place, as a domestic animal found wandering

Astur and **astur** (see **Aster**)

Ata a member of an Indonesian tribe of Mindanao

atta unsorted wheat flour or meal, in India

ate (see **ait**)

ate blind impulse or reckless ambition

Ati a predominantly pagan Negritoid people on Panay, Philippines

eighty the next whole number after seventy-nine

atimy public disgrace, usually with deprivation of civil rights

atomy a tiny and often contemptible creature or object; an extremely gaunt emaciated body

atom (see **Adam**)

atomy (see **atimy**)

atta (see **Ata**)

attar (see **adder**)

attar a perfume obtained from flowers

odder more unusual

otter an aquatic fish-eating mustelid mammal

attle (see **addle**)

aube an often Provençal love lyric usually dealing with a parting of lovers at dawn

obe a subdivision of a phyle or clan in ancient Laconia

audience a group or assembly of listeners

audients catchumens in the early stages of instruction for admission to the church but not yet as applicants for baptism

auger a boring tool

augur to predict

aught (see **Aht**)

aught zero

ought should

augur (see **auger**)

aul (see **Aoul**)

aune a unit of cloth measure in Paris equal to 46.79 inches

own belonging to oneself or itself; to have legal or natural title to

aunt (see **ant**)

auntie (see **antae**)

aural of the ear

oral of the mouth

orle in heraldry, a border within a parallel to but not touching the edge of the field

aureole the luminous area surrounding bright light

oriole a colorful American bird

aureolin cobalt yellow

aureoline golden in color

auricle the upper chamber of the heart; an earlike lobe

oracle a divine revelation

aurore (see **aroar**)

aurous relating to or containing gold

orris the Florentine iris, or its fragrant rootstalk; gold or silver braid or lace used on 18th century clothing

austenite a solid solution in gamma iron of carbon and sometimes other solutes

austinite a mineral consisting of a basic calcium zinc arsenate

Austria a country in central Europe

Ostrea the type genus Ostreidae including oysters that retain eggs in the parent's gills during early development

ostria a warm southern wind on the Bulgarian coast

Ostrya a small widely distributed genus of trees having fruit resembling cones, including the hop hornbeam

autarchic relating to absolute sovereignty

autarkic relating to self-sufficiency

auteur a filmmaker whose individual style and complete control over all elements of production give a film her/his personal and unique stamp

hauteur an arrogant or condescending manner

autograft a tissue or organ transplanted to another part of the same body
autographed wrote one's signature

autonomous possessing self-government
autonymous naming itself

autosight an automatic sighting device
autosite that part of a double fetal monster that nourishes both itself and the parasitic twin

avert to turn away or aside, especially in order to escape something dangerous or unpleasant
evert to overthrow or upset; to turn outward or inside out

avulsion a tearing away of a structure of a part accidently or surgically
evulsion a rooting, casting, or plucking out

aw (see **ah**)

away distant in space or time
aweigh hanging perpendicular just clear of the ground

awe (see **ah**)

aweigh (see **away**)

awful extremely unpleasant
offal waste material

awl (see **aal**)

awn a slender bristle that terminates the bract of a spikelet, such as in wheat
on a preposition denoting position atop something

ax(e) (see **acts**)

axal around, in the direction of, or along the axis
Axel a one-and-a-half-turn jump in skating
axil the angle between a branch or leaf and the axis from which it arises
axle a shaft on which a wheel revolves

axes cutting tools or implements consisting of relatively heavy edged and sharp heads fixed to handles
axis a straight line about which a body rotates

axil (see **axal**)

axin an oleaginous and waxy product yielded by the large Mexican cochineal and used as a soothing ointment
axon a nerve-cell process that is typically single and long and which, as a rule, conducts impulses away from the cell body

axis (see **axes**)

axle (see **axal**)

axon (see **axin**)

ay (see **a** or **ai**)

aye (see **ai**)

ayin the 16th letter of the Hebrew alphabet
ion an atom or group of atoms when combined in a radical or molecule that carries an electrical charge

azimene in astrology, a weak deficient degree which when ascendant at birth causes a physical defect
azimine an azimono compound

Group I

aberrance - aberrants
aboideau - aboideaux
abri - abris
abstinence - abstinents
acceptance - acceptants
acinous - acinus
adolescence - adolescents
adulteress - adulterous
affirmance - affirmants
airdrop - air-drop
alkalis - alkalize
allegiance - allegiants
alumnae - alumni
ambience - ambients

amino - ammino
angulous - angulus
annunciate - enunciate
an(o)estrous - an(o)estrus
anorchous - anorchus
anthropophagous - anthropophagus
appendance - appendants
appurtenance - appurtenants
assistance - assistants
assonance - assonants
astringence - astringents
attendance - attendants
attractance - attractants
axil - axile

Group I and II

ambience   äⁿbyäⁿs
ambients   'a(a)mbēən(t)s

announce   ə'naůn(t)s
enounce   ē'naůn(t)s

anthropopgeny   -jənē
anthropogony   -gənē

Group II

aa   'ä,ä
aha   ä'hä

Aaronic   a'ränik
ironic   i'ränik

abac   'äbak
aback   ə'bak

abacas   'abə,käs
abacus   'abəkəs

abbe   a'bā
abbey   'abē

abbess   'abəs
abyss   ə'bis

abhorred   əb'hȯrd
aboard   ə'bȯrd

accede   ak'sēd or ək'sēd
axseed   'ak(s),sēd

accrue   əkrü
ecru   'ekrü

acerose   'asə,rōs
acerous   'asər,əs

acetal   'asə,tal
acetyl   ə'sēdᵊl

acinous   'asə,nəs
acinus   'asⁿəs

addict   'a,dikt
attic   'atik

adduce   ə'd(y)üs
educe   ē'd(y)üs

adduct   'a,dəkt
educt   'ē,dəkt

aer   'äər
air   'er

aesthetic   es'thedik
ascetic   ə'sedik

affluent   'aflüənt
effluent   'eflüənt

afflux   'a,fləks
efflux   'e,fləks

affright   ə'frīt
afrite   ə'frēt

Africans   'afrikənz
Afrikaans   'afrə,känz

afterward   'aftərwərd
afterword   'aftər,wərd

agar   'ägər
auger   'ȯgər

ager   'äjər
agger   'ajər

aggression   ə'greshən
egression   ē'greshən

agnail   'agnāl
agnel   ,an'yəl

agust   'əgəst
august   ə'gəst

ahl   'äl
all   'ȯl

aigrette   ā:gret
egret   'ēgrət

airan   ī'rän
Iran   i'rän or i'ran

aire   'ärə
aura   'òrə
ora   'ōrə

aition   'īdē,än
idaein   ī'dēən

alem   'ä,lem or 'al,em
alum   'aləm or ə'ləm

alight   ə'līt
alite   'ā,līt

align   ə'līn
A-line   'ā,līn

allocator   'alə,kād·ər or 'alə,kātər
allocatur   ,alə'kād·ər or ,alə'kā,tər

allure   ə'lùr
Alur   'ä,lùr
alure   ə'lùr

alluvium   ə'lüvēəm
eluvium   ē:lüvēəm
illuvium   i:lüvēəm

aloe   'alō
alow   ə'lō

amandin   'äməndən
amandine   'ämən,dēn

amend   ə'mend
amende   'a'mänd

amice   'a,məs
amiss   ə'mis

amor   'ä,mòr
amour   ,ä'mùr

ample   'ampəl
ampul   'am,pəl

amula   'amyələ
amulla   'aməla

Anabas   'anabas
anabasse   ,ana'bas

anaclasis   ə'nakləsəs
anaclisis   ə'naklisis

analogy   ə'naləjē
enallage   en'alajē

Andean   'andēən
indienne   'andē,en

angary   'aŋgərē
angry   'aŋgrē

anil   'anəl
anile   'a,nīl

annual   'anyəl
annule   'anyül

Ansar   'an,sär
answer   'ansər

anthropophagi   ,anthrə'päfəjī
anthropophagy   ,anthrə'päfəjē

aperitif   ə'perə'tēf
aperitive   ə'perədiv

aphagia   ə'fājēə
aphasia   ə'fāzhēə

apiin   'āpēən
Apion   'āpē,än

Apios   'āpē,äs
apiose   'āpē,ōs

aplomb   ə,plōm
aplome   'a,plōm

appel   a'pel
apple   'apəl

apprise   ə'prīz
uprise   'əp,rīz

apses   'apsəz
apsis   'apsəs

argil   'är,jəl
Argyle   'är,gīl

Armenian   är'mēnēən
Arminian   är'minēən

arrha   'arə
era   'erə

arses   'ärsəz
arsis   'ärsəs

artist   'ärdəst
artiste   är'tēst

ascribe   ə'skrīb
escribe   e'skrīb

astir   ə'stər
Astur   'astər

atlantes   at'lantēz
Atlantis   at'lantis

attrited   ə'trītəd
attritted   ə'tritəd

auks   'ȯks
ox   'äks

aura   'ȯrə
ora   'ōrə

aurate   'ȯ͵rāt
orate   ȯ'rāt

Auster   'ȯster
ouster   'au̇stər

autoscope   'ȯtō͵skōp
otoscope   'ōdə͵skōp

auxin   'ȯksən
oxen   'äksən

awed   'ȯd
odd   'äd

awner   'ȯnər
honor   'änər

B

ba   an eternal divine soul in Egyptian religious belief
baa   a sheep's bleat
bah   an expression of disdain
bas   a bet in roulette on one of the vertical columns paying 2 for 1

baa   (see ba)

baaed   bleated, as sheep
bad   unfavorable or derogatory
bade   made an offer

baaed   bleated, as sheep
bod   the body (by shortening)

Baal   any of several Canaanite and Phoenician chief dieties
baal   a false god
bael   a thorny citrus tree of India
bail   to deliver from arrest; to clear water from a boat
bale   a large bundle of goods; pain or mental suffering

baas   master
Bos   a genus of ruminant mammals including wild and domestic cattle
boss   raised ornamentation; a super intendent or overseer

bosse   an African tree having glabrous oblong pointed leaflets

Baatan   a province of the Philippines
bataan   a valuable Philippine timber tree
Batan   a people inhabiting the Batan islands of the Philippines
baton   a stick with which a conductor leads a musical group

babble   to utter meaningless sounds as though talking
Babel   a lofty or towering structure; an excessively grandiose or visionary scheme or project
babel   a confusion or medley of sounds, voices, or ideas

Babhan   a Hindu of a high caste of the Aryo-Dravidian ethnic type
bobbin   any of various small round cylindrical devices on which threads are wound

bac   a vat or cistern
back   in the rear; endorse or support

bacc(h)ar   a plant of grasslands variously identified as Cyclamen europaeum
backer   a supported

bacchanal a drunken revelry

bacchanale a ballet marked with voluptuous dances

bach to live as a bachelor

batch a quantity of persons or things considered as a group

bacillary shaped like a rod

basilary (in biology) relating to or situated at the base

back (see **bac**)

backer (see **bacc[h]ar**)

bad (see **baaed**)

badder more unfavorable or derogatory

batter a mixture of flour, liquid, and other ingredients; to beat repeatedly

baddy a hoodlum or other malefactor; an undesirable or negative event (slang)

batty resembling a bat; mentally unstable

bade (see **baaed**)

bael (see **Baal**)

bael a thorny citrus tree of India

bile a yellow or greenish viscid alkaline fluid excreted by the liver

baetyl a roughly shaped stone worshipped as of divine origin

beadle a messenger in the service of a law court

beetle an insect of the order Coleoptera

betel a climbing pepper plant

bietle a deerskin jacket worn by Apache women

baffed made a stroke with a golf club so the sole of the club strikes the ground and lofts the ball

baft a coarse stuff originally made of cotton

bag to catch; a container made of flexible material, usually closed on all sides except for an opening that may be closed

bague in architecture, the ring or plate of an annulated column

baggie the stomach

baggy loose, puffed out, or hanging like a sac or pouch

bague (see **bag**)

bah (see **ba**)

bahr a body of water

<u>**bar**</u> a straight piece of metal or wood; to confine or shut out

<u>**barre**</u> a handrail ballet dancers use during exercises

Bhar a caste of agricultural laborers in India

baht the basic monetary unit of Thailand

bhat a member of an Indian caste of bards and entertainers

bot(t) the larva of the botfly; a plug of clay for closing the taphole of a cupola in founding

bail (see **Baal**)

bailer a person who attaches handles to pails or buckets

bailor a person who delivers goods to another in trust

baler a person or machine that bales

bailey a medieval castle's outer wall

bailie a magistrate of a Scottish barony similar to a sheriff

bailor (see **bailer**)

bais yellow mists composed of airborne loess or fine sand that is produced in China and Japan during the spring and fall

biz business (by shortening)

bait a lure to attract fish, animals, or persons

bate to reduce the force of intensity

Bete a member of the Phi Beta Kappa academic honor society

bete in certain card games, to subject to a penalty for failure to fulfill one's contract

beth the second letter of the Hebrew alphabet

baiting heckling, hounding, or attacking in speech or writing, usually with malice

bating with the exception of; cleaning depilated leather hides with tryptic enzymes

bai-u relating to the spring or early summer rainy season in China and Japan
bayou a minor waterway that is tributary to a river or another body of water
bio biography (by shortening)
byo a cradle

baize a coarsely woven woolen or cotton napped fabric
bays compartments in a bar; wall openings or recesses; barks at
beys district governors in the Ottoman Empire

balas a ruby spinel of pale rose-red or orange color
ballas a nearly spherical aggregate of diamond grains used as an industrial diamond

balata a hard substance produced by drying the milky juice of a bully tree
ballata a medieval Italian song accompanied by or alternating with dancing

bald lacking all or a significant portion of hair
balled formed into a round mass
bawled cried out loudly

baldie a small double-ended fishing boat used on the east coast of Scotland
baldy a white-headed pigeon of Australia; a person that is bald

bale (see **Baal**)

baleen a horny substance growing in the mouth of whales that forms a fringelike sieve to collect and retain food
baline a coarse woolen or cotton material used in packing
Bilin the Cushitic language of the Bogos

baler (see **bailer**)

baline (see **baleen**)

ball a round mass
baule the theoretical amount of nitrogen or a mineral necessary to produce ½ the maximum possible crop yield
bawl to cry out loudly

ballas (see **balas**)

ballata (see **balata**)

balled (see **bald**)

baller a laundry worker who irons parts of garments that cannot be ironed on or with a flat press
bawler a person who cries out loudly without restraint

ballet(t) a part-song often in stanzas with a refrain
ballot a ticket or sheet of paper containing a list of names for use in casting a vote

ballocks testicles (slang)
bollix to involve in bewildering entanglements
bollocks young or castrated bulls; large iron-strapped gin blocks fitted under the topmost crosstrees to take the topsail tyes

ballot (see **ballet[t]**)

balm a healing ointment
baum to court the favor of someone; to flatter (slang)
bomb a projectile carrying an explosive charge
bombe a frozen molded dessert

ban a provincial governor of former times in Croatia, Hungary, or Slavonia
bon a broad bean; a kidney bean

banat a province under the jurisdiction of a ban
bonnet a woman's head covering of cloth or straw usually tied under the chin with ribbons

banc a bench on which court judges sit
bank a portion of earth above the surrounding level; a business establishment that accepts deposits of and loans money

band an item which confines or constricts movement; an organized group of people
banned prohibited

bands items that confine or constrict movement; organized groups of people

banns a notice of proposed marriage proclaimed in church or a public place

<u>**bans**</u> prohibits

bandy a carriage or cart used in India and drawn by bullocks

bundy a small often crooked Australian tree with pendulous branches

bank (see **banc**)

banket the auriferous conglomerate rock of the Transvaal

banquette a raised way along the inside of a trench on which soliders and guns are posted to fire on the enemy

banned (see **band**)

banns (see **bands**)

banquette (see **banket**)

bans (see **bands**)

bans former provincial governors in Hungary, Croatia, or Slavonia having military powers in time of war

bonds agreements binding one or more parties' devices for holding or tying something together

bons broad beans; kidney beans

bonze a Buddhist monk of the Far East

banyan an East Indian tree the branches of which send out numerous trunks that grow into the soil

bunion an enlargement of the first joint of the great toe

baos African board games usually played by moving pebbles along two rows of holes

boughs tree branches

bouse to haul by means of tackle

bouws Indonesian units of land area each equal to 1.75 acres

<u>**bows**</u> bends down; the forward parts of ships or boats

bar (see **bahr**)

barb a sharp projection extending backward, as from a fishhook or arrowhead

barbe a short lace scarf worn at the throat or on the head

Barbary a coastal region in North Africa

barberry a prickly shrub of the genus Berbis

barbery a barber's craft

barbe (see **barb**)

barbel a slender tactile process on the lips of certain fishes; a large European freshwater fish with four barbels on its upper jaw

barble one of the small projections of the mucous membrane that marks the opening of the submaxillary glands under the tongue in horses and cattle

barberry (see **Barbary**)

barbery (see **Barbary**)

barbet any of numerous loud-voiced tropical birds having a large stout bill bearing bristles

barbut a steel helmet of the 15th century having a T-shaped face slit

barble (see **barbel**)

barbut (see **barbet**)

bard a poet

barred shut or kept out exposed to view

byard a leather strap crossing the breast and used by men to drag wagons in coal mines

<u>**bare**</u> exposed to view

bear a large heavy mammal; to carry a load

ber an edible drupaceous fruit from the tree of the genus Ziziphus; a Chinese date

baretta a rutaceous evergreen shrub of Texas

biretta a square head covering worn by ecclesiastics

barf vomit

barff to protect iron or steel with a coating of iron oxide

baric pertaining to atmospheric pressure, especially as measured by a barometer

barrack a building to house military service personnel

baring the surface soil removed from ore or rock

bearing producing or yielding

barings the small coal made in undercutting coal seams

bearings manners in which one comports oneself; eversion of the vagina at parturition in the ewe

baritone a male singing voice between bass and tenor (seldom barytone)

barytone (a word) having an unaccented final syllable, especially in Greek grammar

Barkie a bread of sheep

barkie a little sharp explosive cry uttered by dogs, foxes, and squirrels

barky covered with or resembling the exterior dead cellular structure of woody roots and stems

barney a small car attached to a cable and used on slopes in a mine

barny suggesting a barn especially in size or characteristic smell

baron a member of the peerage; a man of great power in some activity

barren devoid or lacking something, as vegetation; sterile

baroness a wife or widow of a baron

barrenness state of unproductivity; emptiness

baroque relating to or having the characteristics of a style of artistic expression prevalent especially in the 17th century

berok a pig-tailed ape, a macaque of the Malay peninsula

barrack (see **baric**)

barre (see **bahr**)

barred (see **bard**)

barrel a round bulging vessel of greater height than breadth usually made of staves bound with hoops

beryl a hard mineral consisting of a silicate of beryllium and aluminum

barren (see **baron**)

barrenness (see **baroness**)

barret a small cap

barrette a bar-shaped clip for holding hair in place

bourette an irregular slubbed yarn made usually of silk waste

barrier an obstruction

berrier a person who picks small pulpy edible fruit

burier a person or animal that buries or conceals something

barry in heraldry, divided into an even number of horizontal bars of two tinctures arranged alternately

barye the absolute cgs unit of pressure equal to one dyne per square centimeter

barry a baritone saxophone

berry a small pulpy edible fruit

bury to inter a corpse; to conceal

barye (see **barry**)

barytone (see **baritone**)

bas (see **ba**)

bas enough or stop, often used as an interjection in India

boss a cow or other bovine animal, used chiefly in calling such animals

bus a large motor-driven vehicle designed to carry passengers

buss to kiss; a rugged square-sailed fishing boat

basal fundamental; relating to the foundation, base, or essence

basil any of several aromatic plants

base a foundation

bass a low pitched sound

beth the second letter of the Hebrew alphabet

based formed a foundation

baste to sew with long loose stitches; to moisten with liquid during cooking

baseman a person stationed or positioned at a base, as in baseball

bassman a person who plays a bass viol or sings a bass part

bases foundations

basis a fundamental ingredient or essence

basses persons or instruments able to create the lowest pitched sounds

basest of the most inferior quality

bassist a contrabass player or a bass singer

basi a valuable Philippine timber tree; a fermented Philippine beverage

bassi bass singers

bossy inclined to domineer; a cow or calf; studded

basil (see **basal**)

basilary (see **bacillary**)

basilican resembling a basilica by having a nave and aisles with clerestory

basilicon an ointment composed of rosin, yellow wax, and lard

basin an open usually circular vessel

bason a bench, with a plate heated by a fire underneath, on which felt is formed

basis (see **bases**)

bask to derive pleasure or enjoyment

Basque one of the people inhabiting the western Pyrennes region on the Bay of Biscay in Spain

basque a woman's tight-fitting bodice

bason (see **basin**)

Basque and **basque** (see **bask**)

bass (see **base**)

basses (see **bases**)

bassi (see **basi**)

bassist (see **basest**)

bassman (see **baseman**)

baste (see **based**)

bat a stout solid stick; a flying mammal

batt a sheet of material for use in making felt or insulation (seldom: bat)

bataan (see **Baatan**)

Batan (see **Baatan**)

batch (see **bach**)

bate (see **bait**)

bating (see **baiting**)

baton (see **Baatan**)

baton a policeman's billyclub or truncheon

batten a strip of wood used for nailing across two other pieces

batt (see **bat**)

battel the account for college expenses at Oxford University

battle to engage in combat

batten (see **baton**)

batter (see **badder**)

batterie a ballet movement consisting of beating together the feet or calves of the legs

battery the act of battering or beating; the pitcher and catcher of a baseball team; a device for producing electric current

battle (see **battel**)

battu in ballet, to strike repeatedly in dance

battue driving or drawing out game from cover by beating woods and bushes

batty (see **baddy**)

bauble a trinket, geegaw, or plaything

bobble to make an error or mistake; to fumble

baud a unit to measure signaling speed in telegraphic code

bawd a person who keeps a house of prostitution

baule (see **ball**)

baule the theoretical amount of nitrogen or a mineral necessary to produce ½ the maximum possible crop yield

bole any cylindrically shaped object or mass

boll a plant's pod or capsule, as cotton or flax

Bolle a cultivated variety of white poplar with a pyramidal habit

bowl a rounded hollow vessel; to throw a ball down a green or alley, as in tenpins

baum (see **balm**)

bawd (see **baud**)

bawl (see **ball**)

bawled (see **bald**)

bawler (see **baller**)

bawn a fortified court of a castle; a fold for livestock

Bon a pre–Buddhist animist religion of Tibet; a popular Japanese festival

Bonn a city in western Germany

bonne a French maidservant

bay-bay a tropical American shrub or small tree with racemose flowers and flesh fruits

bye-bye used to express farewell

bayou (see **bai-u**)

bays (see **baize**)

bazaar a place for the sale of merchandise

bizarre odd, extravagant, eccentric, or weird

bb a shot pellet about .18 inches in diameter

beebee the youngest member of a family or brood

bibi a Hindu mistress of a house

be to exist

bee a social colonial hymenopterous insect; a gathering of people to accomplish some purpose

beach a shoreline of ocean, sea, or lake

beech a smooth gray-barked tree

bead a small often round piece of material that is pierced for threading on a string or wire

bede a miner's pick

beader a device or person that makes a bead or strings beads

beater a device or person that beats or whips something

beadle (see **baetyl**)

beady resembling beads

bidi a cheap locally made cigarette, in India

bean the seed of a climbing leguminous plant

been existed

bin a four-stringed musical instrument of India with a long bamboo fingerboard

beanie a potbelly; a blackjack

beany a small round tight-fitting skullcap worn especially by school boys and collegians; marked with an oil-flavor suggestive of beans

beenie a bombadier navigator

bene well

bear (see **bare**)

beard hair growing over the face

beered drank or indulged in beer

beardie a small vigorous shaggy collielike sheepdog of Scottish origin

beardy having a growth of facial hair, particularly about the chin and jaws

bearing (see **baring**)

bearings (see **barings**)

beast a creature

beest a specialized secretion of a cow's mammary glands after calving

beastie a small creature

bheesty a water carrier for a house hold or regiment in India

beat to strike repeatedly

beet a biennial plant with a bulbous root

beater (see **beader**)

beau a man who goes steadily with a woman; an escort

beaux men who go steadily with a woman or specific women; escorts

<u>**bo**</u> a hobo; a fig tree of India

boh a leader of roving bands of criminals in India and Burma who rob and murder

boo marijuana (slang)

<u>**bow**</u> a weapon used to propel an arrow; an implement used to play a stringed musical instrument

Beaune a red table wine

bone the hard part of a vertebrate's skeleton

beaut a beautiful thing

bute phenylbutazone, a potent crystalline drug used to reduce pain and inflammation in rheumatic diseases and gout

Butte a city in southwestern Montana

butte an isolated hill or mountain with steep sides

beaux (see **beau**)

beaux men who go steadily with a woman or specific women; escorts

<u>**bows**</u> weapons used to propel arrows

becken large concave brass plates that produce clashing musical tones, (cymbals)

beckon to extend attraction, interest, allure, or appeal

bedash to splash with color or rain

berdache an American Indian transvestite assuming more or less permanently the role and social status of a woman

bedded deposited in layers or stratified

betted wagered

bedder a person who fixes beds; a plant grown in a bed

better to improve; in a more excellent manner

bettor a person that wagers or gambles (seldom **better**)

bedding bed clothes; a bottom layer

betting wagering

bede (see **bead**)

bee (see **be**)

beebee (see **bb**)

beech (see **beach**)

beeheaded eccentric; crazy

beheaded severed the head or crown from

been (see **bean**)

been existed

ben a seed of an East Indian or African tree

been existed

bin an enclosed storage place

beenie (see **beanie**)

beer a fermented beverage made from malted grain and hops

bier a stand on which a corpse or coffin is placed

byrrh a dry, slightly bitter French aperitif with a light orange flavor

beered (see **beard**)

beery influenced by beer drinking; convivial

birri a woolen cape or cloak worn with a hood by Romans

bees social colonial hymenopterous insects; gatherings of people to accomplish a purpose

bise a cold dry wind of southern Europe

beest (see **beast**)

beet (see **beat**)

beetle (see **baetyl**)

beflour to dust with powder made of ground grain

beflower to adorn with blossoms

beheaded (see **beeheaded**)

bel a thorny citrus tree of India

bell a hollow spherical metallic device that resonates when hit with a clapper

Belle a variety of white-fleshed peach of outstanding beauty

belle a popular or attractive girl or woman

bema the part of an early Christian and modern Eastern Orthodox church that contains the altar and synthrnon
bima(h) a platform in a Jewish synagogue bearing the reading desk

ben (see **been**)

bench a long seat
bensh to say a blessing or recite prayers

bends constrains or strains into a tense condition
Benz Benzedrine (slang)

bene (see **beanie**)

benet the third of the four minor orders in the Roman Catholic church; an exorcist
bennet a yellow-flowered avens

Beni a Negro people of southern Nigeria
ben(n)e an East Indian annual erect herb
Benny a man's overcoat
benny an amphetamine tablet used as a stimulant (slang); a closefitting benjamin overcoat (slang)

bennet (see **benet**)

Benny and **benny** (see **Beni**)

bensh (see **bench**)

Benz (see **bends**)

benzene a flammable, volatile, toxic aromatic liquid hydrocarbon
benzine a flammable, volatile petroleum distillate consisting chiefly of aliphatic hydrocarbons

benzil a yellow crystalline diketone made by oxidizing benzoin
benzyl the univalent radical derived from toluene by removing one hydrogen atom from the side chain

benzine (see **benzene**)

benzyl (see **benzil**)

ber (see **bare**)

berdache (see **bedash**)

berg an iceberg
burg(h) a village

berley bait scattered on the water to attract fish
burley thin-bodied air-cured tobacco
burly strongly built; a burlesque

Berlin the capital of Germany
berlin a 4-wheeled 2-seated covered carriage
berline an enclosed automobile body having at the rear of the driver's seat a glass partition with usually one movable window

Bern(e) the capital of Switzerland
birn a socket on a clarinet into which the mouthpiece is fitted
burn to consume fuel

berok (see **baroque**)

berrier (see **barrier**)

berry (see **barry**)

berth a sleeping accommodation on a ship, plane, or train
birth the act of being born

beryl (see **barrel**)

Bete and **bete** (see **bait**)

betel (see **baetyl**)

beth (see **bait** or **base**)

betted (see **bedded**)

better (see **bedder**)

betting (see **bedding**)

bettor (see **bedder**)

beurre buttered, as "peas au buerre"
birr an onward rush, as of a wind or onslaught in battle
buhr a projection resembling a tooth on a millstone
bur a small rotary cutting tool
bur(r) a prickly envelope of some fruits and plants

beys (see **baize**)

bhabar a valuable Indian fibergrass used for making mats, rope, and paper

bobber a fishing float; a ruddy duck; a member of a bobsled team

b(h)ang the leaves and flowering tip of hemp
bong the deep resonant sound of a bell

bhangi a Hindu sweeper or scavenger
bungee an auxiliary spring device; an elasticized cord

Bhar (see **bahr**)

bharal a wild sheep having down-curved horns and living at high elevations in the Himalayas and Tibet
birl to revolve or cause a floating log to rotate by treading on it
birle to ply with drink; to carouse (seldom **birl**)
burl a hard woody tree growth
burral inferior land lying beside outfields
burrel a variety of pear having soft and melting flesh

bhat (see **baht**)

bheesty (see **beastie**)

Bhora a modern Shi'ite sect of western India retaining some Hindu elements
bora an occasional violent cold north to northeast wind that blows over the northern Adriatic sea; a rite in which Australian aborigine boys are initiated into manhood

bhut an especially malevolent spirit or ghost in India
boot a covering for the foot and leg that is usually made of leather or rubber

bi having sexual desire, commonly on an unconscious level, for members of both sexes
buy to purchase
by next to
bye the position of a tournament participant who faces no opponent in a particular round
'bye goodbye (by shortening)

bib a cloth worn around the chest
Bibb a variety of dark green lettuce with a small head
bibb a piece of timber bolted to the hounds of a ship's mast to support the trestletrees

bibi (see **bb**)

bibless being without a piece of cloth worn across the chest and often tied around the neck to protect clothing during eating
biblus a substance prepared from the pith of the papryus plant

bichir a large primitive fish found in the upper Nile
bitcher a person who complains, gripes, or grouses about something

bichy a kola nut
bitchy suggestive of malice or arrogance

bidder the maker of a bid, as in contract bridge; a person who invites or issues a mild order
bitter a strong, pungent, or unpleasant taste; acrid; grievous

bidding an offer of a price; an invitation or summons
bitting the shape of the bit of a key that causes it to actuate the lock

biddy an elderly housemaid or cleaning woman in a dormitory; an adult female domestic fowl
bitty made up of bits; scrappy; small or tiny

bide to continue in some state or condition
byed declined to bet or make a bid in a card game

bider a person who continues in some state or condition
biter one who seizes with the teeth

bidi (see **beady**)

biding waiting, tarrying, or awaiting one's pleasure

bighting arranging, laying, or fastening a rope in a curve or loop
biting seizing with the teeth

bier (see **beer**)

bietle (see **baetyl**)

biga a two-horse chariot of ancient Mediterranean countries
bigha any of various Indian units of land area varying between one-third and one acre

bight a curve or loop in a rope, hose, or chain
bite to seize with the teeth
byte a group of adjacent binary digits that a computer processes (binary digit eight)

bighting (see **biding**)

bile (see **bael**)

Bilin (see **baleen**)

billed charged a customer for merchandise; offered on a program
build to construct

billian a valuable timber tree of Borneo having heavy hard antproof wood
billion a thousand millions

bima(h) (see **bema**)

bin (see **bean** or **been**)

binds makes secure by tying
bines twining stems or flexible shoots

binnacle a container for a ship's compass and a lamp
binocle a binocular telescope, field glass, or opera glass

bio (see **bai-u**)

bird a warm-blooded egg-laying feathered vertebrate, usually able to fly
burred rough and prickly

birdie a golf score one under par on a hole
birdy abounding in birds

biretta (see **baretta**)

birl (see **bharal**)

birle (see **bharal**)

birma the Santa Maria tree, an evergreen tropical American tree
Burma a country in southeast Asia that changed it official name to the Union of Myanmar in 1989

birn (see **Bern[e]**)

birr (see **beurre**)

birri (see **beery**)

birth (see **berth**)

Biscayan a native or resident of Biscay province, Spain
biscayen a military musket or the ball used in it

bise (see **bees**)

bit a small quantity; the part of a steel bridle that is inserted in a horse's mouth
bitt a post fixed on a ship's deck around which lines are made fast

bitcher (see **bichir**)

bitchy (see **bichy**)

bite (see **bight**)

biter (see **bider**)

biting (see **biding**)

bitt (see **bit**)

bitter (see **bidder**)

bitting (see **bidding**)

bitty (see **biddy**)

biz (see **bais**)

bizarre (see **bazaar**)

blackie a black duck; a Canada goose
blacky somewhat dark-colored or blackish

blasted produced sounds of undesired loudness

blastid an enchinodrem or fossel of the class *Blastoidea*

blays a small European cyprinid fish
blaze a bright flame or intense light

bleater an animal or person that makes a sound suggestive of the call of sheep; any of several game birds that resemble the woodcock
bleeder a person that draws or gives blood

blend to mix or combine
blende any of several minerals with somewhat bright nonmetallic luster

blew produced an air current
Blue the University of Michigan football team
blue a color between green and violet, as a clear sky or deep sea

blewits an edible agaric (fungus) that is pale lilac when young
bluets a light blue color; any of several North American plants of the madder family

blight a plant disease or injury; to cause to deteriorate
blite any of several herbs, as the strawberry blite

bloc a combination of persons, groups, or nations for a common interest
block a solid piece of wood, metal, or stone

blooey out of order or awry (slang)
bluey a blue crab; any of several Australian lizards; a legal summons

Blue and **blue** (see **blew**)

bluetongue an African horse sickness; a serious virus desease of African sheep
blue-tongue a lizard of Tasmania

bluets (see **blewits**)

bluey (see **blooey**)

bo (see **beau**)

boar an uncastrated male swine
Boer a South African of Dutch or Huguenot descent
bore to pierce or drill a hole

board a piece of sawed lumber; to enter a ship, plane, bus, or train; a group of persons
bord a straight passageway driven at right angles to the main cleavage of coal in a mine
bored pierced or drilled a hole; devoid of interest

boarder a person provided with regular meals and or lodging
bordar a feudal tenant bound to menial service to a lord
border an outer part or edge

boardroom a room designated for meetings of a board which usually contains a large conference table
bordroom a space off a passageway from which coal is being or has been mined

boast to say or tell something intended to give others a high opinion of oneself
bosed tested ground by noting the sound of percussion from the blow of a heavy hammer

boat a small vessel propelled by oars, paddles, sail, or engine
bote compensation for injury to a person or honor

boating the act or sport of one who uses small watercraft
boding an omen or ominous premonition about the future

bobber (see **bhabar**)

bobbin (see **Babhan**)

bobble (see **bauble**)

boca a river mouth or harbor entrance
bocca a vent at the side or base of an active volcano from which lava flows

bocce or **bocci(e)** a bowling game of Italian origin
botchy full of defects: poorly done

boce a brightly colored European fish of the family Sparidae

Bos a genus of ruminant mammals including wild and domestic cattle

bose to test the ground by noting the sound of percussion from the blow of a heavy hammer

Boche a German, usually used disparagingly

bosh pretentious nonesense or silliness; the lower sloping part of a blast furnace

bocks bookbinding leathers made from sheepskin

box a square or oblong container

bod (see **baaed**)

bode to indicate by signs or be an omen of

bowed bent or curved

boding (see **boating**)

Boer (see **boar**)

Boer a South African of Dutch or Huguenot descent

booer a person who shouts disapproval or contempt

boor a rude, clumsy, insensitive, or boring person

bogey in golf, to shoot a hole in one stroke over par; a small stone

bogie tobacco in small twisted ropes

boh (see **beau**)

bolar resembling clay

bowler a player who delivers the ball to the batsman in cricket; a person who plays tenpins

bolas weapons consisting of two or more stone or iron balls attached to the ends of a cord which are used to ensnare animals

bolus a large rounded mass in the form of a pill or chewed food

bowless being without a weapon made of a strip of flexible material with a cord that connects the two ends

bold fearless in meeting danger or difficulty

boled having a cylindrical shape

bolled having or producing pods or capsules, as in a plant

bowled played the game of bowls or tenpins

bolder more fearless in meeting danger or difficulty

boulder a detached mass of rock

bole (see **baule**)

boled (see **bold**)

boll (see **baule**)

Bolle (see **baule**)

bolled (see **bold**)

bollix (see **ballocks**)

bollocks (see **ballocks**)

bolly a cotton pod or capsule that has remained unopened or partly opened usually as a result of frost injury

bowly a large usually rectangular sunken pool or well in India that serves as a public water supply

bolter an animal that is given to suddenly breaking away

boulter a line to which many hooks are attached for deep water bottomfishing

bolus (see **bolas**)

bomb (see **balm**)

bombard to attack with explosive projectiles or other explosive weaponry

bombarde a powerful reed stop of 32- or 16-foot pitch in a pipe organ

Bombay a city in India

bombé having an outward swelling curve in furniture

bombe (see **balm**)

bombous of a convex rounded surface

Bombus a genus of bees comprising the typical bumble bees

bombus a humming or buzzing noise in the intestines or ears

Bon (see **bawn**)

bon (see **ban**)

bon the broad or kidney bean; the stiff dried hand-cleaned but not completely degummed fiber of ramie
Bonn a city in western Germany

bonds (see **bans**)

bone (see **Beaune**)

bon(e)y skinny or scrawny; full of bone
Boni a Bush Negro people of the interior of French Guiana

bong (see **b[h]ang**)

Boni (see **bon[e]y**)

Bonn (see **bawn** or **bon**)

bonne (see **bawn**)

bonnes French maidservants
bunds embankments used to control the flow of water; politically oriented associations of people
buns round or oblong breadrolls; knots or coils of hair

bonnet (see **banat**)

bons (see **bans**)

bonze (see **bans**)

boo (see **beau**)

boobie a woman's breast (slang)
booby an awkward foolish person; any of several gannets of tropical seas
Bubi a Bantu-speaking people of the island of Fernando Po, West Africa

boo-boo a stupid or careless mistake
boubou any of several large African shrikes; a long, loose fitting brightly colored garment worn by both sexes in parts of Africa

booby (see **boobie**)

booer (see **Boer**)

boogie to dance the boogie-woogie; Negro, usually used disparagingly
Bugi an Indonesian people of the southern part of Sulawesi island

book a collection of folded sheets bearing printing or writing that have usualy been bound together into a volume
bouk the division between the reticular and abomasum in the stomach of a ruminant

bookie a person who determines odds and receives and pays off bets; a person who makes books
booky inclined to rely on knowledge obtained from books; bookish

bool a hoop for rolling
boule a game similar to roulette; inlaid decoration developed under Louis XIV
buhl inlaid decoration using tortoise shell, yellow metal, and white metal in cabinet work

booly a company of herdsmen wandering with their cattle
boule a legislative council of ancient Greece

boon an often timely and gratuitous benefit received and enjoyed; the woody portion of the stem of flax or hemp after the removal of fiber by retting
Boone a chert formation of the Mississippian geological series in the western Ozarks

boor (see **Boer**)

boor a rustic or peasant typically rough, crude, and insensitive
bourg a town or village

boos shouts of disapproval or contempt
booze an intoxicating drink
bouse carouse (also **bowse**)

boot (see **bhut**)

bootee an infant's sock of knitted or crocheted wool (also bootie)
booty plunder or spoils of war

buddhi the faculty of intuitive discernment or direct spiritual awareness in the beliefs of Hinduism and Buddhism

booze (see **boos**)

bora (see **Bhora**)

boraks something that ridicules, mocks, or scorns
borax a mineral used in glass, ceramics, agricultural chemicals, and as a water softener

bord (see **board**)

bordar (see **boarder**)

border (see **boarder**)

bordroom (see **boardroom**)

bore (see **boar**)

bored (see **board**)

born brought into existence
borne endured or tolerated
bourn(e) an intermittent stream

borough a village, township, or town
burro a small donkey
burrow a hole in the ground

Bos (see **baas** and **boce**)

bose (see **boce**)

bosed (see **boast**)

bosh (see **Boche**)

boss (see **baas** and **bas**)

bosse (see **baas**)

bossy (see **basi**)

botany the science of plants
botonny a cross having a cluster of three balls or knobs at the end of each arm

botchy (see **bocce**)

bote (see **boat**)

botonny (see **botany**)

bot(t) (see **baht**)

boubou (see **boo-boo**)

bouché stopped with the hand, as in French horn playing
bouchée a small patty or creampuff filled with creamed meat or fish
boucher a hand axe or crude stone implement used by paleolithic man

Bougainvillaea a genus of ornamental tropical American woody vines
Bougainvillia a widely distributed genus of marine hydrozoans

boughs (see **baos**)

bought a twist or turn in the grain of a bowstave
bout a round in a game or encounter

bouk (see **book**)

boulder (see **bolder**)

boule (see **bool** and **booly**)

boule a game similar to roulette; a pear-shaped mass of some substance formed synthetically in a Verneuil furnace
boulle inlaid cabinetwork decoration developed under Louis XIV

boullion a broth made by slowly boiling meat in water
bullion gold, silver, or other metal in the shape of bars or ingots

boulter (see **bolter**)

bourdon the drone bass, as in a bagpipe or hurdy-gurdy
burden something carried

bourette (see **barret**)

bourg (see **boor**)

bourn(e) (see **born**)

bouse (see **baos** and **boos**)

bout (see **bought**)

bouws (see **baos**)

bow (see **beau**)

bowed (see **bode**)

bowl (see **baule**)

bowled (see **bold**)

bowler (see **bolar**)

bowless (see **bolas**)

bowly (see **bolly**)

bows (see **baos** and **beaux**)

box (see **bocks**)

boy a male child

buoy an object floating in water and moored to the bottom to serve as a channel marker

bracked sorted or inspected merchandise

bract a somewhat modified leaf associated with the reproductive structures of a plant

brae glacier or ice cap

braies breeches or trousers worn during medieval times

bray a loud harsh cry characteristic of a donkey

brey a conventionalized heraldic representation of a pair of barnacles

braes glaciers or ice caps

braise to cook slowly in fat and little moisture in a tightly closed pot

brays utters a loud harsh cry characteristic of a donkey

braze to solder with an alloy

breys conventionalized heraldic representation of pairs of barnacles; softens skins or leather by working with the hands

brys buttermilk paps usually made with barley and eaten with sugar and syrup

Brahma an Asian breed of very large domestic fowls; any large vigorous heat resistant and tick-resistant Indian cattle

Brahmah an hydraulic machine that produces enormous pressure

Brahman any of several breeds of Indian cattle

Bremen a city in northwest Germany

braid a cord or ribbon, usually with three or more interwoven strands

brayed uttered a loud harsh cry characteristic of a donkey

breyed softened skins or leather by working with the hands

braies (see **brae**)

brail the feathers at a hawk's rump; a rake-like tool to harvest clams

Braille the system of tactile symbols by which blind persons read and write

brale a conical diamond indenter with an angle of 120 degrees that is used in the Rockwell hardness test

braise (see **braes**)

brake a device to arrest motion of a mechanism, often by friction; to apply such a device

break to split into pieces

braker a worker who rolls dough for baked goods or macarone products

breaker a plow with a moldboard arrangement for turning over virgin soil

brakie (or brakey) a member of a train crew whose duties include operating hand brakes (slang)

braky abounding with brambles, shrubs, or ferns

brale (see **brail**)

brand a mark made with a stencil or hot iron; to apply such a mark

branned cleansed of oil, especially with bran

branded impressed indelibly

brandied preserved in an alcoholic liquor distilled from wine or fermented fruit juice

brands marks of simple easily recognized pattern made by a hot iron, stencil, or strap; a class of goods associated with a single or manufacturer or firm

brans broken coats of the seeds of wheat, rye, or other cereal grain separated from the kernels

branned (see **brand**)

brans (see **brands**)

brasil a tree of Texas and adjacent Mexico yielding a yellow dye
Brazil the largest country in South America both in area and population
brazil the wood of a South American tree, brazilwood

brass an alloy of copper and a base metal, usually zinc or sometimes tin
brasse a European bass

brassie a wooden golf club soled with some metal
brassy resembling brass; coarse and impudent

brattice an often temporary partition used in a mine to control ventilation
brattish relating to, or suggestive of a spoiled child

bray (see **brae**)

brayed (see **braid**)

brays (see **braes**)

braze (see **braes**)

Brazil and **brazil** (see **brasil**)

breach an infraction or violation of some standard or law
breech short pants covering the hips and thighs; the buttocks

bread food made of flour dough or grain meal
bred reared or inculcated with certain traditions

break (see **brake**)

breaker (see **braker**)

bream a European freshwater cyprinoid fish
brim the edge or rim of a cup or hat

breast the front of the chest
Brest a seaport and city at the western extremity of France

bred (see **bread**)

breech (see **breach**)

breed to propagate sexually
bride a small joining that resembles a bar and is used to connect various parts of a lace pattern

brees girls or young women
breeze a steady light or moderate air current
Bries soft perishable cheeses ripened by mold

Bremen (see **Brahman**)

Brest (see **breast**)

brew to produce or bring about by mixing ingredients
bruh a pigtailed macaque of the East Indies

brewed produced or brought about by mixing ingredients
brood the young of animals hatched concurrently; to incubate eggs; to dwell moodily on a subject

brewhaha a serving of brew (slang)
brouhaha a confused medley of sounds

brews produces or brings about by mixing ingredients
bruhs pigtailed macaques of the East Indies
bruise an injury caused by a blow not breaking the injured surface
bruzz a wheelwright's corner chisel

brey (see **bray**)

breyed (see **braid**)

breys (see **braes**)

brickie a bricklayer (slang)
bricky tipsy

bricks a building or paving material made of molded clay
brix the percentage of sugar concentration by weight according to the Brix scale

bricky (see **brickie**)

bridal a nuptial festival or ceremony

bridle a headgear by which a horse is controlled

bride (see **breed**)

bridle (see **bridal**)

Bries (see **brees**)

bril a unit of subjective luminance
brill a European flatfish related to the turbot

brilliance sparkling with luster
brilliants old sizes of type (approximately 3½ point) smaller than diamond

brim (see **bream**)

brisk moving quickly; alert, lively, or sprightly
brisque an ace or ten in certain card games, as in bezique

Britain Great Britain (by shortening)
Briton a member of one of the peoples inhabiting Britain prior to the Anglo-Saxon invasions
britten the red-necked grebe, a shorebird

brix (see **bricks**)

bro brother (slang)
broh a pigtailed macaque of the East Indies

broach to turn dangerously broadside to the waves; to introduce a subject for discussion
brooch a fastening device now used chiefly for ornamental jewelry

broad-boughed a tree broadly or widely branched
broad-bowed something, such as a ship, possessing a broadly curved bow

brocard an elementary principle or maxim
brokered functioned as negotiator or intermediary

broch a prehistoric circular stone tower found on the Orkney and Shetland islands and the Scottish mainland
brock a badger

broh (see **bro**)

brokered (see **brocard**)

brome a grass of the genus Bromus, as awnless bromegrass
brougham a vehicle similar to a carriage or automobile with the driver's seat outside

bromous pertaining to an unstable acid believed to be formed in solution by action of bromine water on silver nitrate
Bromus a large genus of grasses native to temperate regions

bronks unbroken or imperfectly broken range horses of western North America
Bronx a borough of New York City

brooch (see **broach**)

brood (see **brewed**)

brooded sat on or incubated eggs for the purpose of hatching; pondered
bruited made celebrated by general mention or publicity

brookie a brook trout
brooky full of creeks

broom a sweeping implement; any of various leguminous shrubs
brougham a vehicle similar to a carriage or automobile with the driver's seat outside
brume mist, fog, or vapor

brougham (see **brome** or **broom**)

brouhaha (see **brewhaha**)

brownie a good natured goblin; a member of the Girl Scouts between ages seven through nine
browny verging on the color brown

brows foreheads
browse to gaze; to look over casually

bruh (see **brew**)

bruhs (see **brews**)

bruise (see **brews**)

bruit to publicize or tout
Brut a medieval chronicle of Britain
brute utterly lacking in sensitivity or
 higher feelings

bruited (see **brooded**)

brume (see **broom**)

Brut (see **bruit**)

brute (see **bruit**)

bruzz (see **brews**)

brys (see **braes**)

Bubalis a genus of African antelopes including the hartebeest
Bubalus a genus of Bovidae comprising
 mud-wallowing buffaloes of Asia

Bubi (see **boobie**)

buccal relating to the cheeks
buckle an ornamental fastening device; to
 warp, bend, or heave

bucco the dried leaves of certain plants of
 the genera Barosma and Diosma used as
 a diuretic and diaphoretic
bucko a person who is domineering and
 bullying, especially officers of sailing
 ships

buckie an alewife fish that is smoked for
 food
bucky exhibiting characteristics of the
 male animal

buckle (see **buccal**)

bucko (see **bucco**)

bucky (see **buckie**)

bud an undeveloped shoot on a tree, bush,
 or flower
but except for that
butt to strike with the head or horns

budded commenced growth from a small
 lateral or terminal protuberance on the
 stem of a plant consisting of undeveloped shoots
butted placed end to end; struck with the
 head or horns

budder a person who inserts buds in plant
 stocks
butter a creamy spread; to cover with lav-
 ish praise or flattery

buddhi (see **bootee**)

buddle an inclined trough or platform on
 which crushed ore is concentrated by
 running water which washes out the
 lighter and less valuable portions
buttle to serve or act as a butler

buddy full or suggestive of buds; a close
 friend
butty a worker or middleman who takes
 an allotment of work by contract at so
 much per ton of coal or ore for execution; an archer's shooting companion

buffe woman singers of comic roles in
 opera
buffet a counter for refreshments and food

buffo a male singer or comic roles in
 opera
Bufo a large genus of toads that contains
 the common toads of America and Europe
bufo any toad of the genus *Bufo*

Bugi (see **boogie**)

buhl (see **bool**)

buhr (see **buerre**)

build (see **billed**)

bullace a small wild or half-domesticated
 European plum
bullous resembling or characterized by
 large vesicles or elevation of cuticles
 usually containing serum

bullae small leather or metal cases containing amulets and suspended by a cord
 around the neck; blisterlike or bubble-
 like prominences of a bone
bully a person given to browbeating and
 threatening; of the best quality, excellent, or first-rate

bullion (see **bouillion**)

bullous (see **bullace**)

bullseye a reddish small-scaled Australian food fish
bull's-eye the center of a target

bully (see **bullae**)

bulto a bundle of fibers for roop making
bultow a long heavy fishline consisting of one or more skates of gear that is anchored at either end

bunds (see **bonnes**)

bundy (see **bandy**)

bungee (see **bhangi**)

bunion (see **banyan**)

bunkie a bunkmate (slang)
bunky full of nonesense

bunnia one of a cast of Hindu merchants and traders
bunya an Autralian coniferous tree
bunyah a cocique, a tropical American oriole

buns (see **bonnes**)

bunya (see **bunnia**)

bunyah (see **bunnia**)

buoy (see **boy**)

bur (see **beurre**)

burden (see **bourdon**)

bureau a low chest of drawers, often with a mirror
buro the policy-forming committee of the Communist part of the former U.S.S.R.

burger a flat cake of ground or chopped meat fried or grilled and served between slices of bread
Burgher a Ceylonese of mixed blood, specifically of Dutch descent
burgher a resident of a town

burg(h) (see **berg**)

burghal relating to a municipal corporation

burgle to burglarize

Burgher and **burgher** (see **burger**)

burgle (see **burghal**)

burier (see **barrier**)

burl (see **bharal**)

burley (see **berley**)

burly (see **berley**)

Burma (see **birma**)

burn (see **Bern[e]**)

burnie a partially smoked marijuana cigarette
burny inclined to burn
byrnie a coat of mail

buro (see **bureau**)

burral (see **bharal**)

burred (see **bird**)

burrel (see **bharal**)

burro (see **borough**)

burrow (see **borough**)

bur(r) (see **beurre**)

bury (see **barry**)

bus (see **bas**)

buss (see **bas**)

bussed kissed; transported by bus
bust a sculptured representation of the upper part of the human figure; to punch or break open

but (see **bud**)

bute (see **beaut**)

butt (see **bud**)

Butte and **butte** (see **beaut**)

butted (see **budded**)

butter (see **budder**)

butteris a steel instrument for paring horse hoofs
buttress a projecting structure of masonry

or wood for supporting or giving stability to a wall

buttle (see **buddle**)

buttress (see **butteris**)

butty (see **buddy**)

buy (see **bi**)

by (see **bi**)

byard (see **bard**)

bye (see **bi**)

'bye (see **bi**)

bye-bye (see **bay-bay**)

byed (see **bide**)

byo (see **bai-u**)

bypassed detoured around
bypast something that is past or bygone

byrnie (see **burnie**)

byrrh (see **beer**)

byte (see **bight**)

Group I

bacchanal - bacchanale
bacchant - bacchante
baggie - baggy
bar - barre
bargainer - bargainor
belligerence - belligerents
bivalence - bivalents
blender - blendor
boosy - boozy
borts - bortz
broad-gage - broad-gauge
brunet - brunette
bulbous - bulbus
buret - burette
burka - burqa
byssin - byssine

Group I and II

biographee bī'ägrə‚fē
biography bī'ägrəfē

bourg 'bůrg
burg(h) 'bərg

Group II

Bacchae 'bak‚ē
baccy 'bakē

bade 'baad
bayed 'bād

baht 'bät
bought 'bȯt

bailee bā'lē
bailey 'bālē

balks 'bȯks
box 'bäks

ballad 'baləd
ballade ba'läd

bal(l)on ba'lōn
balloon bə'lün
balun 'ba‚lən

bandar 'bəndər
bander 'bandər

banzai 'bän'zī
bonsai 'bän‚sī

bar 'bär
barré bä'rā

baratte bə'rat
barret bə'ret

barbel 'bärbəl
barbell 'bär‚bel

barbet 'barbət
barbette bär'bet

baren 'bä‚ren
baron 'barən

baritone 'barə‚tōn
baryton 'barə‚tän

barré bä:rā
beret bə'rā

baton bə'tän
beton bā'tȯn

Baumer 'bȯmər
bomber 'bämər

bawdy 'bȯdē
body bädē

beery 'birē or 'biri
biri 'bērē

Begar 'bā,gär
beggar 'begər

béguin bāgaⁿ
Beguine bə'gēn

below bē'lō
bilo 'bēlō

Berlin bər'lin
birlinn 'berlin

beryl 'berəl
birl 'bərl

besot bə'sȯt
besought bə'sät

binnacle 'binəkəl
binocle 'binokl

blanket 'blaŋkət
blanquette blänket

blowen 'blōən
blown 'blōn

boor 'bōr
boar 'bu̇r

Boran bō'rän
boron 'bō,rän

bot(t) 'bät
bought 'bȯt

bourgeois 'bu̇(r)zh,wä
bushwah 'bu̇sh,wä

bourse 'bu̇rs
burse 'bərs

bowyer 'bōyər
boyar bō'yär

brickle 'brikəl
bricole bri'kōl

brut 'brʊ̇et
brute 'brüt

buffi 'büfē
buffy 'bəfē

buhlwork 'bül,wərk
bulwork 'bu̇l,wərk

bulbil 'bəlbəl
bulbul 'bu̇l,bu̇l

Bulgar 'bu̇l,gär
bulgur 'bu̇l:gu̇r

bustee 'bə,stē
busty 'bəstē

C

C a high level, highly structured, problem-oriented programming language, bearing a strong resemblance to PASCAL
sea a body of salty water
si a music syllable in the sol-fa sequence
caam the heddles of a loom
calm stillness or quietude

caama a southern African fox
cama a cowboy's bedroll
comma a punctuation mark
kaama a large African antelope
Kama the Hindu god of love
kama in Hinduism, enjoyment of the world of the senses as an end of humanity

caaming setting the reed in weaving by properly placing the warp yarns
calming quieting or soothing

caapi a vine of northwestern South America
copje a small hill, especially on the African veld
copy a reproduction of original work
kappie a sunbonnet
kopje a small hill found expecially on the African veld

caatinga a stunted rather sparse forest in northeastern Brazil that is leafless in the dry season
Cotinga the type of genus of birds called Cotingidae that are related to the manakins
cotinga a bird of the family Contingidae

cache a hiding place
cash ready money

cachou an aromatic pill or pastille made of licorice, various aromatics, and gum that is used to sweeten the breath
cashew a tropical American tree important chiefly for its nut
cashoo an extract of the heartwood of an East Indian acacia; a variable color averaging auburn

cacky sticky or muddy; to void excrement
khaki a durable cotton or woolen cloth used for military uniforms; a light yellowish brown color

cacoon a tropical American plant
cocoon an envelope that larvae of many insects form about themselves prior to changing to a pupa
kokoon a brindled gnu

cadalene a colorless liquid hydrocarbon obtained by dehydrogenating cadinene
Catalan a native or inhabitant of Catalonia, an eastern region of Spain
Catalin a thermosetting plastic made of a cast phenol-formaldehyde resin

caddish like a person without gentlemanly instincts
cattish like a cat; spiteful

caddy a person who assists a golfer; any container for storing frequently used things when they are not in use
catty having characteristics resembling those of a cat; stealthy; agile

cade an animal left by the mother and reared by a human
quayed furnished with a landing place alongside navigable water

cadet a pupil in a military school; a grayish blue color
cadette a member of the Girl Scouts aged 12–14

Caecilian a member of the family Caeciliidae, which includes small slender wormlike burrowing amphibians
Sicilian a native or inhabitant of Sicily

Caesar a Roman emperor; a powerful ruler
seizer a person or animal that takes by force
seizor a person who takes possession of a freehold estate

caffa a rich silk cloth with printed or woven designs popular in the 16th century
Kafa a native of the Kafu region in southwestern Ethiopia
Kaffa a grayish reddish brown color

Cain a red or reddish yellow color; trouble, disturbance, or uproar
caine cocaine (by shortening)
cane a hollow or pithy jointed stem; a walking stick

caique a light skiff used on the Bosporus
kike a Jew, usually taken to be offensive

Cairo the capital of Egypt
Chi-Rho a Christian monogram and symbol formed by the first two letters of the Greek word for Christ

cak(e)y having or tending to form crusts or lumps
keiki a child; an immature plant

cala a picnic ham, a shoulder of pork with much of the butt removed commonly smoked and often boned
Calla a genus of bog herbs
calla a familiar house plant or green house plant
callow lacking bird feathers

calabar the gray fur of a Siberian squirrel (also **caliber**)
calabur a tropical American shrub or small tree
caliber a tube's internal diameter

calc a branch of mathematics (by shortening); a small portable calculator (by shortening)
calque a linguistic borrowing from another language

calculous affected with gravel or stone
calculus a branch of mathematics dealing with the limit concept; a concretion of salts around organic matter

calendar a tabular chronological register of events, things, or persons
calender to press material between rollers or plates to make or smooth into sheets

calf the fleshy hind part of the leg below the knee; a young of domestic cattle
calve to give birth to a calf
coff coffee (by shortening)
cough to expel air from the lungs suddenly and explosively
Kaf a mountain range in Moslem mythology that encircles the earth and where lives a mythical bird of wisdom
kaph the eleventh letter of the Hebrew alphabet
koff a two-masted vessel with spritsails used by the Dutch and Dane

caliber (see **calabar**)

caliginous misty, dark, or obscure
kaligenous forming alkalies

calix an ecclesiastical chalice
calyx the outer set of floral leaves making up a flower's external part

calk a pointed device worn on a shoe to prevent slipping (seldom **caulk**)
Cauc Caucasian (by shortening)
cauk to secure by a tenon
caulk to make a seam watertight or airtight (seldom **calk**)
cawk an opaque compact variety of the mineral barite

call to summon
caul a covering network

Calla and **calla** (see **cala**)

callous unfeeling; a protective condition of mental or emotional insensitivity
callus a hardened layer of skin

callow (see **cala**)

calm (see **caam**)

calmant a sedative
comment a note or observation intended to explain, illustrate, or criticize

calmer more tranquil, serene, or placid
colmar a fan fashionable during Queen Anne's reign

calming (see **caaming**)

calmly in a calm, quiet, or composed manner
comely having a pleasing appearance

calot a close-fitting cap without brim or visor
calotte a large glacier not confined to a single valley

calque (see **calc**)

calques linguistic borrowings by one language from another
calx friable residue left when a mineral or metal has been subjected to roasting

caltrap a heraldic representation of a military caltrop
caltrop any of several plants having stout spines on the fruit or flower heads

calumniation slandering
columniation the use of arrangement of columns in a building

calve (see **calf**)

calve to give birth to a calf

<u>cave</u> the sum which each player puts on the table at the beginning of play in such card games as brelan and bouillette

calvous lacking all or most of the hair on the head

calvus a cumulonimbus cloud having its upper portion changing from a rounded cumuliform shape to a diffuse, whitish, cirriform mass with vertical striations

calx (see **calques**)

calyx (see **calix**)

cam a rotating or sliding piece of machinery

<u>cham</u> a local chieftan, especially in Afghanistan, Iran, and some areas of central Asia

cama (see **caama**)

camara the hard and durable wood of the tonka-bean tree

camera a chamber, room, or hall; a light-proof box fitted with a lens for taking photographs

camas(s) an American plant of the genus Camassia of the western U.S.

camus a short and flat or concave nose; pug-nosed

came moved toward something; arrived: a slender grooved rod of cast lead used to hold glass panes in a window

kame a short ridge of stratified drift deposited by glacial meltwater

camera (see **camara**)

campaign a connected series of determined operations or systematic efforts designed to bring about a particular result

campane in heraldry, a bell

campi grounds and buildings of universities, colleges, or schools

campy comically exaggerated

Camptosaurus a small unspecialized bipedal duck-billed dinosaur

Camptosorus a fern having lanceolate fronds that root at the tips

campy (see **campi**)

camus (see **camas[s]**)

can know how to; a container

cann a bulbous drinking mug

Cannes a city and resort area in southeast France on the Mediterranean sea

khan a local chieftain in some areas of central Asia; a rest house in some Asian countries

can know how to

Chen a genus of geese, including the snow goose

ken the range of comprehension or perception

Canada a country in northern North America; a Canada goose

Kannada the major Dravidian language of Mysore, south India

canapé an appetizer consisting of savory food atop a cracker or bread

canopy a covering for shelter or protection

cancellous having a spongy or porous structure

cancellus a screen or rail typically of stone grating or latticework used to enclose or separate a part of a church and the altar or choir

cand the transparent or translucent mineral fluorite

canned enclosed or preserved in a container; put a stop or end to

cane (see **Cain**)

canions close-fitting ornamental knee-pieces joining the upper and lower parts of the leg covering worn by men in Elizabethan England

canyons deep narrow valleys with steep sides

cann (see **can**)

cannable suitable for canning or preserving

cannibal an animal that devours its own kind

canned (see **cand**)

Cannes (see **can**)

cannon a metal tubular weapon for firing projectiles

Canon an ecclesiastical decree, regulation, or code

canon one of the clergy of a medieval cathedral or large church

cannibal (see **cannable**)

cannonry cannonading or artillery

canonry a body of canons

Canon and **canon** (see **cannon**)

canonry (see **cannonry**)

canopy (see **canapé**)

cant jargon; an inclination or slope; to cut at an angle

can't contraction of cannot

quint a segment of three playing cards of the same suit

quinte a protective parry in fencing

canter a three-beat gait that is smoother and slower than a gallop

cantor a choir leader; a singer of Jewish liturgical music

Cantharis a brilliant green blister beetle common in southern Europe

cantharus a basin or stoup containing holy water; a deep cut of ancient Greece with a high stem and loop-shaped handles

cantor (see **canter**)

canvas to cover or furnish with canvas

canvass a personal solicitation of votes or opinions; a full discussion

canyons (see **canions**)

cap a covering for the head, typically fairly tight-fitting, brimless, and relatively simple

kapp a unit of magnetic lines of force

capa a fine grade of Cuban tobacco

cappa a cape that is part of ecclesiastical or academic garb

coppa an Italian sausage made chiefly of pork butts

kappa the tenth letter of the Greek alphabet

cape a judicial writ, now abolished, relative to a plea of lands or tenements

kepi a military cap with a closefitting band, a round flat top sloping toward the front, and a visor

KP kitchen police, enlisted personnel detailed to assist cooks in a military mess

capelin a small salmonoid marine fish

capeline a woman's hat with a small crown and a wide, soft brim

Capella a genus of birds containing the snipes

kapelle the choir or orchestra of a royal or papal choir

capital a stock of accumulated goods; money; a column's uppermost member

capitol the building in which a legislative body meets

capot the winning of all the tricks in piquet and other games

cappo a usually long and hooded cloak or overcoat of rough cloth worn especially by travelers and soldiers

cappa (see **capa**)

cappo (see **capot**)

cappae capes especially as parts of ecclesiastical or academic garb

cappy having a tallow taste because of butterfat oxidation

kappie a sunbonnet

caprin any of the esters of glycerol and capric acid

caprine suggestive of a goat

captain a military officer; a leader or chief

captan a white to cream colored powder used as a fungicide on food plants and flowers

car a vehicle moving on wheels

kar an inland lake or glacier pot formed by the direct erosive action of ice

carab a beetle

Carib an Indian people of northern Brazil extending northward to Belize

carob a leguminous tree of the Mediterranean that yields edible pods

carat a unit of weight for precious stones

caret a mark on written material indicating where something is to be inserted

carrot a biennial plant with a tapering root used as a vegetable

karat a unit of fineness for gold equal to ¹⁄₂₄ part of pure gold (seldom **carat**)

carate a disease endemic in tropical America that is characterized by the presence of various colored spots

karate a Japanese martial art of self defense

carbeen an Australian eucalypt

carbene a component of bitumen soluble in carbon disulfide

carbine a short-barreled lightweight rifle

carbine any short-barreled lightweight rifle

carbon a nonmetallic chiefly tetravalent element

carbinyl the univalent radical corresponding to any alcohol derived from methanol

carbonyl the bivalent radical CO occurring in aldehydes, ketones, esters, and amides

carbon (see **carbine**)

carbonyl (see **carbinyl**)

card to cleanse, disentangle, and collect together animal or vegetable fibers; a flat thin piece of paperboard

carred carried or placed in an automobile

carded mounted on a card; disentangled and prepared fibers for spinning

carted carried or conveyed in a cart

carder a person that attaches cards to articles for display or sale

carter a person who is engaged in vehicle transport; a teamster

caret (see **carat**)

Carian a native or inhabitant of ancient Caria, a division of southwest Asia Minor

carrion the dead and putrefying flesh of an animal

Carib (see **carab**)

caries tooth decay

carries transports while supporting or holding

Carys substages of the Wisconsin glacial stage

karris large gum trees of western Australia

Carinthian of or relating to the Austrian province of Carinthia

Corinthian of, relating to, or characteristic of Corinth, Greece; a gay profligate licentious man; of or belonging to the lightest and most ornate of the three Greek orders

carman a car driver

carmen a song, poem, or incantation

carmine a vivid red color

carnalite a person of marked sensual appetites

carnallite a hydrous potassium-magnesium chloride

carob (see **carab**)

carol to sing joyously; a song

carrel a small alcove in a library for individual study

Karel relating to Karelia, a region of northwestern Russia adjoining eastern Finland

kerril a sea snake of the Asiatic coast from the Persian Gulf to Japan

keryl a mixture of alkyl radicals derived from kerosene

carom to rebound; a rebound at an angle

Carum a genus of biennial aromatic herbs

carom a billard shot in which the cue ball strikes each of two object balls; a glancing off

cherem one of three forms of ecclesiastical excommunication pronounced by a rabbi

carpal pertaining to the wrist

carpel a structure in a seed plant comprising the innermost whorl of its flower

carred (see **card**)

carrel (see **carol**)

carries (see **caries**)

carrion (see **Carian**)

carrot (see **carat**)

car(r)ousel a merry-go-round

karrusel an escapement designed to reduce position errors in a watch

carry to transport while supporting or holding

Cary a substage of the Wisconsin glacial stage

karri a large gum tree of western Australia

kerrie a knobkerrie, a rather short wooden club with a heavy round knob at one end that may be thrown as a missile or used in close attack

Kerry an Irish breed of small, hardy, long-lived black cattle noted for their milk

carryon luggage that may accompany a person in the passenger compartment

carry-on to act in a foolish, excited, or improper manner

karyon the nucleus of a cell

cart a small, usually lightweight wheeled vehicle

carte a chart, map, or diagram; a bill of fare; a playing card

kart a miniature motorcar used for racing

quart a sequence of four playing cards of the same suit

quarte a fencer's parry or guard position; a sequence of four playing cards of the same suit

carted (see **carded**)

cartel a vountary often international combination of independent private enterprises supplying like commodities

kartel a wooden bed or hammock

carter (see **carder**)

Carum (see **carom**)

Cary (see **carry**)

Carys (see **carries**)

cash (see **cache**)

cashew (see **cachou**)

cashoo (see **cachou**)

cask a barrel-shaped container made of staves, headings, and hoops

casque head armor; a process or structure suggesting a helmet

casket a coffin or repository

casquet a light piece of armor covering the head

casquette a cap with a visor

casque (see **cask**)

casquet (see **casket**)

casquette (see **casket**)

cassette a light tight magazine for holding sensitized film of plates for use in a camera

cossette a strip or slice; a chip

Cassia a genus of herbs, shrubs, and trees native to warm regions (usually 'kasēə)

cassia any of the coarser varieties of cinnamon bark

Kasha a softnapped twilled fabric of fine wool and hair

cast to throw; to form in a mold; a group of actors

caste a social division or class

caster a person who throws; a wheel or wheels mounted in a frame and free to swivel

Castor a genus of mammals comprising the beavers

castor a beaver skin

castoff the lateral offset of the stock of a longgun that enables the shooter's eye to be brought in line with the sights

cast-off thrown away or aside

Castor or **castor** (see **caster**)

cat a shrub cultivated by the Arabs for its leaves which act as a stimulant narcotic when chewed or used in tea

cot a bed made of canvas stretched on a frame

cotte a tight-fitting garment resembling a cotehardie, a long-sleeved thigh-length medieval garment

Kot an extinct people once living along the Agul river in Siberia

xat a carved pole erected as a memorial to the dead by some Indians of western North America

cat a carnivorous quadruped that has long been kept by humans as a domesticated pet

kat a shrub cultivated by Arabs for its leaves, which act as a stimulant narcotic

Catalan (see **cadalene**)

Catalin (see **cadalene**)

catarrh inflammation of a mucous membrane characterized by congestion and secretion of mucus

kitar an Arabian guitar

kuttar a short dagger

Qatar an independent emirate on the Persian gulf, (infrequently **Katar**)

catch to capture or seize

ketch a fore-and-aft-rigged boat

cate a dainty or choice food

kate a pileated woodpecker

catfoot a biennial cudweed

cat-foot to move in a manner suggesting a feline

cattish (see **caddish**)

catty (see **caddy**)

Cauc (see **calk**)

caucus meeting of an organization's leaders to decide plans

coccous composed of spherical bacteria

Coccus the type genus of *Coccidae* including certain typical scales

coccus one of the two carpels that resemble achenes in an umbelliferous plant

caudal relating to the tail or toward the hind part of the body

caudle a drink made of warm ale or wine and mixed with other ingredients

caught captured or seized

cotte a tight-fitting garment resembling a cotehardie, a long-sleeved thigh-length medieval garment

Kot an extinct people once living along the Agul river in Siberia

cauk (see **calk**)

caul (see **call**)

caulk (see **calk**)

caulker a worker who forces sealing matter into seams or joints with a caulking tool to make them watertight

cocker in archery, a ground quiver; a person who handles fighting roosters; a cocker spaniel

kakar a small deer of southeastern Asia and the East Indies

Caurus a northwest wind, which in Italy is stormy

chorus an organized company of singers who perform in concert

cause something that affects a result

caws utters a harsh, raucous cry characteristic of a crow

Kaws the most southerly group of Lolo-speaking Tibeto-Burman people forming a large part of the hill tribes of Shan state, Myanmar

causes brings into existence

Causus a genus of nocturnal venomous African snakes

cave (see **calve**)

cavel a cudgel or staff

cavil to object or criticize adversely for trivial reasons

caw a harsh raucous throaty outcry, such as a crow's call

Kaw a Siouan people of the Kansas river valley

cawk (see **calk**)

caws (see **cause**)

cay a small low island or emergent reef

k a unit vector parallel to the Z axis

qua in the character, role, or capacity of

quai a person lying along the Seine river in Paris; a landing on the left bank of the Seine river in Paris noted for its bookstalls

quay a landing place alongside navigable water for loading and unloading

cay a small low island or emergent reef

key a device inserted in a lock or bolt to open it

ki any of several Asiatic and Pacific trees or shrubs of the genus *Cordyline*

quay a landing place alongside navigable water for loading and unloading

cay a monkey of the genus Cebus

chi the 22nd letter of the Greek alphabet

Kai a people on the Huon Gulf of the Territory of New Guinea

kye a mean and unworthy fellow

ceca cavities open at one end, as anatomical blind pouches

sika any of several deer of the eastern Asiatic mainland closely related to the Japanese deer

cedar a coniferous tree

ceder one who yields or withdraws

cedor an assigner of a debt or claim

cedre a moderate olive green color

seater a person who puts in seats; a tool for adjusting something (as a valve) into its seat

seeder an implement used to plant seeds

cedent an assigner of a debt or claim

sedent sitting, especially of a statue

ceder (see **cedar**)

cedor (see **cedar**)

cedre (see **cedar**)

cedrin colorless, bitter, crystalline substance, the active principle of cedron

cedrine of or pertaining to cedar or the cedar tree

cees things having the shape of the letter C

C's $100 dollar bills (slang)

psis plural of the 23rd letter of the Greek alphabet

seas bodies of salty water

sees perceives with the eye

seize to confiscate; to grasp or clutch

sis plural of the seventh tone of the diatonic scale

Szis members of a people found mainly in the Sadon area of the Myanmar-China frontier

ceil to line a ship's bottom and sides with planking; to make a ceiling

ciel a light blue color

seal an aquatic carnivorous mammal; to make secure

seel to close a hawk's eyes by drawing threads through its eyelids

cell a single room; a microscopic mass of protoplasm; a transparent sheet of celluloid

sell to exchange goods or services for money or the equivalent

cella the frequently hidden part of a Greek or Roman temple housing a deity's image

sella the mid-line depression on the surface of the phenoid bone in the skull

cellar a storage room or rooms below ground level

sellar involving the midline depression on

the surface of the sphenoid bone in the skull

seller a person who offers a good or service for sale

Celt a member of a division of early Indo-European peoples in Iron-age and pre–Roman Europe

kelt a salmon or sea trout that is weak and emaciated after spawning

Celtis a genus of trees and shrubs, as the hackberry

celtuce a celerylike vegetable derived from lettuce

cense a perfume

cents units of monetary value each equal to ⅟₁₀₀ of the U.S. dollar

scents smells; fills with or yields an odor

sense something to be grasped; a mechanism or faculty of perception, as seeing, hearing, tasting, feeling, or smelling

censer a vessel for burning incense

censor a person who scrutinizes communications to delete unauthorized material

senser a person who perceives something

sensor a device designed to respond to a physical stimulus

censo in Spanish law, an annuity or ground rent

senso a Chinese medicine for dropsy consisting of the dried secretion of a native food

censor (see **censer**)

censorial exercising a censor's function

sensorial preoccupied with or primarily responsive to sensations

censual related to a census

sensual related to or affecting sense organs or the senses

census a count of population, vital statistics, or other information

senses things to be grasped; mechanisms or faculties or perception

cent a unit of monetary value equal to ⅟₁₀₀ of the U.S. dollar

scent a fragrance; to smell; to fill with or yield odor

sent dispatched or transmitted

centare a metric unit of area equal to ⅟₁₀₀ of an acre; a square meter

centaur one of an ancient mythical Greek race dwelling in the mountains of Thessaly and imagined as men with the bodies of horses

center a point around which things revolve or pivot; the middle, core, or nucleus

scenter a person or animal that perceives or detects by smell

centry a substructure on which a masonry arch or vault is built

sentry a soldier standing guard

cents (see **cense**)

cepe an edible mushroom

cyp either of two tropical American timber trees called princewood

seep to enter or penetrate slowly; to ooze

sipe a small traction-producing hook or bracket-shaped groove in an auto tire

cephalin a gregarine trophozoite complete with epimerite and usually attached to the cells of the host

cephalon the anterior shield of a trilobite

'cept aphetic form of accept or except

sept a branch of a family

cepter a cell, group of cells, or organ functioning in the reception of stimuli

scepter a staff or baton borne by a sovereign as a symbol of authority

ceras one of the often brightly colored and branching integumentary papilliae that serve as gills on the backs of nudibranches

cerris the European Turkey oak

serous resembling the watery portion of an animal fluid

cercal relating to a tail

circle a closed plane curve every point of which is equidistant from its center

cercus a pair of segmented appendages near the posterior end of many insects

Circus a genus of hawks comprising the harriers

circus a spectacular public entertainment consisting of acts of skill, trained animals, and clowns

cere a protuberance at the base of a bird's bill

sear to scorch with a sudden application of intense heat

seer a person with extraordinary intuitive or spiritual insight

sere a dried up or withered condition

cereal foodstuff prepared of grain

serial arranged in a spatial or temporal succession of persons or things; appearing in successive parts

ceres a moderate orange color; protuberances at the base of bird bills

Seres a people of eastern Asia mentioned by Greeks and Romans as making silk fabrics

series a spatial or temporal succession of persons or things

ceresin a white or yellow hard brittle wax used as a substitute for beeswax

Saracen a nomadic people of the deserts between Syria and Arabia

sericin a gelatinous protein that cements the two fibroin filaments in a silk fiber

Cereus a genus of cacti of the western U.S. and tropical America, including saguaro

serious grave in appearance

Sirius the Dog Star, in the constellation Canis Major, and the brightest star in the heavens

ceria an oxide of cerium

Syria a country in southwestern Asia

ceric relating to or containing the element cerium in the tetravalent state

xeric low or deficient in moisture to support plant life

cerin a crystalline triterpenoid that is extracted from cork

cerine a mineral consisting of a hydrous silicate cerium and allied metals

cerise a moderate red color

siris any of several trees of the genus Albizzia, such as the silk tree

cerous relating to or containing the element cerium

cirrus a wispy white cloud

scirrhus a hard cancerous tumor

seeress a prophetess

serous resembling serum

cerris (see **ceras**)

cerulean of sky blue color

c(o)erulein a xanthene dye obtained by heating gallein with concentrated sulfuric acid

Cervus a genus of deer

service performance of work ordered or paid for by another

cession yielding to another

session a period devoted to a certain activity

cessionary an assignee or grantee of property, claim, or debt under a deed of conveyance

sessionary recurring or renewed at each session

cetaceous relating to the Cetacea which comprises whales, dolphins, and porpoises

setaceous consisting of, or resembling bristles

cete a group of badgers

seat something to sit in; an assigned sitting place

cetin a crystalline fat

seton a suture

cetyl a univalent radical that occurs in waxes

setal relating to slender, typically rigid or bristly and springy organs or parts of animals and plants

settle to establish a residence or community

Ceylon an island south of India which became the independent republic Sri Lanka in 1972

salon a usually spacious or elegant living room

cha(a)c one of the Mayan gods of rain and fertility

chock a wedge or block for steadying a body or holding it motionless; as completely as possible

chafer any of various beetles, including the June beetle

chaffer to discuss terms or haggle over the price

chair furniture to accommodate a sitting person

chare an odd job or task

cher attractive

chaise a light carriage or pleasure cart

shays slow, wood-burning, geared locomotives used for hauling logs to a mill

sheas rough-barked tropical African trees

chalet a remote herdsman's hut in the Alps

challis a lightweight soft clothing fabric

cham champagne (by shortening)

sham a trick that deludes

cham (see **cam**)

Chamaeleon a large genus of lizards including most of the Old World chameleons

chameleon a fickle person who is given to expedient or facile change in ideas or character

chamar a fan typically made of a yak's tail or peacock feathers

chummer a person that scatters chum in fishing

chameleon (see **Chamaeleon**)

chamois a small agile goatlike animal on

mountain ridges of Europoe and in the Caucacus

shammy a bag used by Autralian miners as a container for gold dust

Champagne an historic French province

champagne a white sparkling wine that undergoes the first fermentation in a cask and the second in a bottle

champaign an expanse of level open country

champain in heraldry, a broken or deflected line in an ordinary

chance an activity or event that occurs unpredictably

chants hymnlike repetitive melodies

chancre a primary sore or ulcer

shanker a person who makes or fastens on shanks

chant(e)y a song sung by sailors, often in rhythm with their work

shanty a small poorly built dwelling

chants (see **chance**)

chap a fellow; sore roughening of the skin

chape the metal piece at the back of a buckle that fastens it to a strap

chap a jaw or the fleshy covering of the jaw

chop to cut into with an implement

chape (see **chap**)

chaps a pair of joined leather leggings worn over trousers(s)

(s)chappes yarns or fabrics of spun silk

chard a beet with large yellowish-green leaves

charred converted to charcoal or carbon by exposure to heat

chare (see **chair**)

charpie lint

sharpie a long narrow shallow-draft sailboat; an exceptionally keen alert person

charque jerked meat

sharky infested with elasmobranch fish (sharks)

charred (see **chard**)

chartreuse a variable color averaging a brilliant yellow green; several vegetables arranged and cooked in a mold
Chartreux any of a breed of short-haired domestic cats of French origin

chary hesitant and vigilant about dangers and risks
cherry a fruit-bearing tree or shrub; a small smooth-skinned edible fruit

chased followed rapidly and intently
chaste abstaining from sexual intercourse

chat to talk in a light and familiar manner
chert an impure flintlike rock

château a large country house
Chatot an extinct Muskogean people of Florida west of the Apalachicola river

chatelain a governor or warden of a castle or fort
chatelaine an ornamental chain, pin, or clasp worn at a woman's waist

Chatot (see **chateau**)

chauffeurs persons employed to operate motor vehicles
chauffeuse a low-seated French fire side chair
shofars ram's horn blown at high Jewish observances

chaus an Old World wildcat, possibly the Kaffir cat
chiaus a cheat or swindler; a Turkish messenger or sergeant
chouse to drive or herd livestock roughly; to chase, harass, or stir up

chay any of various traveling or pleasure carriages
chez in the home or business place
shay a slow, wood-burning, geared locomotive used for hauling logs to a mill
shea a sea butter tree

cheap inexpensive
cheep to make a small birdlike sound or to chirp

cheapie something that costs very little money or effort to produce
cheepy inclined to make small bird-like sounds

check to impede progress; a bank draft
Czech a native of the Czech Republic

checker a person who marks, counts, tallies, or examines materials or products
chekker a stringed keyboard instrument of the 14th and 15th centuries

cheeky having well-developed cheeks; impudent or brazenfaced
chikee a stilthouse of the Seminole Indians that is open on all sides and thatched

cheep (see **cheap**)

cheepy (see **cheapie**)

cheer lightness of mind and feeling; gaiety
chir an East Indian resinous timber pine

chekker (see **checker**)

chela a claw, as on a crab or lobster
quila a grass of southern South America that resembles bamboo

chelae claws, as on a crab or lobster
keelie a common small Eurupean falcon, a kestrel

Chen (see **can**)

chenier a wooded ridge or sandy hummock in a swampy region
shinnery a thick interlacing growth of scrub oak in the West and Southwest

cher (see **chair**)

cherem (see **carom**)

Chermes a genus of aphids that feed chiefly on spruce and balsam
Kermes a genus of scales comprising those that form kermes, and various related North American and Australian scales
kermes dried female bodies of various scaled insects used as red dye

kermis entertainment usually given to raise money

cherry (see **chary**)

chert (see **chat**)

chesil a collective name for small pebbles, gravel, or shingle
chessel a cheese vat or mold

chevee a flat gemstone with a smooth depression
chevet the apsidal eastern termination of a church choir

chew to crush or grind in the mouth
Chuje an Indian people of northwestern Guatemala

chews crushes or grinds in the mouth
choose to select with free will
tchus expressions of distaste

chez (see **chay**)

Chi Chicago (by shortening)
shy easily frightened; timid

chi (see **cay**)

chiaus (see **chaus**)

chic artistic cleverness
sheik(h) a head of an Arab family, tribe, or village
Shik a people of Turkmenistan regarded as of Arabian origin

chic cleverly stylish
schick a drunk, in Australia

chic(c)ory a thick-rooted, usually blue-flowered perennial herb
chickery a poultry hatchery

chickee a small or young chicken
chikee a stilthouse of the Seminole Indians that is open on all sides and thatched

chickery (see **chic[c]ory**)

chico the marmalade tree or its fruit
chicot the Kentucky coffed tree or its seeds

chigger a six-legged larval mite that at-taches itself to various vertebrates to suck blood
jigger to jerk up and down; a measure used in mixing drinks

chikee (see **cheeky** or **chickee**)

chil an Indian kite (a bird)
chill to make cold

Chile a South American country
chili a thick sauce made principally of meat, tomatoes, and hot peppers (chilies)
chilly noticeably cold

chill (see **chil**)

chilly (see **Chile**)

Chilo a genus of small slender dull colored nocturnal moths
Kyloe a breed of small very hardy beef cattle from the Highlands of Scotland having thick shaggy hair

chinca a South American rodent related to, but larger than, a chinchilla
chinche a skunk

'chine an automobile or motor vehicle (by shortening **machine**)
sheen a bright or shining condition
Shin a major Japanese Buddhist sect growing out of Jodo
shin the 22nd letter of the Hebrew alphabet

ching a Chinese scripture
jing a mild oath, as in the phrase "by jing"

chins lower portions of the face lying beneath the lower lip
chintz a firm glazed cotton fabric of plain weave
chintze to caulk

chir (see **cheer**)

Chi-Rho (see **Cairo**)

chirr the short especially vibrant or trilled and repetitive sound characteristic of certain insects, like grasshoppers and cicadas
churr a whirring noise characteristic of

some birds such as the nightjar or partridge

chitin the amorphous horny substance forming part of the hard outer covering of insects
Chiton a genus of mollusks
chiton the basic garment of ancient Greece; a mollusk of the order Polyplacophora

chive a perennial plant related to the onion
sheave a pulley block's grooved wheel
shiv a knife
shive a small fragment of plant matter

Chivey a small whitefish occurring in lakes in Alaska, Canda, and parts of northern U.S.
shivy containing small fragments of plant matter

chlor a yellowish green color
chlore to treat with a dilute solution of bleaching powder

chlorin any of several derivatives of chlorophyll obtained by hydrolysis
chlorine a common nonmetallic gaseous element

chlorogenin a steroidal sapogenin obtained from a soap plant
chlorogenine an alkaloid found in a tree bark

chock (see **cha[a]c**)

choir an organized group of singers
quire four sheets of paper folded into eight leaves

cholate a salt or ester of cholic acid
collate to assemble according to an orderly system; to bring together for close comparison

choler a ready disposition to anger and irritation
coaler something (as a railroad or ship) chiefly employed in transporting or supplying coal

choler a ready disposition to anger and irritation

collar a neckband; a ring placed on an object, as a pipe

cholic of or pertaining to bile secreted by the liver
colic a paroxysm of acute abdominal pain in man or animals localized in a hollow organ or tube and caused by a spasm, obstruction, or twisting

choline a crystalline or syrupy liquid base widely distributed among animal and plant products
colleen an Irish girl

chondre a rounded granule of cosmic origin usually consisting of enstatite or chrysolite
condor a very large American vulture found in elevated parts of the Andes

choose (see **chews**)

chop (see **chap**)

chorale a hymn or song sung by a choir or congregation
coral a skeletal deposit produced by certain anthozoan polyps
corol the inner set of floral leaves

chorale a hymn or psalm sung by a choir or congregation
corral an enclosure for confining livestock

chord a combination of two or more tones sounded together
cord a slender flexible cylindrical construction of several threads or yarns spun together
cored removed the axial portion, as of an apple

chordae a longitudinal flexible rod of cells that acts as a specific inductor of neural plate formation
chordee painful erection of the penis common as a lesion of gonorrhea

chordal relating to music characterized more by vertical harmony than linear contrapuntal motion
cordelle a towline used on keelboats on U.S. and Canadian rivers

chordate having a notochord
cordate shaped like a heart

chordee (see **chordae**)

chorea any of various nervous disorders having marked uncoordination of various parts of the body
Correa a small genus of Australian shrubs
correa any plant of the genus Correa
keriah a Jewish ritual of rending one's garment at the funeral of a near relative as a symbol of mourning
Korea a country in eastern Asia, divided into North Korea and South Korea since 1948

choree a trochee in classical prosody
karree a southern African plant of the genus *Rhus*
kere a reading that in the traditional Jewish mode of reading the Hebrew bible is substituted for one actually standing in he consonantal text

chorine a chorus girl
Corine narcotics

chorion the highly vascular outer embryonic membrane of higher vertebrates
Korean a native or inhabitant of North or South Korea

chorus (see **Caurus**)

chose a piece of personal property
shous Chinese characters signifying longevity that are often used in decoration
shows puts on view or displays

chott a shallow saline lake of northern Africa (also **shott**)
shot directed the propelling of a missile
shott a young hog of either sex, especially less than one year old

chou a soft cabbage-shaped ornament or rosette of fabric used in women's wear
choux darlings, used as a term of endearment
shoe an outer covering for the foot

shoo to scare or drive away
shu in Confucianism, reciprocity or mutual considerateness in all actions

chough an Old World bird, as the jackdaw
chuff a miser; a brick cracked by rain during burning

chouse (see **chaus**)

choux soft cabbage-shaped ornaments or rosettes of fabric used in women's wear
shoes outer coverings for the foot
shoos scares or drives away

choux (see **chou**)

Chow a heavy-coated blocky powerfully built dog
chow a mixed balanced animal ration of food; military food (slang)
ciao hello or goodbye, in Italian

chrism a consecrated oil that is generally mixed with balm or balm and spices
chrisom a white cloth, robe, or mantle put upon a person at baptism

christcross a personal cipher used in place of a signature
crisscross a ploy in football in which the paths of two offensive players cross, as in a pass pattern

chrome to surface with chromium
crome to catch or kill something by hooking or hitting it with a stick or implement; to overpower or subdue

chromogen a pigment-producing microorganism
chromogene a gene, used to distinguish the nuclear gene in an otherwise ambiguous context from the cytogene

chromophil staining readily, in biology
chromophyll a plant pigment

chronical of long duration or frequent recurrence
chronicle an historical account of facts or events arranged chronologically; to prepare such an account

chrysal a transverse line of crushed fibers in the belly of an archery bow beginning as a pinch
crissal having feathers that cover a bird's cloacal opening

Chrysis a type genus of brilliantly colored wasps
crisis a decisive moment

Chrysochloris a genus of African golden moles
chrysochlorous of a golden green color

chucker a person who throws with a short arm action
chukker a playing period in a polo game

chuff (see **chough**)

Chuje (see **chew**)

chukker (see **chucker**)

chummer (see **chamar**)

Chün relating to a type of Chinese pottery produced in a great variety of colors in Honan province during the Sung period
June the 6th month of the Gregorian calendar

churr (see **chirr**)

chute a narrow walled passageway
shoot to set off an explosive charge or discharge a weapon
shute in weaving, the weft

ciao (see **Chow**)

cibol a Welsh onion or shallot
sibyl a female prophet

cicely any of several herbs of the family Umbelliferae
Sicily an island in the Mediterranean sea west of Italy

Cidaris the type genus of Cidaridae, a family of sea urchins
cidaris the royal tiara of ancient Persian kings
siderous relating to or containing iron

cider a beverage made from apples

citer a person who calls upon or quotes by way of evidence
sider a person living in or on a specified side, as an east-sider
sighter a person who tests the accuracy of sights on small arms

ciel (see **ceil**)

cig a cigarette (slang)
sig a signature, as a newspaper's logotype

cilia minute hairlike processes
Psyllia a genus of jumping plant lice

Cilicia an ancient region in Asia Minor
Silicea a class of Porifera including all sponges not placed in Calcarea

ciliary pertaining to or designating certain structures of the eye
cil(l)ery the carved foliage ornamenting the head of a column

cilicious made of hair
siliceous related to silica

cilium an eyelash; a minute hairlike process
psyllium fleawort, an Old World plantain

cil(l)ery (see **ciliary**)

cilly a predicatable message-key used in cryptography
Scilly a group of small islands off the southwest coast of England
silly trivial, trifling, or frivolous

cinch to guarantee or assure; a strong girth strap for a pack or saddle
sinh the hyperbolic sine

cingle a girdle, belt, or girth
single a separate individual in order of a large class of similar objects

cingular shaped like a ring
singular relating to a single or individual unit; uncommon

cinque the number five in dice or cards
sank became submerged

cinque the number five in dice or cards
sink to become submerged
sync(h) synchronized

cinter a substructure on which a masonry arch or wall is built
sinter a deposit formed by the evaporation of spring or lake water

cionid any of relatively large simple ascidians
cyanide a compound of cyanogen usually with a more electropositive element or radical

cipher a symbol denoting the absence of quantity or magnitude; a method to transform a text so as to conceal its meaning (rarely, to bevel)
sypher to overlap the chamfered edges of planks or make a flush joint, as for a bulkhead

circle (see **cercal**)

circulus one of the usual concentric ridges on a fish scale, each representing an increment of growth
surculus a shoot originating from the roots or lower part of a plant's stem; a sucker

Circus and **circus** (see **cercus**)

cirral relating to a curllike tuft
seral relating to an ecological dry period

cirrhosis a chronic progressive disease of the liver
psorosis a virus disease of citrus trees
sorosis a women's club

cirrhus a mucusbound ribbonlike mass of spores that is exuded from a fungus
cirrus a white filmy variety of cloud usually formed in the highest cloud region at altitudes of 20,000 to 40,000 feet
seeress a female prophet

cirrus (see **cerous**)

cis having certain atoms or groups on the same side of the molecule
<u>**sis**</u> sister (by shortening)
siss a prolonged sibilant or hissing sound

cisor an incisor tooth (by shortening)
sizer a person who determines or sorts by sizes or checks for sizes

cist a wicker receptacle for carrying sacred utensils in ancient Rome
cyst an abnormal closed sac in a body
sissed hissed

cist a neolithic grave lined with stone slabs
kissed touched with the lips
kist a clothes or linen trunk

cistern an artificial reservoir or tank for storing water or other liquids
sistern sisters, used especially in religious contexts

cit a city inhabitant
sit to rest in a position in which the body is essentially vertical and supported chiefly on the buttocks

cite to bring to mind; to call to attention
cyte a maturing germ cell
sight something seen
site a location or space of ground

cited brought to mind; called to attention
sided having right or left lateral parts
sighted having vision or being able to see

citer (see **cider**)

citizen an inhabitant of a city or town, usually entitled to civil rights and privileges
cytisin a bitter crystalline very poisonous alkaloid

citrene a right-handed hydrocarbon occurring in celery-seed oil
citrine a semiprecious yellow stone resembling topaz; resembling lemon or citron

citrin a crystalline water-soluble flavonoid concentrate originally prepared from lemons
citron a citrus fruit resembling a lemon but larger and without a terminal nipple

citrine (see **citrene**)

citron (see **citrin**)

citrulin a purgative yellow resinous preparation of the colocynth apple
citruline a crystalline amino acid formed

as an intermediate in the conversion of
ornithine to arginine

civilian a resident of a country who is not
on active duty in one of the armed forces

Sevillian of, relating to, or characteristic
of the people of Seville, Spain's 4th
largest city

clabber klabberjass or a similar game derived from it

clobber to load with overglaze enameling;
to strike with crushing force

clack loud confused talk

claque a group hired to applaud at a performance

claimant a person who asserts a right or
title

clamant crying out

claire a small enclosed pond for growing
oysters

Clare a nun of an order founded by Assisi
in the 13th century

clamant (see **claimant**)

clamber to crane, struggle, or climb

clammer a person who digs for clams

clamor a continuous loud noise

clan a social unit, smaller than a tribe but
larger than a family, claiming descent
from a common ancestor

Klan an organization of Ku Kluxers

clang a loud resounding sound like that of
a trumpet or pieces of metal struck together

Klang in music and acoustics, a fundamental with its overtones

claque (see **clack**)

Clare (see **claire**)

clarety a color resembling the dark red of
claret wine

clarity clearness

classed divided or distributed into categories or classifications

clast a grain of sediment, sand, or gravel,
especially as a constituent fragment of
an older rock formation

classes social ranks; denominations

classis an ecclesiastical governing body of
a district

clast (see **classed**)

clatch a clod; a daub of something; a
mess

klatch a gathering characterized by informal conversation

clause a section of discourse or writing

claws sharp nails or talons on an animal's
toes

clavis a glossary which aids interpretation

clavus a rounded or fingerlike part or process, as the club of an insect's antenna;
a vertical purple band on a Roman tunic

claws (see **clause**)

clay a widely distributed colloidal lusterless earthy substance

claye a hurdle

clean-boled having a tree trunk free or
trimmed of branches

clean-bowled in cricket, a ball thrown so
that it does not touch the bat or the batsman

cleek a narrow-faced iron golf club

clique a narrow exclusive circle of persons

clefs characters placed at the beginning of
the musical staff to determine the position of the notes

clefts spaces made as if by splitting; partial splits

Klephts Greeks belonging to the independent armed community formed after the
Turkish conquest of Greece

clews the lower corners of a square sail
(rarely **clues**)

clous points of chief interest or attraction

clues evidence tending to lead a person
toward a problem's solution (rarely
clews)

cluse a narrow gorge cutting transversely
through an otherwise continuous ridge

click a slight sharp noise
clique a narrow exclusive circle of persons
klick a kilometer

climb to rise or go upward
clime a climate

cling to hold to each other cohesively and firmly
Kling a Dravidian probably of Tamil origin of the seaports of southeastern Asia and Malaysia

clip a device which grips or clasps; to cut as with a shears
klip(pe) an outlying isolated remnant of an overthrust rock mass due to erosion

clique (see **cleek** or **click**)

clivis a musical symbol denoting the first of two tones being the higher in pitch
clivus a smooth sloping surface on the sphenoid bone in the skull that supports the broad mass of transverse nerve fibers

clobber (see **clabber**)

cloche a woman's small helmetlike hat; a translucent cover for a young plant
closh a post on a whaling ship fitted with hooks for hanging blubber to be sliced

cloddy of low stature and heavily set, as a dog; full of lumps of earth or clay
clotty having roundish viscous lumps formed by coagulation

clomp to tread clumsily and noisily; a heavy tramping sound
klomp a gathering characterized by informal conversation; a wooden shoe worn in the Low Countries

close to shut or terminate
clothes clothing
cloze related to a reading comprehension test

closh (see **cloche**)

clothes (see **close**)

clotty (see **cloddy**)

clouded obscured; mentally confused
clouted mended with patches; hit forcefully

clouter a person who covers with cloth, leather, or other material; a person who hits a baseball, especially long and hard
clowder a group of cats

clough a narrow valley
clow a floodgate

clous (see **clews**)

clouted (see **clouded**)

clow (see **clough**)

clowder (see **clouter**)

cloze (see **close**)

clucker a person who makes the sound of a brooding hen
Klucker a Ku Klux Klansman

clucks makes the noise of a brooding hen
Klux to maltreat or terrorize in the way thought typical of the Ku Klux Klan

clues (see **clews**)

cluse (see **clews**)

clyster an enema
klister a soft wax used on skis

coach a large, usually closed four-wheeled carriage; a railroad passenger car
Koch a member of a hinduized Mongoloid people of Assam

coachee a carriage driver
coachy like a coach horse, especially in configuration

coacts acts or works together; forces or compels
coax a coaxial transmission line in which one conductor is centered inside and insulated from an outer metal tube that serves as a second conductor

coaks dowels placed in timbers to unite them or keep them from slipping
coax to persuade or influence
cokes residues from carbonized coal

coal a hot ember; a black solid combustible mineral

cole a plant of the cabbage family

Ko(h)l a people of Bengal and Chota Nagpur, India

kohl a preparation used in Arabia and Egypt to darken the edges of eyelids

coaled converted to charcoal by burning; supplied with coal

cold having a temperature notably below an accustomed norm

coaler (see **choler**)

coals hot embers; black solid combusitible minerals

colds respiratory infections

coaly covered or impregnated with coal; a coal heaver

coly any of a small group of fruit-eating African birds comprising the genus Colius

Koli a low-caste people of Bombay, Punjab, and other parts of India

coaming a raised frame around a floor or roof opening to keep out water

combing arranging or adjusting hair with a toothed instrument

coarse ordinary, unrefined, or inferior

course a particular path between two points

coarser more unrefined or inferior

courser a swift or spirited horse

coat an outer garment

cote a shed for small domestic animals

coated covered or impregnated with a durable chemical or rubber compound

coded put into the form of symbols for meaningful communication

coater a person or machine that coats surfaces

coder a person or device that puts information into coded form

coax (see **coacts** or **coaks**)

Cob a breed of short-legged, thick-set horses, often having a high gait and frequently used for driving

cob a male swan; a corncob; to break into small pieces prior to sorting

cobb the great black-backed gull

kob an African antelope related to the waterbuck

cobble to mend or make, as shoes; to pave with cobblestones

coble a flat-floored fishing boat

Kabul the capital of Afghanistan

cocaine a bitter crystalline alkaloid and having a narcotic effect

Cockaigne an imaginary land of extreme luxury and ease where physical comforts and pleasures are always immediately at hand

coccal relating to a plant having berries or seeds; a berry-shaped organism; relating to the type genus of Coccidae that includes certain typical scales

cockal a game played with knuckle-bones

cockle a plant growing in grain fields, as cowherb or cocklebur; a bivalve mollusk

cocci a spherical bacterium

cocky pert, arrogant, or jaunty

kaki a Japanese persimmon

khaki a light yellowish brown color

coccous (see **caucus**)

Coccus and **coccus** (see **caucus**)

Cockaigne (see **cocaine**)

cockal (see **coccal**)

cocker (see **caulker**)

cockle (see **coccal**)

cocks adult males of domestic fowl; positions the hammer of a firearm for firing

coques loops of ribbons or feathers used in trimming hats

cox to steer and direct, as does a coxswain

cockscomb a plant with red, purple, or yellow flowers

coxcomb a vain conceited foolish person who is falsely proud of personal achievements

cocktailed entertained by an informal or semiformal party or gathering
cock-tailed docked and nicked a horse's tail so that the stump sticks up

cocky (see **cocci**)

coco the large, hard-shelled seed of the coconut palm, lined with white edible meat, and containing a milky liquid
cocoa a beverage of milk or water, sugar, and powdered cacao seeds
Koko a group of numerous aboriginal peoples of northern Queensland, Australia
koko an araceous plant, such as taro, cultivated in tropical western Africa

coconut a fruit of coconut palm
cokernut an edible seed of the coquito palm

cocoon (see **cacoon**)

coda a final or concluding musical section
cota a fort formerly common in parts of the Philippines
Kota an artisan and buffalo-herding people of the southwestern India

coddle to pamper; to cook in a liquid just below its boiling point
cottle a clay wall encircling an object to be molded
katel a wooden hammock used in Africa as a bed in a wagon

coddling slowly cooking in a liquid just below its boiling point
codling a young codfish

coded (see **coated**)

coder (see **coater**)

codling (see **coddling**)

coeler pertaining to the sky
sealer a machine or person who makes secure or seals

coenocyte a multi-nucleate mass of protoplasm

coenosite a free or separable symbiotic ecological arrangement

c(o)erulein (see **cerulean**)

coff (see **calf**)

coffer a strongbox for safely storing valuables
cougher a person who expels air from the lungs suddenly and explosively

Cognac a brandy distilled from white wine from the French departments of Charente and Charente Maritime
cognac a moderate brown color
Konyak a people of the Assam-Myanmar frontier area

coif a manner of arranging hair
quaff to drink freely or copiously

coign the corner of a crystal formed by the intersection of three or more faces
coin a piece of metal issued by a government to circulate as money
coyne an Irish chieftain's exaction of food and drink from his tenants for his soldiers
quoin a wedge used on ships to keep casks from rolling

coil an arrangement of something in a spiral or concentric rings
koel any of several cuckoos of India, the East Indies, and Australia

coin (see **coign**)

coir stiff coarse coconut husk fiber
coyer more modestly rejecting approaches or overtures

coke the infusible hard residue from carbonized coal
colk a bowl-shaped, cylindrical, or circular hole formed by a stone's grinding action in the rocky bed of a river or stream

cokernut (see **coconut**)

cokes (see **coaks**)

cokie a cocaine addict
coky resembling coke

cola a line or queue
kola a bitter caffeine-containing seed of a kola tree

colation removal of solids from liquid by straining, especially through filter paper
collation assembly of paper or forms into an orderly system

cold (see **coaled**)

colds (see **coals**)

cole (see **coal**)

Coleus a large genus of herbs having showy and often highly variegated leaves and spicate blue flowers
Colius a genus of birds comprising the Colies, a fruit-eating African bird

colic (see **cholic**)

Colius (see **Coleus**)

colk (see **coke**)

collar (see **choler**)

collard an edible hardy plant of the cabbage family
collared wearing a neckband

collate (see **cholate**)

collation (see **colation**)

colleen (see **choline**)

college a building or group of buildings used in connection with some educational or religious purpose
kalij any of the crested India pheasants that are related to the Chinese silver pheasant

collie a breed of dog
colly to understand and approve (jive talk)

collin a prepared form of gelatin used in tanning analysis
colline any of the ridges of a brain coral

collum a neck or necklike part or process
column a vertical arrangement of items; a supporting pillar or shaft

colly (see **collie**)

colmar (see **calmer**)

Cologne a city in western Germany
cologne a perfumed liquid composed of alcohol and an aromatic
colon a colonial farmer, planter, or plantation owner

Colombia a country in northwestern South America
Columbia the capital of South Carolina; a Salishan people of eastern Washington

Colombian relating to or characteristic of Colombia
Columbian having a black-white color pattern characteristic of the plumage of certain varieties of poultry

colombous related to or containing the metallic element niobium
Colombus the capital of Ohio

colon (see **Cologne**)

colonel a military officer ranking between a brigadier general and a lieutenant colonel
kernel a seed's inner portion; a central or essential part

color a hue, as red, yellow, or blue
culler a person who picks out imperfect items, as defective poultry

Columbia (see **Colombia**)

Columbian (see **Colombian**)

column (see **collum**)

columniation (see **calumniation**)

coly (see **coaly**)

comatic blurred as a result of a state of profound unsciourness caused by disease
komatic an Eskimo sledge with wooden runners

comb an instrument for adjusting, cleaning, or confining the hair
come the dried rootlets produced in malting grain

kolm a Swedish shale exceptionally high in uranium oxide

combing (see **coaming**)

combo combination (by shortening); a group of musicians
kamboh a member of a low caste in the Punjab engaged chiefly in agriculture

comby resembling a comb in structure
Komi a people of north central Russia

come (see **comb**)

come the dried rootlets produced in malting grain
cum along with

comedia a Spanish regular-verse drama
commedia an Italian comedy, as performed in the 16th and 18th centuries

comedic like comedy
cometic relating to or like a comet

comedy a drama of light and amusing character, typically with a happy ending
comity kindly courteous behavior

comely (see **calmly**)

comely having a pleasing appearance
cumbly a blanket made of wood or goat's hair

comet a celestial body with a fuzzy head surrounding a bright nucleus and long tail
commit a card game

cometic (see **comedic**)

comics comedians
comix comic art, often luridly sexual or political in character
kamiks Eskimo sealskin boats

coming passing from one point to another nearer or more central
cumming in brewery, a large squarish vessel about 12-18 inches deep that receives what overflows from the masking-fat or barrel

comity (see **comedy**)

comix (see **comics**)

comma (see **caama**)

commedia (see **comedia**)

comment (see **calmant**)

commie a playing marble made of clay; a communist
Kami a scattered people, speaking a Finno-Uric tongue, dwelling about the headwaters of the Pechona and Northern Dvina rivers
kami a kamikaze pilot (by shortening)

commissariat the organized system by which armies and military posts are supplied with food and daily necessaries
commissariot a county or sheriff's court in Scotland that appoints estate executors

commit (see **comet**)

compellation an act of addressing someone
compilation the gathering together of written material; an accumulation of many things or ideas

complacence secure self-satisfaction
complaisance a pleasing ingratiating deportment

complementary supplementing
complimentary expressing regard or praise

comptroller a public officer who supervises the propriety of expenditures
controller an electric device to govern how electric power is delivered

con an argument on the negative side; to swindle; a convict
conn the control exercised by a person who directs a ship's movements
khan a local chieftain in some areas of central Asia; a rest house in some Asian countries

conceded allowed, admitted, or acknowledged
conceited having an unjustifiably high opinion of oneself

concenter to bring together at a focus or point; to concentrate

consenter a person who agrees with, permits, or concurs

conch a large spiral-shelled marine gastropod mollusk

conk to hit, especially on the head; to break down

concha something suggesting or shaped like a shell

khankah a dervish monastery

Conches resident natives of the Bahamas

conches machines in which chocolate is worked and kneaded

conch(e)s large spiral-shelled marine gastropod mollusks

conscious perceiving, apprehending, or noticing with a degree of controlled thought or observation

concord a state of agreement

Concorde a supersonic passenger aircraft manufactured and operated jointly by England and France

concreter a person who builds or works with a hard strong construction material made by mixing cement material and a mineral aggregate

concretor an apparatus for boiling down crude sugar solutions

concubitous the relation of persons who by tribal custom are predestined mates, or eligible to marry each other

concubitus sexual intercourse

cond to superintend the steering of a ship or airplane

conned swindled

Khond any of several Dravidian peoples of Orissa, India

condor (see **chondre**)

con(e)y a European rabbit; a disky black-spotted reddish-finned grouper

coni conical prolongations of the right ventricles in man and mammals

confectionary a place where elaborate, complex, or ornate items are kept

confectionery sweet edibles

confidant a person with whom one feels free to discuss private or secret matters

confidante a sofa divided by arms into separate seats

confident characterized by a strong belief in oneself

confitent a person who confesses, especially to a priest

confirmation the process of substantiating a factual statement with empirical evidence

conformation the form or outline; shaping

confitent (see **confidant**)

conformation (see **confirmation**)

Congaree a Sioux people in the Congaree valley, California

congeree a large, strictly marine, entirely scaleless eel that is an important food fish

congery a collection or mass of entities

conjury the practice of magic

Congo a territory surrounding the Congo river in West Africa; a dark grayish yellowish brown

congo a ballroom dance of Haitian origin

congou a black tea from China

coni (see **con[e]y**)

conics the theory of conic sections

connex closely connected; constituting one syntactical unit

conjury (see **congery**)

conk (see **conch**)

conker a popular English game in which each player swings a horse chestnut threaded on a string to try to break one held by an opponent

conquer to acquire by force or gain dominion over

conn (see **con**)

connects joins, fastens, or links together

connex in mathematics, the infinity of points and lines

conned (see **cond**)

connex (see **conics** and **connects**)

conquer (see **conker**)

conscious (see **Conches**)

consensual involving or caused by involuntary action or movement correlative with a voluntary action, as the contraction of the iris when the eyelid is opened
consentual involving or carried out by mutual agreement

consenter (see **concenter**)

consentual (see **consensual**)

consequence something that is produced by a cause or follows from a set of conditions
consequents musical restatements of the subject in the canon and fugue; a stream or valley that has developed in harmony with the general slope of an existing land surface

consonance harmony of parts
consonants speech sounds characterized by constriction at one or more points in the breath channel

consulter a person who counsels or advises
consultor an advisor who assists a Roman Catholic bishop

continence self-restraint from yielding to desire
continents divisions of land on Earth

contingence contact or touching
contingents chance occurrences; representational groups

continuance remaining in the same condition or place
continuants ones that continue; determinants of which all the elements are zero except those of a principal diagonal and the two adjacent minor diagonals; consonants that may be prolonged without change of quality

controller (see **comptroller**)

convects transfers heat by convection
convex curved, as the exterior of a sphere

conventical relating to a convent or nunnery
conventicle an assembly, meeting, or convention, especially of a society or body of persons

convex (see **convects**)

coo the call of a pigeon or dove
coup a successful stratagem; a blow or stroke

cooch a pseudo–Oriental female dance common in carnivals and fairs
couch a board covered with flannel on which sheets of handmade paper are pressed

cookee a cook's helper, especially in a logging camp
cookie small sweet cake

coolamon an Australian vessel of bark or wood resembling a basin and used for carrying and holding water
Kulaman a people inhabiting southern Mindanao, Philippines

coolie an unskilled laborer, usually in the Far East
cool(l)y without passion or ardor; with indifference
coulee a small stream
Kulli of or pertaining to a prehistoric culture of southern Baluchistan

coom grease exuding from axle boxes or bearings
cwm a deep steep-walled basin high on a mountain, usually shaped like half a bowl and often containing a small lake

coonie a cowhide stretched under a wagon as a carrying device, especially for fuel; a person of Acadian French heritage
coony showing astuteness and cleverness

cooped deprived of free motion by cramped quarters

couped in heraldry, cut off short at the ends so as not to extend to the edges of the field

cooper a ship equipped to supply liquor and tobacco to fishing fleets in the North sea in the 19th century
coper a machine for notching girders
couper a lever in a loom for lifting a harness

coops small enclosures for animals
coupes two-door automobiles with one seating compartment; desserts

coops cooperatives (by shortening)
coopts chooses or elects into a body or group as a fellow member

coos soft low cries or calls, as of a dove or pigeon
cooze a female considered as a sexual object (slang); a vagina (slang)
coups highly successful strategems

coopts (see **coops**)

cooze (see **coos**)

cop a police officer; a tube or quill on which thread or year is wound
kop a South African hill

copek money, especially a silver dollar
kope(c)k a Russian unit of value equal to one-hundreth of a ruble (rarely copeck)

coper (see **cooper**)

copje (see **caapi**)

coppa (see **capa**)

coppa an Italian pork sausage seasoned with cayenne pepper
koppa a letter in the early Greek alphabet

copped rising to a top or head; acquired; stolen, especially on the spur of the moment; captured
Copt an Egyptian of the native race descended from ancient Egyptians, especially a member of the Coptic church

cops policemen; a conical mass of yarn wound on a tube
copse a thicket or grove of small trees

Copt (see **copped**)

copy (see **caapi**)

copyright the exclusive, legally secured right to write, print, publish, and sell artistic works
copywrite to create and write advertising or publicity copy

coques (see **cocks**)

coquet to deal playfully instead of seriously
coquette any of several tropoical hummingbirds of the genus *Lophornis*

cor the heart (in prescriptions)
core the central part of a body
corps an organized subdivision of a military establishment; a group having a common activity
khor a watercourse or ravine

Cora a genus of basidiolichens widely distributed on soil and trees in Central and South America; a Taracahitian people of the states of Jalisco and Nayarit, Mexico
cora a gazelle found from Iran to North Africa
corah plain undyed India silk
kora a large gallinule of southeastern Asia and the East Indies; a 21-string musical instrument of African origin resembling a lute

coral (see **chorale**)

coralline like coral in color and form
corolline relating to or resembling a corolla

corbeille a basket of flowers or fruit
corbel an architectural member which projects from within a wall and supports weight

corcir any of the colors imparted by the dye archil, varying from moderate red to dark purplish red
corker a person that puts tapered or cylindrical stoppers in bottles or other containers; a person or thing of excellent or remarkable quality

cord (see **chord**)

cordate (see **chordate**)

cordelle (see **chordal**)

cordobán cordovan leather
Cordovan a native or resident of Chich projects **cordovan** a dark grayish brown color

core (see **cor**)

cored (see **chord**)

Corine (see **chorine**)

Corinthian (see **Carinthian**)

Cork a county and city in Ireland
cork the outer tissues of the stem of the cork oak
corke any of the colors imparted by the dye archil varying from moderate to dark purplish

corker (see **corcir**)

cormous bearing or producing thick rounded modified underground stem bases, as the gladiolus
cormus the entire body or colony of a compound animal, as coral

corni French horns
corny relating to corn; trite; mawkishly sentimental

cornice a decorative band concealing curtain fixtures
corniche a road built along the edge of an overhanging precipice or along the face of a cliff
Cornish an English breed of domestic fowl; a Celtic language of Cornwall, England, extinct since the late 18th century

cornice a decorative band concealing curtain fixtures
Cornus a genus of shrubs and small trees of the family *Cornaceae*
cornus the dried bark of the root of the flowering dogwood

corniche (see **cornice**)

Cornish (see **cornice**)

Cornus and **cornus** (see **cornice**)

corny (see **corni**)

corol (see **chorale**)

corollate having a corolla, the inner set of floral leaves immediately surrounding the sporophylls
correlate one of two related things viewed in terms of its relationship to the other

corolline (see **coralline**)

corps (see **cor**)

corral (see **chorale**)

Correa and **correa** (see **chorea**)

correlate (see **corollate**)

Cortes a Spanish parliament or parliaments
cortez any of several Central American timber trees of the genus Tabelula

corydalis an herb native to north temperate regions and southern Africa
Corydalus a genus of large megalopterous insects, as dobsons

coscet a class of peasant landholders
cosset to treat as a pet; a lamb reared without a dam's aid
cossette a strip or slice, as of potato

cose to make oneself cozy
coze to chat

cosign to jointly sign a document
cosine a trigonometry term

cosset (see **coscet**)

cossette (see **cassette** and **coscet**)

cot (see **cat**)

cota (see **coda**)

cote (see **coat**)

Cotinga and **cotinga** (see **caatinga**)

Coto a Tucano people of eastern Ecuador; a Chibchan people of Costa Rica

coto the bark of a tree of northern Bolivia formerly used as an astringent and stomachic

koto a long Japanese zither having 13 silk strings

cotte (see **cat** or **caught**)

cotted provided shelter for; matted
cottid a fish of the family *Cottidae*

cotter a wedge-shaped or tapered piece used to fasten together parts of a machine or structure; a cotter pin
Kadir a primitive somewhat negroid jungle-dwelling people inhabiting the Deccan plateau in southern India
quatre the four at cards or dice

cottid (see **cotted**)

cottle (see **coddle**)

cotty entangled or matted
Kati a Kafir people of easternmost Kafiristan in the Hindu Kush mountains of Afghanistan

couac a strident tone sometimes produced by a reed instrument when the reed is out of order or the instrument is blown incorrectly
quack the characteristic duck cry or call; a medical charlatan

couch (see **cooch**)

couche in heraldry, inclined
couchee a reception given in the late evening, especially by nobility

coudé a telescope constructed that reflects light along the polar axis to focus at a fixed place
coudee a measure of length varying between 17.5–20.7 inches

cough (see **calf**)

cougher (see **coffer**)

could knew how to or had the skill to achieve something
cud the portion of food regurgitated by a ruminating animal from its first stomach to be chewed a second time
khud a ravine or precipice

coulé in music, a slur; a gliding dance step
coulee a small stream

coulee (see **coolie**)

council a deliberative assembly
counsel opinion, advice, or direction

council(l)or a council member
counselor an adviser

counsel (see **council**)

counselor (see **council[l]or**)

counter a device used in keeping accounts and in playing games
counto(u)r a pleader in an English court; a sergeant-at-law

coup (see **coo**)

coupe a ballet step
cupay a common tropical American tree (the pitch apple) having coarse evergreen leaves

couped (see **cooped**)

couper (see **cooper**)

coupes (see **coops**)

coups (see **coos**)

courant a newspaper name
currant a small seedless raisin; an edible acidic fruit of several plants of the genus Ribes
current occurring in the present; a continuously flowing part of a fluid or electricity

courier a messenger
currier a person who works tanned hides into salable form; a person who combs a horse

course (see **coarse**)

courser (see **coarser**)

courtesy well-mannered conduct or consideration for others
curtesy the future potential interest that a husband has in real estate in which his wife has an estate of inheritance

cous an herb of the northwestern U.S. having edible roots

kouse a tall cereal grass that is probably of East Indian origin, pearl millet

cousin a child of one's aunt or uncle

cozen to deceive by artful wheedling or tricky dishonesty

covariance the arithmetic mean or the expected value of the product of the deviations of corresponding values of two variables from their respective mean

covariants the functions of both coefficients and variables of quantities that retain their form when the quantities are transformed linearly

coven an assembly of witches

covin a collusive agreement between persons to the detriment of another

coverall a one-piece combination of overalls and shirt

cover-all comprehensive

cow a mature female of wild or domestic cattle

kou a tree of the Pacific islands whose wood is used for making household utensils

coward a person who shows ignoble fear

cowered cringed in abject fear of something

cowherd a person who tends cattle or cows

cowl a hood or hooded sleeveless garment

cowle a written grant or engagement in India, especially of safe-conduct or amnesty

cox (see **cocks**)

coxcomb (see **cockscomb**)

coy shy; showing marked, often playful or irritating reluctance to make a definite or committing statement

koi a carp, a soft-finned freshwater fish

coyer (see **coir**)

coyne (see **coign**)

coyote a small wolf native to western North America extending to Alaska and New York

coyotey mangy-looking

coze (see **cose**)

cozen (see **cousin**)

crabber one who carps or complains; a kind of boat used in crab fishing

craber the European water vole

crackie a broken or chipped playing marble

cracky having cracks; a mild oath; odd or eccentric

cracks narrow breaks or thin slits; loud earsplitting roars

Crax the type genus of Cracidae, which includes long-legged birds such as curassows and guans

cracky (see **crackie**)

Cracow the former capital of Poland

crakow 14th and 15th century European footwear made with an extremely long pointed toe

craft artistic dexterity

kraft a strong paper

crakow (see **Cracow**)

crampette the chape of a sword scabbard

crampit a sheet of iron on which a player stands to deliver the stone in curling

crance a band on the outer edge of a bowsprit to which the bobstays and bowsprit shrouds are fastened

krantz a sheer cliff or precipice in southern Africa

crankie a bend, turn, twist, or crinkle

cranky out of working order; given to fretful fussiness

crapaud a large toad esteemed as food in parts of the Caribbean area

crappo any tree of the genus *Carapa*

crape a band worn on a hat or sleeve as a sign of mourning

crepe a small very thin pancake; a lightweight fabric with wrinkled surface

crappie a North American sunfish

crappy markedly inferior in quality; lousy

crappie a North American sunfish

croppy an Irish rebel in 1798 who wore short hair as a token of sympathy with the French Revolution; a long iron rod used in making cylinder glass to transfer the cylinder to a flattening stock

crappo (see **crapaud**)

crappy (see **crappie**)

craton a relatively immobile area of the earth's crust that forms the nuclear mass of a continent or the central basin of an ocean

kraton a region that has remained undisturbed while an adjacent area has been affected by mountain-making movements

crawl to move slowly with the body close to the ground; to draw along

kraal a village of southern Africa; an enclosure for keeping turtles or lobsters alive in shallow water

kral a title or early rulers of Slavonic countries equivalent to a king

crawley a coralroot of dry woodlands in eastern and central North America

crawlie a small burrowing crayfish

crawly creepy

Crax (see **cracks**)

crays spiny lobsters of Australia

craze a transient infatuation or fad

creak a high, typically subdued rasping or grating noise

Creek the Creek Confederacy, an American Indian confederacy organized around the Muskogee people of Georgia and eastern Alabama before their removal to Oklahoma

creek a natural stream of water normally smaller than a river

cream the yellowish part of milk that rises to the surface

crème a sweet liqueur

creamie a white or clear playing marble

creamy full of or containing the yellowish part of milk

crease a line, groove, or ridge made by folding a pliable substance

creece watercress or garden cress

creases ridges made by folding pliable material

krises Malay or Indonesian daggers often with scalloped cutting edges and serpentine blades

creat an East Indian herb having bitter juice variously used in medicine

create to bring into existence

crécy prepared with carrots

cressy abounding in cresses, such as watercress

Cree an Indian people ranging from James Bay in Ontario, Canada, to Montana

qre a traditional Jewish mode of reading the Hebrew bible that is substituted for one actually standing in the consonantal text

creece (see **crease**)

Creek and **creek** (see **creak**)

creek a natural stream of water normally smaller than a river

cric the ring which turns inward and condenses the flame of a lamp

crick a painful spasmodic muscular condition

Crees an Indian people ranging from James Bay south to Montana

crise a moment of risk or stress; a crisis

crème (see **cream**)

crenel(l)ate embattled or having repeated indentations like those in a battlement

crenulate having the margin cut into minutely rounded scallops

crepe (see **crape**)

cressed abounding in cress, such as water cress
crest the top of a structure or a natural formation

cressy (see **crécy**)

crest (see **cressed**)

Cretan a native or inhabitant of the island of Crete in the eastern part of the Mediterranean sea
cretin a person showing marked mental deficiency, often because of a thyroid deficiency

crevasse a wide and deep opening or chasm; a breach in a river's levee
crevice a narrow recess or slit

crewed acted as a member of a group engaged in a common endeavor
crude a natural or raw state; marked by uncultivated simplicity

crewel worsted, slackly twisted yarn used for embroidery
cruel sadistic; stern, rigorous, or grim

crewelist a person who does embroidery
cruelest most sadistic or stern

crewman a member of a group engaged in a common activity
crumen a suborbital gland in deer and antelope that secretes a waxy substance
Kruman a member of the Kru people

crews serves as a crew member
cruise a journey for the sake of traveling without destination
crus French vineyards that produce wine grapes
cruse a small vessel for holding liquid
krewes private social clubs that sponsor balls and parades as part of the Mardi Gras festivities
Krus members of an indigenous Negro people of Liberia skilled as boatmen

cric (see **creek**)

crick (see **creek**)

crill the narcotic crack
krill planktonic crustaceans and larvae that constitute the principal food of whalebone whales

Crioceras a genus of Cretaceous ammonites with complexly plicated septa
Crioceris a large cosmopolitan genus of beetles including the asparagus beetle

crise (see **Crees**)

crisis (see **Chrysis**)

crispen to become crisp or brittle
crispin a shoemaker or cobbler

criss a wooden stand with curved top on which crest tiles are shaped
kris a Malay or Indonesian dagger, often with scalloped cutting edges and a serpentine blade

crissal (see **chrysal**)

crisscross (see **christcross**)

croc crocodile (by shortening); a hook-shaped iron projection fastened to the stock of a harquebus
crock a thick earthernware pot or jar

croes in early Scottish law, satisfactions in an amount for killing a person
Cros persons of mixed Indian, white, and black ancestry, especially in southeastern North Carolina and eastern South Carolina
cros satisfactions in amounts suitable to the rank of the parties involved, in early Scottish laws, for killing a man
Crows members of a Siouan people inhabiting the region between the Platte and Yellowstone rivers
crows large glossly black birds; makes a sound characteristic of a cock
croze a groove near either end of a barrel stave into which the barrel head is inserted

crokinole a game resembling squails

croquignole a method used in waving the hair by winding it on curlers

crome (see **chrome**)

crone a withered old woman

crosne a Chinese artichoke

crooks implements having a bent or hooked form

crux a determinative point at issue; a main or central feature

crool to make a repeated low, liquid, or gurgling sound

cruel sadistic; stern, rigorous, or grim

croon to make a continued moaning sound; to sing in a soft composing manner

kroon Estonia's basic monetary unit from 1928–1940

croppy (see **crappie**)

croquignole (see **crokinole**)

Cros and **cros** (see **croes**)

crosne (see **crone**)

cross a structure consisting of an upright with a transverse beam; to intersect

crosse the stick used in the game of lacrosse

crossbill having a bird beak adapted to extracting seeds from fruits and tree cones by means of strongly curved and overlapping mandibles

cross-bill a bill of exchange given in return for another

crosse (see **cross**)

crotal a small spherical metal rattle on a harness

crotale one of a pair of small cymbals or rods used like castanets by dancers in antiquity

crotyl the butenyl radical

crotals reddish brown colors

crottels excrement, especially of hares

crotin a mixture of poisonous proteins found in the seeds of a small Asiatic tree

Croton a genus of herbs and shrubs, as spurges

croton a plant of the genus Croton

crottels (see **crotals**)

crotyl (see **Crotal**)

croup spasmodic laryngitis in infants and children

croupe a leap of a horse with the hind legs well under the belly

crowder a person who plays or manipulates a large number of people

cruder marked by more uncultivated simplicity

Crows and **crows** (see **croes**)

croze (see **croes**)

crucks the two curved timbers forming a principal roof support in primitive English house construction

crux a determinative point at issue; a main or central feature

crude (see **crewd**)

cruder (see **crowder**)

cruel (see **crewel** and **crool**)

cruelest (see **crewelist**)

cruise (see **crews**)

crumen (see **crewman**)

crunchie an infantry soldier; a lesbian

crunchy crisp, brittle, or friable; having a healthy diet

crus (see **crews**)

cruse (see **crews**)

crustacean belonging to the class of Arthropoda comprising lobsters, crabs, and shrimp

crustation the process of forming crust

crux (see **crooks** or **crucks**)

crystallin either of two globulins in the crystalline lens of the eye in vertebrates

crystalline composed of crystals or fragments of crystals; resembling crystal

C's (see **cees**)

ctene a ciliated swimming plate of a phylum (Ctenophora) of marine animals resembling jellyfish
teen relating to persons between ages 12 and 20

cu a cumulous cloud (by shortening)
cue to signal to begin action; a hint; a tapered rod used to strike a billiard ball
'que barbeque (by shortening)
queue a line of persons or vehicles; a tail-like braid of hair

cubical a shape with six equal square sides
cubicle a small room or compartment

cubit any of various ancient units of length based on the length of the forearm to the tip of the middle finger
qubit quantum bit (shortened); a binary digit manipulated by a (thus far) theoretical quantum computer

cuckoo a European bird; to repeat monotonously, as does a cuckoo
cucu either of two American shore birds, the greater or lesser yellowlegs
kuku a New Zealand fruit dove

cucujo a luminous click beetle of the West Indies
cucuyo either of two triggerfishes; a fire beetle

cud (see **could**)

cudding chewing the cud
cutting penetrating with a sharp-edged instrument

cuddle to hold close for comfort
cuttle to fold finished cloth in pleats; a cuttlefish

cue (see **cu**)

cuir a light yellowish brown color
queer strange, curious, or peculiar

cuirie a hardened leather piece for protecting the breast, worn over mail

query to question; an inquiry

cuisse defensive plate armor for the thighs
quis a European woodcock

culler (see **color**)

cully a companion or mate (slang); to impose on or cheat
Kulli relating to a prehistoric culture of southern Baluchistan

culpa actionable negligence or fault
kalpa a duration of time in Hinduism covering a complete cosmic cycle

cum (see **come**)

<u>**cumal**</u> a standard of value in ancient Ireland often equal to from three to ten cows
cumhal a female slave in native Irish law until the end of the 10th century

cumbly (see **comely**)

cumenyl any of three univalent radicals derived from cumene by removal of one hydrogen atom
cuminyl the univalent radical derived from the para isomer of cymene

cumhal (see **cumal**)

cuminyl (see **cumenyl**)

cumming (see **coming**)

cumulous increasing in size or strength by successive additions
cumulus a massy cloud form usually occuring at elevations between 2,000 and 15,000 feet; the projecting mass of granulosa cells that bears the developing ovum in a Graafian follicle

cupay (see **coupe**)

cupper a person who draws blood from the surface of the body by forming a partial vacuum over a spot; a device for making cup leathers for use in hydraulic cylinders and pumps
kupper the saw-scaled viper, a small fierce and aggressive desert-dwelling viper found from North Africa to India

cupola a rounded vault raised on a circular or other base and forming a roof or ceiling

cupulo the bony apex of the cochlea

cur a mongrel or inferior dog; a surly, low, or cowardly person

curr to make a murmuring sound, as a dove

Ker a malignant spirit in Greek religion and mythology

curaçao an orange-flavored liqueur

curassow an arboreal bird of South and Central America

curd the part of milk coagulated by souring or being treated with certain enzymes

curred made a murmuring sound, as of doves

Kurd one of a numerous pastoral and agricultural people of the high plateau region of Turkey, Iran, Iraq, and Syria

curdle to cause to coagulate or congeal, as milk

curtal a tenor or bass musical instrument of the oboe type

kirtle a garment resembling a tunic reaching the knees and worn by men until the 16th century

curr (see **curr**)

currant (see **courant**)

curred (see **curd**)

current (see **courant**)

currier (see **courier**)

curser a person who utters maledictions

cursor part of a mathematical instrument that moves back and forth; a movable spot of light on the screen of a visual display terminal

curses utters malediction, execration, or an oath

cursus a pattern of cadence at the end of a sentence in medieval Latin prose

cursor (see **curser**)

cursus (see **curses**)

curtal (see **curdle**)

curtesy (see **courtesy**)

curve a bending without angles

kirve to undercut coal in a mine

curvet a leap of a horse in which at one point all four legs are in the air simultaneously

curvette a gemstone with a raised cameo-like design carved on its hollowed surface

cuter more attractive or prettier

cutor a prosecutor (by shortening) or district attorney

cutler a person that makes, deals in, or repairs cutlery

cuttler a person that folds cloth in pleats after it has been finished

cutor (see **cuter**)

cutting (see **cudding**)

cuttle (see **cuddle**)

cuttler (see **cutler**)

cwm (see **coom**)

cyan any of a group of colors of greenish-blue hue

Cyon a genus of Asiatic wild dogs, including the dhole

(s)cion a detached living portion of a plant prepared for union with a stock in grafting; a descendant

Sion the city of God (also Zion); utopia

cyanide (see **cionid**)

cyanidin an anthocyanidin formed by hydrolizing cyanin

cyanidine any of three parent compounds, $C_3H_3N_3$ containing a ring of three carbon and three nitrogen atoms

cyanin a violet crystalline anthocyanin pigment found in rose petals and the cornflower

cyanine any of several usually unstable dyes that are important in photography

cyanite a mineral consisting of an aluminum silicate

syenite a phanerocrystalline intrusive igneous rock composed of dominant alkaline feldspar

Cyclamen a genus of widely cultivated Eurasian plants; a very dark reddish purple

cyclamin a white amorphous saponin, formerly used as a purgative

cyclamine a cyclic nitrogenous base, as pyrrole

cyclar moving in cycles or at definite periods

cycler a person that rides or travels on a bicycle, tricycle, or motorcycle

cycle to ride a bicycle, tricycle, or motorcycle

Seckel an small American reddish-brown sweet juicy pear

Sicel a member of an ancient people occupying part of Sicily

sickle an agricultural cutting implement consisting of a hook-shaped metal blade with a short handle

cycle an interval of time in which a regularly recurring succession of events is completed; a bi-, tri-, or motorcycle

psychal relating to the mind

cycler (see **cyclar**)

cygnet a young swan

signate having markings like letters; designated

signet an identifying or authenticating mark or stamp

cyke a cyclorama (by shortening)

psych to psycholanalyze; to overcome an opponent as a result of analyzing psychologically

syke in heraldry, a rounded barry-wavy of six argent and azure

cylix a drinking cup having two looped handles on a shallow bowl set on a slender foot

siliques narrow elongated many-seeded

capsules characteristic of the *Cruciferae* family of herbs

cyma a projecting molding whose profile is a double curve

sima basic igneous rock whether solid or molten

cymbal a large concave brass plate producing a brilliant clashing musical tone

symbol something representing something else

cynical given to faultfinding, sneering, and sarcasm; given to or affecting disbelief in commonly accepted human value and in man's sincerity of motive

sinical of or relating to a sine or sines, or founded on sines

cynicism disbelief in commonly accepted human values and in man's sincerity of motive

Sinicism anything peculiar to the Chinese

cynocephalous having a head or face like that of a dog

Cynocephalus a genus of mammals including the flying lemurs

cynocephalus a baboon

Cyon (see **cyan**)

Cyon a genus of Asiatic wild dogs, including the dhole

psion in subatomic physics, a psi particle

(s)cion a detached living portion of a plant prepared for union with a stock in grafting; a descendent

cyp (see **cepe**)

cyp either of two tropical American timber trees called princewood

sip to drink a small quantity

cypress a tree of the genus Cupressus

Cypris a genus of small ostracod crustaceans that live in stagnant fresh water

cypris a developmental form of barnacles in which the shell is bivalved

Cyprus an island in the Mediterranean sea

cyst (see **cist**)

cyst(e)in a crystalline amino acid occurring as a constituent of many proteins
Sistine a pale blue color
sistine relating to any of the popes named Sixtus; relating to the Sistine chapel

cyte (see **cite**)

Cysticercus a genus of parasitic tapeworm larvae
cystocercous having a space in the tail into which the body can be retracted

cytisin (see **citizen**)

cystocercous (see **Cyticerus**)

cytology the branch of biology concerned with the study of cells
sitology the science of nutrition and dietetics

czar an emperor, king, or other person having absolute authority
Saar a coal-producing and industrial region in southwest Germany

Czech (see **check**)

Group I

calicle - calycle
camphene - camphine
cancellands - cancellans
cannequin - cannikin
caracul - karakul
cassena - cassina
chamois - shammy
charivari - shivaree
chatoyance - chatoyants
chemic - chemick
child - Childe
china - quina
chrism - chrisom
chymous - chymus
cirrous - cirrus
citrous - citrus
clairvoyance - clairvoyants
clanger - clangor

closeup - close-up
coalescence - coalescents
coccous - coccus
codeminance - codeminants
coiffeur - coiffure
competence - competents
compleat - complete
concomitance - concomitants
concurrence - concurrents
condescendence - condescendents
confidants - confidence
confluence - confluents
conical - conicle
constance - constants
consulter - consultor
convalescence - convalescents
copperbottomed - copper-bottomed
Cordelier - cordeliere
correspondence - correspondents
couturier - couturiere
creamery - crémerie
crenelet - crenellate
critic - critique
crotalin - crotaline
crout - kraut
crowhop - crow-hop
culture - Kultur
custodee - custody
cysteine - cystine

Group I and II

coaxal kō'aksəl
coaxial kō'aksēəl

comedian kə'mēdēən
comedienne kə'mēdē،en

Covenanter :kəvə:nantər
covenanter :kəvə:nantər
covenantor ،kəvə،nan'tȯr

custodee :kəstə:dē
custody 'kəstədē

Group II

cabal   kȧ'bal or ka'bəl
cabble   'kabəl
cobble   'käbəl

cabinet   'kab(ə)nȧt
cabinette   'kabə̇,net

cacur   'kā,kər
caker   'kākər

caddy   'kadē
qadi   'kädē

caesura   sē'zhu̇rə
scissura   si'zhu̇rə

cairn   'karn
kern   'kərn

calander   kə'landər
calendar   'kalȧndər

calk   'kȯk
cock   'käk

call   'kȯl
col   'käl

callee   kȯ'lē
collie   'kälē

caller   'kȯlər
collar   'kälər

caloric   kə'lȯrik
choleric   kə'lerik

camper   'kam,pər
quimper   'kam:per

canaster   kə'nastər
canister   'kanȧstər

cancellous   'kansələs
cancellus   kan'seləs

candelilla   ,kandə'lēyə
kandelia   kan'dēlyə

cane   'kān
kain   'kīn

cangue   'kaŋ
kang   'käŋ

canna   'kanə
kana   'känə

cans   'kanz
kans   'käns

cantal   kä^n tȧl
cantle   'kantᵊl

canton   'kantən or 'kan,tän
quinton   kä^n tōⁿ

captain   'kaptȧn
captan   'kap,tan

caput   'kä,pu̇t
kaput   kä'pu̇t

caracal   'karə,kal
karakul   'karəkəl

carbineer   :karəbȧ:nīr
carbiner   ,karə'bēnər

careen   kə'rēn
carene   'ka,rēn

carot(te)   kə'rät
carrot   'karət

carotene   'kerə,tēn
keratin   'kerəd•ȧn

carrion   'karēən
carry-on   'karē,än
kerion   'kirē,än

carry   'kerē
karree   kə'rē

catch-up   'ka,chəp
catsup or ketchup   'kachəp

cater   'kādər
heder   'khādər

caudal   'kȯdᵊl
coddle   'kädᵊl

caught   'kȯt
cot   'kät

cauloid   'kȯ,lȯid
colloid   'kä,lȯid

cavalier   'kavə,lir
caviller   'kavələr

caw   'kȯ
ka   'kä

cawed 'kȯd
cod 'käd

census 'sensəs
senses 'sensəz

cerasin 'seraˌsin
ceresin 'serəsən

cerate 'sirˌāt
cirrate 'siˌrāt
serrate 'seˌrāt

ceratin 'serətən
serotine 'seraˌtən

cercle 'serkl
circle 'sərkəl

cere 'sir
sir 'sər

cerin 'sirən
cerine 'sirˌən
serene səˈrēn
serine 'siˌrēn or 'siˌrən

cero 'serō
serow 'səˈrō

cerotene 'serōˌtēn
serotine 'serōˌtin

chace 'chȧs
chase 'chās

chador 'chədər
chatter 'chadər

chagrin shəˈgrin
shagreen shəˈgrēn

chalice 'chaləs
challis 'shalē

chalk 'chȯk
chock 'chäk

chevret shəvˈrā
chevrette shəvˈret

chic 'shēk
chick 'chik

chime 'chīm
chyme 'kīm

chlorogenin 'klōrəˈjenən
chlorogenine klōˈräjənən

choree 'kōrˌē
Coree 'kōrē

chucker 'chəkər
chukar chəˈkär

cider 'sīdər
siddur 'sidər

cillosis siˈlōsis
psilosis sīˈlōsəs

citrin 'sitrən
citrine 'sitrēn

clawed 'klȯd
clod 'kläd

clysis 'klīsəs
clyssus 'klisəs

cnicin 'nīsin
Nicene 'nīˌsēn

coarser 'kȯrsˌər
corsair 'kȯrˌser

coaster 'kōstər
coster 'kästər

coenurus sēˈnyu̇rəs
senoras sēnˈyōrəs

Cohen 'kōən
cone 'kōn
koan 'kōˌän

coir 'kȯir
core 'kōr

cola 'kōlə
colla 'kōlyə

coleus 'kōlēəs
colias 'kōlēˌas

colin 'kälən
colleen 'käˌlēn

color 'kələr
colure 'kəˈlu̇r

columbin kəˈləmbən
columbine 'käləmˌbīn

comers 'kəmərz
Commers kȯ'mers

comity 'kämət•ē
committee :kə'mit|ē

commence kə'mənts
comments 'kä.ments

commerce 'kämərs
commers kȯ'mərs

commissaire 'kämə.sar
commissar 'kämə.sär

company 'kəmpənē
compony kəm'pōnē

compare kəm'par
quimper kam:per

conation kō'nāshən
connation kä:nāshən

conceal kən'sēl
konseal 'kän.sēl

concord 'kän.kȯrd
conquered 'käŋkərd or 'kȯŋkərd

concours kōⁿ'kȯr
concourse 'kän.kȯrs

concur kän'kər
conquer 'kaŋ.kər

condemn kən'dem
contemn kən'tem

congé 'kän.jā
congee 'kän.jē

conger 'kängər
conjure 'känjər

Congo 'käŋgō
Kongo 'käŋgō

consign kən'sīn
consigne .kȯn'sen.ye

consol 'kän.säl
console kən'sōl
consul 'känsəl

cooler 'külər
couleur kü'lər

Coos 'küs
coos 'küz

copies 'käpēz
coppice 'käpəs

cora 'kōrə
corah 'kōra

coralline 'kȯrə.līn
corylin 'kärilin

Cordelier .kȯrdəler
Cordeliére .kȯrdᵊl'yer

corespondent 'kō.rə'spändənt
correspondent .kȯrə'spändənt

coria 'kōrēə
Korea kə'rēə

Cos 'käs
cose 'kōz

cosset 'käsət
cossette kä'set

coteau kō'tō
coto 'kōdō

couleur kü'lər
couloir .kü'lwär

couple 'kəpəl
cupel kyü'pəl

courant 'kȯrənt
current 'kərənt

coyne 'kȯinē
Koine 'kȯi.nē

crasis 'krāsəs
krasis 'kräsəs

crate 'krāt
krait 'krīt or kə'rīt

cribble 'kribəl
crible krē'blä

critic 'kritik
critique kri'tēk

cuckhold 'kək.hōld
cuckold 'kəkəld

Cuman kyü'man
cumene 'kyümēn
cum(m)in 'kəmᵊn

cunette   kyü'net
cunit   'kyünət

Curete   kyə'rēt
curet(te)   kyə'ret

curie   'kyůrē
curry   'kərē

curtain   'kər,tᵊn
curtein   ,kər'tān

custodee   'kəstə,dē
custody   'kəstədē

cutter   'kətər
kuttur   kə'tär

cymas   'siməz
cymous   'siməs

cynosure   'sīnə,shůr
sinecure   'sīnə,kyůr

D

---

da a valuable fiber plant of the East Indies now widespread in cultivation

dah a large Burmese knife; a dash in radio or telegraphic code

dace a small European cyprinoid fish

dais a raised platform

Dacian relating to Dacia or its inhabitants, an ancient Roman province in central Europe

dation the legal act of giving or conferring

Dactylis a genus of two or three perennial chiefly Eurasian grasses

dactylus the part consisting of one or more joints of the tarsus of certain insects

dah (see **da**)

dahl the pigeon pea, a tropical woody herb

doll a small-scale figure of a human being

daim a fallow deer

dam a female parent; a barrier preventing the flow of liquid

damn to condemn

daim a fallow deer

dame a woman of rank, station, or authority; a female (slang)

daimons attendant, ministering, or indwelling powers or spirits; supernatural

beings whose natures are intermediate between that of a god and a human

diamonds native crystallized carbon valued as precious stones with a hardness of 10 (the maximum) on the Moh scale

dairy a room, building, or establishment where milk is kept and butter or cheese is made

derry a meaningless refrain or chorus in old songs

dais (see **dace**)

dais a raised platform

dice to cut into small pieces; small cubes, each face of which is marked with one to six spots

dise merchandise or goods (by shortening)

daisy any of numerous composite plants having flower heads with well-developed rayed flowers

dazy stupified as by a blow; made numb or stunned

dak to transport by relays of persons and horses

dhak an East Indian tree

doc a doctor (by shortening)

dock a place for loading and unloading materials; the solid part of an animal's tail; to cut short

dalli a tropical American tree whose wood is used for staves and its seed yields a wax

dally to waste time; to twist a rope around a saddle horn in roping an animal

dalli a tropical American tree whose wood is used for staves and its seed yields a wax

dally to twist a rope around a saddle horn in roping an animal

dolly a small wheeled platform used to move freight, a child's toy

dally (see **dalli**)

dam (see **daim**)

dame (see **daim**)

damine belonging to or like the fallow deer

dayman a worker paid by time rather than piecework

dammar a resin derived from various evergreen trees

damner a person who condemns

damn (see **daim**)

damner (see **dammar**)

Dan a people of the border region between the Ivory Coast and Liberia

dan the expert level in the Oriental arts of self-defense and games

dawn to begin to grow light; to become apparent

don to put on clothing; a college or university teacher

Tan one of a boat-dwelling people in China

dance to perform either alone or with others a rhythmic and patterned succession of steps usually to music

daunts saps the courage of and subdues through fear

Dandie a breed of terrier originating in the Scottish borders, having short legs, long body, and rough coat

dandy a man who gives fastidious and ex-

aggerated attention to dress or personal appearance

Dane a native of Denmark

deign condescend to give or offer

daos large Philippine trees; large heavy knives used by the Burmese

dauws Burchell's zebras

dhows Arabian lateen-rigged boats

dows large heavy knives used by Myanmers

dowse to plunge into water or immerse; to use a divining rod

taos unitary first principles from which all existence and change spring

dar an Indian timber tree with soft red wood

darr a black tern of Europe

dartars a mange affecting the head of sheep and caused by a mite

darters any of numerous small American freshwater fishes closely related to the perches

dasi a female Hindu who is a slave, servant, or of low caste

dassi a hydrax

dation (see **Dacian**)

daub to coat with something that smirches or stains

dob the penis (slang)

dauber a worker who seals with clay the doors of kilns in which brick and tile are burned; a plasterer

dobber a dabchick or other small grebe

dauby crudely executed; smeary

dobby a loom attachment resembling a jacquard for weaving small figures

dauer a spore-like state akin to hibernation

Daur a member of certain Manchu-Tungus people of the Amur basin related to the Manchus

dour stern, severe, harsh, or forbidding

dower the portion of or interest in the real

estate of a deceased husband that is given by law to his widow during her life

daughter a female offspring

dodder to tremble or shake; a parasitic seed plant

dotter a person who makes dots or locates optical and focal centers, axes, and terminal points in ground lenses

daunts (see **dance**)

Daur (see **dauer**)

dauws (see **daos**)

davit a fixed or movable crane projecting over the side of a ship or hatchway and used especially for hoisting ship's boats, anchors, or cargo

davite a sulfate of aluminum

dawn (see **Dan**)

dayman (see **damine**)

days periods of 24 hours; times between sunrise and sunset

daze to stupefy or make numb

deys ruling officials of the Ottoman Empire in northern Africa

dazy (see **daisy**)

de either of two hollow semicylindrical metal electrodes in a cyclotron

di a music syllable in the sol-fa sequence

deader more deprived of life

debtor a person indebted or obligated to another

deaf lacking or deprived of a sense of hearing

def in music, splendid or superlative; without question, or definitely (by shortening)

deal to distribute, as cards to a player; a business transaction

deel a long robe-like garment worn in Mongolia and wrapped around the waist with a long sash

diel involving a 24-hour period that usually includes a day and the adjoining night

deanery the office, position, or residence of a dean

denary based on or proceeding by tens

dear regarded fondly; expensive

deer a ruminant animal of the family Cervidae

deasil right-handwise or clockwise

decile any one of nine numbers in a series that divides a distribution of individuals in the series into ten groups of equal frequency

decyl any of numerous radicals derived from the decans by removing one hydrogen atom

desyl a univalent radical derived from desoxybenzoin

deasil right-handwise or clockwise

diesel a vehicle driven by a diesel engine

debtor (see **deader**)

decade a period of ten years

decayed underwent decomposition; declined in strength or vigor

decal decalomania (by shortening), the process of transferring designs from specially prepared paper to china, glass, or marble and permanently affixing them thereto

deckle the detachable wooden frame around the outer edges of a paper maker's hand mold

decan any of the three divisions of ten degrees in each sign of the zodiac

Deccan a breed of coarse-wooled sheep of southern India

decken large masses thrust over other rocks by recumbent anticlinal folds

dekan one of 36 equal subdivisions of the equatorial belt of the celestial sphere

decanal of or relating to a dean or deanery

dekanal related to one of 36 equal subdivisions of the equatorial belt of the celestial sphere, in ancient Egyptian astronomy

decayed (see **decade**)

Deccan (see **decan**)

decile (see **deasil**)

decken (see **decan**)

deckle (see **decal**)

decks ship platforms extending within the hull from side to side and stem to stern
dex the sulfate of dextroamphetamine

decyl (see **deasil**)

decyl any of numerous radicals derived from the decans by removing one hydrogen atom
diesel a vehicle driven by a diesel engine

dee a metal ring for holding a saddle strap or belt
<u>**dit**</u> a short usually didactic sometimes satirical poem in old French literature

deel (see **deal**)

deelie a thing whose name is unknown or forgotten; a thingumbob
dele to delete in printing and editing

deem to form an opinion; to believe
deme a local population of closely related organisms

deer (see **dear**)

def (see **deaf**)

deference a yielding of judgment or preference out of respect for another
deferents imaginary circles surrounding the earth in whose periphery either one or more celestial bodies or the centers of their epicycle are supposed to move

deign (see **Dane**)

dekan (see **decan**)

dekanal (see **decanal**)

del in mathematics, an operator upon a function of three variables

dell a small secluded natural valley

delation accusation or denouncement
dilation expansion; the action of enlarging an organ or part of the body

dele (see **deelie**)

delegation the act of investing with authority to act for another
deligation bandaging or binding up

Delhi a city in India
deli ready-to-eat food products; a delicatessen (by shortening)

deligation (see **delegation**)

dell (see **del**)

Delphin related to the Delphin classics
delphine related to dolphins

delphinin a violet crystalline anthocyanin pigment
delphinine a poisonous crystalline alkaloid

deluded deceived or tricked
diluted reduced in strength or quality; watered down

demarch a ruler of a commune in modern Greece
demark to determine the boundary of

deme (see **deem**)

demean to lower in status or reputation
demesne land attached to a mansion; a range of interest or activity

demesne land attached to a mansion; a range of interest or activity
domain the possessions of a sovereign, feudal lord, nation, or commonwealth

demies scholars on the foundation at Magdalen College, Oxford
demise to transmit by succession or inheritance

demoded no longer fashionable
demoted reduced to a lower grade or rank

denary (see **deanery**)

dense crowded very close together; mentally dull

dents depressions made by a blow or pressure

dental relating to teeth

dentil one of a series of small rectangular blocks forming a molding below the cornice

dentile the condition of being saw-toothed; a small tooth

dents (see **dense**)

depravation corruption; perversion

deprivation taking something away from

deric of or pertaining to the skin

derrick any of various hoisting apparatus employing a tackle rigged at the end of a beam

derma the sensitive vascula inner mesodermic layer of skin

dharma in Hinduism, social custom regarded as one's duty; the body of cosmic principles by which all things exist

derrick (see **deric**)

derry (see **dairy**)

descension in astrology, the part of the zodiac in which a planet's influence is thought to be least

dissension disagreement; a breach of friendship

descent moving from a higher to a lower level or state

dissent differ in opinion

desert a reward or punishment deserved or earned

dessert a course served at the close of a meal

desmacyte one of the long fusiform cells forming a fibrous network in sponge cortex

desmocyte any of certain elongated interstitial cells

desman an aquatic insectivorous mammal of Russia resembling a mole

desmine a mineral of the zeolite family consisting of a hydrous silicate of aluminum, calcium, and sodium

desmon an immune body

desmocycte (see **desmacyte**)

desmon (see **desman**)

dessert (see **desert**)

desyl (see **deasil**)

detour a deviation from a direct course or usual procedure

detur a specially bound book awarded to a student for meritorious work

deuce the face of a die or playing card bearing two spots or pips; a tie score in tennis

douce in music, soft or smooth

Deusey a Duesenberg automobile (by shortening)

doozy a remarkable example of its kind; fancy or splendid

deviser a person who plans or designs

devisor a person who bequeaths property in a will

divisor a number by which the dividend is divided

dew moisture condensed on the surface of a cool body

do to perform

doux champagne containing at least seven percent sugar by volume

due owing or in debt

Dewar a glass or metal container with at least two walls with the space between them evacuated to prevent heat transfer

dewer a textile machine operator who brushes or sprays water on cloth during the finishing process

doer a performer or actor

dour stern, severe, harsh, or forbidding

dur any of several major musical keys

dewed dampened as if with dew

dude an overfastidious person in dress and manner; a tenderfoot or novice

dewer (see **Dewar**)

dewks a family unit in which both husband and wife work and have children (or DEWKS for Dual-Employed with Kids)
dooks inclines at a mine for hauling
doucs variegated colored monkeys of China
dukes noblemen

dex (see **decks**)

dextran any of numerous polysaccharides that yield only glucose on hydrolysis
dextrin(e) any of various water-soluble dextrorotatory polysaccharides obtained from starch

deys (see **days**)

dghaisa a small boat resembling a gondola that is common in Malta
Disa a genus of showy tropical African terrestrial orchids
disa a plant of the genus *Disa*

dhai a wet nurse or midwife in India
die to expire or perish; a small cube, each face of which is marked with from one to six spots
dye coloring matter

dhak (see **dak**)

dhan property or wealth, particularly the village cattle, in India
done completed a task
dun dark or gloomy; to ask for repeatedly, as an overdue payment

dharma (see **derma**)

dhauri an East Indian red-flowered shrub; an East Indian tree used for timber, tanning, and a source of gum
dory a flat-bottomed boat with high flaring sides

dhikr the ritual formula of a Sufi (an ascetic Muslim) brotherhood recited devotionally in praise of Allah
dicker to haggle or bargain; the number ten, especially of hides or skins

dhobi a member of a low caste of India employed as launderers
dobe a brick or building material of sun-dried earth and straw

dhole a fierce wild dog of India
dol a unit for measuring pain intensity
dole to distribute material, such as food, clothing, or money to the needy

dhoni a fishing or coastwise trading boat of India
donee a recipient of a gift

dhoon a valley in the Siwaik hills of India
doon a large tree of Sri Lanka
dun a fortified residence in Ireland and Scotland
dune a hill or ridge of sand

dhoop an Indian plant; the pitch derived therefrom
dupe a person easily deceived because s/he lacks discriminatory powers

dhoti a long loincloth worn by Hindu men
doty timber infected by incipient or partial decay often with discoloration
dudie a diminutive fop, dandy, or tenderfoot

dhows (see **daos**)

dhuti a long loincloth worn by Hindu men
dooty excrement (slang)
duty obligator tasks, conduct, service, or functions enjoined by order or custom

di (see **de**)

dial the graduated face of a time piece; a disk or knob for operating a machine; to operate a machine by means of a dial
diel involving a 24-hour period that usually includes a day and the adjoining night

diamonds (see **daimons**)

diane a triaene sponge with one ray reduced or absent
diene a chemical compound containing two double bonds

diaphane the art of imitating stained glass with translucent paper

diaphony dissonance; part writing or singing in two, three, or four parts

diarist a person who keeps a daily record of events

direst most ominous or sinister

dicast a member of the highest court of law of ancient Athens who performed the functions of both jury and judge

die-cast to make by forcing molten metal into a die

dice (see **dais**)

Diceras a genus of Jurassic mollusks comprising clams, oysters, and mussels

dicerous having two tentacles or antennae

dicker (see **dhikr**)

die (see **dhai**)

die-cast (see **dicast**)

diehard an old Scottish breed of terrier

die-hard a person who offers extreme resistance to change

dieing cutting or shaping with a die

dyeing imparting a new and often permanent color to

dying expiring or perishing

diel (see **deal** or **dial**)

diemaker a worker who makes cutting and shaping dies

dyemaker a worker who mixes and brews coloring matter

diene (see **diane**)

dier a person or animal that expires or quits

dire ominous or sinister

dyer a person who colors articles

diesel (see **deasil** or **decyl**)

diesis a semitone in the Pythagorean music scale that is less than half a whole step and is designated as 256/243

diocese the circuit or extent of a bishop's jurisdiction

dike a bank, usually of earth, constructed to control or confine water (rarely **dyke**)

dyke a female homosexual

diker a person who makes or works on dikes

duiker any of several small African antelopes having short straight horns

dyker a two-branched candlestick used in the Eastern Church

dilation (see **delation**)

dildo a West Indian spiny cactus

dildoe an object serving as a penis substitute for vaginal insertion and stimulation

diluted (see **deluded**)

dime a petty sum of money

disme a U.S. ten-cent coin struck in 1792

dine to eat a meal

dyne a unit of force in the cgs system

ding to talk, urge, or impress with tiresome repetition; to make a ringing sound

ting an ancient Chinese ceremonial vessel

dinghy a small boat propelled by oars, sails, or a motor

dingy crazy; groggy or dazed

dink(e)y small or insignificant; a small locomotive

diocese (see **diesis**)

dipterous having two wings or winglike appendages

Dipterus a genus of Devonian dipnoan fishes of America and Scotland having ganoid scales

dire (see **dier**)

direst (see **diarist**)

dis any of several superhuman female beings in Norse mythology

dix a certain score of ten points in pinochle

Disa and **disa** (see **dghaisa**)

disburse to distribute; to expend from a fund

disperse to send or drive into different places

discreet tactful or prudent

discrete constituting a separate entity

discussed investigated a question by reasoning or argument

disgust a marked aversion or repugnance

dise (see **dais**)

disgust (see **discussed**)

dislimb to dismember by cutting off limbs or parts

dislimn to dim or reduce the light

disme (see **dime**)

disperse (see **disburse**)

dissension (see **descension**)

dissent (see **descent**)

dissipater a person who expends energy aimlessly or foolishly; one who drinks alcoholic beverages excessively

dissipator a part of a glacier in which the loss by melting exceeds the gain from the accumulation of snow

distributer a person who deals out or apportions

distributor a device that directs the secondary current from the induction coil to the spark plugs of a multicylinder engine in their proper firing order

districts territorial divisions marked off or defined for administrative, electoral, judicial, or other purposes

distrix a disease of the hair that involves split or divided ends

dit (see **dee**)

<u>**dits**</u> dots in radio or telegraphic code

ditz a silly inane person; a frivolous ninny

divertisement a diversion, amusement, or recreation

divertissement an instrumental musical

composition having from four to ten movements and written as a chamber work

divisor (see **devisor**)

dix (see **dis**)

do (see **dew**)

dob (see **daub**)

dobber (see **dauber**)

dobby (see **dauby**)

dobe (see **dhobi**)

doc (see **dak**)

docile tractable or obedient

dossal an ornamental cloth hung behind and above the altar

dossil lint or a small roll of pledget for keeping a wound or sore open

dock (see **dak**)

dodder (see **daughter**)

doddle coarse bran obtained from wheat; a tree cut back to the trunk to promote growth of a dense head of foliage

dottle unburnt and partially burnt tobacco caked in a pipe's bowl; to keep apart by thimbles, as in glost firing

dodo a large heavy flightless extinct bird

Doto a genus of nudibranch mollusks with tuberculated cerata

doer (see **Dewar**)

<u>**does**</u> adult females of various mammals, as deer and rabbits

<u>**dos**</u> first tones of the diatonic scale

doughs mixtures of flour and other ingredients sufficiently stiff to knead and roll

doze to sleep lightly or intermittently

doggie an infantry soldier

doggy straight, lustrous, and inferior quality wool

dol (see **dhole**)

dolce soft or smooth

dolci sweet desserts

dole (see **dhole**)

doler a person who gives food, money, or clothing to the needy
dolor mental suffering or anguish

doll (see **dahl**)

dolly (see **dalli**)

dolman a woman's wide-sleeved coat or jacket
dolmen a prehistoric monument consisting of upright stones supporting a horizontal base

dolor (see **doler**)

Dom a member of a Hindu caste of untouchables
dom a doom palm, a large African fan palm important as a soil stabilizer in desert regions
dome a vaulted circular roof or ceiling
domn Lord

domain (see **demesne**)

dome (see **Dom**)

domini owners or principals as distinguished from either users or agents
dominie a pastor of the Reformed Dutch Church

domn (see **Dom**)

don (see **Dan**)

donar a girl, especially a steady girl friend or fiancée (slang)
donor a person who gives, presents, or donates

done (see **dhan**)

donee (see **dhoni**)

donjon the strongest and most secure part of a medieval castle, often used as a place of residence
dungeon a close dark prison or vault commonly underground

donné a person dedicated to missionary work
donnée the main assumption(s) on which a work of literature or drama is based

donor (see **donar**)

dooks (see **dewks**)

dooley an outdoor toilet (slang); a sweet potato (slang)
doolie a first-year cadet at the U.S. Air Force Academy
dooly a palanquin, a litter borne on the shoulders of people
duly properly, regularly, or sufficiently

doom judgment or decision of condemnation
doum a doom palm

doon (see **dhoon**)

door an opening in a room or building
dor an insect that flies with a buzzing noise
dorr a glacial trough crossing a ridge

doorman a person that tends the door of a hotel, apartment house, or other building
dormin abscisic acid, a growthinhibiting plant hormone

dooty (see **dhuti**)

doozy (see **Deusey**)

dopey feeling and acting in a dazed state; mentally dull
dopie a person who takes drugs (slang)

dor (see **door**)

dormin (see **doorman**)

dorr (see **door**)

dorsal belonging to or situated near or on the back of an animal or of one of its parts
dorsel a basket to be carried on a person's back or, in pairs, by a horse or other beast of burden

dory (see **dhauri**)

dos (see **does**)

dos property settled by the husband on his spouse at the time of marriage

dose a measured portion of additive, medicine, or labor

dossal (see **docile**)

dossil (see **docile**)

Doto (see **dodo**)

dotter (see **daughter**)

dottle (see **doddle**)

doty (see **dhoti**)

douar an Arabian village consisting typically of a group of tents encircling an open space
duar a tract of land in India leading to a mountain pass

douce (see **deuce**)

doucs (see **dewks**)

doughs (see **does**)

doughty marked by fearless resoluteness and stoutness in a struggle; able or strong
dowdy lacking neatness, charm, or smartness in apparel or appearance

doum (see **doom**)

dour (see **dauer** and **Dewar**)

doux (see **dew**)

dowdy (see **doughty**)

dower (see **dauer**)

downie a tranquilizer or barbituate (slang)
downy soft, quiet, or soothing

dows (see **daos**)

dowse (see **daos**)

doze (see **does**)

draffs the damp remains of malt after brewing that are often used as appetizers or supplements in animal rations
drafts outlines, composes, or prepares; selects an individual for some special purpose

drain to make gradually dry or empty
draine a missal thrush

drias a large European herb the root of which is emetic and cathartic; a deadly carrot
Dryas a small genus of arctic and alpine tufted plants
dryas any plant of the genus Dryas

drogh to transport by means of a small drogher, a small coasting vessel used in the West Indies
drogue a sea anchor; a towed aero dynamic drag device

droop to have a slouched or bent posture; to decline in spirit or courage
drupe a one-seeded indehiscent fruit, as a cherry or peach

dropsie a marble game
dropsy an abnormal accumulation of serous fluid in connective tissue; lethargy or laziness

Drupe (see **droop**)

Dryas and **dryas** (see **drias**)

dual consisting of two parts
duel a combat between two persons
dule a group of doves

dualist an adherent or advocate of dualism
duelist a person who engages in duels

duar (see **douar**)

dub to dignify or give new character to by a name, title, or description
dubb the Syrian bear

duchy the territory or dominions of a duke or duchess
Dutchy characteristically Dutch

ducked lowered the head quickly; avoided
duct a pipe, tube, or channel

ducks lowers the head quickly; avoids; swimming birds
ducts pipes, tubes, or channels
dux a theme of a fugue or canon

duct (see **ducked**)

ductal of or belonging to a pipe, tube, or channel by which a substance is conveyed

ductile capable of being fashioned into a new form

ducts (see **ducks**)

dude (see **dewed**)

dud(h)een a short tobacco pipe made of clay

dudine a female dude or tenderfoot; an ultrafashionable woman

dudie (see **dhoti**)

dudine (see **dud[h]leen**)

due (see **dew**)

duel (see **dual**)

duelist (see **dualist**)

duiker (see **diker**)

dukes (see **dewks**)

dule (see **dual**)

duly (see **dooley**)

dun (see **dhan** and **dhoon**)

dunce a dull-witted or stupid person

dunts in ceramics, cracks made while firing, or afterward by too rapid a temperature change

duncur a common Old World duck that greatly resembles the American redhead

Dunker a member of one of the denominations deriving from an original German Baptist group that practics trine, immersion, love feasts, and simplicity of life

dune (see **dhoon**)

dungeon (see **donjon**)

Dunker (see **duncur**)

dunts (see **dunce**)

dupe (see **dhoop**)

dur (see **Dewar**)

dural relating to the dura mater

duryl a univalent radical derived from durene

dustee the offspring of a white and a fustee; a person who is of 1/32 negro ancestry

dustie a person addicted to inhaling powdered narcotics (slang)

dusty marked by or covered with fine dry pulverized particles of earth or other matter

Dutchy (see **duchy**)

duty (see **dhuti**)

dux (see **ducks**)

dye (see **dhai**)

dyeing (see **dieing**)

dyemaker (see **diemaker**)

dyer (see **dier**)

dying (see **dieing**)

dyke (see **dike**)

dyker (see **diker**)

Dynastes a genus of large chiefly tropical lamellicorn beetles, including the rhinocerous beetle

dynasties groups or classes of individuals having power in some sphere of activity and able to select their successors

dyne (see **dine**)

Group I

dactylous - dactylus
debutant - debutante
decandence - decadents
deformity - difformity
demission - dimission
dependence - dependents
descendance - descendants
despondence - despondents
deterrence - deterrents
devest - divest

deviance - deviants
dextran - dextrin(e)
dicephalous - dicephalus
diestrous - diestrus
dipterocarpous - Dipterocarpus
discous - discus
dissentience - dissentients
dissidence - dissidents
dominance - dominants
dropkick - drop-kick
dryasdust - dry-as-dust

Group I and II

depositary   də'päzə,terē
depository   də'päzə,tōrē

distale   də'stalē
distally   'distəlē

Group II

daiquiri   'dīkərē
dichoree   dīkə'rē

daub   'däb
daube   'dōb

dawdle   'dȯdəl
doddle   'dädəl

deacon   'dēkən
decan   'dekən

debauch   də'bäch
debouch   də'baůch

decalet   'dekə,let
decollate   'dekə,lāt
decollete   dā'kälə,tā

decease   də'sēs
disease   də'z|ēz
disseize   də'sēz

decollate   də'kä,lāt
decollete   dā'kälə,tā

decouple   'de,kəpəl
decuple   'dekəpəl

decry   də'krī
descry   də'skrī

defuse   'dēfyüz
diffuse   də'fyüz

delead   de'led
deled   'de,lēd

delusion   də'lüzhən
dilution   də'lüshən

dental   'dentᵊl
dentelle   den'tel

depose   dē'pōz
depots   'dē,pōz

dessert   də'zərt
dissert   də'sərt

deter   dē'tər
detur   'dē,tər

deva   'dāvə
diva   'dēvə

d(h)oui   'dōnē
donee   dō'nē

diaper   'dīpər
diapir   'dīə,pir

diareal   'dī,arēəl
diarrheal   'dīə,rēəl

dictate   'dik,tāt
diktat   dik'tät

diplomat   'diplə,mat
diplomate   'diplə,māt

discoursive   də'skȯrsiv
discursive   də'skərsiv

discus   'diskəs
discuss   də'skəs

dissimilation   də'simə,lāshən
dissimulation   də'simyə,lāshən

distant   'distənt
distent   də'stent

divers   'dīvərs
diverse   'dī,vərs

dobby   'däbē
doby   'dōbē

doer   'düǝr
douar   dü'wär
dower   'daůǝr

doggy   'dȯge
dogie   'dōgē

dore   dȯ'rā
dory   'dȯrē

doublet   'dǝblǝt
doublette   ˌdǝ'blet

doup   'daůp
dupe   'düp

draftee   draf'tē
drafty   'draftē

dramas   'drämǝz
dromos   'drämǝs

dually   'düǝˌlē
duly   'dülē

dulls   'dǝlz
dulse   'dǝls

E

eager having or characterized by strong and urgent interest, desire, ardor, enthusiasm, or impatience

eagre a tidal flood, flow, or bore (seldom **aegir** or **eager**)

egger a person that collects wild bird eggs for gain; any of various moths of the *Lasiocampidae* family (also **eggar**)

earn to receive an equitable return for work done or service rendered

ern(e) a white-tailed sea eagle

urn a footed vase or vessel for holding liquids, ashes, and ballots

ease (see **aes**)

eaten taken in through the mouth as food

Eton resembling clothing or appearance of boys at Eton College

eau a watery solution, as of perfume

oe a violent whirlwind off the Faroe islands

oh an expression for various emotions; zero

owe to be indebted

eave a roof's lower border that over hangs a wall

eve evening (by shortening)

eboe a Central American tree the seeds of which yield eboe oil

Ibo a group of Negro tribes on the lower Niger river

echappé a ballet movement in which the dancer jumps and lands on the toes or balls of the feet

échappée a melodic ornamental musical tone

ectocarpous having reproductive organs developed from the ectoderm

Ectocarpus the type genus of Ecoto carpacae containing numerous more or less branched filamentous brown algae

eddo the edible root or stem of the taro root

Edo a Negro tribe in southern Nigeria

edition (see **addition**)

Edo (see **eddo**)

eek an expression of surprise or fright

eke to supplement; to live from day to day with difficulty

e'er (see **air**)

eerie (see **aerie**)

effect (see **affect**)

effective (see **affective**)

effector (see **affecter**)

effusion (see **affusion**)

egger (see **eager**)

ego the self; selfesteem
Igo a Japanese game for two persons

eh (see **a**)

eight (see **ait**)

eighty (see <u>ate</u>)

Eire (see **aerie** and **aire**)

Eire of or from the republic of Ireland
era a period set off or typified by some prominent figure or characteristic

Eire of or from the republic of Ireland
eyra a solidcolored reddish wildcat regarded by some as a color phase of the jaguarundi and by others as a separate species

eke (see **eek**)

el an elevated railway
ell an extension at a right angle to a building

Elaps a genus of venomous snakes
elapse to slip or glide away
illapse flowing into, as a river or a large number of individuals

elation high spirits
illation inference

elegit a judicial writ of execution whereby a defendent's goods and lands are delivered to the plaintiff
illegit contrary to or violating a law or regulation (slang)

elicit to draw or bring out
illicit unlawful

elision (see **allision**)

ell (see **el**)

elude (see **allude**)

eluded (see **alluded**)

elusion (see **allusion**)

eluted (see **alluded**)

Elysian (see **allision**)

em (see **am**)

'em (see **am**)

emanant emerging from a source, used especially of mental acts
eminent noteworthy or conspicuous

embarras an obstruction, such as snags or packed masses of tree trunks or driftwood
embarrass to place in doubt, perplexity, or difficulties

emboli foreign or abnormal particles circulating in the blood
emboly a process of gastrula formation by simple infolding of the blastula wall that is typical of embryos

embraceor a person guilty of influencing a court, jury, or other office(r) corruptly
embracer a person who clasps in the arms, usually as a gesture of affection; to welcome or accept eagerly

emend (see **amend**)

emerge to rise from an enveloping fluid; to come out into view
immerge to plunge into

emergence the recovering of consciousness, as after anesthesia
emergents any of various plants (as bulrushes) rooted in shallow water and having most of the vegetative growth above water

emersed rising above a surface of surrounding leaves, as a water lily
immersed completely imbedded in or sunk below the surface

eminent (see **emanant**)

emission something sent forth; discharged; released
immission placing a small piece of the host into consecrated wine

emission something sent forth; discharged; released
omission leaving out or failing to include

emit to send out; to express
omit to leave out

emotion (see **amotion**)

emplastic sticky, gluey, or adhesive
implastic not plastic or readily molded

emu a large Australian ratite bird
imu an Hawaiian cooking pit

en (see **an**)

encyst to form or become enclosed in a cyst or capsule
insist to hold firmly to something

end (see **and**)

ends (see **ands**)

endue to put on; to provide
undo to cancel; to unfasten; to destroy someone's reputation
undue inappropriate or improper

enfold to surround with a covering; to embrace
infold to fold inward or toward one another
unfoaled a mare which has not produced an offspring; an unborn colt or filly
unfold to spread out or lay open to view

engrain to color in imitation of a wood's grain
ingrain an innate quality or character

enhyrdos a hollow nodule of chalcedony containing water
enhydrous containing fluid drops

enrapt absorbed in ecstatic contemplation
enwrapped enfolded with material
unwrapped opened to view; unrolled

ens (see **ands**)

ensure to make certain or safe
insure to underwrite
unsure lacking confidence or assurance

enterocele a hernia containing a portion of the intestines
enterocoele a body cavity that originates by outgrowth from the archenteron

entrada an expedition or journey into unexplored territory
intrada a musical introduction or prelude, especially in 16th and 17th century music

Entrance a solemn procession through the body of the church to the bema in Eastern Church liturgy
entrance the bow or entire forepart of a ship below the water line
entrants persons that enter, say a competition

enumerable countable even though infinite
innumerable characterized by a vast or countless number

enunciate (see **annunciate**)

envoi a concluding or parting remark
envoy a messenger, agent, or representative of a sovereign government

enwrapped (see **enrapt**)

ephemeris a tabular statement of the assigned places of a celestial body for regular intervals
ephemerous of interest or value for only a short time; transient

epic heroic; a long narrative poem
epoch a memorable event or date; a new beginning

equation (see **aquation**)

er an expression of hesitation
err to make a mistake

era (see **Eire**)

ere (see **air**)

erecter a person who buids or constructs
erector a combination of lenses or prisms

in an optical instrument for making the image appear erect instead of inverted

ergodic the path followed by energy

ergotic pertaining to or derived from a fungous disease of rye, other cereals, and wild grasses

eria (see **area**)

Erica a large genus of low manybranched evergreen shrubs

erika a reddishbrown dye used on cotton, wool, and silk

erics payments imposed on a slayer and his/her kin for homicide in medieval Irish law

Eryx a genus comprising the typical sand snakes

Erie (see **aerie**)

erika (see **Erica**)

ern(e) (see **earn**)

erose (see **aerose**)

erosive (see **arrosive**)

err (see **air** and **er**)

errant (see **arrant**)

erred made a mistake; deviated from a standard

urd a spreading hairy annual bean widely cultivated in warm regions

error (see **airer**)

ers a vetch grown in Mediterranean and Asiatic countries

erse characteristic of Gaelicspeaking people of Scotland

erupt to force out or release suddenly and often violently

irrupt to enter forcibly or suddenly; to intrude

erythrin a mineral consisting of a hydrous cobalt arsenate

erythrine a colorless crystalline substance extracted from certain lichens and yielding certain red compounds

Eryx (see **erics**)

es a unit of quantity of electricity in an electrostatic system

ess resembling the shape of the letter S

escaladed climbed up or over

escalated carried, as if on a moving staircase

eschar a scar

esker a long narrow ridge of sand or debris deposited near a glacier

espier (see **aspire**)

ess (see **es**)

essay (see **assay**)

estray (see **astray**)

eta (see **Aeta**)

ethel ancestral land

ethyl a univalent hydrocarbon radical derived from ethane (C_2H_6)

Eton (see **eaten**)

euonymous suitably named

Euonymus a genus of evergreen shrubs, small trees, or vines of north temperate regions

euonymus any plant of the genus Euonymus

Eurya a genus of Asiatic evergreen trees and shrubs with foliage resembling holly

urea a highly soluble crystalline nitrogenous compound formed in nature by the decomposition of protein

Uria a genus of guillemots comprising the murres

eve (see **eave**)

evert (see **avert**)

evulsion (see **avulsion**)

ewe a female sheep, goat, or smaller antelope

yew a shrub or tree with rich evergreen foliage

you the second person pronoun; the one(s) being addressed

yu precious jade

ewe the female of the sheep
yo used by sailors as a signal to commence hauling on a rope

ewer a vaseshaped pitcher with handle and spout
your of or belonging to you
you're the contraction of you are

ewes female sheep, goats, or smaller antelopes
use to put into action or service
yews shrubs or trees with rich evergreen foliage
youse the plural of you (substandard)

ex formerly
x to cancel or obliterate; a ten-dollar bill (slang)

exceed (see **accede**)

except (see **accept**)

excess (see **access**)

excided cut out or excised
excited aroused or increased the activity of

exciter a dynamo or battery that supplies the electric current used to produce a magnetic field in another dynamo or motor
excitor an afferent nerve arousing increased action of the part that it supplies

excurses journeys or passes through
excursus a dissertation that is appended to a work that contains a more extended exposition on some topic

exercise to discharge an official function; something practiced to develop power or skill
exorcise to drive out (an evil spirit) by adjuration

exitus an export duty; the fatal termination of a disease; an excretory outlet
exodus a mass departure; the part of a Greek drama following the last song of the chorus

exorcise (see **exercise**)

exotic not native to the place where found; strange; romantic or glamorous
ixodic relating to or caused by ticks of the genus Ixodes

expatriate a person who lives in a foreign country
ex-patriot a person who formerly loved his/her country and defended and promoted its interests

exponence correlation between an abstract linguistic category and its specific elements
exponents persons who champion or advocate; expounders or explainers

expos any shows, displays, or expositions (by shortening)
expose to lay open to view or lay bare

eye (see **ai**)

eyed having eyes; watched carefully
I'd the contraction of I had or I would
ide a European freshwater cyprinid foodfish

eyelet a small usually round hole
islet a small island

eyer a person who watches carefully
ire anger or wrath

eyra (see **Eire**)

eyre (see **air**)

Group I

efference - efferents
effuence - effuents
ellipses - ellipsis
enhydros - enhydrous
ensure - insure
epigenous - epigynous
epigonos - Epigonus
epigram - epigramme
equipollence - equipollents
equivalence - equivalents
erysipelas - erysipelous
escallop - scallop

estrous - estrus
euryalae - Euryale
Eutopia - Utopia - utopia
exigence - exigents
existence - existents
exodus - exodusts
expectance - expectants
expedience - expedients
experience - experients
eyetie - itie

Group I and II

eradiation   ē,rādē'ashən
irradiation   ə,rādē'ashən

escallop   ə'skäləp
scallop   'skäləp

especial   ə'speshəl
special   'speshəl

espy   ə'spī
spy   'spī

Group II

earing   'iriŋ
erring   eriŋ

effete   e'fēt
Ephete   'e,fēt

efficient   ə'fishənt
officiant   ə'fishēənt

eidolism   'idō,lizəm
idolism   'īdəl,izəm

elegance   'elēgəns
elegants   ālāgänz

elopes   ə'lōps
elops   'e,läps

elusion   ə'lüzhən
elution   ə'lüshən

eluviate   ē'lüvē,āt
illuviate   i'lüvē,āt

embarras   :änbə:rä
embarrass   em'barəs

emigrate   'emə,grāt
immigrate   'imə,grāt

eminent   'emənant
imminent   'imənənt

empres   'ēmprəs
impress   əm'pres

empyreal   'em,pirēəl
imperial   'im,pirēəl

enervate   ə'nərvət
innervate   i'nər,vāt

ensoul   ən'sōl
insole   'in,sōl

enthrone   in'thrōn
inthrown   'in,thrōn

Equidae   'ekwə,dē
equity   'ekwədē

equites   'ekwə,tēz
equities   'ekwətēz

errands   'erəndz
errants   'erəntz

Eunuch   'yünək
unique   'yü,nēk

excite   ek'sīt
exite   'ek,sīt

excyst   ek'sist
exist   eg'zist

exert   eg'zərt
exsert   ek'sərt

expiree   ek:spi:rē
expiry   ek'spīrē

expos   'ekspōz
expose   ik'spōz or ek'spōz

extorsion   eks'tȯrshən
extortion   ek'stȯrshən

F

faces front parts of human heads

phasis a stage or interval in a development or cycle

facet a plane surface produced on a precious stone

fascet a carrying tool used in glass manufacturing

facks tells the truth (slang)

facts assertions purporting to have objective reality

fax facsimile (by shortening)

faddish resembling an object or style followed widely but briefly

fattish somewhat overweight or obese

faddy a person's father (slang)

fatty corpulent, greasy, or sticky

fade to lose freshness, vigor, color, or health

fayed fitted closely together

faded lost freshness, vigor, color, or health

fated determined or controlled by fate or destiny

feted entertained or celebrated

fagan a stick for poking holes in the side of a charcoal pit

Fagin an adult who instructs others in crime

fail to fall short of success or achievement in something expected, attempted, desired, or approved

faille a semilustrous closely woven fabric with good draping qualities

faille a semilustrous closely woven fabric with good draping qualities

file a hardened steel smoothing tool; to arrange in a particular order

phial a small container for liquids

fain gladly, willingly, or happily

fane a temple

feign to pretend or sham; to assert as if true

faint to swoon; barely perceptible; lacking courage or spirit

feint a false or deceptive act; a trick

fair attractive in appearance; pleasing to hear; just or equitable; not stormy or foul

fare a transportation charge; the range of food or stock

phare a lighthouse or beacon to guide seamen

fairer in a more equitable, attractive, or agreeable manner

farer a traveller

fairy a tiny mischievous creature of folklore

ferry to convey by ship or airplane over water or to a shipping point

fait a legal deed

fate foreordination, destiny, or lot

fete a festive celebration or entertainment

faker a fraud or pretender

fakir a swindler

fallacious deceptive or misleading

phallaceous resembling a family of fungi comprising the true stinkhorns

false untrue or disloyal

faults defects or imperfections; fractures in the earth's crust

fane (see **fain**)

fanner a person who circulates air by fanning

phanar Greek officials of Turkey, as a class

farce a light satirical or humorous dramatic composition; a ridiculous show

farse an interpolation inserted in a liturgical formula

farci a stuffed roast or fowl dish
Farsi a native of Fars, Iran

farcy a chronic ultimately fatal disease of cattle
Farsi a native of Fars, Iran

farding painting the face with cosmetics
farting expelling intestinal gas from the anus

fare (see **fair**)

farer (see **fairer**)

farming engaging in the business of raising crops or livestock
pharming a fraudulent scheme in which computer thieves redirect a person to an imposter Web page or phony site (even if the victim types a legitimate address in the Web browser) with the intention of stealing that individual's personal information

faro a banking game
farrow a litter of pigs
Pharaoh a ruler of ancient Egypt

farse (see **farce**)

Farsi (see **farci** and **farcy**)

farting (see **farding**)

fascet (see **facet**)

fate (see **fait**)

fated (see **faded**)

father a male parent
fother to cover with oakum to temporarily stop a leak in a ship's hull

fattish (see **faddish**)

fatty (see **faddy**)

faults (see **false**)

faun a half man half goat rural deity
fawn a young deer; to court favor by cringing or exuding an overly flattering manner
Fon a Negro people of Benin in West Africa

phon a unit of loudness

faux artificial, imitation, or fake
foe enemy or adversary

favous pitted like a honeycomb
favus a contagious skin disease caused by a fungus occuring in humans on hairy surfaces

fawn (see **faun**)

fawned to give birth to a young deer
fond loving or affectionate

fax (see **facks**)

fay to fit closely together
fey behaving in an excited irresponsible manner; mad; a visionary

fayed (see **fade**)

fays fits closely together; white persons (slang)
faze to disturb the composure of or disconcert (rarely **feaze**)
phase a stage or interval in development or a cycle

feared was afraid or frightened of
fyrd the national militia in England prior to the Norman Conquest

feast an elaborate meal
feest untidy, unkempt, or filthy; disgusted with

feat a specialized act or deed
feet an arthropod's limbs; units of measure each equal to twelve inches

fee a fixed charge for admission or services rendered
fi a music syllable in the sol-fa sequence

feeder a person who gives or provides food; a source of supply
fetor stench or fetidness

fees admission charges; compensation for professional services
feeze to disturb, worry, or beat
fis the fourth tones sharped of the diatonic scale

phis the 21st letter (plural) of the Greek alphabet

feest (see **feast**)

feet (see **feat**)

feeze (see **fees**)

feign (see **fain**)

feint (see **faint**)

fella a fellow (informal)
fellah a peasant or agricultural laborer in several Arabicspeaking countries

fellen a sprawling Old World poisonous plant, otherwise called bittersweet
felon a person who has committed a felony; a severe inflammation on a finger or toe

felloe the rim of a wheel supported by spokes
fellow a companion, comrade, or associate

felon (see **fellen**)

felt cloth or wool and fur fibers; sensed or perceived a stimulus by tactile sensation
veldt an African grassland

femerell a small open structure on a roof for ventilation
femoral relating to or located near the femur or thigh

feminin a colorless crystalline water-soluble hormone, theelin, that stimulates changes characteristic of oestrus
feminine characteristic of or appropriate or peculiar to women

femoral (see **femerell**)

fence a barrier to prevent escape or intrusion
fents cloth remnants

fends protects, repels, or defends
fens low peaty lands covered wholly or partly with water
foehns warm dry winds blowing down a mountain side

fennel a perennial European herb imperfectly naturalized in North America and cultivated for the aromatic flavor of its seeds
phenyl a univalent radical derived from benzene by removal of one hydrogen atom

fens (see **fends**)

fents (see **fence**)

feoff to put in possession of a lease hold
fief a feudal estate; something over which one has rights or exercises control

fer marijuana (by shortening reefer)
fur a piece of the dressed pelt of an animal

feral existing in a state of nature or untamed; suggestive of a beast of prey
ferrule a band of metal around the end of an object to strengthen it or prevent splitting
ferule an instrument used to punish students

fern a vascular plant constituting the class Filicineae
foehn a warm dry wind blowing down a mountain side

ferrule (see **feral**)

ferry (see **fairy**)

ferule (see **feral**)

fess confess (by shortening)
fesse a buttock

fessed confessed (by shortening)
fest an informal meeting or gathering

fete (see **fait**)

feted (see **faded**)

fetor (see **feeder**)

feudal founded upon or involving the relationship of lord and vassal; constituting a ruling class
futile serving no useful purpose, fruitless

feuar a person who holds a grant of land

fewer a smaller number of persons or things

few not many
phew an expression of discomfort or distaste

fewer (see **feuar**)

fey (see **fay**)

fi (see **fee**)

fibrin a white insoluble fibrous protein formed from fibrogen by the action of thrombin, especially in the clotting of blood
fibrine consisting of fibers

fiche a sheet of microfilm usually containing several rows of images (microfiche, by shortening)
fish any of numerous coldblooded strictly aquatic waterbreathing craniate vertebrates

fidded in sailing, secured and supported in place with a square bar of wood or iron
fitted shaped to conform to the lines of something else

fie an expression of disgust or dislike
phi the 21st letter of the Greek alphabet

fief (see **feoff**)

fila filaments or threadlike structures
phyla major taxonomic units comprising organisms sharing a fundamental pattern of organization and presumably a common descent

filander a kangaroo native to the Aru islands
Philander a genus of marsupials including the wooly opossums
philander any of several mediumsized wooly opossums of Central and South America; to make love frivolously

filar possessing threads across the field of view
filer a file clerk; a worker who smooths or shapes with a file

phylar relating to a phylum, a major taxonomic unit comprising organisms sharing a fundamental pattern of organization

file (see **faille**)

filé powdered young sassafras leaves
filet a lace with geometric designs; a piece of boneless fish or meat

filer (see **filar**)

filet (see **filé**)

filiform having the shape of a thread or filament
phylliform having the shape of a leaf

filleted rounded off with a narrow strip of ornamental material
phyllade one of the reduced leaves in a quillwort

fillipeens nuts with two kernels each; gifts given as a forfeit
Philippines an archipelago of 7,083 islands in the Pacific Ocean southeast of China

Filipena a female native of the Philippine islands
philopena a game in which a man and a woman who have shared the twin kernels of a nut each try to claim a gift from the other as a forfeit at their next meeting by fulfilling specific conditions

filly a young female horse or woman
Philly relating to Philadelphia, Pennsylvania

filter a porous article to separate liquid or gas from matter in suspension
philter a potion credited with magical power

filum a filament or threadlike structure
phylum a major taxonomic unit comprising organisms sharing a fundamental pattern of organization and presumably a common descent

fin a membranous appendage resembling a wing or paddle in fish and certain aquatic mammals
Finn a native or inhabitant of Finland

finally eventually; conclusively; decisively

finely precisely; admirably; in an impressive or elegant manner

find to come upon or locate

fined punished by assessment of a monetary penalty

finds comes upon by searching or effort

fines finely crushed or powdered material; monetary penalties imposed as punishment

fined (see **find**)

finely (see **finally**)

fines (see **finds**)

finick to become excessively dainty or refined in speech or manner

Finnic relating to the Finns

finish to bring to an end or terminate

Finnish relating to Finland or its inhabitants

Finn (see **fin**)

Finnic (see **finick**)

finnie to lay claim to; to latch on to

finny having or characterized by membraneous appendanges resembling a paddle in fish

Finnish (see **finish**)

finny (see **finnie**)

fireboat a boat equipped for fighting fire

firebote a tenant's right to take from land occupied by the tenant sufficient wood to maintain fires in the tenant's house

firelight the illumination from a domestic fire or campfire

fire-light to engage in a night hunt in which torches or other illumination devices are used

fireplow to make furrows to protect against fires

fire-plow a stick that is rubbed in a wooden groove to produce fire

firm securely or solidly fixed in place; a business unit or enterprise

firme a cross pattee that extends to each side of the shield or covers the entire shield

firry made of or abounding in any of several evergreen trees

furry consisting of or resembling the fine soft thick hairy covering of mammals

firs evergreen trees

furs fine soft thick hairy coverings of mammals; pieces of a dressed animal's pelt

furze a spiny evergreen shrub common throughout Europe

fis (see **fees**)

fish (see **fiche**)

fisher a person or animal that fishes; a large dark brown somewhat vulpine arboreal carnivorous mammal

fissure a narrow crack or cleft

phisher an identity thief; a person who lures another person to phony internet websites in order to steal passwords, account information, or other sensitive and private data.

fishery a fishing establishment

fissury abounding in fissures or cleavages

fissure (see **fisher**)

fissury (see **fishery**)

fit shape to conform to the lines of something else

phit any sound suggesting one made by a rifle bullet

fitted (see **fidded**)

fizz to effervesce; a hissing sound

phiz the face (by shortening physiognomy)

Fjäll a Swedish breed of small white polled dairy cattle

fjeld a barren plateau of the Scandanavian plateau

flack a professional publicity worker or press agent (slang); the recurrent sound of striking, as of loose tire chains on pavement

flak bursting shells fired from antiaircraft guns; abusive criticism

flacks professional publicity workers or press agents (slang); recurrent sounds of striking, as of loose tire chains on pavement

flax a plant whose long silky bast fibers are the source of linen

flagellate to whip, scourge, or flog; having or bearing various elongated filiform appendages of animals

flageolet a small flute resembling a treble recorder

flair a discriminating sense; instinctive discernment

flare to flame up brightly

flayer a person who strips off the skin or the surface of

flak (see **flack**)

flamboyance the quality or state of being ostentatious

flamboyants showy tropical trees native to Madagascar, but now widely planted

flan a large open pie usually with straight sides filled with custard

flawn a tropical Asiatic grass used more recently in America as a lawn grass

flare (see **flair**)

flask a somewhat narrownecked container

flasque an heraldic bearing narrower than a flanch

flavan an aromatic heterocycle compound from which all flavonoids are derived

flavin a yellow dye extracted from the bark of the quercitron tree

flavine a yellow crystalline base obtained artificially

flawn (see **flan**)

flax (see **flacks**)

flay to strip off the skin or the surface of
vley a temporary lake

flayer (see **flair**)

flea a wingless bloodsucking insect
flee to run from

flèche a slender spire above the intersection of a church's nave and transcept

flesh parts of an animal body composed chiefly of skeletal muscle, fat, and connective tissue

flecks spots, blemishes, or flakes
flex to bend repeatedly

flee (see **flea**)

Flem a member of the Germanic people inhabiting northern Belgium

phlegm viscid mucus secreted in abnormal quantity in respiratory passages

flesh (see **flèche**)

fleuret a light fencing sword

fleurette a small decorative floral motif

fleury having the ends of the arms of a cross broadening out into the heads of fleursdelis; in heraldry, having the heads of fleursdelis projecting out from the edge

flurry a spasmodic agitation or nervous commotion

flew moved through the air

flu influenza (by shortening), an illdefined transitory disease

flue an enclosed passageway for directing a gas or air current

flews pendulous lateral parts on a dog's upper lip

flues enclosed passageways for directing a gas or air current

flex (see **flecks**)

flicks light sharp strokes, often with something flexible; quick sudden movements; movies (slang)

flics police officers, especially in Paris (slang)

flix flax, a slender erect annual plant

flighting a system of flights, as on a conveyor belt

flyting a dispute or exchange of personal abuse or ridicule in verse form

flix (see **flicks**)

flocks natural assemblages of animals, as sheep or geese
flocs wooly masses formed by aggregation of fine suspended particles
Phlox a large genus of American herbs
phlox any plant of the genus Phlox

floe a floating ice sheet
flow to issue or run in a stream

flooder something that floods
flutter to move about agitatedly, irregularly, or with great bustle

floor the lower inside surface of any hollow structure
flor a coating of microorganisms that is allowed to form on the surface of some sherry wines

florescence being in a state of bloom or flourishing
fluorescence the emission by a substance of electromagnetic radiation, especially of visible light

florin an old gold coin first struck in Florence in 1252 weighing about 54 grains
fluorene a colorless crystalline cyclic hydrocarbon that has a violet fluorescence
fluorine a nonmetallic univalent element belonging to the halogens

flour finely ground meal of wheat or other cereal grain
flower the part of a seed plant that normally bears reproductive organs

flow (see **floe**)

flower (see **flour**)

flu (see **flew**)

flue (see **flew**)

flues (see **flews**)

fluorene (see **florin**)

fluorescence (see **florescence**)

fluorine (see **florin**)

flurry (see **fleury**)

flutter (see **flooder**)

fly to move in or pass through the air with wings; a winged insect
vlei a marsh

flyboy a worker who removes printed sheets from a handpress
fly-boy an aircrewman or airplane pilot

flyting (see **flighting**)

foaled brought forth a young horse
fold to lay one part over another part; a sheep pen

foamie a beer drinker
foamy frothy

focal relating to or having a focus or central point
phocal relating to or resembling seals

foe (see **faux**)

foehn (see **fern**)

foehns (see **fends**)

foes enemies or adversaries
phose a subjective visual sensation

fold (see **foaled**)

Fon (see **faun**)

fond (see **fawned**)

fono a Samoan council constituting the central political structure of a village, district, or island
phono a phonograph player (by shortening); spelling based on pronunciation (by shortening **phonology**)

foodie a person fond of culinary products
footie an action of flirting or becoming friendly or intimate
footy paltry or insignificant; foolish or simpleminded

for sent to; in connection with; to the extent that
fore previous, former, or earlier; situated in front of something else
four a number between three and five

foram one of the order of Rhizopoda comprising large chiefly marine protozoas
forum a public meeting place for open discussion

forced compelled, coerced, or constrained
Forst a white wine of the Palatinate region in Bavaria

forcene in heraldry, a rearing horse
forescene a preliminary view, sight, or vista
foreseen anticipated or known beforehand

forcite a variety of dynamite
forecite to call to attention preliminarily
foresight an act or the power of foreseeing; foreknowledge

fore (see **for**)

forecite (see **forcite**)

forehanded mindful of the future; thrifty or prudent
four(-)handed having four hands; designed for execution by four hands or four persons

foreheaded characterized by a brow
four(-)headed having extraordinary mental power

fores things that occupy a front or anterior position
fours races for the four-oared shells, with or without coxswain

forescene (see **forcene**)

foreseen (see **forcene**)

foresight (see **forcite**)

forestage the part of the platform on which actors or musicians perform that is nearest the audience, and which usually projects beyond the curtain
fore-stage the part of the upper deck of a vessel foreward of the foremast

forewarn to caution in advance
foreworn exhausted by effort

foreword a preface
forward situated in advance of or before something; toward the future

foreworn (see **forewarn**)

form the shape and structure of something
forme a low bench on which shoemakers formerly sat when working; a pattern for the upper of a shoe

formal following or according to established form, custom, or rule
formyl the radical HCOof formic acid that is also characteristic of aldehydes

formally in a prescribed or customary form; explicitly
formerly in a previous time

forme (see **form**)

formerly (see **formally**)

formyl (see **formal**)

Forst (see **forced**)

fort a strong or fortified place
forte a person's strong point

forte in music, loudly
forty a number between 39 and 41

forth onward in time or place
fourth the number four in a countable series

forty (see **forte**)

forum (see **foram**)

forward (see **foreword**)

fother (see **father**)

foul offensive to the senses; wet and stormy, as weather; an infringement of a game's rules
fowl a gallinaceous bird, as a chicken or turkey

fouler one of the several rounds fired before a rifle match to warm the barrel
fowler a person who hunts wild fowl for sport or food

fouling a deposit of powder or metallic fragments in the bore of a gun after firing
fowling the sort of hunting wild game-birds

founderous likely to cause a person to become disabled

foundress a female that establishes or builds

four (see **for**)

four(-)handed (see **forehanded**)

four(-)headed (see **foreheaded**)

fours (see **fores**)

fourth (see **forth**)

fowl (see **foul**)

fowler (see **fouler**)

fowling (see **fouling**)

frage the lowest bid in a card game, such as skat

frog any of various smoothskinned web-footed tailless agile leaping amphibians

fraid afraid (shortened slang); a ghost or spectre

frayed unraveled or worn

fraise a fluted reamer; in heraldry, a strawberry blossom; an obstacle used in fortifications

frays commotions; wears off by rubbing

fraze a small milling cutter used to cut down the ends of canes or rods to receive a ferrule

phrase a mode or form of speech; a group of words or musical notes expressing a thought

franc the recent basic monetary unit of France, Belgium, and Luxembourg

Frank a member of one of the West Germanic peoples entering the Roman provinces in A.D. 253

frank candid or open

frap to draw tight

frappe an iced and flavored semi-liquid mixture served in a glass

fraser an heraldic representation of a strawberry blossom

frazer a person who cuts or shapes to receive a ferrule

phraser a person who utters finesounding but often meaningless and unoriginal phrases

frater a monastery's refectory

freighter a ship or airplane used chiefly to carry goods

phrator a member of a social tribal subdivision or totemic clan

fratry the residental quarters of a monastery

phratry a social tribal subdivision or clan

fray a clerical title in various religious orders in Spanish countries

fry to cook in a pan or griddle over high heat, often in hot fat

frayed (see **fraid**)

frays (see **fraise**)

fraze (see **fraise**)

frazer (see **fraser**)

frazil ice crystals or granules formed in turbulent water

frazzle to reduce to a state of extreme nervous or physical fatigue; to upset

freak an odd, unexpected, or seemingly capricious action or event; a person with a physical oddity

freek frequency (slang)

phreak to use an electronic device without paying the appropriate charge or toll

freedom a quality or state of not being coerced or constrained

fretum an arm of the sea; a strait

freek (see **freak**)

frees liberates; rids of something

freeze to become congealed by extreme cold, as water at zero degrees Centigrade

Friese a descendant of those that inhabit principally the Netherlands province of Friesland and the Frisian islands in the North Sea

frieze in architecture, a sculptured band

between the architrave and cornice; a heavy roughsurfaced durable fabric; to embroider with gold

freezer an insulated compartment or room equipped to maintain the temperature below 32°F

frieser a person who embroiders with gold

freighter (see **frater**)

frequence a condition occurring frequently or often

frequents familiarizes oneself with another's thoughts or writings

fret to cause to suffer emotional wear and tear; irritation; to decorate with interlaced designs

frett in ceramics, frit

frette a hoop of wrought iron or steel shrunk on a castiron gun to strengthen it

fretum (see **freedom**)

friable easily pulverized or reduced to powder

fryable capable of being cooked in a pan or griddle over direct heat

friar a member of a religious order

fryer something used in frying; a young chicken

Friese (see **frees**)

frieser (see **freezer**)

frieze (see **frees**)

frits materials from which glass is made

Fritz a German, often used disparagingly

fritz to ruin, spoil, or interfere with; to cause to malfunction

fro backward, as "to and fro"

froe a steel wedge for cleaving or splitting logs

frow a woman or housewife

froes steel wedges for cleaving or splitting logs

frows women or housewives

froze became congealed by extreme cold

frog (see **frage**)

fronds leaves of a palm or fern

frons the upper anterior part of the head capsule of an insect

frore frosty, cold, or frozen

frower a person who uses a steel wedge for splitting logs

frow (see **fro**)

frower (see **frore**)

frows (see **froes**)

froze (see **froes**)

fry (see **fray**)

fryable (see **friable**)

fryer (see **friar**)

fu marijuana (slang)

phoo an expression of contempt, repudiation, or astonishment

fuge an early 19th century hymn characterized by polyphony and imitation

fugue a contrapuntal musical composition in which one or two melodic themes are repeated by successively entering voices

fuhrer a person in authority or leader

furor an angry fit or rage; hectic activity

Ful a member of a pastoral and nomadic people scattered from Senegal to Cameroon

full completely filled

fulgid in zoology, denoting fiery red with metallic reflections

fulgide the anhydride of fulgenic acid

full (see **Ful**)

fund a quantity of resources maintained as a source of supply; a sum of money set aside for a specific purpose

funned indulged in banter or play

funds money on deposit which is held at a specified place on which checks or drafts can be drawn

funs indulges in banter or play

funned (see **fund**)

funs (see **funds**)

fur (see **fer**)

furor (see **fuhrer**)

furred lined, trimmed, or faced with fur

fyrd the national militia in England prior to the Norman Conquest

furry (see **firry**)

furs (see **firs**)

furze (see **firs**)

fusel an acrid oily liquid having an unpleasant odor

fusile a rhomboidal heraldic bearing longer in proportion to its width; a light flintlock musket

fussed created or was in a state of restless activity

fust the shaft of a column or pilaster

fustee an offspring of a white and mustee (or octoroon); a person of $1/16$ negro ancestry

fusty moldy, illsmelling, or without freshness; oldfashioned or rigidly conservative

futile (see **feudal**)

fyrd (see **feared** or **furred**)

Group I

faerie - fairy
faineance - faineants
feme - femme
fermenter - fermentor
fiancé - fiancée
figurant - figurante
finestill - fine-still
flocculants - flocculence - flocculents
frau - frow
fucous - fucus
furor - furore

Group II

facial 'fāshəl
fascial 'fashəl

facundity fa'kəndədē
fecundity fē'kəndədē

fagot 'fagət
fagott fä'gȯt

fairy 'ferē
Ferae 'fe₁rē

fanatic fə'nadik
phonetic fə'nedik

farci 'fär₁sē
farcy 'färsē

farrier 'farēər
ferrier 'ferēər

faucet 'fäsət
fossette fä'set

fern 'fərn
firn 'firn

file 'fīl
phyle 'fīlē

fili fi'lē
filly 'filē

foams 'fōmz
fomes 'fōmēz

forced 'fȯrsd
forest 'fȯrəst

foreigner 'fȯrənər
forerunner 'fȯr'rənər

forgone fȯr'gȯn
fourgon färgō^n

formulate 'fȯrmyə₁lāt
formylate 'fȯrmə₁lāt

fourrier 'fu̇rēər
furrier fu̇rēər

freezer 'frēzər
friseur frē'zər

frison frē'zō^n
frisson frē'sō^n

furfural ˈfərfəˌral	**fusel** ˈfüzəl
furfuryl ˈfərfərəl	**fusil** ˈfyüzəl

G

gabel a deep notch in a ridge

gable the vertical triangular portion of the end of the cornice or eaves to the ridge of the roof

gabian petroleum or mineral naphtha

gabion a hollow cylinder of wickerwork or strap iron, like a basket without a bottom, that is filled with earth and used in building fieldworks, mining, or as shelter from fire

gable (see **gabel**)

gadded went or wandered about especially idly or for trivial purposes

gadid a fish of the family *Gadidae*

gade a gadoid fish, especially a rockling

gayed behaved gaily; made bright or cheerful

gadid (see **gadded**)

gadid a fish of the family *Gadidae*

gated supplied with an opening for passage in an enclosing wall, fence, or barrier

Gael a Scottish Highlander

gail wort in the process of fermentation that is added to a stout or ale

gale a strong air current with a speed of 32 to 63 mph

Gaelic characteristic of the Celtic Highlanders of Scotland; the Goidelic speech of the Celts

Gallic French, especially in quality; relating to Gaul or the Gauls

gaff an iron hook with a handle used in fishing and logging; an ordeal

gaffe a social or diplomatic blunder or clumsy mistake

gage a personal belonging cast on the ground to be taken up by an opponent as an agreement of combat; any of several small cultivated plums of European origin

gauge a measurement according to some standard or system; an instrument for testing and measuring

gagor in law, a person who pledges or secures something

gauger a person who inspects the dimensions of parts in a machine shop

gail (see **Gael**)

gain to obtain or increase; a resource or advantage acquired or increased; profit

gaine a support beneath a sculptured bust or head

gainer a fancy competitive dive

gainor tillage or husbandry

gait a manner of moving on foot

gate an opening in an enclosing fence, wall, or barrier

gaiter a leg-covering reaching from the instep to the ankle, mid-calf, or knee

gater a person that attends to the hole through which liquified metal is poured in the process of casting iron

gator alligator (by shortening)

gala a gay and lively celebration

Gal(l)a any of the several groups of Cushitic-speaking peoples occupying Kenya, Tanzania, and Uganda

galla any of certain nut galls from oaks that are used in pharmacy for their astringent properties

gallow to put to flight by frightening

galant relating to or composed of the light and elegant free homophonic style of musical composition in the 18th century

gallant notably marked by courtesy and attentiveness to women especially in a spirited, dashing, or elaborate way

gale (see **Gael**)

galena a mineral consisting of lead sulfide

Gallina related to an ancient New Mexican culture characterized by painted pottery

galipot a crude turpentine oleoresin exuded on the bark of the cluster pine tree

gallipot a small ceramic vessel with a small mouth used to hold medicine

gall bile; something bitter to endure; brazen boldness with impudent assurance

Gaul a member of the Celtic people that inhabited ancient Gaul

ghol a sciaenid fish of the Indian coast

goll an expression of astonishment (by shortening **golly**)

Gal(l)a and **galla** (see **gala**)

gallant (see **galant**)

Gallas any of several groups of Cushitic-speaking peoples occupying British East Africa and southern Ehtiopia

gallows a structure consisting of any upright frame with a crosspiece used in punishment by hanging

gallein a metallicgreen crystalline phthalein dye

galleon a heavily built squarerigged sailing ship of the 15th to early 18th centuries

galley a short crescentshaped sea going ship of classical antiquity propelled chiefly by oars; the kitchen of a ship or airplane; an oblong tray to hold set type

Galli a suborder of Galliformes consisting of the megapodes, currasows, pheasants, turkeys, and related birds

gallie any of various large North American woodpeckers

gally to put to flight by frightening

Gallic (see **Gaelic**)

gallie (see **galley**)

Gallina (see **galena**)

gallipot (see **galipot**)

gallop a fast natural threebeat horse's gait; to go at great speed

galop a lively dance in duple measure performed with sliding steps

gallow (see **gala**)

gallows (see **Gallas**)

gally (see **galley**)

galop (see **gallop**)

gam a school of whales; a friendly conversation

gamb(e) in heraldry, a leg or shank

gamme an entire range from one extreme to another

gama a tall coarse American grass valuable for forage

gamma the third letter of the Greek alphabet

gamb(e) (see **gam**)

gambet the redshank, a common Old World limicoline bird

gambit a remark, comment, or tactical maneuver designed to launch a conversation or make a telling point

gamble to play games of chance for money or other stakes

gambol playful leaping, frolicking, or cavorting

gamin a roguish impudent boy; an urchin

gamine a girl of ingratiating qualities, typically slight build, and a pert saucy air or wistful elfish charm

gammon a ham or flitch of cured bacon; to fasten to a ship's stem by lashings; to deceive or fool

gamma (see **gama**)

gamme (see **gam**)

gammon (see **gamin[e]**)

gang a group of persons drawn together by a common interest, tastes, or activity

gang(ue) worthless rock or vein matter in which valuable metals or minerals occur (seldom **gang**)

gantlet a stretch where two lines of railroad track overlap

gauntlet a glove designed to protect a hand from injury; a challenge to combat

gap a break in continuity; an intervening distance

gape to open the mouth wide (although usually 'gāp)

garbel the plank(s) in a wooden ship and the plate(s) in a metal ship lying next to the keel

garble to mix up through accident, ignorance, or intention

garret a room on the top floor of a house; an attic

garrot the goldeneye duck; a tourniquet

gar(r)ote(e) a Spanish method of execution by strangulation using an iron collar

garnet a brittle and transparent to semitransparent mineral that is used as a semiprecious stone

garnett to remove foreign substances from wool or cotton, or to reduce waste to fiber

garrot (see **garret**)

gar(r)ote(e) (see **garret**)

garrulous loquacious, talkative, or wordy

Garrulus a large genus of Old World jays including the common jay of Britain and Europe

garter a circular elastic band worn to hold up a stocking or shirt sleeve

guarder a person who watches or protects

Gascon a Romance speech of the area between the Garenne river and the Pyrennes

gascon a braggart

gaskin a part of the hind leg of a horse between the stifle and the hock

gatch a plaster used especially in Persian architectural ornamentation

gotch drooping or cropped, as of an animal's ears

gate (see **gait**)

gateau a fancy cake filled with custard and glacéed fruits and nuts

gato an Argentine composition in lively ¾ time for singing and dancing

gated (see **gadid**)

gater (see **gaiter**)

gato (see **gateau**)

gator (see **gaiter**)

gaud a showy bit of jewelry or finery

God the supreme ultimate reality

god a superhuman person or being

gaufre a very thin crisp wafer baked with a wafer iron

gofer an employee whose duties include running errands

goffer to crimp, plait, or flute linen or lace with a hot iron

gopher a burrowing rodent; a burrowing land tortoise

gaufre a very thin crisp wafer baked with a wafer iron

goffer to crimp, plait, or flute linen or lace with a hot iron

golfer a person who plays the game of golf

gauge (see **gage**)

gauger (see **gagor**)

gaugliar relating to, or like a small cystic tumor containing viscid fluid

gauglier more lanky or loosely built

Gaul (see **gall**)

gauntlet (see **gantlet**)

gay excited and merry; bright and lively in appearance

Ge Gaia, the earth goddess in Greek mythology

guay in heraldry, a horse without a harness and rearing on its hind legs

gayed (see **gade**)

gays makes bright and cheerful; homosexuals

gaze a steady intent look or stare

Ge (see **gay**)

geal relating to or caused by the earth

jheel a pool, marsh, or lake especially remaining after inundation

gean the fruit of a wild or cultivated sweet cherry

gene a complex protein molecule that transmits hereditary characteristics

jean a durable twilled cotton cloth

gear personal belongings or equipment; a toothed wheel used in machinery

Gir a breed of mediumsized dairy type Indian cattle

gees turns a horse or draft animal to the right

jeez a mild exclamation of surprise or wonder (slang)

gel a semisolid substance

jell to take shape; to achieve distinctness

gelid extremely cold or icy

jellied brought to the consistency of jelly

gemmae sexual reproductive bodies that become detached from a parent plant

gemmy have characteristics desired in a gemstone

genapp to singe so as to remove loose fibers

genappe a smooth worsted yarn used with silk in braids and fringes

gene (see **gean**)

genet a small European carnivorous mammal related to the civet

jennet a female donkey; a small Spanish horse

genus a class, kind, or group marked by one or more common characteristics

genys the lower outline of a bird's bill

geophilous living or growing in or on the ground

Geophilus a cosmopolitan genus of geophilomorph centipedes

ger a circular tent consisting of skin or felt stretched over a collapsible lattice framework and used by the Kirghiz and Mongols

grr an exclamation expressing dislike

germ a small mass of living substance capable of developing into an animal, plant, organ, or a part

jerm a small Levantine sailing vessel with one or two masts and lateen sails

German a native or inhabitant of Germany; a person who speaks the German language

german a dance consisting of capriciously involved figures intermingled with waltzes

germen germ cells and their precursors; a primary sex gland, such as an ovary or testis

Gerres the type genus comprising longbodied compressed marine fishes with protusible mouths and large silvery scales

jerries railroad section workers; Germans (slang)

gest(e) a notable deed or action

jessed attached two short leather straps to a hawk's legs, in falconry

jest a prank or act intended to provoke laughter; a jeering remark

just exactly or precisely; having a basis in fact or well-founded

ghat in India, a mountain range, mountain pass, or landing place on a river bank

got gained possession, acquired, or obtained

ghee a semifluid clarified butter made in

India and neighboring countries from buffalo milk

Gi a people of the border region between the Ivory Coast and Liberia

gi a lightweight, twopiece garment worn by practitioners of the Oriental martial arts

ghol (see **gall**)

ghol a sciaenid fish of the Indian coast
goal an objective or aim

ghoul a legendary evil being that robbed graves and fed on corpses
gool an illmannered offensive introvert (slang); a goal
gul something resembling a rose in form

ghurry the 60th part of a day, or 24 minutes
gurry refuse from cutting up a whale

Gi and **gi** (see **ghee**)

Ghuz a descendent of certain early Turkish invaders of Persia
goos viscid or sticky substances

gib a castrated male cat; a removable machined metal plate that holds other mechanical parts in place
guib a small harnessed antelope of western Africa

gibber to speak rapidly, inarticulately, and often foolishly
jibber a balky horse

gibbous the moon when seen with more than half the apparent disk illuminated
gibbus the hump of the deformed spine in Pott's disease

gig a gigolo (by shortening)
jig to give a rapid, jerky up-and-down or to-and-fro motion, as in dancing or fishing

gil an insecure or phony person (slang)
gill an organ in fish for obtaining oxygen from water

gild to overlay with a thin covering of gold

gilled having an organ for obtaining oxygen from water
guild persons associated in a kindred pursuit

gilder a person whose occupation is to overlay with gold or gilt
guilder a member of a modern guild or association of artisans; the recent basic monetary unit of The Netherlands

gilgai one of the shallow holes that honeycomb parts of the soil in interior Australia, attributed to the burrowing of pademelons
gilguy a rope temporarily used as a guy or lanyard

gill (see **gil**)

gill a U.S. liquid measure equal to ¼ pint
jill a female ferret

gilled (see **gild**)

gilt false glitter; a young female swine
guilt a state of one who has committed an offense

gimbal a device that permits a body to incline freely in any direction so that it will remain level when its support is tipped
gimble to make a face or grimace

gimel the third letter of the Hebrew alphabet
gimmal joined work whose parts move within each other

gimmal made of consisting of interlocked rings or links
gymel vocal part writing in medieval music in which the voices usually progress in parallel thirds

gimp a flat narrow braid used as trimming or decorative finish for upholstery and clothing; a limp or bobble
guimpe a wide usually stiffly starched cloth used to cover the neck and shoulders of some nuns

gimpy crippled or limping

gympie an Australian nettle tree having foliage and twigs covered with stinging hairs

gin any of several machines, as a cotton gin; a strong alcoholic liquor
jinn a supernatural spirit
Kin a Tatar people that founded an 11th century dynasty in China

ginney an Italian (slang), usually used disparagingly
Guinea a coastal region in West Africa
guinea an English gold coin circulated from 1663 to 1813, equivalent to 21 shillings in 1717

ginny affected with a strong alcoholic liquor
jinni Islamic spirits believed to inhabit the earth
jinny a block carriage on a crane that sustains pulley blocks

Gir (see **gear**)

giro a rotating winged aircraft
gyro a gyroscope or gyrocompass

girt bound by a cable; prepared or ready; geared; a heavy timber framed into the second floor corner posts as a footing for roof rafters
girth a band or strap encircling the body of a horse or other animal to fasten a saddle, pack, or other article on its back

gist the main point or material part
just exactly or precisely; having a basis in fact or well-founded

glace a frozen dessert
glass an amorphous inorganic usually translucent substance consisting typically of a mixture of silicates

glacier a large body of ice moving slowly down a slope or valley
glazier a person who cuts and sets glass, as in windowpanes

glacis a slope used for defense against attack; a buffer state

glasses a device used to correct defects of vision; drinking receptacles

glacis a slope used for defense against attack; a buffer state
glassie a marble made of glass
glassy suggestive of glass; having a dull fixedness of expression

glair(e) a sizing liquid made from egg white and vinegar
glare a harsh uncomfortably brilliant light

glands secreting organs of animals or plants
glans the conical vascular body forming the extremity of the clitoris or penis

glare (see **glair[e]**)

glass (see **glace**)

glasses (see **glacis**)

glasseye a walleyed pike
glass-eye any of several African forest warblers

glassie (see the second **glacis**)

glassy (see **glacis**)

glaucous having a powdery or waxy coating that gives a frosted appearance
Glaucus a genus of slender elongate pelagic nudibranches with three pairs of lateral lobes

glaze a smooth slippery coating of thin ice; a fine translucent glassy film
gleys bluish grey or olivegray sticky layers of clay formed under the surface of certain waterlogged soils

glazier (see **glacier**)

gleys (see **glaze**)

Glis a genus comprising the common Old World dormice
gliss a rapid series of connective notes played on a stringed instrument by sliding one or more fingers across adjacent strings or keys (slang for glissando)

glissile capable of gliding

glycyl the univalent acyl radical of glycine

gloam the twilight

glome the prominent rounded part of the frog of a horse's hoof

glögg a sweetish Swedish hot punch served usually at Christmas

glug a gurgling sound

glome (see **gloam**)

gloom partial or total darkness; a state of melancholy or depression

glume one of two empty bracts at a spikelet's base in grasses

glossae tongues; fused lobes of the labium of an insect

glossy having a shiny or lustrous surface

glossed gave a soft glowing luster or glistening brightness to

glost clayware with glaze applied but not yet fired

glossy (see **glossae**)

glost (see **glossed**)

glows becomes incandescent; shines with suffused radiance

gloze to make a false or perverse interpretation

glucide any of a class of carbohydrates comprising both the glycoses and glycosides

gluside saccharin

glug (see **glögg**)

glume (see **gloom**)

gluside (see **glucide**)

glutenin glutelin found in wheat

glutinin a blocking antibody

glutenous characteristic of the tenacious, tough, elastic protein in flour that gives cohesiveness to bread dough

glutinous gluey or sticky

glutinin (see **glutenin**)

glutinous (see **glutenous**)

glycyl (see **glissile**)

gnarred snarled or growled

knarred knotty or gnarled

nard rhizomes of several pharmaceutically useful plants

gnash to grind or strike the teeth together

nash to leave or quit a place or group (slang)

gnatty infested with gnats

natty trimly neat and tidy

gnaw to chew on with teeth

naw no (slang)

gnawer an animal that gnaws or chews with teeth

knaur a knot or burl on wood

knorr a single-sail medieval ship of northern Europe

nor or not, used with neither as a negative correlative

gneiss laminated or foliated metamorphic rock, as granite

<u>**nice**</u> refined, cultured, pleasant, or satisfying

gnir a ball of dust

near within a short distance or time

gnome an ageless often deformed dwarf of folklore; a dry wizened little old man; a maxim or proverb

Nome an Alaskan seaport city

nome a musical composition of ancient Greece

gnomic expressive of pithy wisdom concerning the human condition

nomic generally valid, as a statement

gnomon an object on a sundial that casts a shadow

nomen a grammatical form with functions of a noun

gnu a large compact blocky African antelope

knew comprehended, understood, or perceived

new recent, fresh, or modern
Nu TibetoBurman inhabitants of the upper Salween river region in Yunnan
nu the 13th letter of the Greek alphabet

go to move; a Japanese game
Ko a 12th century Chinese porcelain distinguished by dark clay and fine crackle

goad a rod pointed at one end used to urge on an animal
goed past tense of go (slang)

goal (see **ghol**)

goaled scored a point in a game
gold a malleable, ductile, yellow metallic element

gob a lump or mass of indefinite or variable shape; a large amount
gobbe a tropical leguminous African creeping herb also known as Bambarra groundnut

Gobi an east Asian desert mostly in Mongolia
gobi the lenticular mass of sedimentary deposits that occupies a down warp basin
goby any of numerous spinyfinned fishes

God and **god** (see **gaud**)

goed (see **goad**)

goer a person or animal that moves
gore to pierce with a pointed instrument or animal horn; thick or clotted blood; a triangular piece of land or cloth

gofer (see **gaufre**)

goffer (see **gaufre**)

Gola an African people of Liberia and Sierra Leone
gola a warehouse for grain in India
golah the people of one country dispersed into other countries

gold (see **goaled**)

golfer (see **gaufre**)

goll (see **gall**)

gon a railroad gondola; a thief (slang)
gone passed from a point; departed or left

goo a viscid or sticky substance; sickly sentimentality
gou a freshwater drum (the gasper goufish, shortened)
goût artistic or literary good taste

google to access the Google internet website search engine for information regarding specific topics or persons
googol a number equal to 1 followed by 100 zeroes, or 10^{100}

gool (see **ghoul**)

goos (see **Ghuz**)

goote a branch of a plant prepared for air layering
goutte a small pear-shaped figure occasionally borne as an heraldic charge

gopher (see **gaufre**)

gorce any obstruction in a river preventing passage of vessels
gorse juniper; furze, a spiny ever green shrub

gore (see **goer**)

gored pierced with a pointed instrument or animal horn
gourd a hardrinded inedible fruit of vines
gourde the basic monetary unit of Haiti; formerly a dollar in Louisiana

gorilla an anthropoid ape
guerrilla a member of an independent group engaged in predatory excursions in wartime

gorse (see **gorce**)

got (see **ghat**)

gotch (see **gatch**)

gou (see **goo**)

gourd (see **gored**)

gourde (see **gored**)

goût (see **goo**)

goutte (see **goote**)

grace a short prayer before or after a meal; charming or attractive characteristics

graisse a disease of white wines and cider

grade a degree of value or quality; a stage in a process

grayed became dull or cheerless

grader a worker or machine that sorts products according to certain specifications; a person who evaluates students' test papers

grater a device for reducing material to small bits of abrasion

greater larger or more prominent

graff a trench used in fortifications, as a moat

graph a diagram comparing one variable to another

graft the point of insertion of a scion in plant stock; acquisition of money or position by dishonest or questionable means

graphed plotted a curve or line on a graph

graham made wholly or largely of whole wheat flour

gram a metric unit of mass and weight

grain the unhusked or threshed seeds or fruits of various food plants including the cereal grasses

graine the eggs of the silkworm

graisse (see **grace**)

gram (see **graham**)

Granat any of several azo dyes giving red colors

granat a small bridge or culvert; a strong red or reddish orange color

granite a natural igneous rock formation of visibly crystalline texture

Granth the sacred scriptures of the Sikhs

grunt a deep short sound characteristic of a hog

graph (see **graff**)

graphed (see **graft**)

graser a device that uses gamma rays to produce a highenergy beam

grazer an animal that feeds on growing herbage

grassie the redbacked parrot of Australia

grassy covered or abounding with grass

grater (see **grader**)

grave an accent mark indicating a vowel is pronounced with a fall in pitch

Graves red or white table wines

gray to become dull or cheerless

greige woven fabric as it comes from the loom and before it is submitted to the finishing process

grès a piece of ceramic stoneware, especially when decorated

griege a variable color averaging a grayish yellow green

grayed (see **grade**)

grays becomes dull or cheerless

graze to feed on growing herbage

grèses pieces of ceramic stoneware, especially when decorated

grazer (see **graser**)

grease an oily substance; to influence with bribes

Greece a country in southeastern Europe

gr(i)ece in heraldry, a step in a series

gris(e) a costly gray fur used decoratively on medieval costumes

greased smeared with a thick lubricant; smoothed or made easy of passage; affected with a chronic inflammation of the skin of the fetlocks and pasterns, as a horse

grieced in heraldry, standing on steps

greater (see **grader**)

greave armor for the leg below the knee

grieve to mourn or feel sorrow

greaves refuse of tallow melting used as dog food

grieves mourns or feels sorrow

Greece (see **grease**)

greeney a green finch
greeny an inexperienced person

greige (see **gray**)

grès (see **gray**)

grèses (see **grays**)

grew developed or increased
grue a shiver; gruesome quality

gr(i)ece (see **grease**)

grieced (see **greased**)

griege (see **gray**)

grieve (see **greave**)

grieves (see **greaves**)

griffes in architecture, ornaments at the base of a column projecting from the torus toward a corner of the plinth; persons of mixed black and American Indian ancestry
griffs white persons newly arrived in the Orient (slang)
grifts lives by one's wits; practices methods of obtaining money illicitly

griffin a white person newly arrived in the Orient; an untried Chinese racing pony; a fabulous bird typically having the head, forepart, and wings of an eagle and hindparts and tail of a lion
Griffon a breed of small shortfaced compact dogs of Belgian origin; a breed of mediumsized longheaded sporting dogs originating in Holland
Griffon a breed of small shortfaced compact dogs of Belgian origin; a breed of mediumsized longheaded sporting dogs originating in Holland
griffone a woman of ¾ negro and ¼ white ancestry

griffs (see **griffes**)

grifts (see **griffes**)

grills cooking utensils; broils; distresses with continued questioning

grilse a young mature Atlantic salmon returning from the sea to spawn for the first time

grim stern or forbidding in action or appearance
grimme a small African antelope

grimaced distorted one's face
grimmest fiercest in dispoition or anger; most unyielding and relentless

grimme (see **grim**)

grimmest (see **grimaced**)

grind any of several small-toothed whales related to the dolphins
grinned drew apart or back the lips usually in merriment or good humor

grip to seize tightly; a spasm of pain; a suitcase
grippe an acute febrile contagious viral disease similar to influenza

gris(e) (see **grease**)

grisly dreadful or terrible
gristly containing tough fibrous matter
grizzly a large powerful brownish yellow bear

gros a heavy durable crossribbed silk fabric
grow to spring up and come to maturity

groan a deep harsh sound indicative of pain or grief
grown arrived at maturity; cultivated

grocer a dealer in foodstuffs
grosser ruder, coarser, or more vulgar

grommet an eyelet of material set into a perforation to strengthen the inner circumference of material surrounding the perforation
grummet a cabin boy on a ship (also **gromet**)

groom a person in charge of tending horses; a bridegroom
grume a thick viscid fluid, as a blood clot

grosser (see **grocer**)

grough impure commercial potassium nitrate

gruff rough or stern in manner, speech, or aspect

grow (see **gros**)

growan decomposed granite
grown arrived at maturity; cultivated

grown (see **groan**)

grr (see **ger**)

grue (see **grew**)

gruff (see **grough**)

grume (see **groom**)

grummet (see **grommet**)

grunt (see **Granth**)

Grus the type genus of Gruidae consisting of the typical cranes
gruss a finely granulated rock that has not decomposed by weathering

guan any of various large tropical American birds, somewhat resembling turkeys, that are highly regarded for sport and food
Kuan a type of Chinese porcelain pottery of the Sung period in the 12th century

guarder (see **garter**)

guay (see **gay**)

guddle to grope for fish in their lurking places
guttle to eat or drink greedily and noisily

guerilla (see **gorilla**)

guessed formed an opinion from insufficient evidence; conjectured
guest a person to whom hospitality is extended

Guhr a loose earthy deposit from water occurring in the cavities of rocks
Gur a branch of the NigerCongo language family centered in the upper Volta river valley in Ghana and the Upper Volta territory in West Africa
gur an unrefined brown sugar made especially from jaggery palm sap

guib (see **gib**)

guide to lead or steer
guyed steadied with a rope or chain; ridiculed goodhumoredly

guild (see **gild**)

guilder (see **gilder**)

guile crafty or deceitful cunning
gyle beer produced at one brewing

guilt (see **gilt**)

guimpe (see **gimp**)

Guinea and **guinea** (see **ginney**)

guise external appearance, shape, or semblance
guys ropes or chains attached to steady or brace something

gul (see **ghoul**)

gull(e)y a small valley or gulch
gullie a tern (seabird)

gumbee a small marble
gumby a drum made of skin stretched over a piece of hollowed tree

gumbo the okra plant or its edible pods
gumboe a small marble
gum-bow a slingshot

gumby (see **gumbee**)

gundi a short-tailed hystricomorphous rodent of North Africa
gundy a high-boiling distillate separated in refining shale oil

Gur and **gur** (see **guhr**)

gurry (see **ghurry**)

Guti a mountain people ruling Sumer and Akkad near Babylon in the 24th century B.C.
gutty in heraldry, an ornamental pattern of drops argent

guttae two or more in a series of ornaments in a Doric entablature; gray to brown tough plastic substances obtained from the latex of several Malaysian sapotaceous trees

gutty having courage or fortitude; having a significant or challenging substance or quality; in heraldry, an ornamental pattern of drops argent

guttle (see **guddle**)

gutty (see **guttae** and **Guti**)

guyed (see **guide**)

guys (see **guise**)

gyle (see **guile**)

gymel (see **gimmel**)

gympie (see **gimpy**)

gyro (see **giro**)

gyve to bind or restrain with fetters
jive a special slang jargon

Group I

gager - gagor
galaks - Galax
ganging - gangion
gecko - Gekko
granter - grantor
grievance - grievants

Group I and II

gluten 'glüt^ən
glutin 'glütin

guarantee :garən:tē
guaranty :garəntē

Group II

gala 'galə
galah gə'lä

galerie gal'rē
gallery 'galrē

galette gə'let
gal(l)et 'galət
gullet 'gələt

Galeus 'gālēəs
galleass 'galēəs

Galium 'gālēəm
gallium 'galēəm

gally 'gȯlē
golly 'gälē

gambet 'gambət
gambette gam'bet

gar 'gär
guar 'gwär

garbill 'gär,bil
garble 'gärbəl

garnet 'gärnət
garnett gär:nət

garrott gȧrō
garrot(t)e ga'rōt

gauzy 'gȯzē
Ghazi 'gä,zē

gebur ge'bur
Gheber 'gabər

geese 'gēs
gies 'gēz

genae 'jē,nē
genie 'jēnē

German 'jərmən
germon zhermōⁿ

ghouls 'gülz
gules 'gyülz

gizzard 'gizərd
Guisard gē'zärd

glazer 'glāzər
glazier 'glāzhər

glossae 'glä,sē
glossy 'gläsē

gluten 'glüt^ən
glutin 'glütin

gnawed 'nȯd
nod 'näd

Gobelin 'gōbələn
goblin 'gäblən

Golo 'gō͵lō
goloe gō'lō

goody 'gu̇dē
Guti 'gu̇dē

gook 'gük or 'gu̇k
guck 'gək

gorgeous 'gȯrjəs
gorges 'gȯrjəz

Gouda 'gu̇də
gutta 'gu̇də

grantee 'gran͵tē
granthi 'grantē

grazer 'grāzər
graizer 'grāzhər

greisen 'grīzən
grison 'grizən

groat 'grōt
grot 'grät

Guiana gē'anə
Guyana gī'anə

gusla 'güslə
gusli 'güslē

guttie 'gət͵tī
gutty 'gədē or 'güdē

H

haab the 365-day year of the Maya calendar
hob a level projection at the back or side of a fireplace on which something to be kept warm can be placed

haaf deepsea fishing grounds off the Shetland and Orkney Islands
haff a long shallow lagoon separated from the open sea by a narrow sandbar or barrier beach
half one of two equal parts into which a thing is divisible
have to feel compulsion, obligation, or necessity with respect to

hache an axe or hatchet
hash a mixture, jumble, or hodgepodge; a dish usually consisting of leftover meat chopped into small pieces, mixed with potatoes, and browned

hachure a short line used in mapmaking for shading and denoting surfaces in relief; a contour line
hasher a worker who feeds unmarketable

meat into a hashing machine so it may be used for byproducts; a waiter or waitress (slang)

hackee a chipmunk
hackie a cab driver
hacky a short and dry manner of coughing

hade an angle made by a rock fault plane or vein with the vertical
hayed cut and cured grass for hay

Hadean characteristic of the abode of the dead or hell
Haitian characteristic of the people or the island of Haiti

haded in geology, deviated from the vertical, as a vein, fault, or lode
hated felt extreme enmity toward

haem an iron-containing pyrrole derivative
hem a finished edge of a cloth article

haff (see **haaf**)

hagi a Japanese bush clover

hoggy a towpath driver for the early 19th century barge transportation system in parts of the eastern U.S.

haik a voluminous piece of cloth worn as an outer garment in northern Africa
hake a fish related to cod

haik a voluminous piece of cloth worn as an outer garment in northern Africa
hike to march, walk, or tramp
hyke an exclamation used to urge dogs onward in a chase

hail precipitation in the form of small ice balls; to salute or greet
hale healthy or sound; to haul, pull, or draw

hair a threadlike outgrowth on an animal's epidermis
hare a longeared gnawing animal
hayer a person that cuts and cures grass, then hauls it to storage
herr mister or a gentleman, in German

hairier covered with more hair
harrier a hunting dog; a crosscountry runner

hairing removing or covering with slender threadlike outgrowth of the epidermis
haring moving swiftly
herring a valuable food fish

hairy covered with hair
harry to assault or ravage

Haitian (see **Hadean**)

hake (see **haik**)

hala a screw pine native from southern Asia west to Hawaii
hollow a depression, a low, or an excavated place

hale (see **hail**)

half (see **haaf**)

half-soled repaired or renewed a shoe by putting on a new partial sole
half-souled partially possessing a psychical or spiritual nature

halide a binary compound of a halogen with a more electropositive element or radical
hallowed consecrated or blessed

hall a large assembly room; a passageway; a large building
haul to pull, drag, or transport

hallo a call used to attract attention
hallow to make holy; to venerate
halo containing halogen (by shortening)
hello an expression or gesture of greeting
hollo a call of encouragement or jubilation

hallocks rectangular wood veneer berry boxes with straight sides and a raised bottom
hallux the first or preaxial digit of the hind limb; the big toe

hallow (see **hallo**)

hallowed (see **halide**)

hallux (see **hallocks**)

halo (see **hallo**)

halve to divide in two equal parts
have to possess or hold

Hamburg a city in northern Germany
Homburg a man's hat of smooth-finished felt with a stiff curled ribbonbound brim and a high tapered crown creased lengthwise

hamus in biology, a hook or curved process
jemez a group of Tanoan Amerindian peoples of New Mexico

hance a ship's curved contour
hanse a trading association in foreign countries; an entrance fee into a merchant guild

handmade produced by hand
handmaid a female servant

hands terminal parts of a vertebrate's forelimb when modified for grasping
Hans an Athaspakan people of the Yukon

river district in east central Alaska and the Yukon territory of Canada; members of a people now comprising the dominant culture group of China

handset a telephone mouthpiece and earpiece mounted on a single handle
hand-set consisting of or printed or cast from individual pieces of type assembled with fingers

handsome attractive or having an impressive and pleasing appearance; of considerable value
hansom a twowheeled covered carriage

hangar an enclosed area for housing and repairing aircraft
hanger a device from which something is hung; a person who hangs articles

Hans (see **hands**)

hanse (see **hance**)

hansom (see **handsome**)

harass to annoy continually or plague; to raid
harras a herd of stud horses

hardtop an automobile with a metal roof
hard-top a hard-surfaced area or road

hardy strong or robust; resolute
hearty exhibiting vigorous good health; exuberant

hare (see **hair**)

haring (see **hairing**)

harras (see **harass**)

harrier (see **hairier**)

harry (see **hairy**)

hart a stag or male deer
heart a muscular organ which acts as a pump to maintain blood circulation

hash (see **hache**)

hasher (see **hachure**)

hatcher a device to which eggs are trans-

ferred from the incubator shortly before they are due to hatch
hatchur a short line used in map-making for shading and denoting surfaces in relief; a contour line (see **hachure** for an alternate pronunciation)

hated (see **haded**)

Hati in Egyptian religion, the physical heart
Hatti a pre–Hittite people of contral Anatolia in Asia Minor

haughty disdainfully proud or overbearing; arrogant
hottie an attractive or sexually promiscuous person of the opposite sex, usually a woman (slang)

haul (see **hall**)

haus irregularly spreading or shrubby trees widely distributed on tropical shores
house to provide with living quarters; to store in a secure place
hows ways in which something is or can be done
how's the contraction of how is, how has, or how was

haute highclass, hightoned, or fancy
oat a cereal grass cultivated for its edible seed

hauteur (see **auteur**)

have (see **haaf** or **halve**)

hawer a speaker who pauses while collecting his or her thoughts
hoar frost or rime; a grayish coating
hoer a person that works the soil with a hoe
whore a female prostitute

hawksbill a carnivorous sea turte of tropical and subtropical seas
hawk's-bill the pawl for the rack in the striking mechanism of a clock

haws pauses made by a speaker when collecting his or her thoughts

hawse the distance or space between a ship's bow and its anchor

hayed (see **hade**)

hayer (see **hair**)

hays cuts and cures grass for hay

haze dull or cloudy; to subject a person to unnecessary or ridiculous treatment

he(h)s the fifth letter of the Hebrew alphabet (plural)

heighs expressions of cheeriness

heis games of cat's-cradle

heys expressions of interrogation or attentiongetting

<u>**headward**</u> in the direction of the head

headword a word or term often in distinctive type placed at the beginning of a chapter or entry

heal to restore to health or cure

heel the hind part of a foot; to cause a boat to list

he'll the contraction of he will

heald a weaving harness or heddle

healed restored to health or cured

heeled caused a boat to list

healer a person or circumstance that cures or heals

heeler a local worker for a political boss; a dog that urges lagging animals onward by nipping at their heels

hear to perceive with the ear

heer an old unit of measure for linen and woolen yarn of about 600 yards

<u>**here**</u> at this point in space

heard apprehended with the ear

herd several of one kind of animal together; to lead or gather animals into a group

hearse a vehicle for conveying the dead; a usually triangular wooden or metal frame used in the Tenebrae service during Holy Week and normally designed to hold 15 candles

herse a frame to dry skins, as for parchment

hirse broomcorn millet

hearsed conveyed in a hearse; buried

hurst a grove or wooded knoll; a sandbank in a river

heart (see **hart**)

hearty (see **hardy**)

heated raised the temperature of

heeded had regard for or paid attention to

heater a device that generates or retains heat or warmth

heder an elementary Jewish school in which children are given religious instruction often in Hebrew

heeder a person who pays attention to circumstances, things, or people

heaume a large helmet supported by the shoulders

holm an evergreen oak of southern Europe

hom a sacred plant of the ancient Persians

home a principal place of residence

heaumer a maker of medieval helmets

homer to hit a baseball enabling the batter to make a complete circuit of the bases and score a run

hecks wooden gratings set across a stream to obstruct the passage of fish; devices on a vertical frame for controlling warp threads in textile manufacturing

hex to practice witchcraft on; hexagonal in shape

he'd the contraction of he would or he had

heed to have regard for or pay attention to

heder (see **header**)

heed (see **he'd**)

heeded (see **heated**)

heeder (see **heater**)

heel (see **heal**)

heeled (see **heald**)

heeler (see **healer**)

heer (see **hear**)

he(h)s (see **hays**)

heigh an expression of cheeriness
hi a greeting
hie to hasten
high tall or having considerable upward
  extension

heighs (see **hays**)

heinous hatefully or shockingly evil;
  abominable
highness the quality or state of being
  high; a person of honor

heir (see **air**)

heiress (see **arras**)

heirless (see **airless**)

heirship (see **airship**)

heis (see **hays**)

held retained in one's keeping
helled behaved in a noisy and often dis-
  solute way; caroused

helicin a glucoside obtained by partial oxidation of salicin
helicine pertaining to the helix of the ear;
  curled, spiral, or helicoid (in designating
  certain small arteries of the penis)

he'll (see **heal**)

helled (see **held**)

hello (see **hallo**)

hem (see **haem**)

hep one, used in counting cadence in
  marching
hut a temporary structure used as living
  quarters or for storage

herb a plant or plant part valued for its
  medicinal, savory, or aromatic qualities
urb an urban area

herd (see **heard**)

herding the actual work of taking care of
  livestock
hurting painful or distressing

herds groups of several people or animals
  of one kind
hurds coarse parts of flax or hemp adhering to the fiber after separation

here (see **hear**)

herl a barb of feather used in dressing an
  artificial fly
hurl to throw, toss, or cast

heroin a bitter white crystalline narcotic
  made from morphine
heroine a principal female character in a
  drama, novel, or event

herr (see **hair**)

herring (see **hairing**)

herse (see **hearse**)

hertz a unit of frequency equal to one
  cycle per second
hurts injuries or damages

heterogenous not originating with the
  body
heterogynous having females of more
  than one kind

heteronomous subject to or involving
  different laws of growth
heteronymous having different designa-
  tions

heugh an exclamation expressing surprise
hoo an expression of emotional reaction; a
  call
Hu an ancient Tatar people of northwest
  China
who what person(s)
whoo the cry of an owl

hew to cut with a heavy cutting instrument; to adhere, conform, or stick to
hue a color or complexion
whew an expression of relief, amazement,
  or discomfort; to make a halfformed
  whistling sound

hewer a person who cuts or fells with hard rough blows

huer a person who shouts an alarm or signal

hure the head of a bear, boar, or wolf

hex (see **hecks**)

heys (see **hays**)

hi (see **heigh**)

hic a sound of a hiccup

hick an awkward unsophisticated person

hickey a pimple; a defect in a negative or printing plate

hicky unsophisticated, awkward, or provincial

hide to conceal, put out of sight, or keep secret; an outer covering of an animal

hied hastened

hie (see **heigh**)

hied (see **hide**)

high (see **heigh**)

highdried a red herring

high-dried deprived of an unusually high percentage of its moisture by baking or drying

higher taller or having greater upward extension

<u>**hire**</u> to employ for wages

highline a high-voltage electric transmission line

high-line being a fisherman or fishing boat with a large or the largest catch

highly in or at an elevated place, level, or rank

hyle in philosophy, whatever receives form or determination from outside itself

highness (see **heinous**)

hike (see **haik**)

hila scars on a seed marking the point of attachment of the ovule to the funiculus

Hyla a large genus of archiferous amphibians comprising the typical toads

hyla any amphibian of the genus Hyla

hillie a small pinch of dirt on which a marble is sometimes elevated

hilly abounding with natural elevations of land; difficult or obscure

him the objective case of he

hymn a song of praise or joy

hip the laterally projecting region of each side of the lower or posterior part of the mammalian trunk; extremely alert and knowing

hipp hippopotamus (by shortening)

hipe in wrestling, a means of throwing an opponent

hype a narcotic addict; to promote or publicize extravagantly

hipp (see **hippie**)

hippie a baby's diaper

hippy having or resembling large haunches or hips

hire (see **higher**)

hirse (see **hearse**)

hissed made the sound by which an animal indicates alarm, fear, irritation, or warning

hist an expression or sound used to attract attention

Ho a people of the northeastern part of the Indian subcontinent south of the Ganges plain

ho an expression of surprise, delight, or derision

hoe an agricultural implement

Hoh an Indian people of the Olympic Peninsula, Washington

whoa a command to a draft animal to stop or stand still

hoar (see **hawer**)

hoard to accumulate something

hoared frosted or rimed; grayishly coated

horde a loosely organized group of individuals, animals, or insects; a swarm

whored acted as a prostitute

hoarse rough sounding, grating, or rasping

horse a large solidfooted herbivorous mammal

hoarsen to make or become rough sounding, grating, or rasping

whoreson a coarse fellow; an illegitimate child

hob (see **haab**)

hobo a migratory worker; a vagrant

jobo a tropical American tree sometimes cultivated for its edible yellow plumlike fruit

hocker a person who pledges security for a loan

hougher a person who hamstrings cattle

hockey a game played on the ice by two sixperson teams

hocky having faulty tarsal joints, as a dog

hocks tarsal joints or regions in the hind limbs of digitigrade quadrapeds, as a horse; restraints of goods usually as pledges for loans

hocs a card game in which a holder gives certain cards any value

hoks small pens to contain animals

hox to pester or annoy by following

hocky (see **hockey**)

hocs (see **hocks**)

hoe (see **Ho**)

hoer (see **hawer**)

hoes works the soil with a hoe

hos expressions of surprise, delight, or derision

hose a cloth leg covering; a flexible tube for conveying fluid or gas

hoggy (see **hagi**)

Hoh (see **Ho**)

hokey characterized by or the product of fakery or false value

hokie a large marble

hoks (see **hocks**)

hold to maintain possession of; to grasp; a ship's interior below decks

holed made an opening in something; drove an animal into a hole

holds maintains possession of; grasps; a ship's interior below decks

holes openings

wholes complete amounts or sums

hole an opening

whole entire or total; free of defect

holed (see **hold**)

holes (see **holds**)

holey having a hole or full of holes

Holi a Hindu spring festival characterized by boisterous and ribald revelry

holy hallowed, sacred, or venerated

wholly to the full extent

hollo (see **hallo**)

hollo a call of encouragement or jubilation

hollow empty; a depression; false or deceitful

hollow (see **hala**)

holm (see **heaume**)

holy (see **holey**)

hom (see **heaume**)

hombre a man, fellow, or guy

ombre shaded, especially of fabrics with a dyed or woven design in which the color is graduated from light to dark

Homburg (see **Hamburg**)

home (see **heaume**)

homer (see **heaumer**)

homily a discourse on a religious or moral theme

hommilie a calf or dehorned cow

hon sweetheart, dear, or honey

Hun a member of a nomadic Mongolian

people; a German soldier in World Wars I and II

honeysweet a white woolly perennial herb of the desert region in the U.S.

honey-sweet sweet with or as if with the viscid material produced by bees

hoo (see **heugh**)

hooey something false or unacceptable; hokum

Huey a U.S. military heliocopter, model HU-1B

hui a partnership, club, syndicate, or community gathering in Hawaii

hookie a meaningless expression or mild expletive

hooky truant; full of or covered with metal or tough curved material for holding something

hoop a strip of wood or metal bent in circular form and united at the ends

whoop an expression of eagerness, exuberance, or jubilation; to arouse sentiment for

hooper a person or machine that forms strips of wood or metal into circular form

whooper a large white nearly extinct North American crane; a whooping crane

hoos expressions of emotional reaction; calls

hoose verminous bronchitis of cattle, sheep, and goats

whos what persons

who's the contraction of who is, who was, or who has

whose relating to what person(s)

horde (see **hoard**)

horney a constable or sheriff

hornie a horn agate marble

horny hard or callous; easily excited sexually

horse (see **hoarse**)

horsed handled roughly; played; provided with a horse

horst part of the earth's crust separated by faults

hos (see **hoes**)

hose (see **hoes**)

hostel a public house for entertaining or lodging travelers

hostile marked by malevolence, antagonism, or unfriendliness

hosteler a person who lodges or entertains guests or strangers

hostler a person who takes care of horses at an inn or stable; a person who takes charge of a railroad locomotive after a run

hostile (see **hostel**)

hostler (see **hosteler**)

hostler a person who takes care of horses at an inn or stable; a person who takes charge of a railroad locomotive after a run

hustler an active, enterprising, sometimes unscrupulous individual

hottie (see **haughty**)

hougher (see **hocker**)

hour (see **Aor**)

house (see **haus**)

houseboat a yacht, barge, or boat outfitted as a dwelling or for leisurely cruising

housebote wood allowed to a tenant for repairing a house

Hova the dominant native people of central Madagascar

Jova an important division of the Piman peoples of northeastern Sonora, Mexico

howel a plane used by a barrel or cask maker

Howell a game of duplicate bridge in which matchpoint scoring is used

howl to utter a loud sustained doleful sound characteristic of dogs and wolves

how'll contraction of how will or how shall

hows (see **haus**)

how's (see **haus**)

hox (see **hocks**)

hsin the cardinal Confucian virtue of faithfulness or veracity
<u>**shin**</u> the front part of a leg below the knee

Hu (see **heugh**)

hue (see **hew**)

huer (see **hewer**)

Huey (see **hooey**)

hui (see **hooey**)

<u>**hum**</u> an isolated residual hill or mass of limestone
whom what person or persons, when used as an object of a verb

human characteristic of mankind
humin a darkcolored insoluble amorphous substance formed in many chemical reactions
Yuman a language family of the Hokan stock in Arizona, California, and Mexico; belonging to a culture of western Arizona about A.D. 700–1200

humbles brings down the pride or arrogance of a person
umbels racemose inflorescences characteristic of the family Umbelliferae, which includes anise, carrot, and parsley
umbles entrails of an animal used as food

humeral belonging to the shoulder or situated in the region of the humerus
humoral relating to a bodily humor, now often used of endocrine factors as opposed to neural or somatic

humerus the longest bone of the upper arm or forelimb
humorous jocular or funny

humin (see **human**)

humoral (see **humeral**)

humorous (see **humerus**)

humpie a humpback salmon; a hump back sucker (fish); a mooneye (fish)
humpy covered with protuberances; a California wrasse (fish)

Hun (see **hon**)

hurdle an obstacle or barrier
hurtle to propel violently, move rapidly, or dash headlong

hurds (see **herds**)

hure (see **hewer**)

hurl (see **herl**)

hurley an Irish game resembling field hockey
hurly confusion or uproar

hurst (see **hearsed**)

hurting (see **herding**)

hurtle (see **hurdle**)

hurts (see **hertz**)

hustler (see **hostler**)

hut (see **hep**)

hydrocele an accumulation of serous fluid in a sacculated cavity, especially the scrotum
hydrocoele the watervascular system of an echinoderm, or the pouch or cavity in the embryo from which it develops

hydrous containing water
Hydrus a fabulous water serpent; a Southern constellation

hyke (see **haik**)

Hyla and **hyla** (see **hila**)

hyle (see **highly**)

hymn (see **him**)

hype (see **hipe**)

hypogenous growing on a leaf's lower side

hypogynous inserted on the axis below
the carpels in a flower

Group I

hamulous - hamulus
hemidactylous - hemidactylus
hippish - hyppish
hoax - hokes
hocker - hougher
horsecollar - horse-collar
humous - humus
hydrocephalous - hydrocephalus

Group II

hairy 'herē
here 'he‚re or 'hir

haje 'häjē
hajji 'hajē

haka 'häkä
Hakka 'häk'kä

halling 'häliŋ
hauling 'hȯliŋ

harpes 'här‚pēz
harpies 'härpēz

hartin 'här‚tin
hearten 'här‚tən

hawed 'hȯd
hod 'häd

hawk 'hȯk
hoc(k) 'häk

hawker 'hȯkər
hougher 'häkər

heterogeneous :hetərə:jēnēəs
heterogenous :hetə:räjenəs

highbred 'hī‚bred
hybrid 'hībrəd

hilum 'hīləm
hylam 'hī‚läm

homage '(h)ämij
ohmage 'ōmij

hostal 'hōstəl
hostel 'hästəl

hummus 'həməs
humus 'hyüməs

Hungary 'həngərē
hungry 'hungrē

hymeneal 'hīmə‚nēəl
hymenial hī'mēnēəl

I

I (see **a(a)h** and **ai**)

i (see **ai**)

Ibo (see **eboe**)

icer (see **Aissor**)

I'd (see **eyed**)

ide (see **eyed**)

Idaean characteristic of the ancient Greek
goddess Rhea or Cybele with whom Mt.
Ida was associated

idaein an anthocyanin pigment obtained
in the form of a greenish brown crystalline chloride

idem the previously mentioned or as mentioned above

item a detail or particular

ideogram a symbol used in a system of
writing to represent a thing but not a
particular word for it

idiogram a diagrammatic representation
of a chromosome complement

ideograph a symbol used in a system of writing to represent a thing but not a particular word for it (the identical definition as ideogram)

idiograph a mark or signature peculiar to an individual

idle not occupied; unemployed

idol a symbol of a deity, being, or thing used as an object of worship

idyll a descriptive work usually dealing with pastoral or rural life

if so long as or on condition that

iff if and only if, in mathematics

Igo (see **ego**)

ileac of or pertaining to intestinal obstruction characterized by lack of peristalsis and leading to severe colicky pain and vomiting

iliac of, pertaining to, or situated near the broad upper portion of either hip bone

ileum the last division of the small intestine constituting the part between the jejunum and large intestine

ilium the dorsal and upper one of three bones composing either lateral half of the pelvis

illium an alloy containing 60% nickel, 25% chromium, plus some copper, manganese, silicon, and tungsten

iliac (see **ileac**)

ilium (see **ileum**)

I'll (see **aisle**)

illapse (see **elapse**)

illation (see **elation**)

ill-born brought forth by birth with great trouble or difficulty

ill-borne not well, or poorly endured or tolerated

illegit (see **elegit**)

illicit (see **elicit**)

illiterate (see **alliterate**)

illium (see **ileum**)

illuded (see **alluded**)

illuminate (see **aluminate**)

illumine (see **alumen**)

illusion (see **allusion**)

immanent confined to consciousness or to the mind; indwelling, inherent, or intrinsic

imminent near at hand or impending

immerge (see **emerge**)

immerse (see **amerce**)

immersed (see **emersed**)

imminent (see **immanent**)

immission (see **emission**)

impartable capable of being communicated or transmitted

impartible not subject to division

impassable incapable of being traveled on or crossed

impassible unfeeling or impassive; incapable of suffering or of experiencing pain

impatience restlessness or chafing of spirit

Impatiens a large genus of widely distributed annual plants

implastic (see **emplastic**)

impressed aroused strong feeling about; applied with pressure

imprest a loan or advance of money

imu (see **emu**)

in a preposition indicating a place with respect to time or space

inn a public house for lodging, feeding, and or entertainment of travelers

incenter the center of the circle inscribed in a triangle, or of a sphere inscribed in a tetrahedron

incentor a person who or that which stirs up, spurs, or urges on incite to stir up, spur, or urge on; to instigate

insight discernment or understanding

inciter a person that instigates

insider a person having access to confidential information because of his/her position; a person recognized or accepted as a member of some group

incubous leaves so arranged that the anterior margin of each overlaps the posterior margin of the next younger

incubus an evil spirit believed to lie on sleeping persons; a nightmare

indict to formally accuse

indite to compose a poem or story

indie an organization, such as a motion-picture studio, that is independent (slang); a selfemployed person

Indy pertaining to the capital of Indiana or the "Indianapolis 500" car race

indiscreet imprudent, inconsiderate, or untactful

indiscrete not separated into distinct parts

indite (see indict)

Indy (see indie)

infirmation the process of making invalid, as opposed to confirmation

information knowledge of a particular event or situation; news or intelligence

influence an act or power to produce an effect on

influents tributary streams; animals having an important effect on an ecological community's balance

infold (see enfold)

information (see infirmation)

ingrain (see engrain)

inlaw place under the protection of the law

in-law a relative by marriage

inn (see in)

innumerable (see enumerable)

insider (see inciter)

insight (see incite)

insist (see encyst)

insolate to place in sunlight

insulate to separate or shield from conducting bodies to prevent transfer of electricity, heat, or sound

insolent haughty, contemptuous, or brutal in behavior or language

insulant a material that retards the passage of temperature, electricity, or sound

installation giving possession of an office, rank, order with the usual ceremonial rites; something that is set up for use or service

instillation gradual introduction a drop at a time

instance a case, illustration, or example

instants points of time

instillation (see installation)

insulant (see insolent)

insulate (see insolate)

insure (see ensure)

intendance the care, control, or management of an administrative department

intendence attendance; presence; attention

intense extremely marked or pronounced; strained or deep

intents proposed ends or objects; meanings

intension connotation; determination or intentness

intention a purpose, aim, or objective

intents (see intense)

intercession an interposition between parties at variance with a view to reconciliation; a mediation

intersession a period between two academic terms or conference meetings

interdental situated between the teeth

interdentile in architecture, the space between two dentils under the corona of a cornice

intern an advanced student or recent graduate in a professional field who receives practical experience under the supervision of an experienced worker

in-turn a moving curling stone that rotates clockwise

interned confined within prescribed limits; impounded; acted as an intern

inturned turned inward; introverted

interosseous situated between bones

interosseus a muscle arising from the metacarpals (in the hand) and metatarsals (in the foot)

interpellate to question formally a governmental policy or decision

interpolate to insert between other things or parts

intersects pierces or divides by passing through or across

intersex an individual that exists between a typical male and a typical female

intersession (see **intercession**)

intersex (see **intersects**)

interval a space of time between recurrences of similar conditions or states; a space between things

intervale lowlying grassland and fields along a watercourse

intrada (see **entrada**)

intrait one of a class of extracts prepared from plants in which the enzymes are destroyed before drying

in-tray a shallow wood, metal, or plastic basket used for holding incoming material

in-turn (see **intern**)

inturned (see **interned**)

invade to overrun with a view toward conquest or plunder; to enter in a hostile manner; to permeate

inveighed complained vehemently

inverter a device for converting direct current into alternating current

invertor a muscle that turns a limb or part inward

io a large hawk that is Hawaii's only indigenous raptorial bird

iyo a Philippine woody vine; the stiff coarse bast fiber of an African palm

ion (see **ayin**)

ire (see **eyer**)

irrupt (see **erupt**)

isle (see **aisle**)

islet (see **eyelet**)

isotac a line on a map connecting points where ice melts at the same time in the spring

isotach a line on a map connecting points of equal wind speed

istle a fiber obtained from various tropical American plants

iztle a type of obsidian used by the Mexican Indians to make knives and arrow points

item (see **idem**)

its of, associated with, or belonging to it or it has

it's the contraction of it is or it has

ius a legal principle, right, or power

use the act of employing something

youse your, or substandard version of you

ixodic (see **exotic**)

iyo (see **io**)

iztle (see **istle**)

Group I

idrialin - indrialine
ileal - ilial

illuminance - illuminants
impatience - impatients
impenitence - impenitents
impertinence - impertinents
impotence - impotents
incidence - incidents
incompetence - incompetents
independence - independents
indifference - indifferents
indigence - indigents
indolence - indolents
ingredience - ingredients
inhabitance - inhabitants
innocence - innocents
insignificance - insignificants
insistence - insistents
insolence - insolents
insurance - insurants
insurgence - insurgents
intelligence - intelligents
intendance - intendants
intervenience - intervenients
intolerance - intolerants
intransigence - intransigents
intrigant - intrigante
invariance - invariants
iridescence - iridescents

Group I and II

indemnitee ən'demnə‚tē
indemnity ən'demnətē

Group II

idea 'iːdēə
itea id•ēə

immortal 'i'mȯrdəl
immortelle 'i‚mȯr‚tel

inapt ən‚ept
inept ə'nept

incendive in'sendiv
incentive in'sentiv

incipit 'insəpət
insipid ən'sipəd

incision ən'sizhən
insition in'sishən

incus 'in‚küs
incuse 'in‚kyüs

ingenious ən'jēnyəs
ingenuous ən'jenyəwəs

insole 'in‚sōl
insoul ən'sōl

J

jacinth a plant of the genus Hyacinthus
jacinthe a moderate orange color

jack a portable device for raising or lifting heavy objects
jak a large East Indian tree

Jacobean representing an early 17th century style of architecture, furniture, literature, or drama
Jacobian a determinant in which the elements of the first column are partial derivatives of the first of a set of n functions with respect to each of n independent variables, those of the second column are partial derivatives of the second of a set of n ... etc.

jaeger a large, spirited, rapacious bird inhabiting northern seas
yager a largebore rifle formerly used in the U.S.

Jaggie the army Judge Advocate General
jaggy tipsy from alcoholic drink

Jain an adherent of Jainism, a dualistic religion founded in India during the 6th century B.C.

jane a girl or woman (slang)

jak (see **jack**)

jam to press into a close or tight position; a product made by boiling fruit and sugar into a thick consistency
jamb an upright piece forming a side of an opening, as a doorway

jambeau a piece of plate armor for the leg between the knee and ankle; a spikefish
jambo a rose apple tree of the tropics

jane (see **Jain**)

jasmine any of numerous usually limber and often climbing shrubs of temperate and warm regions that usually have extremely fragrant flowers
jazzmen performers of American music developed from religious and secular songs, blues, ragtime, and other popular music

Jat an IndoAryan people of the Punjab and Uttar Pradesh
jot the smallest amount; to write briefly or hurriedly

jaun a small Calcutta conveyance similar to a sedan chair for transporting a person on the carriers' shoulders
john a fellow, guy, or chap; a toilet

jay a noisy, vivacious bird of the crow family; a simpleton
jeh a female demon in Zoroastrianism

jazzmen (see **jasmine**)

jean (see **gean**)

jeered spoke or cried out with derision or mockery
jird any of several North African gerbils

jeez (see **gees**)

jeh (see **jay**)

jeld castrated
jelled congealed or set (gelled is an alternate spelling)

jell (see **gel**)

jelled (see **jeld**)

jellied (see **gelid**)

jemez (see **hamus**)

jen the cardinal Confucian virtue of benevolence toward one's fellowman
run to go by moving the legs quickly

jen the cardinal Confucian virtue of benevolence toward one's fellowman
wren a small brown singing bird

jennet (see **genet**)

jerm (see **germ**)

jerries (see **Gerres**)

jes an African insectivorous animal about the size of a stoat but similar in form and habits to an otter
jess a short leather strap used in falconry that is secured to each leg of a hawk

jessed (see **gest[e]**)

jest (see **gest[e]**)

jet a forceful rush of liquid, gas, or vapor through a restricted opening
Jeth the second month of the Hindu calendar

Jew-bait to persecute or harass members of the Jewish faith
jubate fringed with long pendent hairs like a mane

jewel a precious stone; an ornament
jhool trappings for a horse, elephant, or other animal
joule a unit of work or energy equal to .7375 footpounds

Jewry part of a population that adheres to Judaism
jury a group of persons sworn to give a verdict on some matter

jheel (see **geal**)

jhool (see **jewel**)

jibber (see **gibber**)

jig (see **gig**)

jigger (see **chigger**)

jill (see **gill**)

jing (see **ching**)

jinks pranks or frolics; moves quickly with sudden turns or changes of direction

jinx something that is felt or believed to bring bad luck

Jynx a genus of woodpeckers

jinn (see **gin**)

jinni (see **ginny**)

jinny (see **ginny**)

jinx (see **jinks**)

jird (see **jeered**)

jive (see **gyve**)

jobo (see **hobo**)

john (see **jaun**)

jook an establishment having a jukebox

juke to make a sound or call like a partridge

jot (see **Jat**)

joule (see **jewel**)

joule a unit of work or energy equal to .7375 footpounds

jowl a jaw; a hog's boneless cheek meat; loose flesh surrounding a lower cheek and jaw

joust a combat between two persons on horseback

juiced supplied with the extractable fluid contents of plant cells or structures

joust a combat on horseback between two persons

just reasonable, equitable, or fair

Jova (see **Hova**)

jowl (see **joule**)

juba an Haitian dance of African origin having drum and stick accompaniment

jubba(h) a long outer garment resembling an open coat, having long sleeves, and formerly worn in Muslim countries

jubate (see **Jew-bait**)

jubba(h) (see **juba**)

judding vibrating with intensity

jutting projecting or protruding

juey a large swift-moving dull-grayish land crab; a great land crab

whey the serum or watery part of milk

juggler a person skilled in acts of manual dexterity

jugular relating to the throat, neck, or jugular vein (substandard speech)

juice the extractable fluid contents of plant cells or structures

jus a legal principle, right, or power

juiced (see **joust**)

juke (see **jook**)

June (see **Chün**)

junkie a person addicted to heroin or morphine; a person who operates a small boat, especially for the purpose of transporting stolen or illegal merchandise

junky extremely inferior; rotten

Jur a member of a tribe on the White Nile

jure jurisprudence; a right; to impanel as a juror

jurel any of several carangid food fishes of warm seas, as the blue runner and crevalle

xurel a saurel which includes several elongated compressed fishes having a series of bony plates extending the full length of the lateral line

jury (see **Jewry**)

jus (see **juice**)

just (see **gest(e)**, **gist**, and **joust**)

jutting (see **judding**)

Juvenal a writer resembling or suggestive of the Roman poet Juvenal in his use of biting satire and pungent realism

juvenile psychologically immature or undeveloped; young

Jynx (see **jinks**)

Group I

jivetime - jive-time
jogtrot - jog-trot
jurisprudence - jurisprudents

Group II

Jews 'jüz
juice 'jüs

jingal 'jingȯl
jingle 'jingəl

juba 'jübə
jubba(h) 'jübə or jəbə

K

k (see **cay**)

kaama (see **caama**)

Kabul (see **cobble**)

Kadir (see **cotter**)

Kaf (see **calf**)

Kafa (see **caffa**)

Kaffa (see **caffa**)

Kai (see **cay**)

kains sarongs
kinds natural groupings without taxonomic connotations

Kaiser a head of an ancient or medieval empire; the Austrian sovereign from 1804 to 1918; the ruler of Germany from 1871 to 1918
kayser a unit of length equal to the reciprocal of 1 centimeter (in spectroscopy)

kakar (see **caulker**)

kaki (see **cocci**)

kaligenous (see **caliginous**)

kalij (see **college**)

kalpa (see **culpa**)

Kama and **kama** (see **caama**)

kamboh (see **combo**)

kame (see **came**)

Kami (see **commie**)

kamiks (see **comics**)

Kannada (see **Canada**)

kapelle (see **Capella**)

kaph (see **calf**)

kapp (see **cap**)

kappa (see **capa**)

kappie (see **caapi and cappae**)

kar (see **car**)

karat (see **carat**)

karate (see **carate**)

Karel (see **carol**)

karree (see **choree**)

karri (see **carry**)

karris (see **caries**)

kart (see **cart**)

kartel (see **cartel**)

karusel (see **car[r]ousel**)

karyon (see **carryon**)

Kasha (see **Cassia**)

kat (see **cat**)

katar (see **catarrh**)

kate (see **cate**)

katel (see **coddle**)

Kati (see **cotty**)

Kaw (see **caw**)

Kaws (see **cause**)

kaya a Japanese tree with light red bark and yellow lustrous closegrained wood
Khaya a genus of African timber trees with wood closely resembling mahogany
khaya any tree of the genus Khaya

k(a)yak a fully deckedin Eskimo skin canoe propelled by a doublebladed paddle
kyack a packsack swung on either side of a pack saddle

kayser (see **Kaiser**)

kecks retching sounds
kex a Mayan therapeutic rite in which a sick person pledged to offer food in return for health

keed a kid (slang)
keyed adjusted, attuned, or fitted; furnished with instruments to open locks

keel the longitudinal timber extending from stem to stern along the center of a ship's or boat's bottom
Kiel a city in northern Germany

keelie (see **chelae**)

keesh graphite that separates on a slow cooling of molten cast or pig iron
quiche a baked custard pie

keiki (see **cak[e]y**)

kelt (see **Celt**)

ken (see **can**)

keno a game resembling lotto and bingo
kino the dried juice obtained from the trunk of an East Indian tree; a motion picture theater in Europe

kepi (see **cape**)

Ker (see **cur**)

kerasin a cerebroside which yields liquoceric acid
kerasine horny or corneous

kere (see **choree**)

keriah (see **chorea**)

Kermes or **kermes** (see **Chermes**)

kermis (see **Chermes**)

kernel (see **colonel**)

kerrie (see **carry**)

kerril (see **carol**)

Kerry (see **carry**)

keryl (see **carol**)

Ket a people of the middle Yenisei region of Siberia
quête a collection of money, such as a payment to a street musician or a strolling player

ketch (see **catch**)

ketol a compound that is both a ketone and an alcohol
kitol a crystalline alcohol obtained from wholeliver oil containing vitamin A

kex (see **kecks**)

key (see **cay**)

keyed (see **keed**)

khaki (see **cocci**)

khan (see **can** and **con**)

khan a local chieftan or man of rank especially in Afghanistan and Iran
skarn contact metamorphic rock rich in iron

khankah (see **concha**)

Khaya and **khaya** (see **kaya**)

Khond (see **cond**)

khor (see **core**)

khud (see **could**)

ki (see the 2nd **cay** sequence)

kibbets forms a syndicate of small capitalists to furnish money needed for a business venture

kibbutz to look on at a game and make critical or distracting comments, or offer unwanted advice

kicker a person or animal that thrusts out a foot or feet with force

kikar the gum arabic tree (an acacia) that yields gum arabic

kidded made fun of usually good-humoredly

kitted gave birth to a smaller fur-bearing animal, as a cat

kiddle a barrier that extends across a river designed to deflect water and fish through an opening across which a fishnet is stretched

kittel a white cotton robe worn by Orthodox Jews on special occasions

kiddy a small child

kitty a kitten; a fund in a poker game

Kiel (see **keel**)

kikar (see **kicker**)

kike (see **caique**)

kill to put to death; to put an end to

kiln an oven or furnace

Kin (see **gin**)

kindal an Indian tree with hard gray wood resembling walnut

kindle to start a fire; to awaken or intensify to awareness

kinds (see **kains**)

kino (see **keno**)

kirtle (see **curdle**)

kirve (see **curve**)

kissar a fivestringed lyre of northern Africa

kisser the face (**slang**)

kissed (see **cist**)

kisser (see **kissar**)

kissie come to rest against or on top of, as in the game of marbles or other game piece

kissy a call to cows or calves

kist (see **cist**)

kitar (see **catarrh**)

kitchen a place for cooking and preparing meals

Kitchin a business cycle formed by a 3½-year recession during a prosperity phase

kitol (see **ketol**)

kitted (see **kidded**)

kittel (see **kiddle**)

kitty (see **kiddy**)

Klan (see **clan**)

Klang (see **clang**)

klatch (see **clatch**)

Klepths (see **clefs**)

klick (see **click**)

Kling (see **cling**)

klip(pe) (see **clip**)

klister (see **clyster**)

klomp (see **clomp**)

Klucker (see **clucker**)

Klux (see **clucks**)

knack a clever or adroit way of doing something

nak the stigmatic point of the fruit of the mango

knaggy covered with gnarled, knotty protuberances

naggie an agate playing marble

naggy a little nag, as a pony; characterized by being persistently annoying, fault finding, or scolding

knarred (see **gnarred**)

knaur (see **gnawer**)

knave an unscrupulous person

nave the main part of a church's interior; a block or hub in a wheel's center into which the axle is fitted

knead to mix into a blended whole by repeatedly working and pressing the mass, as bread dough

kneed struck or touched with the knee

need to want or desire; poverty

kneader a person who mixes into a blended whole by repeatedly working and pressing the mass

neater freer from whatever clutters, blurs, or confuses

knee the joint in the midpart of a leg

ne(e) originally or formerly called

kneed (see knead)

kneel to bend the knee

neele any of several grasses of the genus Lolium, including bearded darnel

knell to ring a bell with slow solemnity

nell the second highest trump in various card games

knew (see gnu)

knickers loosefitting kneelength pants gathered at the knee with a band; small balls of baked clay used as marbles

nickers neighs, as a horse; persons who notch objects; fabulous water monsters or water sprites; 18th century night brawlers of London who broke windows with a halfpence

knight a person on whom a sovereign has conferred a dignity or title; a chess piece

night the time from dusk to dawn

knighthood the rank or profession of a person on whom a sovereign has conferred a dignity or title

nighthood a condom (slang)

knit to form fabric by interlocking yarn in a series of connected loops; to consolidate

nit a parasitic insect's egg, as a louse

knitted formed fabric by interlocking yarn in a series of connected loops; consolidated

nited bright, glossy, or lustrous

knitter a person or machine that makes knit goods

nitter an insect that deposits its eggs on horses

knob a small rounded projecting mass

nob to strike in the head; in cribbage, the jack of the same suit as the starter card

knobby having protuberences, projections, or protrusions

nobby a stick sometimes used by anglers for stunning or killing fish

knocks strikes or raps

nocks notches in arrows to accommodate the bowstring

nox a unit of lowlevel illumination measurement equal to 10^{-3}lux; nitrogen oxide that is emitted by an energy source into the atmosphere (by shortening)

knorr (see gnawer)

knot a fastening made by intertwining pliant rope or tubing; a unit of nautical or air speed; a sandpiper

nat a class of spirits in Burmese folklore

naught nothing

naut a sea mile of 2,029 yards used as a measure for submarine cables

not negative; in no manner

knote the point where ropes and cords meet from angular directions in funiculars

note to record or fix in the mind or memory

knotting fancywork made by twisting and looping thread into knots to form designs

nodding bending downward or forward

knotty full of difficulties or complications; gnarled or nobby

naughty guilty of misbehavior or disobedience

noddy a stupid person; a card game resembling cribbage

knout a flogging whip with a lash of leather thongs twisted with wire
newt any of various small semi-aquatic salamanders
Nut the goddess of the sky, in Egyptian religion

known comprehended or understood
None the canonical ninth hour

knows comprehends or understands
noes denials; negative votes
No(h)s classic Japanese dance-dramas that are heroic in subject and in the use of measured chants and movements
nose a prominent part of a mammal's face which bears the nostrils

knubs waste silk usually taken from a cocoon's outside
nubs knobs or lumps; cores or gists of an argument

knut a fop or dandy of the late 19th and early 20th centuries
nut a hardshelled dry fruit or seed; a perforated block of metal with an internal screw thread for attachment to a bolt

Ko (see **go**)

kob (see **Cob**)

Koch (see **coach**)

koel (see **coil**)

koel any of several cuckoos of India, the East Indies, and Australia
kohol a preparation used in Arabia and Egypt to darken the edges of eyelids

koff (see **calf**)

Ko(h)l (see **coal**)

kohl (see **coal**)

kohol (see **koel**)

koi (see **coy**)

Koko and **koko** (see **coco**)

kokoon (see **cacoon**)

kola (see **cola**)

Koli (see **coaly**)

kolm (see **comb**)

komatic (see **comatic**)

Komi (see **comby**)

Konyak (see **Cognac**)

kooky crazy, offbeat, or eccentric
Kuki any of numerous hill people in southern Assam, India

kop (see **cop**)

kope(c)k (see **copek**)

kopje (see **caapi**)

koppa (see **coppa**)

kora (see **Cora**)

Koran the book forming the basis of the Islamic world
korin a gazelle of West Africa

Korea (see **chorea**)

Korean (see **chorion**)

korin (see **Koran**)

Kot (see **cat** and **caught**)

Kota (see **coda**)

koto (see **Coto**)

kou (see **cow**)

kouse (see **cous**)

KP (see **cape**)

kraal (see **crawl**)

kraft (see **craft**)

kral (see **crawl**)

krantz (see **crance**)

kraton (see **craton**)

krewes (see **crews**)

krill (see **crill**)

kris (see **criss**)

krises (see **creases**)

krona the basic monetary unit of Iceland and Sweden

krone the basic monetary unit of Denmark, and of Austria from 1892 to 1925

kroon (see **croon**)

Kruman (see **crewman**)

Krus (see **crews**)

Kuan (see **guan**)

Kuki (see **kooky**)

kuku (see **cuckoo**)

Kulaman (see **coolamon**)

Kulli (see **coolie** or **cully**)

kupper (see **cupper**)

Kurd (see **curd**)

kuttar (see **catarrh**)

Kwa a branch of the NigerCongo language family that is spoken along the coast and a short distance inland from Liberia to Nigeria

qua in the capacity or character of; a European night heron

kweek a grass of the genus Cynodon

quaich a small shallow circular vessel or drinking cup used in Scotland and made of wood, pewter, or silver with two flat ears for handles

quake to shake, vibrate, or tremble

Kweri a people of the southern British Cameroons

query a question or inquiry

kyack (see **k[a]yak**)

kye (see **cay**)

Kyloe (see **Chilo**)

kyphosis an abnormal backward curvature of the spine

Kyphosus a genus that includes the Bermuda chub, a gray percoid fish

Group I

knulling - nulling

Group II

kennel 'kenᵊl
quenelle kə'nel

kettle 'ketl
ketyl 'ketil

kibbutz ki'buts
kibitz 'kibəts

knacker 'nakər
nacre 'nākər

koel 'koəl
kohl 'kōl

L

laager a defensive position protected by a ring of armored vehicles

lager a beer brewed by bottom fermentation and stored in refrigerators

logger a lumberjack; a device that records data automatically

label an identification tag or stamp

labile changeable or unstable; adaptable

lablab hyacinth beans, a large twining vine

lab-lab a mass of microscopic algae used as food by fry

Labrus the type genus of the large and important family of percoid fishes of Labridae, such as the wrasse

labrys an ancient Cretan sacred double ax

lace a fine openwork fabric; to thread or intertwine

laisse an irregular rhythmic system of Old French poetry

laces beats or lashes; adds a dash of alcoholic liquor to food or beverage

lacis a squaremeshed lace with darned patterns

laches negligence or carelessness

lashes whips; binds with rope; moves suddenly or violently

laches negligence or carelessness

latches devices that hold something in place, as a door; grasps

lacis (see **laces**)

lacks wants or is in need of

lacs resinous substances secreted by the lac insect and used as shellac

Lak(h)s members of a division of the Lezghian people in southern Russia on the western shore of the Caspian Sea

laks performances of the male capercaillie (the largest European grouse) during courtship

lax not stringent; easygoing

ladder a structure for climbing up and down; to scale

latter coming after something else

lade to put a load or burden on

laid put or set down

lader a person that loads

later tardier; after

lager (see **laager**)

lagopous having hairy rhizomes suggestive of a hare's foot

Lagopus a genus of northern game birds comprising the ptarmigans and red grouse

laid (see **lade**)

lain rested or remained in a horizontal position

laine a woolen cloth

lane a narrow passageway; an alley

lair a wild animal's living place; a den

layer a person that lays something; a hen that lays eggs; a thickness lying over or under another

lehr a long oven in which glassware is annealed

lais medieval short tales or lyric poems in French literature

lase to emit coherent light

lays puts or sets down

laze to pass in idleness or relaxation

leas pastures or grasslands

leis garlands or necklaces of flowers

les the sixth tones flatted of the diatonic scale

leys pewters containing about 80% tin and 20% lead

Lais a Mongoloid people of the Chin Hills in Myanmar

lie to rest in a horizontal position; to convey an untruth

lye a strong alkaline solution

laisse (see **lace**)

laisse an irregular rhythmic system of Old French poetry

less fewer or smaller

loess an unstratified deposit of loam ranging from clay to fine sand

laitance an accumulation of fine particles on freshly placed concrete

latents scarcely visible fingerprints

Lak(h)s (see **lacks**)

Lak(h)s members of a division of the Lezghian people in southern Russia on the western shore of the Caspian Sea

lax various anadromous fishes of the family Salmonidae

lochs lakes

locks tresses of hair; fastenings for a door or a box

lox liquid oxygen (by shortening); smoked salmon (also 'lax)

lakie a temporary retrograde movement of

the tide, especially in the Firth of Forth, Scotland

laky resembling hemoglobin dissolved in plasma

laks (see **lacks**)

laky (see **lakie**)

lali a large drum made of a hollowed log to summon people in Western Polynesia and Fiji

Lally a concrete-filled cylindrical steel structural column

lolly soft ice that is ground down from floes or formed in turbulent seawater

lam to flee hastily

lamb a young sheep

Lama a genus of mammals that includes the alpaca, guanaco, llama, and vicuna

lama a Tibetan Buddhist priest or monk

llama a South American ruminant

lamb (see **lam**)

lance a weapon of war consisting of a long shaft with a sharp steel head

lants any of several small elongate marine teleost fishes of the genus Ammodytes (sometimes **launce**)

lande an infertile moor

lawned made into or like grass-covered ground

lane (see **lain**)

lang the grass pea, an Old World pea grown chiefly for forage

long extending for a considerable distance; to yearn or pine for

longue a large dark North American char that is an important commercial food fish in northern lakes

lants (see **lance**)

Laos a kingdom of Indochina

louse any of various small wingless usually flattened insects that are parasitic on warmblooded animals

Lapps people of northern Scandinavia and the Kola peninsula of northern Russia

laps folds over or around something; circuits around a racetrack

lapse a trivial fault or oversight; to depart from an accepted standard

lapses goes out of existence

lapsus an accidental mistake in fact, or departure from an accepted norm

lase (see **lais**)

laser a device that uses natural oscillations of atoms to amplify or generate electromagnetic waves

lazar a person afflicted with a repulsive disease

lashes (see **laches**)

Lassa a systemic arenavirus infection that involves most visceral organs, (Lassa fever, by shortening)

Lhasa capital of Tibet

lat a separate column or pillar in some Buddhist buildings in India similar to the Greek stela

lot a portion of land; a considerable quantity or number

lotte any large pediculate fish of the family Lophiidae found along the Atlantic coast of America

latches (see **laches**)

latents (see **laitance**)

later (see **lader**)

Latin a language of ancient Latium and Rome

latten an alloy of or resembling brass that is hammered into thin sheets

latter (see **ladder**)

laud to praise or acclaim

lawed mutilated an animal so as to prevent mischief, as cut the claws from the forefeet of a cat or dog

laun in ceramics, a fine-meshed sieve or silken net through which the clay is passed

lawn untilled ground covered with grass

laureate a recipient of an honor for pre-eminence in one's field
loriot the golden oriole of Europe

laurel a tree or shrub, the leaves of which yield a fragrant oil
lauryl a mixture of alkyl radicals derived from commercial lauryl alcohol
loral related to the space between the eye and bill of a bird, or the corresponding area in a reptile or fish
lorel relating to a body of knowledge

lauter clear or clarified
louder more intense sound; noisier

lawed (see **laud**)

lawn (see **laun**)

lawned (see **lande**)

lawyer a specialist in or a practitioner of binding customs or practices of a community, the law
loir a large European dormouse

lax (see **lacks** and **Lak[h]s**)

laydown a declarer's hand in bridge that is easily able to fulfill the contract
lay-down a turned over object, as a collar

layer (see **lair**)

lays (see **lais**)

lazar (see **laser**)

laze (see **lais**)

lea a pasture or grassland
lee a side sheltered from the wind; dregs or sediment
Li an ethnic group that is culturally a branch of the early Tai people of southern China
li a cardinal virtue in Confucianism consisting of correct behavior as an outward expression of inner harmony; the solmization syllable for the semitone between the 6th and 7th degrees of the diatonic scale

leach to draw out or remove as if by percolation or seepage

leech a carnivorous or blood-sucking annelid worm

leachy permitting liquids to pass by means of percolation
lichi an African antelope somewhat smaller than the related waterbuck
Litchi a genus of Chinese trees cultivated for its edible fruit
litchi the fruit of a Chinese tree

lead a heavy metallic element
led guided or marked the way

leader an individual who goes before or guides
lieder German folk songs
liter a metric unit of capacity equal to 1.057 liquid quarts

leading a covering or framework of a heavy metallic element
letting allowing or permitting

leadoff an offensive hit in boxing
lead-off starting or opening

leads guides or marks the way
Leeds a city in Yorkshire, England

leaf a lateral outgrowth constituting part of a plant's foliage
lief gladly, willingly, or freely

leag a kelp
league a unit of distance varying from 2.4 to 4.6 statute miles; an association of nations or persons united in a common interest

leak an opening that permits escape
leek a biennial herb related to garlic and onion

lean to deviate from a vertical position; free of fat or rawboned
lien a charge on property in satisfaction of a debt

leaner a pitched horseshoe that leans against the stake without ringing it
lienor a person holding a valid lien

leap to project oneself through the air

leep to plaster (as a wall) with cow dung

leas (see **lais**)

lease to rent property from or to another
lis a fleur-de-lis
lisse silk gauze used for dresses and trimmings

leased rented property from or to another
least lowest, smallest, or slightest

leave to withdraw or depart; to abandon; to bequeath
lief gladly or willingly

leaver a person who leaves
lever a rigid device that transmits and modifies motion when a force is applied and it turns about a point, as a crowbar, oar, or canoe paddle
levir the now abolished custom of a husband's brother assuming his place (see **levirate**)
liefer more gladly, willingly, or freely
livre a former French unit of value worth a pound of silver in Charlemagne's reign

lechs prehistoric monumental capstones
leks sites where birds regularly resort for purposes of sexual display and courtship
lex the law

Lecythis a genus of very large South American trees
lecythus a cylindrical or round and squat vase used by ancient Greeks for oils and ointments

led (see **lead**)

lee (see **lea**)

leech (see **leach**)

Leeds (see **leads**)

leek (see **leak**)

leep (see **leap**)

leer to give a lascivious, knowing, or malicious look
lehr a long oven in which glassware is annealed

leet a ceremonial English court
lied a German folksong

leggings coverings for legs, usually of leather or cloth
leggins copulation in which the penis is rubbed between the legs of the receptive partner

lehr (see **lair** and **leer**)

leis (see **lais**)

leister a spear with several barbed prongs for catching fish
lister a person who itemizes articles or costs of materials and labor; a double-moldboard plow that throws a ridge of earth both ways

leks (see **lechs**)

lends gives temporarily to another; loans
lens an optical instrument consisting of a transparent substance with two opposing regular surfaces

leopard a large strong cat with black spots
lepered afflicted with leprosy

Lepas a widely distributed genus of goose barnacles
Lepus a genus comprising the typical hares

leper a person afflicted with leprosy
lepper a horse skilled in jumping

lepered (see **leopard**)

lepidene a crystalline compound made by heating benzoin with hydrochloric acid
lepidine an oily nitrogenous base found in coaltar

lepper (see **leper**)

leptocephalous characterized by or exhibiting abnormal narrowness and tallness of the skull
Leptocephalus a genus of small pelagic fishes

leptodactylous having slender toes
Leptodactylus a genus of toothed toads

Lepus (see **Lepas**)

les (see **lais**)

less (see **laisse**)

lessen to decrease or diminish
lesson a segment of instruction

letdown a source of mood or mental depression; discouragement
let-down a physiological response of a lactating mammal to suckling or allied stimuli

Lethean of, relating to, or causing forgetfulness or oblivion
letheon ether when used as an anesthetic

lets services in racket and net games that do not count and must be replayed; obstructions; allows or permits
let's the contraction of let us
Letts people closely related to Lithuanians mainly inhabiting Latvia

letting (see **leading**)

Letts (see **lets**)

Leucifer a genus of freeswimming slender macruran crustaceans
Lucifer the devil; a person resembling the devil especially in evil or pride

leucine a white crystalline amino acid
loosen release from restraint

leucite potassium aluminum silicate occurring in igneous rock
Lucite an acrylic resin or plastic

leucon a sponge or sponge larva
leukon a body organ consisting of white blood cells and their precursors

leud a feudal tenant in ancient Frankish kingdoms
lewd indecent, obscene, or salacious
lood methaqualone (slang)
looed obligated to contribute an amount to a new pool in the game of loo because of a failure to win a trick
lowed made the usually deep sustained sound characteristic of bovine animals

lude a capsule or tablet of Quaaludes, trademarked brand of methaqualone

leukon (see **leucon**)

levee an embankment to prevent flooding; a fashionable party to honor someone
levy an imposition of a tax, assessment, or fine; conscription for military service

lever (see **leaver**)

leveret a hare in its first year
levirate the marriage of a widow by the brother or occasionally the heir of her deceased husband (see **levir**)

levir (see **leaver**)

levirate (see **leveret**)

levy (see **levee**)

lewd (see **leud**)

lewder more indecent, obscene, or salacious
looter a person that plunders, sacks, or robs
loutre a dark grayish yellowish brown color, such as otter brown
luter a person who seals coke oven doors with cement or a clay mixture

lewdest most indecent, obscene, or salacious; most sexually unchaste or licentious
lutist a maker or player of a stringed musical instrument of Oriental origin

lex (see **lechs**)

leys (see **lais**)

Lhasa (see **Lassa**)

Li and **li** (see **lea**)

liable exposed or subject to an adverse contingency or action; likely
libel a written or oral defamatory statement or representation

liar a person who utters a falsehood; a prevaricator
lier a person who lies or waits, as in ambush
lyre an ancient Greek stringed musical in-

strument resembling a harp; a triangular area of the ventral surface of the corpus callosum between the posterior pillors of the fornix

libel (see **liable**)

lice small wingless parasitic insects
lyse to cause to undergo the gradual decline of a disease process

lichen a thallophytic plant composed of alga and fungus
liken to compare; to represent as similar

lichi (see **leachy**)

licker a person or animal who passes the tongue over
liquor a distilled alcoholic beverage; a cooking broth

lickerish fond of good food; desirous
licorice a dried root of gummy texture with a sweet astringent flavor

licorice a dried root of gummy texture with a sweet astringent flavor
liquorous resulting from or resembling an intoxicated condition

lidder a person who fastens lids on containers
litter the offspring at one birth of a multiparous animal; a stretcher for carrying a sick or injured person; refuse or rubbish

lie (see **Lais**)

lied (see **leet**)

lied conveyed an untruth
lyed treated with a strong alkaline solution

lieder (see **leader**)

lief (see **leaf** and **leave**)

lief gladly, willingly, or freely
live to maintain oneself

liefer (see **leaver**)

liefer more gladly or more freely
liver a large very vascular glandular organ of vertebrates that secretes bile

lien (see **lean**)

lienor (see **leaner**)

liens spleens
lions large carnivorous animals of the cat family
Lyons third largest city in France

lier (see **liar**)

lies rests in a horizontal position; conveys an untruth
lyes strong alkaline solutions
lyse to cause to undergo the gradual decline of a disease process

lieu instead
loo halloo; an ancient card game; a toilet
Loup a member of the Skidi tribe of Pawnee Indians that dwelled from along the Platte river in Nebraska to Arkansas
loup a half mask usually of silk or satin
Lu a Tai ethnic and Buddhist group inhabiting the extreme southwest part of Yunnan province in southern China

lieut a military officer with the rank of lieutenant (slang)
loot plunder or booty
lute a stringed musical instrument with a large pearshaped body; a packing or caulking compound to make joints impervious to gas or liquid

lightening a sense of decreased weight and abdominal tension felt by a pregnant woman on descent of the fetus into the pelvic cavity prior to labor
lightning the flashing of light produced by a discharge of atmospheric electricity from one cloud to another or from Earth to cloud

liken (see **lichen**)

lim a blue pine
limb an animal's projecting appendange; a primary tree branch
limn to draw or paint on a flat surface; to delineate

limber a logger who trims branches or arms from felled trees

limner al illuminator of medieval manuscripts

limbous with slightly overlapping borders, as of a suture

Limbus a region on the border of hell
where souls abide who are barred from
heaven through no fault of their own

limbus the marginal region of the cornea
of the eye by which it is continuous with
the sclera

lime a small globose citrus fruit of the
lime tree; to whitewash with a solution
of lime and water

lyme in heraldry, a leash or a bloodhound

limen the point at which a physiological
or psychological effect begins to be produced

limon a hybrid citrus fruit produced by
crossing a lime and a lemon

limey an English sailor (slang)

limy smeared with or consisting of lime;
viscous

limn (see **lim**)

limner (see **limber**)

limon (see **limen**)

Limousin a French breed of medium-
sized yellowred cattle bred especially
for meat

limousine a large luxurious sedan or
small bus, especially one for hire

limpet a marine gastropod mollusk with a
low conical shell; a person who clings
tenaciously to someone or something

limpid completely free from cloudiness or
other obstacles to the passage of light

limps walks lamely or unsteadily

lymphs pale coaguable fluids that bathe
tissues

limy (see **limey**)

lin a female unicorn in Chinese mythology

linn a tree of the genus Tilia, including
the European linden

llyn a lake or pool

linde a synthetic gemstone, as a sapphire

lindy a jitterbug dance originating in
Harlem

linen a cloth made of flax

linon a fine sheer plainwoven cotton fabric

links a gold course; connecting structures,
as in a chain

Lynx the genus of Felidae comprising the
lynxes

lynx a wildcat, often with tufted ears and
a short stubby tail

linn (see **lin**)

linon (see **linen**)

lintwhite a common small Old World
finch

lint-white of the color of dressed flax

lions (see **liens**)

lippie lipstick (slang)

lippy insolent; brash and arrogant

liquor (see **licker**)

liquorous (see **licorice**)

lira a ridge on some shells resembling a
fine thread or hair

lyra a glockenspiel with a lyre-shaped
frame

lis (see **lease**)

lisse (see **lease**)

lisses silk gauzes used for dresses and
trimmings

lyssas acute virus diseases of warm-
blooded animals that attack chiefly the
nervous system; rabies

lister (see **leister**)

Litchi and **litchi** (see **leachy**)

liter (see **leader**)

literal adhering to the primary or exact
meaning of a term, phrase, or expression

littoral a coastal region including land
and water near the shoreline

litter (see **lidder**)

littoral (see **literal**)

live (see **lief**)

liver (see **liefer**)

livre (see **leaver**)

llama (see **Lama**)

llyn (see **lin**)

Lo a North American Indian
lo an interjection used to draw attention or to express wonder or surprise
low having relatively little upward extension; a deep sustained sound characteristic of cattle

Loa a genus of African filarial worms infesting the subcutaneous tissues and blood of man
loa any worm of the genus Loa
lowa an Indian quail

loach any of a family of small Old World freshwater fishes closely related to the Cyprinidae but resembling catfishes in appearance and habits
loche a freshwater fish related to the cod, such as the eelpout

load a mass or weight; to pack or fill with something
lode an ore deposit
lowed uttered deep sustained sounds characteristic of cattle

loam a clay mixture
loom a device for interlacing sets of thread or yarn at right angles to form cloth

loan something given temporarily to another, as money at interest
lone solitary

loath reluctant to do something contrary to one's tastes or ways of thinking
loathe to feel strong aversion to, detest, or abhor

lobelin a yellowish-green eclectic resinoid used as an emetic and diaphoretic

lobeline a poisonous alkaloid used in treating paralysis of respiratory centers

locale a place or site
lo(w)cal low in calories, as a food or drink

locater a person that determines the position of something or someone
locator a device used to maintain mechanically the relationship between parts of work during assembly or manufacture

lochage the commander of a small division of an ancient Greek army
lockage an act or the process of passing a vessel through an enclosure with gates at each end; a toll paid for passing through a canal lock

loche (see **loach**)

lochs (see **Lakhs**)

lockage (see **lochage**)

locks (see **Lakhs**)

locus a place or locality
locusts migratory grasshoppers that often travel in vast swarms and strip all vegetation from areas through which they pass

lode (see **load**)

loess (see **laisse**)

logger (see **laager**)

logie a piece of imitation jewelry designed for use in theater productions
logy marked by sluggishness and lack of vitality

loir (see **lawyer**)

loir a large European dormouse
Loire the largest river in France

lolly (see **lali**)

lone (see **loan**)

long (see **lang**)

longe a lake trout; a muskellunge; a long rope used to lead or guide a horse in training

lunge a sudden thrust, pass, or plunge forward

longer having greater length; a row of barrels stored fore and aft

longueur a dull or tedious passage or section, as in a book, play, or musical composition

longline a long heavy fishline with numerous baited hooks

long-line of or relating to long-distance communication or transportation

longue (see **lang**)

longueur (see **longer**)

loo (see **lieu**)

lood (see **leud**)

looed (see **leud**)

looie a lieutenant (slang, by shortening)

louis a French gold coin used from 1640 to the Revolution; the French 20-franc gold piece issued after the Revolution

lookdown any of several deep-bodied compressed silvery caranoid fishes

look-down the superficial appearance of paper as seen under reflected light

loom (see **loam**)

loon a fisheating diving bird; a crazy person

lune a hawk's leash; halfmoon shaped

loons fisheating diving birds; crazy persons

lunes fits of lunacy or frenzy

loop the doubling of a line with an aperture between; a turning area for vehicles

loupe a small magnifying glass

loos halloos; toilets

lose to mislay; to fail to win; to fail to keep in sight

loose not securely attached; lacking precision

luce a fullgrown pike (a fish)

loosen (see **leucine**)

loot (see **lieut**)

looter (see **lewder**)

looting plundering or robbing

luting a sealant for packing a joint or coating a porous surface to produce imperviousness to gas or liquid

loral (see **laurel**)

<u>**lore**</u> a body of knowledge or traditions; something learned

<u>**lower**</u> situated further below or under; to bring down; to reduce

lorel (see **laurel**)

lori either of two small nocturnal slow-moving lemurs

lory any of numerous parrots of Australia, New Guinea, and adjacent islands

loriot (see **laureate**)

lory (see **lori**)

lose (see **loos**)

loser a person, animal, or thing that fails to win or lags behind

luser an uninformed user of a computer system

lot (see **lat**)

lotte (see **lat**)

louder (see **lauter**)

loudish rather marked by intensity or volume of sound

loutish clownish or coarse

louis (see **looie**)

Loup and **loup** (see **lieu**)

loupe (see **loop**)

loure a dance in slow triple or sextuple time

Lur a chiefly nomadic Muslim people inhabiting a wild part of the Zagros mountains in Iran

lur a large bronze S-shaped Scandinavian trumpet of the Bronze Age

lure a bait, decoy, enticement, or incentive; to attract or entice

louse (see **Laos**)

loutish (see **loudish**)

loutre (see **lewder**)

low (see **Lo**)

lowa (see **Loa**)

lo(w)cal (see **locale**)

lowdown the actual facts; inside information

low-down contemptible, mean, or base

lowed (see **leud** and **load**)

lower (see **lore**)

lox (see **Lakhs**)

Lu (see **lieu**)

luce (see **loose**)

Lucifer (see **Leucifer**)

Lucite (see **leucite**)

lucks prospers or succeeds through good fortune or change, as "lucks out"

lux a unit of illumination

luxe a quality or state of being sumptuous

lude (see **lewd**)

luffed turned a ship's bow toward the wind or a sail nearer the wind

luft a lieutenant (by shortening "luftenant")

luggar a large dullbrown Asiatic falcon

lugger a person who carries materials

lumbar related to the abdominal areas on either side of the umbilicus and above the inguinal regions; related to the vertebrae between the thoracic vertebrae and the sacrum

lumber timber or logs; to move heavily or clumsily

lumen a cavity or passageway in a tubular organ; the bore of a tube

lumine to illuminate; to give physical light to

lune (see **loon**)

lunes (see **loons**)

lunge (see **longe**)

Lur and **lur** (see **loure**)

lure (see **loure**)

luser (see **loser**)

lute (see **lieut**)

luter (see **lewder**)

Lutheran a follower or adherent of Martin Luther or of doctrines and practices of the Lutheran Church

luthern a dormer window

luting (see **looting**)

lutist (see **lewdest**)

lux (see **lucks**)

luxe (see **lucks**)

lyddite a high explosive composed chiefly of picric acid

lydite basanite, a basaltic extensive rock closely allied to the chert, jasper, and flint; a test or criterion to determine the quality or genuineness of a thing, such as using a touchstone

lye (see **Lais**)

lyed (see **lied**)

lyes (see **lies**)

lyme (see **lime**)

lymphs (see **limps**)

Lynx and **lynx** (see **links**)

Lyons (see **liens**)

lyra (see **lira**)

lyre (see **liar**)

lyse (see **lice** and **lies**)

lysigenic formed by the breaking down of adjoining cells

lysogenic harboring an intracellular form of various bacterial viruses as hereditary materials

lysin a substance capable of dissolving bacteria and blood corpuscles

lysine a biologically important basic amino acid

lysogenic (see **lysigenic**)

lyssas (see **lisses**)

Group I

laggar - luggar
lapan - lapin
lapses - lapsus
leadin - lead-in
lech - letch
legumen - legumin
leporid - leporide
light - lite
lithodomous - lithodomus
longwool - long-wool
lowlife - low-life
lubbard - lubbered
lupous - lupus
lupulin - lupuline
lustering - lustring

Group I and II

liqueur   li'kər
liquor   'likər

Group II

la   'lä
law   'lȯw

languor   'laŋ(g)er
langur   'laŋ'gu̇r
lunger   'ləŋər or 'lənjər

larigo   'lärə,gō
larigot   'larə,gō

larin   'lärən
larine   'la,rən

laten   'lātən
Latin   'latən

lauds   'lȯdz
Lodz   'lädz

laws   'lȯz
Laz   'läz

leaven   'levən
levan   'le,van

lesser   'lesər
lessor   'le,sȯr

leucon   'lü,kän
Lucan   'lükən

liard   lē'är
lierre   lē'er

likeness   'līknəs
lychnis   'liknəs

likin   'lē'kēn
leaking   'lē,kiŋ

linch   'linsh
lynch   'linch

lineament   'linēəmənt
liniment   'linəmənt

linen   'linən
linin   'līnən

lisa   'lēsə
lyssa   'lisə

loggia   'lȯjēə
logia   'lōjēə

longer   'läŋgər
longueur   lȯŋ'gər

looies   'lüēz
lues   'lü,ēz

loose   'lüs
lose   'lüz

loots   'lütz
lutz   'lu̇tz

lorry 'lȯrē
lory 'lōrē

loupe 'lüp
lupe 'lüpā

lunare lu'narē
lunary 'lünərē

luscious 'ləshəs
lushes 'ləshəz

M

ma mother
maa a sheep's bleat
maw a receptacle (as a stomach) into which food is taken by swallowing

maa(e)d bleated like a sheep
mad completely unrestrained by reason and judgment

ma'am madam
malm a soft friable chalky limestone
Mam an Indian people of southwestern Guatemala
mom mother

ma'am madam
mom mother
mum silent; to go about merrymaking in disguise; a chrysanthemum

maar a volcanic crater in a low relief area
mar to injure, deface, or damage

macci stock characters of Roman comedy representing stupid greedy country fellows
maqui a Chilean shrub from whose berries wine is made
Maquis a member of an underground organization
maquis a thick scrubby underbrush along Mediterranean shores

mach the ratio of the speed of a body to the speed of sound; a mach number
moc a moccasin (by shortening)
mock to deride, treat with scorn, or ridicule; to make a sham of

macher an active, usually self-important person; an extremely influential person
mocker a person or bird that imitates or parodys another

mackintosh a lightweight waterproof fabric originally of rubberized cotton
McIntosh a late-ripening variety of brilliant-red apple

mackle a blur on a printed sheet
macle chiastolite, a mineral consisting of andalusite; a twinned crystal

macks pimps (slang)
Macs fellow, used informally to address men whose names are unknown
macs mackinaw coats or jackets
max a weevil that feeds on henequen buds; the maximum (by shortening)

macle (see **mackle**)

maco Egyptian cotton, especially in its natural undyed state
mako a large vigorous shark of the Atlantic

macrocephalous having an exceptionally large head; having the cotyledons of a dicotyledonous embryo consolidated
Macrocephalus a genus of mammals comprising the warthogs

macrurous having a long tail; relating to the Macrura, a suborder of crustaceans comprising shrimps, lobsters, and prawns
Macrurus the type genus of Macroridae, a family of fishes comprising the grenadiers

Macs and **macs** (see **macks**)

mad (see **maa[e]d**)

madam a female head of a house of prostitution

madame a female member of a French royal family

madded made angry; exasperated
madid wet or moist
matted having parts adhering closely together

madder angrier; an herb whose root was formerly used in dyeing

matter the substance of something; a topic under consideration

madding inciting into a raving or frenzied state

matting interweaving or tangling together so as to make a mat; a dull lusterless surface

made manufactured or produced
maid an unmarried girl or woman; a female employed to do domestic work

Madi a negro people of the upper Nile region north of Lake Albert
Mahdi a Muslim leader who assumes a messianic role

madid (see **madded**)

madregal an amberfish of the West Indies and other warm regions
madrigal a polyphonic part-song originating in the 14th century having parts for three or more voices

maerls lime-producing red seaweeds used especially in France to reduce soil acidity
merels an ancient game for two players in which counters are placed at angles

maggot a softbodied legless grub that is the larva of various dipterous insects
magot a Barbary ape; a small grotesque figure of Chinese or Japanese style

magnate a person of influence, distinction, or prominence
magnet something that attracts, especially a body that attracts iron

magot (see **maggot**)

Mahdi (see **Madi**)

Mahri a native or inhabitant of the Mahra region of the Arabian peninsula
Maori a native Polynesian population of New Zealand
Mari a Baluchi people of Baluchistan; a Finnish people of eastern Russia who are forest dwellers and farmers
marri a very large Australian red gum tree

mahsur a large Indian freshwater cyprinid food and sport fish
mosser a person who gathers or works with a plant of the class Musei

mai a slow Japanese folk or theater dance featuring hand gestures
my belonging to me

Maia a nearly cosmopolitan genus of spider crabs
Maya a people of Yucatan, Belize, and northern Guatemala
maya an illusioncreating power of a god or demon

maid (see **made**)

mail postal matter; armor made of metal links or plates
male the sex that usually performs the fertilizing function in generation

mailer a container in which to mail something
malar relating to a cheek or side of the head

main the first in any respect; the principal item
Maine the northeasternmost state in the U.S.
mane neck hair
mein Chinese wheatflour noodles

Mainer a native or resident of the state of Maine
mainour in Old English law, something stolen that is found in the thief's possession

Mainiac or **Main(e)iac** a resident of Maine
maniac a lunatic or a person affected with madness

mainour (see **Mainer**)

mais slow Japanese folk or theater dances featuring hand gestures

mise the issue in a legal proceeding upon a writ of right

Maithili an Indic dialect of north Bihar, India

mightily earnestly, vigorously, or powerfully

maize Indian corn; a light yellow color

Mayes a variety of dewberry important in northern Texas and the Middle West

Mays the fifth month of the Gregorian calendar (plural)

maze intricate passages that ramify and interconnect in confusing ways

maizer a redwing blackbird

maser a device that utilizes the natural oscillations of an atomic or molecular system to amplify or produce electromagnetic waves

mazer a large drinking bowl originally of hard wood that is often footed and silver mounted

mako (see **maco**)

mal a disease or sickness

mall a public area for shopping or leisurely strolling

maul a heavy hammer; to injure by beating

moll a gangster's girlfriend; composed in a minor mode

malacia abnormal softening or loss of consistency of an organ or tissue

Malaysia a constitutional monarchy in southeast Asia

malaise a sense of physical, mental, or moral illbeing or uneasiness

Malays members of people of the Malay peninsula, eastern Sumatra, and part of Borneo

malar (see **mailer**)

Malay a member of the people of the Malay peninsula, eastern Sumatra, and parts of Borneo

mele an Hawaiian poem adapted to vocal music

melee a confused struggle; a diamond, usually less than ⅛-carat, cut from a fragment of a larger stone

Malays (see **malaise**)

Malaysia (see **malacia**)

male (see **mail**)

Male the capital of the Maldives

Mali a republic in west Africa

mal(l)ie a person belonging to a caste in India whose usual occupation is gardening; a person who frequents shopping marts for social contacts and excitement

maulie a fist or hand, in boxing

molle in music, lower by a half step; flat

molly a pampered darling (slang); a spineless weakling; a gangster's girl friend

moly molybdenum, a fusible polyvalent metallic element

mall (see **mal**)

mal(l)ie (see **Male**)

malm (see **ma'am**)

Mam (see **ma'am**)

manacan the dried root of a shrub of Brazil and the West Indies used in the treatment of rheumatism and syphilis

manakin a small bird of Central and South America

manikin a little man, drawf, or pigmy

mannequin a representation of a human figure for displaying or fitting clothes

mannikin a small weaver bird of Africa, Asia, and Australia

mand an East Indian cereal grass

manned furnished with a sufficient force or complement of armed personnel

Mandarin the primarily northern dialect of Chinese used by the court and the official classes under the Empire

mandarin a public office under the Chinese Empire

mandarine a sweet liquer flavored with the dried peel of manarin (orange)

mandrel an axle inserted in a piece of work to support it during machining

mandrill a large fierce gregarious baboon of western Africa

mane (see **main**)

Mangar a people of Nepal

monger a person engaged in the sale of a commodity; a person engaged in petty or discreditable dealings

mangel a large coarse yellow to reddish orange beet extensively grown for cattle food

mangle to cut, bruise, or hack with repeated blows or strokes; to maim

maniac (see **Maniac** or **Main(e)iac**)

manikin (see **manacan**)

manism the worship of the spirits of deceased humans

monism the metaphysical view that only one kind of substance or ultimate reality exists

manned (see **mand**)

mannequin (see **manacan**)

manner a mode of procedure or way of acting; normal behavior

manor a mansion; a lord's house; a large estate

mannikin (see **manacan**)

Mano a Negro people inhabiting the northern tip of the central province of Liberia and adjacent Ivory Coast

mano a handstone used as the upper millstone for grinding grains

mono monotype, a typesetting machine; a bullring attendant; containing one atom, radical, or group of a particular kind

manor (see **manner**)

manteau a loose cloak, coat, or robe

manto a nearly horizontal or gently inclined sheetlike body of ore

mantel a supporting beam, stone, or arch for masonry above a fireplace

mantle a loose sleeveless garment worn over clothing; a part of the earth's interior

manto (see **manteau**)

Mao a plain shirtlike jacket, usually blue or gray with a high collar

mow a contortion of the face or lips especially so as to produce a mocking or derisive expression

Maori (see **Mahri**)

maos peacocks

mows stacks of hay or straw

Maquis and **maquis** (see **macci**)

mar (see **maar**)

marabou a large stork, as an African stork or adjutant bird

Marabout a Muslim monk, hermit, or saint

marabout a tomb or shrine erected to a Marabout

maracan a Brazilian macaw

maroquin a fine very firm flexible leather prepared from goatskin

maray a Pacific round herring

moray any of numerous often brightly colored savage voracious eels

marc a residue remaining after fruit (as grapes) has been pressed

mark something that records position; the recent basic monetary unit of Germany

marque a brand or make of a product; a governmental license granted to a private person to use an armed vessel at sea to plunder the enemy

mare a female horse

Mayer a person who celebrates May Day

mayor the chief magistrate of a municipality

Mari (see **Mahri**)

maria any of several shrubs and trees of tropical America

Moraea a genus of southern African or Australian bulbous or tuberus plants

marid one of the most powerful class of jinn in Mohammedan mythology
married united in wedlock

marine relating to the sea
moreen a strong crossribbed upholstery fabric of wool or wool and cotton

marischal an earl marshal of Scotland from the 15th century to 1716
Marshall the Austronesian language of the Marshall Islands
marshal(l) to arrange or assemble according to some scheme; a military commander
martial warlike; falling under the astrological influence of Mars

mark (see **marc**)

marl a loose or crumbling earthy deposit that contains chiefly calcium carbonate or dolomite
moral ethical or principled; a lesson taught by a story or fable
morel an edible fungus

marli an ornamented raised border on a dining plate
marly resembling clay

marlin a large oceanic gamefish
marline a small tarred twostrand line used to cover wire rope

marly (see **marli**)

maroquin (see **maracan**)

marque (see **marc**)

marquees permanent canopies over entranceways; large field tents formerly used by highranking officers
Marquis an important variety of wheat in the U.S.
marquis a nobleman of hereditary rank
marquise an elliptical gem, ring mounting, or bezel with pointed ends

marri (see **Mahri**)

married (see **marid**)

marrier an official or cleric who performs weddings
merrier more cheerful or joyous

marry to unite in wedlock
<u>**mere**</u> a Maori war club
merry cheerful or joyous

marshalcy the rank or position of a marshal
marshalsea a former English court held before the lord steward and the knight marshal of the royal household

Marshall and **marshal(l)** (see **marischal**)

marshalsea (see **marshalcy**)

marten a slenderbodied carnivorous mammal
martin a swallow or flycatcher

martial (see **marischal**)

martin (see **marten**)

maser (see **maizer**)

masi fermented taro or breadfruit stored in an underground pit
Mossi a people of the west central Sudan
mossie a mosquito, in Australia
mossy overgrown or covered with moss or something like moss; antiquated

Mason a member of a widespread secret society called Free and Accepted Masons
mason a skilled worker who builds with stone or similar material
maysin a very soluble globulin in cornmeal
meson an unstable nuclear particle first observed in cosmic rays

massed gathered into a large quantity
mast a long vertical spar rising from a ship's deck

mat a flat relatively thin article placed on a horizontal surface
<u>**matte**</u> a mixture of sulfides formed in smelting sulfide ores of metals

mater a worker who packs shoes or hosiery in pairs

Mehter a member of an harijan caste of sweepers and scavengers in India
mehter a groom or stable boy in Iran

matey companionable
maty a native assistant servant in India

matte (see **mat**)

matted (see **madded**)

matter (see **madder**)

matting (see **madding**)

mat(t)rass a rounded longnecked glass flask
mattress a pad used as a resting place

maty (see **matey**)

maul (see **mal**)

maulie (see **Male**)

Mauser a certain type of repeating firearm, or for its parts or ammunition
mouser one that catches mice and rats, especially a cat

maw (see **ma**)

max (see **macks**)

Maya and **maya** (see **Maia**)

Mayer (see **mare**)

Mayes (see **maize**)

mayor (see **mare**)

Mays (see **maize**)

maysin (see **Mason**)

mazarin a deep dish often of metal
mazarine a hood worn by women in the 17th century

maze (see **maize**)

mazer (see **maizer**)

McIntosh (see **mackintosh**)

me the objective case of I, a personal pronoun
mi the third note of the diatonic scale

mead a fermented drink of water, honey, malt, and yeast

Mede a native or inhabitant of ancient Media, a kingdom in what is now northwestern Iran
meed a fitting return or just dessert

mealie an ear of Indian corn
mealy soft, dry, and friable

mean displaying petty selfishness; lacking dignity; to have in mind; to signify; an average or measure of central tendency
mesne intermediate in time of occurrence or performance
mien a person's bearing

meanings things a person intends to convey by an act, language, or purpose
meninx any of three membranes that envelop the brain and spinal cord

meat animal tissue used for food
meet to come into contact with or encounter
mete to allot or apportion

meatier more full of meat; furnishing more solid food for thought
meteor a streak of light in the night sky produced by passage through the earth's atmosphere of solid matter in the solar system

medal an inscribed medal commemorating a person or event, or awarded for a deed
meddle to interfere without right or propriety
metal any of a large group of substances that typically are opaque, lustrous, temperature and electrical conductors, and can be fused
mettle qualities and abilities relative to a given situation

meddler a busybody
medlar a small Eurasian tree; a small deciduous tree of southern Africa
metal(l)er a person who places metal sheets on sized work

meddlesome officiously intruding
mettlesome spirited

Mede (see **mead**)

medic a plant of the genus Medicago, which includes the typical clovers; a person engaged in medical work

metic an alien resident of an ancient Greek city who had some civil privileges upon payment of a tax

medlar (see **meddler**)

meed (see **mead**)

meet (see **meat**)

meeter a person who encounters or comes in contact with

meter a unit of length equal to 39.37 inches; an instrument for measuring; a systematically measured rhythm

Mehter and **mehter** (see **mater**)

mein (see **main**)

melded showed or announced a card or combination of cards

melted changed from a solid to a liquid state

mele (see **Malay**)

melee (see **Malay**)

mellow relaxed and at ease; pleasantly convivial; fully matured or aged

Melo a genus of marine shells, usually designated as Cymbium, comprising the melon shells

melo a melodrama (by shortening)

melted (see **melded**)

mends repairs or improves

men's the possessive form of human males

meninx (see **meanings**)

menology an ecclesiastical calendar of festivals celebrated in honor of particular saints and martyrs

monology the habit of soliloquizing

men's (see **mends**)

meow a cat's cry; a spiteful or malicious remark

Miao an aboriginal people of China inhabiting southwestern China into northern parts of Vietnam, Laos, and Thailand

mer a monomeric unit of polymer

murre a narrowbilled auklike bird, as the razorbill

myrrh an aromatic bitter gum resin used as an ingredient of incense and perfume

merc a mercenary soldier (by shortening)

murk darkness, gloom, or thick heavy air

mere (see **marry**)

mere exclusive of anything else

Mir a chief or leader, used especially in India for descendents of Mohammed

mir a Russian village community

mire a fixed mark due north or south of a meridian

merels (see **maerls**)

merer more exclusive of or considered apart from anthing else; purer; barer

mirror a polished or smooth substance that forms images by the reflection of light

merle a bluish grey color of the coats of some dogs

merl(e) a common English black thrush with an orange bill and eye trim

murral a common freshwater snakehead food fish of southeast Asia and the Philippines

Merlin a stocky, sturdy pony

merlin a small European falcon

merlon the solid interval between embrasures of a battlemented parapet

murlin a large brownish black seaweed often eaten as a vegetable in Europe

merrier (see **marrier**)

merry (see **marry**)

mesne (see **mean**)

meso a molecule or compound that is optically inactive because it is internally compensated

miso a paste made of grinding steamed rice, cooked soybeans, and salt that is used in preparing soups and other foods

meso a molecule or compound that is optically inactive

mezzo a manner of engraving on copper or steel (mezzotint, by shortening); a woman's voice of medium compass betwen that of a soprano and contralto (mezzo-soprano, by shortening)

meson (see **Mason**)

metal (see **medal**)

metal(l)er (see **meddler**)

metanym a generic name rejected because it is based on a type of species congeneric with the type of a previously published genus

metonym a word used for another that it may be expected to suggest

mete (see **meat**)

meteor (see **meatier**)

meter (see **meeter**)

methene a bivalent hydrocarbon radical derived from methane

methine a trivalent hydrocarbon radical derived from methane

metic (see **medic**)

metonym (see **metanym**)

mettle (see **medal**)

mettlesome (see **meddlesome**)

meuse a gap through which a wild animal customarily passes

mews utters a cry characteristic of a cat or gull; sheds the horns

mus bridging groups that join central atoms or ions; the twelfth letter of the Greek alphabet (plural)

Muse one's creative spirit (from the Muses of Greek mythology)

muse to fall into a state of deep thought or dreamy abstraction

meute a cage for molting hawks

mute debatable; deprived of practical significance

mewl a whine or cry

mule a hybrid between a horse and an ass; a very stubborn person

mews (see **meuse**)

mezzo (see **meso**)

mhos units of electrical conductance equal to the reciprocal of the ohm

mohs the scale of hardness that is used in grading minerals

mos moments (slang); books or volumes (by shortening duodecimo)

mots pithy or witty sayings

mows cuts down or off

mi (see **me**)

Miao (see **meow**)

micks persons of Irish descent, often used offensively

mix to blend or stir

micropterous having small or rudimentary fins or wings

Micropterus a genus of sunfishes that includes the American freshwater black basses

Midas a genus of South American marmosets comprising the tamarins

mitis tending to be less than average virulent, such as strains of diphtheria bacilli

middy a student naval officer or midshipman

midi a skirt or coat of midcalf length

mien (see **mean**)

might possible or probably; power or authority

mite a small to minute arachnid; a very little bit

mightily (see **Maithili**)

mighty powerful, notable, or extraordinary; extremely

mity infested with mites

mignon a moderate purple color; a filet mignon (by shortening)

mignonne daintily small or petite

mikado an emperor of Japan; a strong to vivid reddish orange

mockado a woolen fabric made chiefly in the 16th and 17th centuries in imitation of velvet

mil a unit of measurement equal to $\frac{1}{1000}$ inch; a monetary unit of property tax assessment

mill a factory for manufacturing activity, as grinding grain

milch a domestic animal bred for or suitable for milk production

milk to shuffle cards by drawing one from the top and one from the bottom and simultaneously allowing them to fall face down on the table; to exploit, bleed, or elicit

mile a unit of linear measure equal to 5,280 feet

myal of or relating to a cult among West Indian blacks akin to obeah

miliary accompanied or marked by an eruption or formation of lesions the size of millet seeds

milliary marking the distance of a mile

milk (see **milch**)

mill (see **mil**)

millefleur having an allover pattern of small flowers and plants

millefleurs a perfume made from extracts of several flowers

millenary a group of a thousand things

millinary women's headwear

milliary (see **miliary**)

millinary (see **millenary**)

million 1000 thousand

milyun either of two soft-fleshed sweet-flavord pepos that are usually eaten as a fruit

millrace a canal in which water flows to and from a mill wheel; the current that drives that wheel

milreis a Portuguese unit of value equal before 1911 to 1,000 reis; Brazil's basic monetary unit until 1942

milyun (see **million**)

mince to cut or chop into small bits

mints places where coins are made; confections flavored with peppermint or spearmint

mind the intellect or brain; to obey; to take care of

mined dug or extracted from the earth

miner a person or machine that extracts ore and coal from the earth

minor of lesser or inferior importance; a person younger than majority age

mini something that is small of its kind

Minni a primitive Mongol people inhabiting the foothill region of the southern Caucasus during pre–Babylonian times

minnie a hand barely strong enough for an opening bid in bridge

minion a servile dependent; a piece of light artillery; a person who is highly esteemed and favored

Minyan having characteristics of a prehistoric Greek civilization noted for its pottery

minyan the required number (ten) of males at least thirteen years old to conduct public Jewish worship

minks slenderbodied semiaquatic carnivorous mammals

minx a pert or flirtatious girl

Minni (see **mini**)

minnie (see **mini**)

minor (see **miner**)

mintie a homosexual (slang)

minty having the flavor of an aromatic plant of the family Labiatae

mints (see **mince**)

minty (see **mintie**)

minx (see **minks**)

Minyan and **minyan** (see **minion**)

Mir and **mir** (see **mere**)

mire (see **mere**)

mirror (see **merer**)

mis dried dung used as fuel
miss fail to hit, reach, or make contact with

misbilled erroneously charged a customer for merchandise or service
misbuild to construct something in error or by mistake

miscreance an opinion or doctrine thought to be false
miscreants those who behave criminally or viciously

mise (see **mais**)

mises various dried dungs used as fuel
misses fails to hit, reach, or make contact with; girls or unmarried women
missus a wife; the mistress of a household

Miskito a people of the Atlantic coast of Nicaraqua and Honduras
mosquito any of numerous two-winged flies

miso (see **meso**)

miss (see **mis**)

miss a young married woman or girl
Mus a genus of rodents including the common house mouse
muss a state of confusion or disorder

missal a book containing what is said and sung at Roman Catholic mass during the year
missel a large European thrush which feeds on mistletoe berries
missile a weapon or object thrown or projected

missed failed to hit, reach, or make contact with

mist moisture in the form of minute particles suspended in the atmosphere; a haze or film
myst an intiate in a mystery

missel (see **missal**)

misses (see **mises**)

missile (see **missal**)

missus (see **mises**)

mist (see **missed**)

mistic a small lateenrigged sailing ship used in the Mediterranean
mystic constituting or belonging to something occult or esoteric

mite (see **might**)

mitis (see **Midas**)

mity (see **mighty**)

mix (see **micks**)

mnemonic assisting or intended to assist memory
pneumonic relating to the lungs or pneumonia

mo a moment (slang)
mow to cut grass close to the ground

moa any of various extinct flightless ratite birds of New Zealand
mohwa any of several East Indian trees of the genus Madhuca

moan a low prolonged sound of pain or grief
Mon the dominant native people of Pgu in Myanmar
mown cut or cropped close to the ground

moat a deep wide trench around a fortified place, often filled with water
mote a small particle or speck

moc (see **mach**)

mock (see **mach**)

mockado (see **mikado**)

mocker (see **macher**)

Mod a meeting to study and perform Gaelic arts

mode a form or manner of expression

mowed cut grass close to the ground

model an example, pattern, or standard

mottle an appearance resembling a surface having colored spots, blotchings, or cloudings

mohels persons who circumcise male infants

moyles types of shoes or slippers

Moho a genus of Hawaiian honey eaters; a depth ranging from 3 to 25 miles beneath the ocean floor

moho any of several Hawaiian honey eaters having pectoral tufts of yellow feathers

Mojo an Arawakan people of northern Bolivia

mojo an irregularly spreading or shrubby tree widely distributed along tropical shores; an erect forest tree of the West Indian uplands

mohr a gazelle of northern Africa

moire a fabric having a wavy watered appearance

Moor a member of a darkskinned people of mixed Arab and Berber ancestry inhabiting ancient Mauretania in northern Africa

moor an extensive area of open rolling land often covered with heather, moss, and grass; to make fast with cables and lines

mor forest humus consisting of a layer of largely organic matter distinct from the mineral soil beneath

more larger in size, quantity, or extent

mohr a gazelle of northern Africa

Moor a member of a darkskinned people of mixed Arab and Berber ancestry

moor an extensive area of open rolling land

more larger in size, quantity, or extent

mower an implement to cut grass or grain

mohs (see **mhos**)

mohwa (see **moa**)

moiles metallic oxide adhering to glass knocked from the end of the blowpipe

moils works with grueling persistence; is in continuous agitation

moire (see **mohr**)

moirés irregular wavy finishes produced on fabric

morays savage voracious often brightly colored eels

mores customs and folkways of a particular group

Mojo and **mojo** (see **Moho**)

Moki a Shoshenean people of Pueblo Indians in northeastern Arizona

moki a trumpeter fish

moky foggy or hazy

mol a molecule (by shortening)

mole a congenital mark or discoloration on the skin; a burrowing mammal

molar a tooth adapted for grinding

moler an animal that catches burrowing mammals of the family Talpidae

mold a pattern or template that serves as a guide for construction

moled made or traversed an underground passage; burrowed or tunneled

mould a membrane-covered opening in bone or between bones

mole (see **mol**)

mole a highly spiced sauce made principally of chile and chocolate

moly a European wild garlic; a mythical herb described by Homer

moled (see **mold**)

moler (see **molar**)

moll (see **mal**)

molle (see **Male**)

molly (see **Male**)

moly (see **Male** and **mole**)

mom (see both **ma'am** entries)

Mon (see **moan**)

monac(h)al relating to or having characteristics of monks or monastic life
monocle an eyeglass for one eye

monger (see **Mangar**)

monism (see **manism**)

mono (see **Mano**)

monocle (see **monac[h]al**)

monogeneous developing without cyclic
change of form; the presumed origin of
all life from one original entity or cell
monogynous having but one wife or mate

monology (see **menology**)

months measures of time corresponding
to the period of the moon's revolution
around Earth
Muntz an alloy of copper and zinc

moo a cow's natural throat noise
moue a little grimace or pout
mu a bridging group joining central atoms
and ions; the twelfth letter of the Greek
alphabet

mood a feeling, temper, or atmosphere
mooed made a cow's natural throat noise

moody subject to or characterized by depression or discontent
muti medicine, in Africa

mooed (see **mood**)

moola(h) money (slang)
mulla(h) a learned teacher or expounder
of the religious law and doctrines of
Islam

Moonie a member or follower of the
Unification Church founded by Sun
Myung Moon
moony shaped like the moon; abstracted
or dreamy
muni a Hindu hermit sage; a bond issued

by a governmental unit (by shortening
municipal)

Moor and moor (see both **mohr** entries)

Moorish relating to or in the style characteristic of the Moors
moreish causing a desire for more; palat-
able

moose a large ruminant mammal of northern North America
mousse a frothy dessert; a food prepared
with whipped cream

mor (see **mohr**)

Mora a small genus of tall half-evergreen
forest trees of northern South America
mora any tree of the genus Mora, especially a tall buttressed tree
morrow the next following day

Moraea (see **maria**)

moral (see **marl**)

morale a state of individual psychological
wellbeing and buoyancy; a sense of
common purpose or degree of dedica-
tion to a common task; esprit de corps
morral a fiber bag usually used as a food
bag for horses

moray (see **maray**)

morays (see **moirés**)

mordant a biting and caustic thought or
style; a chemical that fixes dye
mordent a melodic musical ornament

more (see both **mohr** entries)

moreen (see **marine**)

moreish (see **Moorish**)

morel (see **marl**)

morelles counters or disks used in playing
a board game
morels edible fungi of the genus
Morchella

mores (see **moirés**)

morn the beginning of a day

morne gloomy or dismal

mourn to feel or express deep regret; to grieve

morning the early part of the day before noon

mourning feeling or expressing deep regret or grief

Mornay a white sauce containing cheese, especially Parmesan or Gruyère

morné in heraldry, a lion without teeth, tongue, or claws

morne (see morn)

Moro any of several Muslim peoples of the southern Philippines chiefly of the Sulu archipelago

moro a thick-billed Afro-Asian finch

morro a round hill or point of land

Moro any of several Muslim peoples of the southern Philippines chiefly of the Sulu archipelago

morrow the next following day

Morone a genus of carnivorous fresh and saltwater percoid fishes, including white perch

Moroni the angel who appeared on September 21, 1823, in a vision telling Joseph Smith that a record engraved on golden plates contained the history of the ancient inhabitants of America

morral (see morale)

morris a vigorous dance done by men; an ancient game for two persons

Morus a widely distributed genus of trees comprising the mulberries

morro (see Moro)

morrow (see Mora or Moro)

morsal relating to the grinding or biting surface of a tooth or occlusion of the teeth

morsel a small piece or quantity of food

Morus (see morris)

mos (see mhos)

Moso a people closely related to the northern Lolo and found mainly in the high plateaus and mountains of southwest China

mosso animated and/or rapid, in music

mozo a male servant or domestic; a handyman

mosquito (see Miskito)

mosser (see mahsur)

Mossi (see masi)

mossie (see masi)

mosso (see Moso)

mossy (see masi)

mote (see moat)

moter a person or device that removes small underdeveloped seeds or fragments from cotton

motor a device that imparts motion or is a source of mechanical power

mots (see mhos)

mottle (see model)

moue (see moo)

mould (see mold)

mourn (see morn)

mourning (see morning)

mouse to hunt for or catch mice; explored or snooped

mows stacks of hay or straw

mouser (see Mauser)

mousse (see moose)

mow (see Mao and mo)

mowed (see Mod)

mower (see mohr)

mown (see moan)

mows (see maos, mhos and mouse)

moyles (see mohels)

mozo (see Moso)

mu (see **moo**)

mucks covers with manure or other fertilizing material; clears of manure or filth

mux to make a mess of; a device for multiplex transmission of signals

mudded made turbid

muddied characterized by a confused state

mudder a race horse that runs well on a wet or muddy track; or an athlete that performs well in muddy conditions

mutter to talk indistinctly or with a low voice

muddie a baked clay marble, in the game of marbles

muddy covered with a slimy sticky fluid-to-plastic mixture of dirt or other fine divided particles and water

muddied (see **mudded**)

muddy (see **muddie**)

muhly a grass

muley hornless or polled, as an animal; stubborn or obstinate

mule (see **mewl**)

muleta a small cloth attached to a short tapered stick and used by a matador during the faena

muletta a Portuguese coasting ship with a lateen sail and pointed bow painted with a human eye

muley (see **muhly**)

mulla(h) (see **moola(h)**)

mullar a die cut in intaglio for stamping an ornament in relief

muller a hard relatively flatbased implement for grinding or mixing materials; a pestle

multichord two or more chords sounded together

multicored having more than a single axial portion or core, as a boil

multiply to find the product of, in mathematics

multi-ply composed of several or many layers or strata

mum (see **ma'am**)

mumu filariasis caused by a slender white filaria transmitted in larval form by mosquitoes

muumuu a loose gaily colored and patterned dress worn chiefly in Hawaii

Muncie a city in north central Indiana

Munsee a Delaware Indian people of northern New Jersey and neighboring parts of New York

munds states of peace or security imposed or guaranteed in Anglo-Saxon and early medieval England

muns classes of London street roisterers of the mid17th century

muni (see **Moonie**)

muns (see **munds**)

Munsee (see **Muncie**)

Muntz (see **months**)

murderess a female legally guilty of committing the crime of killing a person

murderous characterized by extreme difficulty

murk (see **merc**)

murlin (see **Merlin**)

murra a material thought to be of semi-precious stone or porcelain used to make costly vessels in ancient Rome

Murrah an Indian breed of dairy type buffaloes with distinctive coiled horns

murrain a pestilence of plague affecting domestic animals or plants

murrhine made of semiprecious stone or porcelain

murral (see **merle**)

murre (see **mer**)

murrhine (see **murrain**)

Mus (see **miss**)

mus (see **meuse**)

muscadin a young French fop, especially one with royalist sympathies during the French Revolution
muscadine a tallgrowing grape of the southern U.S.

Muscat the capital city of (the Sultanate of) Oman
muscat a cultivated vinifera grape used in making wines and raisins
musket a heavy smoothbore large caliber shoulder firearm; a male sparrow hawk

muscle a tissue of modified elongated cells that produces motion when contracted; strength or brawn
mussel a marine bivalve mollusk (seldom **muscle**)

muscleman a person hired to enforce compliance by strongarm methods; a goon
Mus(s)ulman a Muslim

Muse and **muse** (see **meuse**)

musket (see **Muscat**)

muss (see **miss**)

mussed untidy or wrinkled
must is required, compelled, or obliged to
musth a murderous frenzy of a bull elephant usually occurring during rut

mussel (see **muscle**)

Mus(s)ulman (see **muscleman**)

must (see **mussed**)

mustard a plant from whose seeds a pungent yellow condiment is made
mustered convened, assembled, or accumulated; enlisted

mustee the offspring of a white and a quadroon; a person of 1/8 negro ancestry; an octoroon
musty impaired by damp or mildew; moldy

mustered (see **mustard**)

musth (see **mussed**)

musty (see **mustee**)

mute (see **meute**)

muti (see **moody**)

mutter (see **mudder**)

mutual shared in common
mutuel the parimutuel, a system of betting on a (horse) race whereby those who bet on the winner share the total stakes, less a small percentage for the management

muumuu (see **mumu**)

mux (see **mucks**)

my (see **mai**)

myal (see **mile**)

myatonia lack of muscle tone or muscular flabbiness
myotonia a tonic spasm of one or more muscles

myrrh (see **mer**)

myst (see **missed**)

mystic (see **mistic**)

Group I

magnificence - magnificents
malevolence - malevolents
malfeasance - malfeasants
marasmous - marasmus
marcescence - marcescents
mauveine - mauvine
metis - metisse
microcephalous - microcephalus
militance - militants
milktoast - milquetoast
modern - moderne
monoculous - monoculus
monticulous - monticulus
mucous - mucus
multivalence - multivalents

Group I and II

massif   ma:sēf
massive   'masiv

material   mə'tirēəl
materiel   mə:tirē'el

Mousquetaire   :müskə:ter
musketeer   :məskə:tir

myrtle   'mərtᵊl
myrtol   'mərtōl

mystic   'mistēk
mystique   mi'stēk

Group II

Macá   mə'kä
macaw   mə'kȯ

macabi   :mäkə:bē
Maccabee   'makə,bē

madge   'maj
mage   'māj

Mahri   'märē
Maori   'maủrē

maidan   mī'dān
maiden   'mādᵊn

maidou   mī'dü
maidu   'midü

majorat   ,mazhō'ra
majorate   'mājərāt

malign   mə'līn
meline   'me,līn

malo   'malō
mallow   'malō

mammae   'ma,mē
mammee   ma'mē
mammy   'mamē

mana   'mänə
manna   'manə

manhattan   mən'hatᵊn
menhaden   mən'hadᵊn

manila   mə'nilə
manilla   mə'nēlyə

mara   mə'rä
maray   mə'rā

margarite   'märgə,rīt
marguerite   'märgə,rēt

marquessate   'märkwə,zə̇t
marquisette   'märkwə,zet

martineta   ,märtᵊn'ädə
martinete   ,märtᵊn'ādā

maser   'māzər
mazar   mə'zär

matelot   'mat,lō
matelote   'mat,lōt

matross   mə'träs
mattress   'matrə̇s

maud   'mȯd
mod   'mäd or 'mōd

maulie   'mȯlē
molly   'mälē

megameter   ,me'gamēdər
megohmmeter   'me,gōm,mēdər

meridian   mə̇'ridēən
meridienne   mə̇:ride:en
Meridion   mə̇'ride,än

metamer   'medəmər
metamere   'medə,mir

microhmmeter   'mī,krōm,mēdər
micrometer   'mīkrō,medər

midden   'midᵊn
mitten   'mitᵊn

migraines   'mī,grānz
migrans   'mī,granz

milieu   mēl'yü
milu   'mē'lü

mistaken   mə̇'stākən
Mixtecan   mē'stākən

mistakes məˈstāks
mystax ˈmiˌstaks

misti ˈmisˌtī
misty ˈmisti

Mohawk ˈmōˌhȯk
Mohock ˈmōˌhäk

moot ˈmüt
mute ˈmyüt

mootable ˈmüd•əbəl
mutable ˈmyütəbəl

moral ˈmȯrəl
morale mȯˈral
morral məˈral or məˈräl

morceau mȯrˈsō
moreso ˈmȯrsō

morro ˈmōrrō
morrow ˈmȯrō or ˈmȯrə

motif mōˈtēf
motive ˈmōtəv

moutan ˈmü:tan
mouton ˈmüˌtan

mucic ˈmyüsik
music ˈmyüzik

mudar məˈdär
mudder ˈmədər

murein ˈmyu̇rˌēn
murine myüˈrēn

muscle ˈməsəl
mussal məˈsäl

N

nacre an irridescent inner layer of various mollusk shells; mother-of-pearl
naker a kettledrum

nade a grenade (by shortening)
neighed made the loud prolonged calling cry typical of a horse

naggie (see **knaggy**)

naggy (see **knaggy**)

naiad the distinctive aquatic young of mayflies and dragonflies that differ markedly from the adult counterparts
naid any of numerous small fresh water annelids constituting Nais

naissant in heraldry, rising from the middle of an heraldic field, as an animal with only its upper part visible
nascent beginning to exist

nak (see **knack**)

naker (see **nacre**)

nal the giant reed, a tall European grass with woody stems used in making organ reeds
nul in law, not any
null invalid, void, or of no consequence

nance an effeminate male (slang)
Nantes a city in west central France

nani beautiful (in Hawaii)
nanny a female domestic goat; a nursemaid

Nantes (see **nance**)

nao a medium-sized sailing ship of the late middle ages
now at the present time

nap to sleep briefly; a soft fuzzy fibrous surface
nape the back part of the neck
nappe a sheet of water falling down from the crest of a dam

Nara relating to the 9th century Buddhistic renaissance in Japan
narra any of several timber trees of the genus Pterocarpus

naras a spiny southern African desert shrub

naris the opening of the nose or nasal cavity of a vertebrate

narc a narcotics or illegal drug agent, or police officer

nark a decoy or shill, in gambling

nard (see **gnarred**)

naris (see **naras**)

nark (see **narc**)

narra (see **Nara**)

narrow-gage track of less than standard distance between the heads of the rails

narrow-gauge restricted, provincial, or petty

nascent (see **naissant**)

nash (see **gnash**)

nat (see **knot**)

natty (see **gnatty**)

naught (see **knot**)

naughty (see **knotty**)

naut (see **knot**)

naval relating to ships or a navy

navel the midabdomen depression marking the point of attachment of the umbilical cord

nave (see **knave**)

navel (see **naval**)

navies the ships of nations, owners, or gatherings

navys variable colors averaging a grayish purple blue

naw (see **gnaw**)

nay a negative reply or vote

ne(e) originally or formally called

neigh a horse's typical loud prolonged cry

Nayar a people of the Malabar coast of India

nigher nearer in place, time, or relationship; closer

nays negative replies or votes

naze a headland or promontory

neighs typical loud prolonged cries of a horse

near (see **gnir**)

neater (see **kneader**)

nebbie a capsule of Nembutal, a trademark name for a brand of pentobarbital

nebby pitifully ineffectual

necklace a string of beads or other small objects worn about the neck as an ornament

neckless having no neck

neddy a bludgeon or billyclub; a sling shot

netty resembling a meshed arrangement of threads, cords, or ropes

ne(e) (see **knee** or **nay**)

need (see **knead**)

neele (see **kneel**)

neigh (see **nay**)

neighed (see **nade**)

neighs (see **nays**)

nell (see **knell**)

nephrocele hernia of the kidney

nephrocoele the cavity of a vertebrate embryo

nervous tending to produce agitation; jerky, jumpy, or unsteady

nervus nerve

nester an animal that builds or occupies a nest; a homesteader or squatter who takes up rangeland for farming

Nestor a wise elder counselor; a grand old patriarch of a particular field; a genus of large parrots in New Zealand

nestor a homesteader or squatter who takes up rangeland to cultivate

netty (see neddy)

neuma a symbol in musical notation of the middle ages

pneuma an ethereal fiery stuff or universal spirit held by the ancient Stoics to be a cosmic principle

neumatic characterized by symbols in the musical notation of the middle ages, or square symbols in the plainsong notation of the Roman Catholic Church

pneumatic relating to or using air, wind, or other gas; having cavities filled with air

neuter belonging to neither of two usually opposed classes; sexless

nuder more devoid of clothing

new (see gnu)

Newcomb a game resembling volleyball

newcome recently come or arrived

newer more recent or fresher

Nuer a Nilotic people in the Sudan

newk a newcomer, especially in the military

nuke to destroy with nuclear bombs; a nuclearpowered electric generating station

nuque the back of the neck

newsie a young person that peddles newspapers; a newsdealer

newsy given to gossip; filled with news items

Nuzi a dialect of Akkadian used in Iraq

newt (see knout)

nibble a small bite or morsel of food

nybble a group of binary digits (in computing) consisting of four bits or onehalf byte

nice (see gneiss)

Nice a city on the southeast coast of France; a grayishblue color (also called Quimper)

niece a daughter of one's sister, brother, sisterinlaw, or brother-inlaw

nickel a nearly silverwhite hard malleable ductile ferromagnetic metallic element; a five-cent U.S. coin

Nicol a clear calcite prism for producing and analyzing polarized light

nickers (see knickers)

nicks notches

nix not or nothing; to cancel or reject; a supernatural creature in Germanic folklore

Nyx an ancient Greek goddess personifying night

Pnyx the place where regular meetings of the Athenian ecclesia or public assembly of voters were held

Nicol (see nickel)

nide a group of pheasants

nighed approached

nigher (see Nayer)

nidor a strong smell, especially of cooking or burning meat or fat

niter potassium nitrate, especially occurring naturally in northern Chile

niece (see Nice)

niepa an East Indian tree whose bark contains a bitter principle similar to quassia

Nipa a monotypic genus of creeping semiaquatic palms

nipa an alcoholic beverage made from fermented sap of an Australian palm; any palm of the genus Nipa

niggard a miser

niggered divided a log by burning

nigger a steamoperated capstan for warping river steamboats over snags and shallows; any of several darkcolored insect larvae; a negro, usually taken to be offensive

nigre a darkcolored water solution of soap and impurities formed during soap manufacture

niggered (see niggard)

nighed (see nide)

nigher (see **Nayar**)

night (see **knight**)

nighthood (see **knighthood**)

nigre (see **nigger**)

nimbed having a halo around the head
nimmed stolen or filched

Nipa and **nipa** (see **niepa**)

nisse a friendly goblin or brownie of Scandanavian folklore that frequents farm buildings
nyssa a small genus of American and Asiatic trees, including the black gum and tupelo

nit (see **knit**)

nited (see **knitted**)

niter (see **nidor**)

nitrile characterized by the presence of the cynanogen group, CN
nitryl the nitro group, radical, or cation, especially in names of inorganic compounds
nytril a synthetic fiber composed chiefly of a longchain polymer of vinylidene

nitter (see **knitter**)

nix (see **nicks**)

nob (see **knob**)

nobby (see **knobby**)

nocks (see **knocks**)

nocturn one of three principal divisions of the office of matins in Roman Catholicism
nocturne a musical or artistic night piece

nodal relating to or located near a node or nodes
notal belonging to the back; dorsal

nodding (see **knotting**)

noddy (see **knotty**)

noded having or divided into thickened or swollen enlargements; nobbed

noted wellknown by reputation; provided with musical notation or score

nodous knotty
nodus a center or central point; a complication of difficulty; a hinge on the front margin of the wings of insects of the order Odonata
notice an announcement
Notus the ancient Greek personification of the south wind

noes (see **knows**)

nog a beverage made with beaten eggs, usually with alcoholic liquor; to fill in with brickwork
nogg in carpentry, a shave for shaping dowels and handles

No(h)s (see **knows**)

Nome and **nome** (see **gnome**)

nomen (see **gnomon**)

nomic (see **gnomic**)

noncereal a foodstuff prepared without grain
nonserial not arranged in spatial or temporal succession; not appearing in successive parts

None (see **known**)

none not any
nun a woman belonging to a religious order, especially under vows of poverty, chastity, and obedience

nonfeudal not founded upon or involving a lordvassal relationship
nonfutile serving a useful purpose; fruitful

nonserial (see **noncereal**)

nontidal not tidal or involving the tides, as a waterway
nontitle a nondescriptive name, title, or designation; a pseudolegal document that does not substantiate a legal claim to ownership

noon the middle of the day when the sun is on the meridian
nun the 14th letter of the Hebrew alphabet

noose a loop with a running knot that binds closer the more it is drawn; to execute by hanging

nous the highest intellect

nor (see **gnawer**)

nose (see **knows**)

nosy of a prying or inquisitive disposition; intrusive

Nozi an extinct Indian people of the Pitt river valley of northern California

not (see **knot**)

notal (see **nodal**)

note (see **knote**)

noted (see **noded**)

notice (see **nodous**)

Notus (see **nodous**)

nous (see **noose**)

now (see **nao**)

nox (see **knocks**)

Nozi (see **nosy**)

Nu and **nu** (see **gnu**)

nubbie a saffron bun

nubby having a small bunch of fibers; consisting of small or immature ears, as on corn

nubs (see **knubs**)

nuder (see **neuter**)

Nuer (see **newer**)

nuke (see **newk**)

nul (see **nal**)

null (see **nal**)

nulla a hardwood club used by Australian aborigines

nullah a watercourse that is often dry

nun (see **none** or **noon**)

nuque (see **newk**)

Nut (see **knout**)

nut (see **knut**)

Nuzi (see **newsie**)

nybble (see **nibble**)

nymphs minor divinities of nature that are represented by beautiful maidens; women of loose morals; artificial fishing flies

nymss a mongoose, especially the North African mongoose highly regarded for supposedly devouring crocodile eggs

nyssa (see **nisse**)

nytril (see **nitrile**)

Nyx (see **nicks**)

Group I

negligence - negligents
Nellie - nelly
nescience - nescients
nonadherence - nonadherents
nonassonance - nonassonants
nonexistence - nonexistents
nonresidence - nonresidents
nudest - nudist

Group I and II

nebulose   'nebyə‚lōs
Nebulous   'nebyələs

Group II

nasi   'näsē or 'nā‚sī
Nazi   'näzē

nautch   'nȯch
notch   'näch

navy   'nāvē
névé   nā'vā

nectarous   'nektərəs
Necturus   nek'tyu̇rəs

Nobelist nō'beləst
noblest 'nōb(ə)ləst

noel nō'el
nowel 'nōəl

nonpros 'nän:präs
nonprose 'nän:prōz

O

---

oak a tree or shrub of *Quercus*
oke any of three units of weight varying around 2.8 pounds and used in Bulgaria, Egypt, Greece, and Turkey

oar a long wooden pole with a broad flat blade at one end for propelling a boat
o'er the contraction of over
or a conjunction indicating an alternative or choice; either
ore a natural usually unrefined mineral that can often be mined

oat (see **haute**)

oater a horse opera, a movie or show about the frontier days in the U.S. West
Oder a major river of central Europe
odor a scent, fragrance, or aroma

obe (see **aube**)

obeyance (see **abeyance**)

Occident related to or situated in the West, as opposed to the Orient
oxidant an oxidizing agent

ocellate having minute simple eyes or eyespots
oscillate to move to and fro like a pendulum, to vibrate

ocelot a mediumsized American wildcat
osselet a bony outgrowth on the leg of a horse

octroi a tax on commodities brought into a city, especially in certain European countries; a municipal customs duty
octroy to grant or concede as a privilege

od a natural power underlying hypnotism and magnetism and held by some to reside in certain persons and things
odd unusual or peculiar

od a natural power underlying hypnotism and magnetism and held by some to reside in certain persons and things
ode a lyric poem
owed was obligated to pay; was indebted to

odal an estate owned by Scandinavian individuals or families
odyl a force or natural power formerly held by some to reside in certain individuals and things, and to underlie hypnotism and magnetism

odd (see **od**)

odder (see **attar**)

odds the difference favoring one of two opposed things
ods forces or supernatural powers

ode (see **od**)

Oder (see **oater**)

odeum a contemporary theater or music hall
odium hatred and condemnation often marked by loathing or contempt

odor (see **oater**)

ods (see **odds**)

odyl (see **odal**)

oe (see **eau**)

o'er (see **oar**)

offal (see **awful**)

offed moved away from shore or started out to sea; departed or went away

oft often (by shortening), used chiefly in compound adjectives

oh (see **eau**)

OK or **okay** to approve, authorize, or sanction; all right

oke an alcoholic liquor distilled from ti or taro root

oke (see **oak**)

oleo oleomargarine, a butter substitute (by shortening)

olio a miscellaneous mixture of hodge-podge

olive the oblong or ovoid drupaceous fruit that is eaten as a pickle or relish

ollav(e) a learned man in ancient Ireland

ombre (see **hombre**)

omission (see **emission**)

omit (see **emit**)

on (see **awn**)

once one time and no more

wants desires or wishes; suffers from a lack of

wonts customs or habits; has the habit or custom of doing something

one a single unit; the first whole number between zero and two

won gained victory, achieved, prevailed, or succeeded

oner a heavy blow with a fist (slang)

owner a person who has legal or rightful title to something

oohs expressions of amazement, satisfaction, or excitement

ooze soft mud or slime typically in the bed of a river or estuary; to pass slowly or in small amounts through the pores or small openings of a body

whos what persons

who's the contraction of who is, who was, or who has

whose relating to what person(s)

oppose (see **appose**)

oppositive (see **appositive**)

oppressed (see **appressed**)

or (see **oar**)

oracle (see **auricle**)

oral (see **aural**)

orc a cetacean that is widely distributed in the seas of the northern hemisphere; a gampus

orch (or **ork**) an orchestra or orchestration (by shortening)

ordinance an authoritative decree or directive; a public enactment

ordnance military supples

ordinance an authoritative decree or directive; a public enactment

ordonnance an arrangement of a composition's parts with respect to one another and the whole

ordnance (see **ordinance**)

ordonnance (see **ordinance**)

ore (see **oar**)

Oregon a state in northwestern continental U.S.

origan any of various aromatic mints, as wild marjoram

oriel a large bay window

oriole a colorful American bird

origan (see **Oregon**)

orinthorhynchous having a beak like that of a bird

Orinthorhynchus a genus of egg-laying mammals

orinthorhynchus the platypus, a small flat-footed aquatic mammal

oriole (see **aureole** and **oriel**)

orion (see **Arion**)

orle (see **aural**)

orris (see **aurous**)

<u>os</u> an esker, a long narrow often sinuous ridge or mound of sand, gravel, and boulders
ose glycose, a simple sugar

oscillate (see **ocellate**)

ose (see **os**)

osselet (see **ocelot**)

Ossetic (see **acetic**)

Ostrea (see **Austria**)

ostria (see **Austria**)

Ostrya (see **Austria**)

Otis a genus of typical bustards, including the great bustard
Otus a genus of rather smalleared owls

otter (see **attar**)

Otus (see **Otis**)

ouf an expression of discomfort, aversion, or impatience
ouph an elf

ought (see **aught**)

oui yes, in French
we a group including me
wee very small
whee an expression of delight or general exuberance

oui-oui a French person, often used derisively
wee-wee to urinate

ouph (see **ouf**)

our (see **Aor** and **are**)

outcast regarded with contempt or despised; exiled from one's domicile or country
outcaste a person who has been ejected from his/her caste for violating its customs or rules

outlimb an extremity of the body

outlimn to represent or delineate in sharpness of detail above some norm or another person's performance

outpraise to exceed or surpass in commending or applauding
outprays surpasses in entreating, imploring or praying

outright completely; instantaneously
outwrite to surpass in ability to write

outrode traversed on an animal or vehicle better than someone else
outrowed propelled a boat by oars better than another person or group

outsea an open part of a sea or ocean
outsee to surpass in power of vision or insight

outside in the open air; situated outside a particular place
outsighed exceeded another person's grieving or lamenting

outsighs exceeds another person's grieving or sorrowing
outsize a size larger than standard

outsole the exterior or outside sole of a boot or shoe
outsoul a spirit or intelligence exterior to man

outturn an amount of something produced; yield
out-turn a moving curling stone which is rotating counter clockwise

outwrite (see **outright**)

ovendry dried at a temperature at or above 100°–110° centigrade
oven-dry to make free or relatively free of water or liquid in a heated enclosure for baking or roasting

overbilled charged more than the full amount
overbuild to build beyond actual requirements; to supply with buildings in excess of demand

overchute an overhead flume
overshoot to pass swiftly beyond or ahead of; to overstate a case or point

overdo to do too much or in excess
overdue delayed; unpaid; more than ripe

overflour to sprinkle with excess flour
overflower to cover over with flowers; to put forth flowers beyond strength or wellbeing

overhigher exceedingly taller or more above
overhire to employ more personnel than necessary to accomplish a task

overite a mineral consisting of hydrous basic phosphate of aliminum and calcium
overwrite to produce words or symbols on paper in too literary, diffuse, or labored style

overlade to load with too great a burden
overlaid superimposed; covered

overmeddled interferred excessively without right or propriety
overmettled exhibited qualities of courage or ardor exceeding those required by a given situation

overpaid compensated, rewarded, or paid beyond what was due
overpayed allowed an excessive amount of rope or line to run out

overpassed managed to get through; surmounted
overpast ended or over

overpayed (see **overpaid**)

overseas beyond or across oceans or seas
oversees supervises; looks down on

oversew to sew books by a machine that simulates hand overcasting; to top-sew
oversow to plant or scatter too much seed

overshoot (see **overchute**)

oversow (see **oversew**)

overstaid overly sober, sedate, or serious
overstayed remained beyond the time or limits of

overtaught instructed beyond the point of proficiency
overtaut tightened or stretched excessively

overwrite (see **overite**)

owe (see **eau**)

owed (see **od**)

owl (see **aoul**)

own (see **aune**)

owner (see **oner**)

ox (see **Akhs**)

oxen adult castrated males of domestic bovine usually used as draft animals
oxin a crystalline phenolic base that is used in analysis
oxyn a solid product (as linoxyn) formed when a drying oil is oxidized

ox-eyed having oxlike eyes
oxhide the outer skin of an ox
oxide a binary compound of oxygen with an element

oxidant (see **Occident**)

oxide (see **oxeyed**)

oxin (see **oxen**)

oxyn (see **oxen**)

Group I

obedience - obedients
obsequence - obsequents
occupance - occupants
occurrence - occurrents
omnipotence - omnipotents
omniscience - omniscients
operance - operants
ordinance - ordinants

Group II

obdurate   'äbdərāt
obturate   'äbtə,rāt

obliger   ə'blījər
obligor   'äblə,gȯr

Octans   'äk,tanz
octanes   'äk,tānz

ohm   'ōm
om   'ȯm

oho   ō'hō
oo   'ō,ō

OK   ō:kā
oke   'okā

orchestral   ȯr'kestrəl
orchestrelle   ȯrkə'strel

origin   'ȯrəjən
orogen   'ōrəjən

osteal   'ästēəl
ostiole   'ästē,ōl

ostracean   ä'strāshən
ostracion   ä'strashē,än

overate   ōvər,āt
overrate   ōvər,rāt

oxine   'ak,sən
oxyn   'aksən

P

pa   father
pah   an expression of disdain, contempt,
   or disgust
pas   dance step(s) forming a pattern or
   figure

pa   father
paw   a quadruped's foot; to touch clumsily
   or rudely

paar   a depression produced by crustal
   blocks moving apart
par   a common level or value
parr   a young salmon

pace   proceed with a slow or measured
   step; to regulate the speed of
pes   a part resembling a foot

paced   went with a slow or measured step;
   regulated the speed of
paste   a glue or cement; a dough used for
   pastry crust

packed   stowed in a container; carried
pact   a treaty or agreement

packs   bundles of goods; stows in a container; carries
PACS   political action committees, cor-
   porations, or unions that distribute
   money to political candidates (an
   acronym)
pacs   laced heelless sheepskin or felt shoes
   worn inside boots or over shoes in cold
   weather
pacts   treaties or agreements
Paks   individuals from Pakistan (sometimes regarded as offensive)
Pax   a period characterized by the absence
   of major wars
pax   a tablet or board decorated with a
   figure of Christ or a religious person

pact   (see **packed**)

pacts   (see **packs**)

padded   lined, covered, or stuffed with
   material that serves to cushion, protect,
   fill out, or heighten
patted   stroked or tapped gently with the
   hand to soothe, caress, or show approval

padder a person or machine that makes sheets of paper into pads, or places ordered tobacco leaves in boxes

patter to repeat in a rapid manner; a quick succession of slight sounds; a relatively meaningless chatter

paddle a rather short light wooden, metal, or plastic pole with a broad fairly flat blade at one end that is used to propel and stop a canoe or other watercraft

padle a soft thick clumsy marine fish of both coasts of the northern North Atlantic ocean, also called lump fish

paddlefoot a member of the airforce that lacks distinctive rating and is usually occupied with ground duties

paddle-foot a cottontail rabbit

paddy a heavily irrigated piece of land for growing rice

patty a small pie or pasty

paty in heraldry, a cross with the ends splayed or spread out

padle (see **paddle**)

paean a joyously exultant song or hymn

paeon a metrical foot of four syllables with one long or stressed, and three short or unstressed syllables

peon a person in a position of subordination or servility

paeon (see **paean**)

pah (see **pa**)

paid received compensation; discharged an obligation

pate the top of the head

payed allowed a rope or line to run out

pail a bucket

pale deficient in color or intensity; pallid or wan

pain physical or mental discomfort or agony

pane a window or door section

peine punishment (shortening of **peine forte et dure** or hard punishment)

paeon (see **paean**)

pair a set of two items

pare to trim off or peel

pear a fleshy oblong pome fruit

pairer a person who matches like or related articles

parer a mechanical device for peeling fruits and vegatables

pairle an heraldic ordinary in the form of a Y extending to the upper corners and base of the field

parol an oral declaration or statement

parrel a rope loop or sliding collar by which a yard or spar is held to a mast

pairle an heraldic ordinary in the form of a Y extending to the upper corners and base of the field

peril exposure to the risk of being injured, destroyed, or lost

pais in law, the country

pay to discharge an obligation

pe the 17th letter of the Hebrew alphabet

Paks (see **packs**)

palace the official residence of a sovereign

pallas loose outer women's garments formed by wrapping or draping a large square of cloth

palar resembling a stake

paler more deficient in color or intensity

palate the roof of the mouth

palette a thin oval board with a thumbhole on which a painter lays and mixes pigments

pallet a strawfilled mattress; a portable platform for storing materials

pallette a usually rounded plate at the armpit of a suit of armor

Palau the Austronesian language of the Palau islands

pilaf rice cooked in stock and usually combined with meat and vegetables

pale (see **pail**)

paleing soldering
paling the act of building a fence or enclosing with pickets

palely with an effect of dimness or pallor
paly in heraldry, divided into four or more equal parts by perpendicular lines

paler (see **palar**)

palette (see **palate**)

Pali an Indic language found in the Buddhist canon
pali an Indian timber tree; a steep slope in Hawaii
palli a member of a Sudra caste of field laborers

paling (see **paleing**)

pall to lose strength, vigor, or effectiveness
pawl a small doublepoled tent with steep sloping sides
pol a politician (slang)
poll a college or university degree without honors

pallae loose outer garments worn by women in ancient Rome
pally informally intimate
polly a poll parrot
poly a polymorphonuclear leukocyte (by shortening)

pallar a member of a depressed caste in India
pallor a wan or blanched appearance

pallas (see **palace**)

palled covered with a cloak or drape
pawled checked by a pivoted tongue or sliding bolt

pallet (see **palate**)

pallette (see **palate**)

palli (see **Pali**)

pall-mall a 17th century European game resembling croquet
pell-mell mingled confusion or disorder; indiscriminately

pallor (see **pallar**)

pally (see **pallae**)

palm the somewhat concave part of the human hand between the bases of the fingers and the wrist; a plant of the family *Palmae*
pom a pomeranian dog; an ornamental ball or tuft on clothing; the characteristic noise of a small caliber cannon
pomme in heraldry, a rounded green area

palmar involving the palm of the hand
palmer a person wearing two crossed palm leaves to denote having made a pilgrimage to the Holy Land

paly (see **palely**)

pament a tile or brick used to pave malthouse floors
payment something given or received to discharge a debt or obligation

pampas extensive generally grass-covered plains of temperate South America east of the Andes
pompous ornately showy and pretentiously dignified

pamper to treat with excessive care and attention
pampre an ornament of vine leaves and grapes

Pan a genus of anthropoid apes including the chimpanzee
pan a shallow container; to rotate a camera in any direction; to wash earth deposits in search of precious metal
panne a finish for velvet or satin

pan a betel palm leaf; a card game resembling rummy
paon a greenish blue color called peacock blue
pawn to deposit something with another as collateral for a loan; the least powerful chess piece
pon upon (by shortening)

pandit a Brahman expert in Sanskrit and in the science, laws, and religion of the Hindus

pundit a person who announces judgments, opinions, or conclusions in an authoritative manner

pane (see **pain**)

panel a group of persons selected for some service or activity; a distinct part of a surface, as a fender or door

pannel a saddle blanket

paniele a compound racemose influorescence

panniele the brainpan or skull

panne (see **pan**)

pannel (see **panel**)

panniele (see **paniele**)

pans betel palm leaves

pawns the least powerful chess pieces

pons a broad mass of chiefly transverse nerve fibers conspicuous on the ventral surface of the brain

paon (see **pan**)

pap soft pulpy food for infants or invalids

pape the painted bunting, a brightly colored finch of the southern part of the U.S.

papagallo a large brightly colored food fish related to the amberfishes and found from northern California to Peru

papagayo a violet often tornadic northerly wind occurring along the Pacific coast of Central America

pape (see **pap**)

pape the painted bunting, a brightly colored finch of the southern part of the U.S.

pop to strike or knock sharply

pappi appendages or tufts of appendages crowning the ovary or fruit in various seed plants

pappy pulpy, soft, or succulent

par (see **paar**)

Para native rubber obtained from South American trees

para of, relating to, or being a diatomic molecule in which the nuclei of the atoms spin in opposite directions

parra any of several wading birds that chiefly frequent coastal freshwater marshes and ponds in warm regions

parachute the wing membrane of a mammal or reptile

parashoot to attack an invading parachutist by shooting

parade (in rapid speech) a ceremonial formation of troops; to march ceremoniously; a formal display

prayed entreated or implored; made application to

preyed made raids for the sake of booty

parados a bank of earth behind a fortification trench

parodos the first choral passage in an ancient Greek drama recited or sung as the chorus enters the orchestra

paragnathous having both mandibles of equal length with the tips meeting, especially of a bird

paragnathus one of the paired lobes of the hypopharynx in various insects

paragon a model of excellence or perfection

perigon an angle obtained by rotating a half line in the same plane once around the point from which it extends

paraphrase a restatement of a work or section giving the meaning in another form, usually for clearer and fuller exposition

periphrase the use of a negative, passive, or inverted construction in place of a positive, active, or normal construction

parashoot (see **parachute**)

parasite an organism living in or on another organism; a sycophant or toady

Parisite a native of Paris, France

parisite a mineral consisting of a carbonate and flouride of calcium, cerium, and lanthanum

parasite an organism living in or on another organism; a sycophant or toady

pericyte an adventitious cell of connective tissue about capillaries

pard a partner or chum (slang)

parred placed on an equal footing or par; made a golf score equal to par

pardoner a person who forgives or excuses

partner an associate or colleague

pare (see **pair**)

parer (see **pairer**)

Paridae a large family of passerine birds that includes the titmice

parity close equivalence or likeness

parody a literary style characterized by reproducing stylistic peculiarities of a work for comic effect or ridicule

parroty like or of the nature of a zygodactyl bird (parrot)

Paris a small genus of Eurasian herbs; the capital of France

parous having produced offspring

Parus a type genus comprising common titmice

parish an ecclesiastical area committed to one pastor

perish to die; to pass away completely; to become destroyed or ruined

Parisite or **parisite** (see **parasite**)

parity (see **Paridae**)

parlay to transform into something of greater value

parley a discussion or discourse; a conference held to discuss points in dispute

parodic having the character of parody or caricature

parotic adjacent to the ear

parodos (see **parados**)

parody (see **Paridae**)

parol (see **pairle**)

parol an oral declaration or statement

parole a conditional and revocable release of a prisoner serving an unexpired sentence

pyrrole a colorless toxic liquid heterocyclic compound

parolee a prisoner serving an unexpired sentence who is conditionally and revocably released

paroli a betting system in which a bettor leaves staked money and its winnings as a further stake

parotic (see **parodic**)

parous (see **Paris**)

parr (see **paar**)

parra (see **Para**)

parred (see **pard**)

parrel (see **pairle**)

parrot a zygodactyl (two toes in front and two behind) bird

perit a unit of weight equal to $\frac{1}{20}$ droit, formerly used by coiners of money

parroty (see **Paridae**)

parrs young salmon

pars makes a golf score equal to par

parse to divide speech into component parts and describe them grammatically; to analyze critically

parry to turn aside or otherwise avert; to dodge

perry a fermented liquor made from pears

pars (see **parrs**)

parse (see **parrs**)

parshall a device for measuring flow in conduits

partial favorably disposed toward someone or something

Parthenopean of or belonging to Naples, especially to the short-lived republic established there in 1799 by French revolutionary forces

Parthenopian a crab of the genus *Parthenope*

parti the basic concept of an architectural design; a person eligible to enter into marriage and viewed with regard to his/her advantages or disadvantages as a marriage partner for a prospective mate

party persons forming a constituency; a social gathering for entertainment or pleasure

partial (see **parshall**)

partner (see **pardoner**)

party (see **parti**)

Parus (see **Paris**)

pas (see **pa**)

pase a maneuver by a bullfighter with the cape to gain the bull's attention

passé a ballet movement in which one leg passes behind or in front of the other; past one's prime; no longer fashionable

passable able to be crossed, traveled, or passed on; able to pass inspection

passible capable of feeling or suffering

passé (see **pase**)

passed proceeded; went by

past belonging to a former time; gone by

passes proceeds along a specified route or beyond a particular point

passus a division or part of a narrative or poem

passible (see **passable**)

passus (see **passes**)

past (see **passed**)

paste (see **paced**)

pastiche a musical composition or piece of writing made up of selections from different works

postiche false hair or a toupee

pastie small round covering for a woman's nipples

pasty a meat pie or turnover; pallid and unhealthy in appearance; sickly

pat to stroke or tap gently with the hand

patte a decorative band, strap, or belt to fasten garments

patchily in spots, bits, or pieces

pa(t)chouli an East Indian shrubby mint that yields a fragrant oil

pate (see **paid**)

pâte a plastic material for pottery

pot a deep rounded container; a common resource or fund; marijuana (slang)

pott a size of paper about 13" × 16" used in printing

patens metal plates used for bread in the eucharistic service; thin metal disks

patents government grants of a monopoly right to inventors or discoverers of new processes or devices

pattens shoes, often with devices to elevate the foot

Pattons a type of tanks named after General George S. Patton

Pater a recital of the Lord's Prayer in any language except Latin

pater the socially acknowledged or legal father among some primitive people

potter a person who makes clayware or earthenware

patience a capacity to endure pain, adversity, or evil with fortitude; forbearance

patients sick persons awaiting treatment

patte (see **pat**)

patted (see **padded**)

pattens (see **patens**)

patter (see **padder**)

Pattons (see **patens**)

patty (see **paddy**)

paty (see **paddy**)

pau in Hawaii, completed, consumed, or finished

pow a sound of a blow or explosion

pause a temporary stop, hesitation, or respite

paws a quadruped's feet; touches clumsily or rudely

paw (see **pa**)

pawl (see **pall**)

pawled (see **palled**)

pawn (see **pan**)

pawned deposited something with another as collateral for a loan

pond a small body of water

pawns (see **pans**)

paws (see **pause**)

Pax and **pax** (see **packs**)

Pax a period characterized by the absence of major wars

pax a tablet or board decorated with a figure of Christ or a religious person

pocks holes or pits

pox a virus disease characterized by pustules or eruptions; a disease of sweet potatoes

pay (see **pais**)

Paya an Indian people of northern Honduras

pia the delicate and highly vascular membrane of connective tissue investing the brain and spinal cord

pyre a combustible heap usually of wood for burning a dead body as a funeral rite

payed (see **paid**)

payment (see **pament**)

PC's personal computers (by shortening)

Pisces the 12th sign of the zodiac; a variously limited class of vertebrates comprising all the fishes

pe (see **pais**)

peace freedom from civil clamor, confusion, and war; serenity of spirit

piece a fragment or part of a whole

peaceable tranquil, quiet, or undisturbed

pieceable capable of being repaired or extended

peaced became quiet or still

pieced repaired, renewed, or completed by adding component parts or pieces

piste a beaten track or trail made by an animal; a hard packed ski trail

peachy unusually fine; resembling a peach

pichi a small armadillo of southern South America

peak a sharp or pointed end; the top of a hill or mountain; to grow thin or look sickly

peek to look slyly or furtively; to peep

peke a pekingese dog

pique to stimulate by wounding pride, or inciting jealousy or rivalry

peaky pointed or sharp; having peaks; sickly

piki maize bread baked in thin sheets by Indians of the southwestern U.S.

peal to ring a bell or chime

peel to strip off an outer layer; to pare

piel an iron wedge for boring stones

pean an heraldic fur of gold ermine spots on a black field

peen the formed head of a hammer opposite the face; to flatten by hammering

pien the sharp edge or salient angle formed by the meeting of two surfaces

pear (see **pair**)

pearl a dense concretion of calcium carbonate formed around a small foreign particle in various mollusks

perle a soft gelatin capsule enclosing volatile or unpleasant tasting liquids

purl a type of knitting stitch

pearler a person who dives for the dense

concretions that are formed in various mollusks

purler a worker who finishes raw edges of knitted garments with decorative stitching

pearlite a lamellar mixture of ferrite and cementite occurring in steel and iron

perlite volcanic glass with a concentric shelly structure

peas(e) small round edible vegetables produced by a variable annual leguminous vine

pees urinates

pes a part resembling a foot; the ground bass of a canon

peat partially carbonized vegetable matter

pete a metal box sometimes built into a wall or vault to protect valuables against fire or theft (slang)

peavey a stout lever equipped with a sharp spike that is used in lumbering

peavie a newly enlisted person in the Civilian Conservation Corps (slang)

peckie a semi-palmated and other small sandpipers

pecky tedious and intricate, requiring patience and attention to detail

pecks U.S. units of dry capacity equal to 537.605 cubic inches; makes holes in a material with quick movements of the beak

pecs pectoral muscles (slang)

pecky (see **peckie**)

pecs (see **pecks**)

pecten an animal's body part resembling a comb

pectin a colorless amorphous methylated pectic substance used as an ingredient of fruit jellies

pectous resembling the consistency of jelly

pectus a bird's breast

pedal a footactivated lever

peddle to travel about with wares for sale

petal a leafshaped part of a flower

pedaler a person who moves a part or lever with the foot

peddler a person who sells goods in different places

peddle (see **pedal**)

peddler (see **pedaler**)

peek (see **peak**)

peeking looking slyly or furtively; peeping

Peking capital of China (Beijing since 1949)

peel (see **peal**)

Peelite one of a group of 19th century British Tories supporting Peel in the repeal of the Corn Laws

pelite a rock composed of fine particles of clay or mud

peen (see **pean**)

peened drew, bent, or flattened by hammering with the hammer head opposite the face

piend a sharp edge formed by the meeting of two surfaces, as in moldings

peepee to urinate

pee-pee a call to chickens and turkeys

pipi a bivalve mollusk

peer a person of equal standing; to look intently or curiously

pier a structure built on piles into water as a landing place or pleasure resort

Pierre the capital of South Dakota

pir a Muslim saint or spiritual guide

pirr a gust of wind or a flurry

pyr a unit light intensity equal to .954 candles

peerage nobility

pierage the charge for using a wharf for freight handling or ship dockage

peery inquisitive or suspicious

peri a supernatural being, as a fairy or elf

pees (see **peas[e]**)

peewee a small, usually cheap marble
pee-wee a bluet, a delicate plant of the U.S.
pe(e)wee any of various small alivaceous flycatchers

peine (see **pain**)

peke (see **peak**)

Peking (see **peeking**)

pekoe a tea made from the first three leaves on the spray
picot one of the small ornamental loops forming the edging on ribbon or lace

pelisse a long cloak or coat made of, or trimmed or lined with fur
police a government unit concerned with maintaining public order and safety

pelite (see **Peelite**)

pell-mell (see **pall-mall**)

pelorus a navigational instrument resembling a mariner's compass without magnetic needles and having two sight vanes
pylorus the opening in a vertebrate from the stomach into the intestine

penal prescribing, enacting, or threatening punishment
penile relating to the penis

penance sorry or contrition for sin; repentance
pennants nautical flags usually tapering to a point

pence a former British coin representing one penny
pents penthouses or smaller structures joined to a building

pencil an implement for writing, drawing, or marking; a small narrow flag or streamer borne by a man-at-arms in late medieval or Renaissance times
pensile suspended from above

pend to be undecided or unsettled
penned placed in an enclosure to prevent straying; recorded in writing

penni a unit of value Finland equal to one hundreth markka
penny a cent of the United States or Canada; a trivial amount

penetrance the ability of a gene to express its specific effect in the organism of which it is a part
penetrants things that pass into or through, or are capable of doing so

penile (see **penal**)

pennants (see **penance**)

penned (see **pend**)

penny (see **penni**)

pensile (see **pencil**)

pentamerous divided into or consisting or five parts
Pentamerus a genus comprising Paleozoic brachiopods

pents (see **pence**)

peon (see **paean**)

people human beings
pipal a fig tree of India remarkable for its great size and longevity

pepless without energy or spirit
Peplis a genus of chiefly aquatic herbs
peplos a garment worn by women of ancient Greece

per by means of; through
pirr to blow with a whiz; to speed along
purr a cat's low vibrating murmur

perches bird roosts; small fresh water spiny-finned American fish
purchase to buy merchandise by payment of money or its equivalent; a position from which to exert power or leverage

peri (see **peery**)

pericyte (see **parasite**)

perigon (see **paragon**)

peril (see **pairle**)

periodic occurring at regular intervals
periotic situated around the ear

periphrase (see **paraphrase**)

perish (see **parish**)

perit (see **parrot**)

perjury a deliberate giving of false testimony
purgery the part of a sugarhouse where molasses is drained from sugar

perle (see **pearl**)

perlite (see **pearlite**)

permeance the reciprocal of magnetic reluctance
permeants animal influents ranging widely within an ecological community of which they are a part

pern a honey buzzard
pirn bobbins on which filling yarn for weaving is wound before insertion into the shuttle

perpetuance perpetuation or perpetuity
perpetuants in mathematics, a semi variant which cannot be expressed rationally in terms of other semivariants

perry (see **parry**)

perse a dark grayish blue color
purse a receptacle used to carry money and small objects

pertinence relevance
pertinents things belonging to an estate that pass to a new owner of the estate
purtenance the heart, liver, and lungs of an animal

pervade to spread throughout
purveyed obtained or supplied for use; provided

pes (see **pace** and **peas[e]**)

petal (see **pedal**)

pete (see **peat**)

petrel a sea bird
petrol gasoline; petroleum

petti a woman's underskirt that is full and often trimmed and ruffled and of decorative fabric; a half slip
petty minor or subordinate

Peul a member of a Sudanese people of African Negroid stock and Mediterranean Caucasoid admixture
pool a small body of water
poule a prostitute; the third figure of a quadrille

pew a long-handled hooked prong for pitching fish (also pugh)
piu in music, more of something

phallaceous (see **fallacious**)

phanar (see **fanner**)

pharaoh (see **faro**)

phare (see **fair**)

pharming (see **farming**)

phase (see **fays**)

phaser a person who introduces or carries out an activity in stages
phasor a vector whose angle from the polar axis to the radius vector represents a phase or phase difference

phasis (see **faces**)

phasor (see **phaser**)

phenetic relating to classificatory systems and procedures that are based on overall similarity without regard to the evolutionary history of the organisms involved
phonetic representing the sounds and other phenomena, as stress and pitch of speech

phenology a branch of science concerned with relationships between climate and periodic biological phenomena
phonology the science of speech sounds

phenyl (see **fennel**)

phew (see **few**)

phi (see fie)

phial (see faille)

Philander and philander (see filander)

Philippines (see fillipeens)

Philly (see filly)

philogeny the racial history of a specified kind of organism
philogyny fondness for women

philopena (see Filipena)

philter (see filter)

phis (see fees)

phisher (see fisher)

phit (see fit)

phiz (see fizz)

phlegm (see Flem)

Phlox or phlox (see flocks)

phocal (see focal)

phon (see faun)

phonetic (see phenetic)

phono (see fono)

phonology (see phenology)

phoo (see fu)

phose (see foes)

phosphene a luminous impression due to excitation of the retina of the eye by some cause other than the impingement of light rays
phosphine a colorless very poisonous gaseous compound that may ignite spontaneously when mixed with air or oxygen

photogen a light oil obtained by distilling bituminous shale, coal, or peat
photogene an afterimage or retinal impression

phrase (see fraise)

phraser (see fraser)

phrator (see frater)

phratry (see fratry)

phreak (see freak)

phthalic derived from phthalic acid
thallic relating to or containing thallium

phthalin any of a group of colorless compounds obtained by reduction of the phthaleins
thalline a crystalline base derived from quinoline; consisting of or constituting a plant body that is characteristic of the thallophytes

phthiocol a yellow crystalline quinone with vitamin K activity
thiokol any of a series of commercially produced polysulfide rubbers, closely related liquid polymers, or water-dispersed lattices

phyla (see fila)

phylar (see filar)

phyllade (see filleted)

phylliform (see filiform)

phyllin a complex magnesium derivative of a porphyrin or phorbin
phylline leaflike

phylum (see filum)

physocarpous having bladdery fruit
Physocarpus a genus of chiefly North American shrubs

pi the ratio of a circle's circumference to its diameter (3.1416); spilled or mixed type; the 16th letter of the Greek alphabet
pie meat or fruit baked in, on, or under dough

pia (see Paya)

pial related to the membranous connective tissues investing the brain and spinal cord
pile things heaped together; a cylinder or slender rod driven into the ground to support a vertical load

Pica a genus containing magpies

pica a typesetting unit equal to 1/6 inch

pika a small lagomorph mammal inhabiting rocky parts of high mountains; a cony

piced prodded or thrust, say at a bull with a picador's lance

picked selected as being the best obtainable or best for the purpose

Pict one of a possibly non–Celtic people once occupying Great Britain

pich a West Indian shrub or small tree

pitch any of various black or dark-colored viscous semisolid to solid substances or residues in the distillation of tars; to throw or cast

pichi (see **peachy**)

picine of or relating to woodpeckers

piscine relating to or having the characteristics of fish

picked (see **piced**)

pickel an ice ax

pickle a brine or vinegar for preserving or corning fish, meat, or other foodstuffs

picul any of various weights used in China and southeast Asia

pickerel any of several fishes of the genus Esox

picryl the univalent radical derived from picric acid by removing the hydroxyl group

picketer a person posted by a labor organization at an approach to the place of work

picqueter a person who bunches artificial flowers

picketty choppy, as the sea

pickety fussy or hypocritical

pickle (see **pickel**)

picks chooses or selects; heavy curved metal tools with both ends pointed

pics photographs or motion pictures

Picts members of a possibly non–Celtic people who once occupied Great Britain

pix photographs or motion pictures

pyx an ecclesiastical container holding the reserved sacrament on the altar

picnic an outing with food eaten in the open

pyknic characterized by short stature, broad girth, and powerful muscles

picot (see **pekoe**)

picqueter (see **picketer**)

picryl (see **pickerel**)

pics (see **picks**)

Pict (see **piced**)

Picts (see **picks**)

picul (see **pickel**)

pie (see **pi**)

piece (see **peace**)

pieceable (see **peaceable**)

pieced (see **peaced**)

piel (see **peal**)

pien (see **pean**)

piend (see **peened**)

pier (see **peer**)

pierage (see **peerage**)

Pierre (see **peer**)

pierrot a standard comic character of old French pantomime, usually with whitened face and loose white clothes

Piro a Tanoan people of Pueblo Indians in central New Mexico and the state of Chihuahua, Mexico

pignon the nutlike seed of the European stone pine

pinion the distal part of a bird's wing; to disable or restrain by binding the arms; a gear

piñon any of various low-growing nut pines

pika (see **Pica**)

piki (see peaky)

Pila the type genus of the family Pilidae comprising the apple and dextral snails

pila heavy javelins of a Roman foot solider

pyla the opening from the third ventricle into the aqueduct of Sylvius in higher vertebrates

pilaf (see Palau)

pilaf rice cooked in stock and usually combined with meat and vegetables

pillow a head support while resting or sleeping

pilar hairy

piler a person that heaps things up

pylar of or relating to an opening on either side from the cavity of the optic lobe

pile (see pial)

pileous hairy

pileus an umbrellashaped upper cap of many fungi; a cloud resembling a cap that sometimes appears above and partially obscures the bulging top of a cumulus cloud

piler (see pilar)

pileus (see pileous)

piley having a strong development of hair

pily divided into a wedge-shaped heraldic charge

piline hairy

pylon a tower for supporting either end of a wire

pillary resembling or formed into a pillar

pillory a means by which to expose or hold up a person to public ridicule

pillow (see pilaf)

pily (see piley)

pimento the wood of the allspice tree; a vivid red color

pimiento a thick-fleshed sweet pepper

used as a stuffing for olives and as a source of paprika

pincer one of the central incisors of a horse or other equine

pincher one that presses hard between the ends of the finger and thumb

pinion (see pignon)

pinkie a rabbit bandicoot

pinky tinged with pink color

pinnulate having one or more secondary branches of a plumelike organ

pinulate being or having the form of a pentact sponge spicule

piñon (see pignon)

pintoes toes that turn inward

pintos chronic skin diseases endemic in tropical America

pinulate (see pinnulate)

pipal (see people)

pipi (see peepee)

pique (see peak)

piqué a durable ribbed cotton, rayon, or silk clothing fabric; inlaid, as a knife handle; a ballet movement; a glove seam

piquet a twohanded card game

pir (see peer)

pirn (see pern)

Piro (see pierrot)

pirr (see peer and per)

piscan of or relating to fishes

piskun a steep cliff used by American Indians for driving buffalo to their slaughter

Pisces (see PC's)

piscine (see picine)

pishpash an India rice broth containing bits of meat

pishposh nonsense

piskun (see **piscan**)

piste (see **peaced**)

pistil a seed plant's ovulebearing organ
pistol a short firearm fired with one hand, as a revolver

pitch (see **pich**)

pitchi a large shallow elongated wooden receptacle much used by Australian aborigines as a container for food and drink
pitchy coated, smeared, or sticky with pitch

pitiless without mercy or compassion
Pitylus a genus of Central and South American grosbeak birds

piu (see **pew**)

pix (see **picks**)

place a space or area; a specific portion of a surface; to put into, set, or position
plaice a European flounder fish

plack a small billon coin of Scotland
plaque a film of mucus harboring bacteria on a tooth; an inscribed usually metal tablet placed on a building or post

plaice (see **place**)

plain unadorned or simple; an extensive area of level or rolling countryside
plane to make smooth or even; a tree of the genus Platanus; to soar on wings or skim across water

plainer more unadorned or simpler
planar having a flat two-dimensional quality
planer a power tool for surfacing wood

plaining the process of freeing molten glass of bubbles usually with the addition of certain chemical agents
planing making smooth or even

Plains of or belonging to North American Indians of the Great Plains or to their culture
plains extensive areas of level or rolling countryside
planes makes smooth or even; soars on

wings or skims across water; trees of the genus Platanus

plainsman an inhabitant of an extensive area of relatively flat land
planesman a person who operates the bow and/or stern horizontal rudders on a submarine

plait to interweave strands of yarn, fabric, or locks of hair
plat a detailed map of an area; a small tract of land
Platt a colloquial language of northern Germany comprising several Low German dialects
Platte a major river flowing through central Nebraska
platte a resistant knob of rock in a glacial valley or rising in the midst of a glacier

plait to interweave strands of yarn, fabric, or locks of hair
plate a piece of domestic hollowware, as a dish; a flat sheet or metal
Platt a colloquial language of northern Germany comprising several Low German dialects

played engaged in recreational activity or frolicked

plait a braid of hair or straw
pleat a fold of cloth

plaiter a person or machine that interweaves strands of yarn, fabric, or locks of hair
plater a worker that plates metal objects with gold or silver; an inferior race horse

plaiter a person or machine that interweaves strands of yarn, fabric, or locks of hair
platter a large shallow plate; a phonograph record

planar (see **plainer**)

plane (see **plain**)

planer (see **plainer**)

planes (see **Plains**)

planesman (see **plainsman**)

planing (see **plaining**)

plantar related to the sole of the foot

planter a person who cultivates plants; a container in which plants are grown; a farmer

plaque (see **plack**)

plastic pliable, pliant, or adaptable

plastique a technique of statuesque posing in dancing

plat (see **plait**)

platan a treen of the genus Platanus

platen a flat plate usually designed to press against something, as in a printing press

platten to flatten and make into sheets or plates of glass

plate (see **plait**)

platen (see **platan**)

plater (see **plaiter**)

Platt (see both **plait** entries)

Platte and **platte** (see **plait**)

platten (see **platan**)

platter (see **plaiter**)

played (see **plait**)

play-right an author's proprietary right of performance of a musical or dramatic composition

playwrite a person who writes plays

pleader an intercessor; a person who conducts pleas, especially in court

pleater a person that makes pleats in cloth, paper, or other material

pleas appeals or petitions

please a word to express politeness in a request; to give delight, satisfaction, or pleasure

pleat (see **plait**)

pleater (see **pleader**)

pleural related to sides of the thorax

plural more than one

plurel the aggregate resulting from categorizing or statistical analysis

pliers a small pincers with roughened jaws for holding objects or cutting wire

plyers a balance or timbers used in operating a drawbridge; persons working diligently or steadily

plodder a person who proceeds or works slowly, steadily, or unimaginatively

plotter a person or device that marks on a map or display board the positions of airplanes or ships in transit; a schemer

plots conspiracies or intrigues; small areas of ground

plotz to collapse or faint from surprise, excitement, or exhaustion (slang)

plotter (see **plodder**)

plotz (see **plots**)

plum a tree and shrub that bear globular smoothskinned fruit

plumb a small weight attached to a line to indicate vertical direction

plumber a person who installs and maintains piping and fixtures

plummer a block of material serving as a bearing plate

plumbing a natural or artificial system of tubes, conduits, or channels

plumming degradation of a silver photographic image

plummer (see **plumber**)

plumming (see **plumbing**)

plural (see **pleural**)

plurel (see **pleural**)

pluripotence in heraldry, having several flat bars across the ends of the arms in a cross

pluripotents in heraldry, having several rows of interlocking upright and inverted shortstemmed Tshaped panes

plyers (see **pliers**)

pneuma (see **neuma**)

pneumatic (see **neumatic**)

pneumatics spiritual beings held by Gnostics as belonging to the highest of the three classes into which mankind is divided; a branch of mechanics that deals with the mechanical properties of gases
pneumatiques letters or messages transmitted by compressedair dispatch

pneumatophorous having the characteristics of a submerged or exposed root that often functions as a respiratory organ of a swamp or marsh plant
Pneumatophorus a genus of small warm-water mackerels

pneumonic (see **mnemonic**)

Pnyx (see **nicks**)

Po the longest and largest river in Italy
poh an expression of contempt

poak waste (consisting of hair, lime, and oil) that arises from the preparation of skins
poke a quick thrust, jab, or dig
poque ground cone, a parasite on the roots of alder

pocks (see **Pax**)

podded assembled in a protective envelope
potted preserved in a closed jar, can, or container; drunk or inebriated

poe a predominantly glossy black New Zealand honeyeater, also called the parson bird
poi an Hawaiian food made of cooked and pounded taro root

poem a composition in verse form
pome a fleshy fruit (as an apple) with a central core of usually five seeds
pomme in heraldry, a rounded vert

pogey a package of food, candy, or other treats
pogie menhadden, a marine fish of the family *Clupeidae*; black perch, a common surf fish of the Pacific coast

poh (see **Po**)

poi (see **poe**)

pois Hawaiian food made of taro roots
poise easy composure of manner marked especially by assurance and gracious dignity

poke (see **poak**)

pokey a jail; annoyingly slow
pokie type of vitreous ware playing marble
poky spooky, scary, or eerie

pol (see **pall**)

polar related to one of the Earth's poles; diametrically opposite in nature or action
poler a person who propels a boat with a long staff or rod
poller a person who lops or trims trees; a person who asks questions in a poll or canvass

Pole a native or inhabitant of Poland
pole a long slender cylindrical piece of wood or metal
poll a voting at an election; to cut off the head, horns, or treetops

poler (see **polar**)

police (see **pelisse**)

policies definite courses or methods of action selected from among alternatives
pollices thumbs, or the inner most digit of forelimbs

poling a process used in refining some metals such as copper
polling casting ballots at an election

politic expedient or judicious; sagacious in devising or promoting a policy
politick to engage in political discussion or activity

poll (see **pall** and **Pole**)

pollan a whitefish of the Irish lakes
pollen microscopes in a seed plant

poller (see **polar**)

pollices (see **policies**)

polling (see **poling**)

pollster a person who conducts or asks questions in a poll or canvas
polster a cushion plant

polly (see **pallae**)

polster (see **pollster**)

poly (see **pallae**)

polydactylous having more than the normal number of toes or fingers
Polydactylus a genus of fishes found in warm seas

polygenist a person who accepts the doctrine that existing human races have evolved from two or more distinct ancestral types
polygynist a person that practices or advocates having more than one wife or female mate at one time

polygenous consisting of or containing many kinds of elements
polygynous having many pistils

polygynist (see **polygenist**)

polygynous (see **polygenous**)

polymathy the character or attainments of encyclopedic learning
polymythy the inclusion of several stories or plots in one narrative or dramatic work

polypous relating to or characteristic of a polyp
Polypus a genus of octopuses

pom (see **palm**)

pomace a substance resulting from crushing by grinding
pumice a porous powdered volcanic stone used for smoothing and polishing
pummice the head and entrails of a sheep or other animal

pome (see **poem**)

pomme (see **palm** or **poem**)

pommée a cross having the end of each arm terminating in a ball or disk
pommy an English immigrant recently arrived in Australia

pommel an ornamental terminal knob, as a saddle horn; a removable handle on a gymnastic horse
pummel to thump or pound

pommy (see **pommée**)

pompous (see **pampas**)

pon (see **pan**)

pon upon (by shortening)
pun a play on words

pond (see **pawned**)

ponds small bodies of water
pons a broad mass of transverse nerve fibers

pone a player on the dealer's right who cuts the cards
pony a small horse; a translation used as an aid in learning a language

pons (see **pans** and **ponds**)

pontil a solid metal rod used for fashioning hot glass
pontile appropriate for a bridge

pony (see **pone**)

poof an expression of disdain, disapproval, or contempt
pouf something inflated or insubstantial, as clothing or furniture accessories

pooh an expression of contempt, disapproval, or impatience
pugh an interjection used to express disgust or disdain

pooka a mischievous or malignant goblin specter in Irish folklore
puka a hole or tunnel, in Hawaii; either of two New Zealand trees that are sometimes epiphytic

pool (see **Peul**)

pooli a tropical African timber tree

pooly swampy; having many pools

poo-poo excrement or feces

pupu any hot or cold usually bite-size Polynesian-Hawaiian appetizer

poor lacking material possessions, destitute, or needy

pore to look searchingly; a minute opening on an animal or vegetable

pour to diffuse, discharge, or decant

poort a pass between or across mountains

port a place where ships may ride secure from storms; a harbor or haven

Porte formerly the Ottomon court; the government of the Turkish Empire

pop (see **pape**)

popery Roman Catholicism, especially its government and forms of worship

potpourri a general mixture of often disparate or unrelated materials or subject matter

populace the total number of people; the common people

populous numerous; filled to capacity; popular

Populus a genus of trees native to the Northern Hemisphere

poque (see **poak**)

pore (see **poor**)

porous full of holes; capable of absorbing moisture or permeable to liquids

porus a pit on an insect's body connected with its sense organs

porphyrin any of a group of reddish brown to purplish black metalfree usually octa-substituted derivatives of porphin

porphyrine an alkaloid obtained as a bitter amorphous powder from Australian fever bark

port (see **poort**)

Porte (see **poort**)

porus (see **porous**)

positivest most positive

positivist an adherrent of the philosophy of positivism

posthole nothing, empty space, or a nonexistent item (slang)

post-hole to walk in snow, sinking deeply with each step

postiche (see **pastiche**)

pot (see **pâte**)

potence a supporting watchwork bracket; the integrated dominance effect of a group of polygenes

potents in heraldry, rows of interlocking upright and inverted short-stemmed T-shaped panes

potpourri (see **popery**)

pott (see **pâte**)

potted (see **podded**)

potter (see **Pater**)

pouf (see **poof**)

poule (see **Peul**)

pour (see **poor**)

pouter a person that sulks; a domestic pigeon that is characterized by long legs, slender body, erect carriage, and remarkably distensible crop

powder dry pulverized earth or disintegrated matter

pow (see **pau**)

powder (see **pouter**)

pox (see **Pax**)

praise to commend, applaud, glorify, or laud

prase greenish chalcedony

prays entreats or implores

preys makes raids for booty or food

praiss a fluid extract of tobacco

press to squeeze or crowd

pram a small lightweight nearly flatbottomed boat usually with a squared-off bow

prom a formal dance given by a high school or college class

prase (see **praise**)

prau one of several usually undecked Indonesian boats propelled by sails, oars, or paddles

prow the bow of a ship

prayed (see **parade**)

prayer a person who prays; a supplicant

preyer a person, animal, organism that hunts and preys on others

prays (see **praise**)

preaccept to take or suggest taking without protest prior to the actual occurrence

preexcept to omit something prior to another event

preaffect to influence or make an impression on beforehand or in preparation of another event

preeffect to cause to come into being or accomplish prior to another occurrence

precedential having the force or character of a precedent

presidential related to a president

precession a comparatively slow gyration of the rotation axis of a spinning body about another line intersecting it so as to describe a cone

presession occurring before a session of a legislative body, committee, or group

precipitance headlong haste

precipitants agents that cause the formation of a precipitate

precision exactness or definiteness

prescission the act of detaching for purposes of thought

preeffect (see **preaffect**)

preexcept (see **preaccept**)

premier a prime minister; the first in importance or rank; a bluishwhite diamond

premiere a first performance or exhibition

preon any of various hypothetical constituents of a quark or a lepton that determines its particular character

prion an infectous agent about 100 times smaller than a normal virus

prescission (see **precision**)

presence a state of being in one place and not elsewhere

presents donations or gifts

presession (see **precession**)

presidential (see **precendential**)

press (see **praiss**)

pressed crowded, forced, or squeezed

prest a duty formerly paid by a sheriff on his/her account into the exchequer

presser a person or device that shapes, molds, or irons items

pressor involving or producing an increase in blood pressure

prest (see **pressed**)

prevision foresight or foreknowledge

provision a stipulation made in advance

preyed (see **parade**)

preyer (see **prayer**)

preys (see **praise**)

pride a sense of one's worth or selfesteem; a group of lions

pried peered curiously; moved or opened with a lever

prier a person who peers curiously; an inquisitive person

prior earlier in time or order; the rank below an abbot in a monastery

pries moves or opens with a lever

prize something offered or striven for in a contest or competition

primer an elementary instruction book

primmer more formal in manner or appearance; neater or trimmer

prince a male member of a royal family

prints makes an impression or mark on; copies of paintings or photographs

principal the most important or salient; main; a person who has a leading position, as in a school

principle a general or fundamental truth, law, doctrine, or assumption

prints (see **prince**)

prion (see **preon**)

prior (see **prier**)

prize (see **pries**)

procellas a glass manufacturing tool for imparting a characteristic shape to an object as it is rotated by the punty

procellous stormy

profit the excess of returns over expenditures; net income (revenues and gains less expenses and losses)

Prophet the accredited leader of a religious group, as the Mormons or Muhammud, the founder of Islam

prophet a person gifted with extraordinary spiritual and moral insight; a spiritual seer

projicience reference of a perceived quality or modification of consciousness to an external reality

projicients persons who project or thrust forward

prom (see **pram**)

prominence the quality of being notable or eminent

prominents moths of the family Notodontidae

proon to breed

prune to cut down or reduce; a plum

proper appropriate; in accord with established traditions and feelings of rightness

propper a person or device that prevents something from falling or collapsing; a supporter

Prophet and **prophet** (see **profit**)

propodeum a part of the thorax of a hymenopteran

propodium the sixth or penultimate leg joint of a crustacean

propper (see **proper**)

pros arguments favoring a position or argument; affirmative sides of a question or position; professionals (by shortening)

prose a literary medium distinguished from poetry; a language intended primarily to give information or communicate ideas

prosar a service book in the Roman Catholic church of sequences, hymns, or rhythms

proser a person who talks or writes tediously; a writer of prose

prose (see **pros**)

proser (see **prosar**)

protean exceedingly variable; capable of change

protein a natural complex combination of amino acids

proud having or displaying inordinate self-esteem

prowed having a bow, stem, or beak

Provençal relating to Provence, a region of southeastern France

provençale cooked with garlic, olive oil, onion, mushrooms, and herbs

provision (see **prevision**)

prow (see **prau**)

prowed (see **proud**)

prune (see **proon**)

prunell a milled cashmere

prunelle a small yellow dried plum

Psalter the Psalms as printed in the Book of Common Prayer

psalter a translation or version of the Psalms

salter a person that manufactures or deals in sodium chloride; a person or device that applies salt

psaltery an ancient and medieval stringed musical instrument that is played by plucking its stretched strings

saltery an establishment in which fish are salted for market

psammite sandstone

samite a rich medieval fabric of silk interwoven sometimes with gold or silver threads

psephite a coarse fragmental rock composed of rounded pebbles

psephyte a lake bottom deposit consisting mainly of coarse, fibrous plant remains

pseud a person of fatuously earnest intellectual, artistic, or social pretensions

sued brought action against or prosecuted judicially

pshaw an expression of disapproval or disbelief

sha the urial, a wild sheep of the uplands of southern and central Asia

Shah a sovereign of Iran

psicose a syrupy ketohexose sugar in the unfermentable residue of cane molasses

psychos persons with emotional disorders

psion (see **Cyon**)

psis (see **cees**)

psis plural of the 23rd letter of the Greek alphabet

scyes armhold shapes or outlines

sighs expresses weariness, relief, or grief

size the area, magnitude, or volume of something

xis plural of the 14th letter of the Greek alphabet

psittaceous like a parrot

setaceous consisting of or resembling bristles

psora a chronic skin disease characterized by circumscribed red patches covered with white scales

sora a small short-billed North American rail

psoriasis a chronic skin disease characterized by circumscribed red patches covered with white scales

siriasis sunstroke

psorosis (see **cirrhosis**)

psorous pertaining to or affected by the itching disease (psora) of the skin

sorus a cluster of reproductive bodies or spores on a lower plant, such as ferns

psych (see **cyke**)

psychal (see **cycle**)

psychos (see **psicose**)

psychosis a profound disorganization of the mind, personality, or behavior

sycosis a chronic inflammatory disease of hair follicles, especially of the bearded part of the face

Psylla a genus of jumping plant lice

psylla any insect of the family Psyllidae

Scilla a large genus of Old World bulbous herbs comprising the squills

scilla any plant, bulb, or flower of the genus Scilla

Scylla a destructive peril

Psyllia (see **cilia**)

psyllium (see **cilium**)

Ptelea a small genus of North American shrubs or small trees including the hop tree

telea aggregations of teliospores, often stalked

ptere a wing-like organ or part, especially in sponges

tear a drop of fluid secreted by the lacrimal gland near the eye

<u>tier</u> a row, rank, or layer of articles
Tyr the Norse god of war and son of Odin
Tyre principal maritime city of ancient Phoenicia

pteric relating to or resembling a wing
terek a sandpiper of the Old World

Pteris a genus of coarse ferns
teras a grossly abnormal organism
<u>terrace</u> a raised embankment with a leveled top; a gallery or portico

pterocarpous having winged fruit
Pterocarpus a genus of tropical flowers

pteron a side (as of a temple) in classical architecture
Teh(e)ran the capital of Iran

ptisan a decoction of barley with other ingredients
tisane an infusion of dried leaves or flowers that is used as a beverage or for mildy medicinal benefits

pudding boiled or baked soft food with the consistency of custard or thick cream
<u>putting</u> placing in a specified position

puddy short and plump; chubby or squat
puttee a leg covering from the ankle to the knee
putty a pliable cement for fastening glass in sashes

puer a dog dung mixture used in tanning hides and skins
pure free from admixture; containing no added substance

puerer a tannery worker who treats hides to remove lime that was used for unheairing
purer freer from admixture

pugh (see **pooh**)

puisne in law, of a subsequent date or later; junior or subordinate
puny weak, insignificant, or sickly

puka (see **pooka**)

puli an Hungarian breed of intelligent vigorous medium-sized farm dog
pulley a mechanical device for lifting a heavy weight

pumice (see **pomace**)

pummel (see **pommel**)

pummice (see **pomace**)

pun (see **pon**)

pundit (see **pandit**)

punkie a biting dipterous insect of the family Ceratopogonidae
punky decayed, soft, or unsound wood

puny (see **puisne**)

pupal related to the pupa stage in an insect's life cycle
pupil a student; the contractile aperture in the eye's iris

pupu (see **poopoo**)

purchase (see **perches**)

pure (see **puer**)

purer (see **puerer**)

purgery (see **perjury**)

puri a light fried wheatcake of India
purie a transparent clear or colored glass marble without inclusions
purree an Indian yellow color

purl (see **pearl**)

purler (see **pearler**)

purr (see **per**)

purree (see **puri**)

purree an Indian yellow color
purry like a low vibratory murmur of a cat

purse (see **perse**)

purtenance (see **pertinence**)

purveyed (see **pervade**)

<u>put</u> a blockhead or dolt

putt a golf stroke made on or near a putting green

puts sets, lays, or places in a specific position

putz a decoration built around a representation of the Nativity scene; a crèche

putt (see **put**)

puttee (see **puddy**)

putting (see **pudding**)

putty (see **puddy**)

putz (see **puts**)

pyknic (see **picnic**)

pyla (see **Pila**)

pylar (see **pilar**)

pylon (see **piline**)

pylorus (see **pelorus**)

pyr (see **peer**)

pyr a unit of light intensity equal to .954 candles

pyre a combustible heap usually of wood for burning a dead body as a funeral rite

pyre (see **Paya**)

pyric resulting from or associated with burning

Pyrrhic relating to or resembling that of Pyrrhus, king of Epirus

pyrrhic an ancient Greek martial dance; a foot in prosody consisting of two short or unaccented syllables

pyrrole (see **parol**)

pyx (see **picks**)

Group I

palmar - palmer
panfried - pan-fried
pappous - pappus
pediculous - Pediculus - pediculus
pedipalous - pedipalpus

penitence - penitents
pentine - pentyne
percipience - percipients
perivitellin - perivitelline
permanence - permanents
petit - petty
petulance - petulants
phaser - phasor
phosphorescence - phosphorescents
phosphorous - phosphorus
phylostomous - phylostomus
pilous - pilus
pincer - pincher
planar - planer
pledger - pledgor
plumae - plumy
policlinic - polyclinic
pollenize - pollinize
polyvalence - polyvalents
porcelainous - porcelanous
postulance - postulants
preadolescence - preadolescents
precedence - precedents
precisian - precision
predominance - predominants
presidence - presidents
prevalence - prevalents
prodromous - prodromus
proestrous - proestrus
profluence - profluents
protégé - protégée
ptisan - tisane
pungence - pungents
pursuance - pursuants
pyruvil - pyruvyl

Group I and II

paracardiac 'parə+
pericardiac 'perə+

parahepatitis 'parə+
perihepatitis 'perə+

paramastitis 'parə+
perimastitis 'perə+

parametrium 'parə+
perimetrium 'perə+

paraneural 'parə+
perineural 'perə+

paraoral 'parə+
perioral 'perə+

pignon 'pēn,yän
pinon 'pēn,yōn

poser 'pōzər
poseur pō'zər

princes 'prinsəz
princess 'prinsə̇s

promiser 'prämə̇sər
promisor 'prämə̇,sȯr

Group II

paean 'pēən
pion 'pī,än

pacifist 'pasə,fə̇st
passivist 'pasə,və̇st

palea 'pālēə
pallia 'palēə

pall 'pȯl
pol 'päl

papa 'päpə
pawpaw pə'pȯ

paragraph 'perə,graf
perigraph 'peri,graf

parotid pə'rätə̇d
parroted 'parətə̇d

pase 'pä,sā
passe pa'sā or 'päs

pastoral 'pastərəl
pastorale ,pastə'räl
pastourelle ,pastə'rel
pastural 'paschərəl

pau 'paů
pa'u 'pä,ü

pauper 'pȯpər
popper 'päpər

pavilion pə'vilyən
pavillon 'pävē,yōⁿ

pawed 'pȯd
pod 'päd

pearlish 'pərlēsh
perlèche 'per,lesh

peeking 'pēkiŋ
Peking 'pē,kiŋ

pekan 'pekən
Pekin 'pē,kin

penal 'pēnᵊl
pennal 'penəl
pinal pē'näl

perilless 'perəlləs
perilous 'perələs

periodic :pirē:ädik
periotic :perē:ädik

pew 'pyü
phew 'fyü

phenol 'fē,nōl
phenyl 'fēnᵊl

physic 'fizēk
physique fə̇'zēk

physiogeny 'fizēəjenē
physiogony ,fizē'ägənē

picarel ,pikə'rel
pickerel 'pikərəl

picker 'pikər
piqueur pē'kər

picture 'pikchər
pitcher 'pichər

pillory 'pilərē
pilori pə̇'lōrē

pincher 'pinchər
pinscher 'pinshər

pinnae 'pi,nē
pinny 'pinē

pi(c)quet pē'kā
piquette pē'ket

Piro 'pirō
pyro 'pīrō

pisciform 'pisə,form
pisiform 'pīsə,form

pistol 'pistəl
pistole pə'stōl

placate 'plā,kāt
placket 'plakət
plakat plə'kat
plaquette 'pla,ket

plaintiff 'plāntəf
plaintive 'plāntiv

planchet 'planchət
planchette plan'shet

plastic 'plastik or 'plastēk
plastique pla'stēk

Polacks 'pō,läks
pollacks 'päləks
pollex 'pa,leks

pooch 'püch
putsch 'püch

posit 'päzət
posset 'päsət

poulette 'pü:let
pullet 'pulət

precent prē'sent
present prē'zent

Precis 'prēsəs
precise prē'sīs

precisian prē'sizən
precision prē'sizhən

premonition ,prēmə'nishən
premunition ,prēmyə'nishən

promoter prə'mōdər
promotor prō'mōdər

psammon 'sa,män
salmon 'samən

pulley 'pulē
pulli 'pə,lī

puree pyu'rē
purey 'pyurē
puri 'purē
purree 'purē

putti 'pütē
putty 'pədē

putto 'püdē
puttoo 'pətü

pyrite 'pī,rīt
pyrrhite 'pi,rīt

Q

Qatar (see catarrh)

qre (see Cree)

qua (see cay and Kwa)

quack (see couac)

quad a block of type metal; a quadrangle on a college campus
quod a prison (slang)

quadrat a game in which printer's quads are thrown like dice; a small usually rectangular plot laid off for the study of vegetation or animals
quadrate relating to a bony or cartilaginous element of each side of the skull

quaff (see coif)

quai (see cay)

quaich (see kweek)

quaily an upland plover
quale a feeling having its own particular

quality without meaning or external reference

quake (see **kweek**)

quale (see **quaily**)

qualmish affected by scruples, compunction, or conscience

quamish a plant of the genus Camassia of the western U.S.

quarl(e) a large brick or tile

quarrel a dispute, conflict, or altercation; to argue

quart (see **cart**)

quartan recurring at approximately 72-hour intervals, as chills and fever of malaria

quartern a fourth part of various units of measure

quarte (see **cart**)

quarten (see **quartan**)

quartre (see **cotter**)

quarts U.S. liquid measures equal to two pints or ¼ gallon

quartz a mineral consisting of silicon dioxide

quashee any negro

quashy wet or swampy, as land

quay (see the first two **cay** entries)

quayed (see **cade**)

qubit (see **cubit**)

'que (see **cu**)

quean a prostitute

queen a female monarch; a king's wife; the most privileged chess piece

queer (see **cuir**)

queerest strangest, most curious, most eccentric, or most unconventional

querist a person who inquires or asks questions

query (see **cuirie** or **Kweri**)

quester a person that makes a search or goes in pursuit of something or someone

questor an agent of a pope or bishop charged with collecting alms

quetch to break silence or utter a sound

quetsch a dry white Alsatian brandy distilled from fermented plum juice

quête (see **Ket**)

queue (see **cu**)

quiche (see **keesh**)

quickset a single slip or cutting of a plant

quick-set a rapid-setting material

quidder a horse that drops chewed food from the mouth due to an inability to swallow

quitter a person who gives up, admits defeat, or stops trying; a coward

quittor a pus-filled inflammation of the feet of horses

quila (see **chela**)

quince a fruit of a widely cultivated central Asiatic tree

quints sequences of five playing cards of the same suit; quintuplets (by shortening)

quint (see **cant**)

quintain an object to be tilted in a sport during the middle ages

quintan occurring as the fifth after four others

quintin a kind of fine, sheer, plain-woven linen

quintal a metric unit equal to 100 kilograms

quintile any of the four values that divides the items of a frequency distribution into five classes each containing one-fifth of the total number of items

quintan (see **quintain**)

quinte (see **cant**)

quintile (see **quintal**)

Quintillian one of a party of Montanists of the 2nd century A.D.

quintillion a number 10³⁰

quintin (see **quintain**)

quints (see **quince**)

quire (see **choir**)

quis (see **cuisse**)

quite to a considerable extent; rather; positively

quyte a triplet of adjacent nucleotides that is part of the genetic code (also codon)

quitter (see **quidder**)

quittor (see **quidder**)

quod (see **quad**)

quoin (see **coign**)

quotaed divided or fixed by a proportional part or share

quoted spoke or wrote from another's work verbatim and with due acknowlegment

quyte (see **quite**)

Group I

quercin - quercine
quiescence - quiescents

Group II

quadrans 'kwā͵dranz
quadrants 'kwädrənz

R

Ra the great sun god and principal deity of historical Egypt

ra a music syllable in the sol-fa sequence

rah to cheer or express joy, approbation, or encouragement

rath a circular earthwork serving as a stronghold for an ancient Irish chief

raab a plant with slightly bitter dark green leaves, and clustered edible flower-buds (also called broccali **ra[a]b**)

rob to take something away from by force

raad an electric catfish; a legislative assembly in a South African Boer republic prior to British administration

rahed cheered or expressed joy or encouragement

rathed a hill residence that has been fortified with an earthen wall

rod a slender pole for fishing, measuring, hanging, or lightning protection

rodd a crossbow for shooting stones

rabat a polishing material made from potter's clay

rabbet a channel or groove cut from the edge of material

rabbit a small grayish brown mammal related to hares

rabot a hardwood block used for rubbing marble before polishing

rabban a Jewish title or honor higher than a rabbi and given to heads of the Sanhedrin

Rabbin a scholar who developed the Talmudic basis of orthodox Judaism

rabbin a Jew qualified by study of the Jewish civil and religious law forming the halakah to expound and apply it

rabbet (see **rabat**)

Rabbin and **rabbin** (see **rabban**)

rabbit (see **rabat**)

rabot (see **rabat**)

race a speed contest; descendants of a common ancestor

reis monetary units in Portugal before 1911, and in Brazil before 1942

<u>res</u> in law, a particular thing

rack a frame on which articles are placed; a pair of antlers; a device for inflicting pain by pulling or straining

wrack to wreck beyond repair; a piece of wreckage

racket a confusing clattering noise; a light bat used in tennis and badminton

rackett a bass instrument of the oboe family

racquet a grayish brown to grayish yellowish brown color

raddle to interweave; a red ocher; to color with rouge

rattle a rapid succession of sharp clattering sounds; a noisemaker

radiance a deep pink color; vivid brightness; splendor

radiants organisms that have reached their present geographical location as a result of dispersal from a primary place of origin

radical the considerable departure from the usual or traditional; a fundamental constituent of chemical compounds

radicle the lower portion of the axis of a plant embryo or seedling

radish the pungent fleshy root of a plant

rattish resembling or having characteristics of a rat

raffes usually triangular topsails set above square lower sails

raffs coarse, disreputable persons

rafts collections of logs or timber fastened together for transportation by floating

raggee an East Indian cereal grass from whose seeds is ground a somewhat bitter flour that is an Oriental staple food

raggy rough or ragged

rah (see **Ra**)

rah to cheer or express joy, approbation, or encouragement

raw being in or nearly in the natural state

rahed (see **raad**)

raid a hostile or predatory incursion

rayed having lines that appear to radiate from a bright object

raider a person involved in hostile incursions; a fast unarmored lightly armed ship for capturing or destroying merchant ships

rater a person who scores (examination papers) or estimates (premiums on property insurance)

rail a long piece of wood, metal, or other material used as a structural member or support; a wading bird related to the crane; to rant or utter abusive language

ral syphilis (slang)

rayl a unit of specific acoustical impedance equal to the sound pressure of one dyne per square centimeter divided by the sound particle velocity of one centimeter per second

raiment clothing or garments

rament any of the thin brownish often fringed or lacinate scales that are borne upon the leaves or young shoots of many ferns

rain water falling in drops from the atmosphere

reign a monarch's power or rule

rein a line fastened to the bit through which a rider or driver directs a horse or other animal

Rais a Mongoloid people of Nepal who speak Kiranti

rais a Muslim chief, ruler, or ship captain; a person in charge in Muslim countries

reis monetary units in Portugal before 1911, and in Brazil before 1942

rice an annual cereal grass widely cultivated in warm climates for its seeds

raise to lift or set upright; to grow plants or animals

rase to erase; to incise by carving or engraving

rays lines that appear to radiate from a bright object

raze to level to the ground; to destroy

rehs mixtures of soluble sodium salts appearing as an efforescence on the ground in arid or semiarid regions in India

reis monetary units in Portugal before 1911, and in Brazil before 1942

res second notes of the diatonic scale

reys kings or male monarchs that reign over major territorial units

raiser a person who lifts, sets upright, or grows plants or animals

raser a person who erases; a person that forms by carving or engraving

razer a person who demolishes structures

razor a keen-edged cutting instrument

raki a Turkish liqueur distilled usually from fermented raisins

rocky abounding in or consisting of extremely hard dense stones; unstable; hard

ral (see **rail**)

Raleigh the capital of North Carolina; of the style prevalent in Raleigh

rawly in or nearly in a natural state

ram a male sheep; a device for exerting considerable pressure or driving force on another subject

rhamn a buckthorn tree or shrub

rament (see **raiment**)

ramie a tall perennial herb of eastern Asia or its strong lustrous bast fiber

rammy resembling a ram

ramous (or **ramose**) relating to or resembling branches

ramus the posterior vertical part of each lower jaw which articulates with the skull

ran to go by moving the legs quickly

rann a stanza of a song

rance a dull red Belgian marble with blue and white markings

rants talks noisily, excitedly, often extravagantly

ranch an establishment where live stock is raised

ranche a pin pool stroke that leaves only the center pin standing

rancor vehement hatred or ill will

ranker a person who draws up in line or serves in military ranks

randem three horses harnessed to a vehicle, one behind the other

random lacking a regular plan or order; haphazard

rangle bits of gravel fed to hawks

wrangle an angry, bitter, noisy, or prolonged dispute or quarrel

ranker (see **rancor**)

rann (see **ran**)

rants (see **rance**)

rapped struck with a quick sharp blow

rapt lifted and carried up or away; enraptured

wrapped enclosed in a covering

rappel to descend a cliff by means of a double-rope arrangement

repel to drive back, repulse, or turn away

rapport a relationship characterized by harmony and accord

report a record or something that provides information

rapt (see **rapped**)

ras a cape or headland; a ruler of an Ethiopian province; a local Italian Fascist boss

ross the rough often scaly exterior of tree bark

rase (see **raise**)

raser (see **raiser**)

rasse a grizzled black-marked semiarboreal civet

wrasse a brilliantly colored marine fish related to parrot fish

ratal an amount by which a person is rated with reference to assessment

ratel any of several powerful nocturnal carnivorous mammals resembling the badger

rater (see **raider**)

rath (see **Ra**)

rath a car or chariot used to carry an image of a god

rut a track made by the continual passage of anything; sexual excitement in a mammal, especially a male deer

rath a circular earthwork serving as a stronghold for an ancient Irish chief

wrath an enraged feeling expressed vehemently and accompanied by bitterness; righteous indignation and condemnation

wroth moved to intense anger; highly incensed; turbulent

rathed (see **raad**)

rattish (see **radish**)

rattle (see **raddle**)

ravelin a detached work formerly used in forifications

raveling a thread that is detached from a fabric

raven a large glossy black bird

raving irrational, incoherent, wild, or extravagant utterance or declamation

raw (see **rah**)

rawer more unprepared or more imperfectly prepared for use or enjoyment

roar to utter or emit a full loud heavy prolonged sound, as a lion

rawly (see **Raleigh**)

rayed (see **raid**)

rayl (see **rail**)

rays (see **raise**)

raze (see **raise**)

razer (see **raiser**)

razor (see **raiser**)

re regarding or concerning

Ree a Caddo people west of the Missouri river in the Dakotas

ree a female ruff, a European sandpiper

rhe the unit of fluidity equal to the reciprocal of one dyne-second per square centimeter

ri a music syllable in the sol-fa sequence

rig an ancient Irish king

rea a person required to provide an answer in an action or suit in law, equity, or a criminal action

Rhea a genus of large tall flightless South American birds resembling but smaller than the African ostrich

rhea any bird of the genus Rhea; the ramie plant or fibre

ria a long narrow inlet that gradually gets shallower inward

rya a Scandinavian handwoven rug with a deep resilient comparatively flat pile

react to exert a reciprocal or counteracting force or influence

re-act to perform a second time

reactance impedance of an AC circuit that is due to capacitance and or inductance

reactants chemically reactive substances

read mentally formulated words or sentences

red a color

redd the spawn of fish

read to mentally formulate words or sentences as represented by letters or symbols

reed a tall grass with a slender stem; a device on a loom resembling a comb

reader a person who reads; a book for instruction in reading; a textile worker who records a design that is read from a card

reeder a person who thatches with reeds;

a textile worker who tapes a reed or wire on sweatband leathers

rhetor a master or teacher of rhetoric; a person concerned with rhetoric

Reading a city in southeast Pennsylvania

redding material which is, or is used to make red color; a compound used to redden the hearth and sides of a fireplace; the action of arranging, tidying, or clearing up

retting soaking or exposing (as flax) to moisture in order to promote the loosening of fiber from woody tissue by bacterial action

reading looking at or scanning letters or symbols with mental formulation of the words or sentences represented

reeding corrugations on the edge of a coin

ready prepared for something about to be done or experienced

Reddi a Munda-speaking migratory agricultural people of southeast Hyderabad, India

reddy reddish in color

real actual, true, or objective

reel a device to wind yarn, thread, string, or line

riel Cambodia's basic monetary unit from 1954

real actual, true, or objective

rill a very small brook; a rivulet or streamlet

realer more actual or truer

reeler a leather worker who uses a beam machine to transfer hides from one vat of solution to another

realest most actual or truest

realist an adherent or advocate of a philosophical doctrine that universals exist outside the mind

reamer a rotating finishing tool with straight or spiral cutting edges used to enlarge or shape a hole

rimur a complex form of versified saga or treatment of episodes from the sagas popular in Iceland from the 15th century

reams bundles of 500 sheets of book paper or newsprint; widens a hole opening

reems horned wild animals, probably wild oxen

rhemes semantic units or elements of speech

R(h)eims a city in northern France famous for its Gothic cathedral

riems pliable strips of rawhide; thongs

reaper a machine or person that cuts a crop and drops it in unbound piles

reeper a strip of wood used in India as a batten or lath

rear the back part of something; to rise up to an erect position

rier in whaling, a small oil cask of about ten gallons stowed at the end of tiers

reason a horizontal timber over a row of posts supporting a beam

resin any of various hard brittle solid to soft semisolid amorphous fusible flammable substances

rebait to place another lure in a trap or on a fishing line; to attach in speech or writing, usually with malice

rebate retroactive credit, discount, abatement, or refund

rebilled reissued notice to a customer for payment

rebuild to restore to a previous condition

reboard to reenter a ship, plane, bus, or train

rebored pierced or drilled a hole again

rebuild (see **rebilled**)

rec recreation (by shortening)

reck to take heed or thought

wreck a thing that is disabled, shattered, or ruined

receded departed, withdrew, or retreated; granted or yielded again to a former possessor

receipted gave a written acknowledgment of goods or money delivered

reseated sat again; fitted with a new seat, as a chair

reseeded replanted or resowed

recesses interrupts the course or sitting of for a comparatively short period

recessus a cleft in a living body; a sinus

recite repeat from memory or read aloud

re-site to place at another location

reciting repeating from memory or reading aloud, especially before an audience

re-siding placing new siding on a structure

resighting looking carefully again in a certain direction

re-siting placing on a new site

reck (see **rec**)

recks is apprehensive or fearful; considers, deems, or regards

rex a genetic variation of a domestic rabbit and various rodents

wrecks things that are disabled, shattered, or ruined

reclaim to rescue from an undesirable or unhealthy state

re-claim to demand the return of, as a right

recoated covered with a finishing or protective layer

recoded put in the form or symbols of meaningful communication

recoil to fall or draw back under the impact of force or pressure

re-coil to rewind into rings laid within or on top of one another or wound spirally

recover to get or win back

re-cover to provide with new concealment or protection

rect an element analogous to a right line in a geometrical system

wrecked ruined or damaged

recta terminal parts of the intestines

rekhta a very highly Persianized form of Urdu used in Urdu poetry

red (see **read**)

redd (see **read**)

redder having a deeper or more red color

retter a person who soaks flax to loosen fiber from the woody tissue

rhetor a master or teacher of rhetoric

Reddi (see **ready**)

redding (see **Reading**)

reddy (see **ready**)

redeye a rock bass; a smallmouth black bass

red-eye cheap whiskey; a large black Australian cicada

redo to execute again or do over

redue something that is again owed or due

redocks cuts short again; comes or goes again into a wharf or pier

redox oxidation-reduction (by shortening)

reducts to reduce

redux brought back; resurgent

redue (see **redo**)

redux (see **reducts**)

Ree and **ree** (see **re**)

reed (see **read**)

reeder (see **reader**)

reeding (see **reading**)

reedy abounding in or covered with reeds; having the tone quality of a reed instrument

rete a circular plate with many holes on the astrolabe to indicate positions of the principal fixed stars; a network of blood vessels or nerves

reek to emit a strong or disagreeable fume or odor

wreak to bring about, cause, or inflict

reel (see **real**)

reeler (see **realer**)

reemerge to appear again after conceal-ment, retirement, or suppression
reimmerge to plunge into or sink again

reems (see **reams**)

reentrance the action of reentering the earth's atmosphere after traveling into outer space
reentrants indentations between two salients in a horizontal plane

reeper (see **reaper**)

rees female ruffs; Europen sandpipers
res a particular thing, in law
rhes cgs units of fluidity
rigs ancient Irish kings

reffed administered, arbitrated, or refer-eed a game or match
reft a cleft or fissure; seized

refind to recover or rediscover
refined reduced to a fine, unmixed, or pure state; free of impurities

reflects turns, throws, or bends back at an angle; thinks about or considers
reflex a reaction to a stimulus, often un-conscious

reft (see **reffed**)

refuse to show or express a positive un-willingness to do or comply with
re-fuse to melt again; to replace a deto-nating device in

refusion the act of pouring back
re-fusion a second or fresh melting

regal of notable excellence or magnificence; stately; splendid
regle a groove or channel for guiding a sliding door
riegel a low transverse rock ridge on the floor of a glaciated valley

regard consideration, heed, or concern
reguard to protect or shield again from

danger; watch over again to prevent es-cape

regence related to a furniture style preva-lent between about 1680 to 1725
regents persons who govern in the ab-sence, disability, or minority of a sover-eign

regle (see **regal**)

reguard (see **regard**)

reheal to again care or restore to health
reheel to place the rear part of a shoe sole

rehs (see **raise**)

reign (see **rain**)

reimmerge (see **reemerge**)

rein (see **rain**)

reis (see **race, Rais,** and **raise**)

reis a Muslim ruler, chief, or ship captain
rice an annual cereal grass widely culti-vated in warm climates for its seeds

reiter a German cavalry soldier of the 16th and 17th centuries
rider a person who rides a vehicle or form of transportation; an addition to a leg-islative bill
righter a person who does justice or re-dresses wrongs
writer a person who produces symbols or words on paper

rejecter a person that refuses or rejects
rejector a circuit that combines induc-tance and capacitance in parallel

rekhta (see **recta**)

relaid put to set down again
relayed passed along by successive reliefs or relays

relaps folds over or around some thing anew or again
relapse to slip or fall back into a former state of illness; to backslide

relater a narrator or storyteller
relator a private person in whose behalf a mandamus is filed

relayed (see **relaid**)

release discharge from obligation or responsibilty
re-lease to rent or lease again

releaser a stimulus in lower organisms serving as an intiator of complex reflex behavior
releasor a person giving a release

relegate to consign to insignificance or oblivion
religate to bind together

remand to return a case from one court to a lower court or an administrative agency
remanned supplied with people or a crew again or anew

remark an expression in speech or writing
remarque a sketch done on the margin of a plate and removed before regular printing

remittance money sent to another person or place
remittents fevers the symptoms of which temporarily abate and moderate at regular intervals

remitter a person who sends a remittance; a legal principle concerning a person who obtains possession of property under a defective title
remittor a sending back of a case or some portion of a verdict from an appellate or superior court to a trial or inferior court for further proceedings or reconsideration

rends pulls violently from a person or thing; wrenches
reyns an abstract number characteristic of the flow of a fluid in a pipe or past an obstruction, used especially in testing airplane models in a wind tunnel; a unit of dynamic viscosity of a fluid equal to 14.8816 poise; Reynolds numbers (by shortening)
wrens small brown singing birds

repand a plant leaf having a slightly undulating margin
repanned rewashed earth deposits in search of precious metals

repassed crossed or traveled again
repast something taken as food; a meal

repel (see **rappel**)

repleaded filed a new legal petition appropriate under the circumstances
repleted stuffed or filled to satiety; replenished

report (see **rapport**)

repress to check by or as if by pressure or coercion
re-press to again exert steady pressure on

reroot to reattach or replant a tree or shrub
reroute to replan an itinerary

res (see **race**, **raise** and **rees**)

resail to sail again
resale selling again or as second hand

research to investigate exhaustively
re-search to look into or over again

reseated (see **receded**)

reseeded (see **receded**)

resew to stitch again
resow to replant with seed

re-siding (see **reciting**)

resighting (see **reciting**)

resin (see **reason**)

resinate to impregnate or flavor with various hard brittle solid to soft semisolid amorphous fusible flammable substances
resonate to produce or exhibit the ability to sound or echo back

resister a person who strives or reacts against
resistor a device used in an electrical circuit for protection or control

re-site (see **recite**)

re-siting (see **reciting**)

resold sold again or as second hand
resoled put a new sole on a shoe

resonate (see **resinate**)

resow (see **resew**)

respondence answering or correspondence

respondents the prevailing parties in a lower court

responser the part of a transponder that transmits a radio signal
responsor the receiver coomponent of an interrogator

rest relaxation, repose, or leisure for body or mind
wrest to move by violent wringing or twisting movements

restaur the legal recourse that insurers have against each other
restore to put or bring back

resteal to again take another's property illegally
resteel to equip with new steel

restore (see **restaur**)

resultance something that results as a consequence, effect, or conclusion, as a resolution of a legislative body
resultants mathematical vector sums

retailer a merchant middleman who sells goods mainly to ultimate consumers
retailor to remake or alter to suit a special need or purpose

retard to delay or impede progress
retarred recovered with tar
ritard a gradually slackening musical tempo

retch to strain to vomit
wretch a miserable person

rete (see **reedy**)

retracked traced or tracked again
retract to draw or pull back; to remove; to withdraw

retread a person returned to military service after a period as a civilian
re-tread to refurnish with a new thickened face of a tire

retreat to retire, withdraw, or recede
re-treat to reconsider

retter (see **redder**)

retting (see **Reading**)

revere to regard with profound respect and affection
revers a lapel on women's garments

review to inspect or examine
revue a light theatrical entertainment

reviver a stimulant; a person who restores, reestablishes, or reintroduces something
revivor revival under law of a suit that is abated

revue (see **review**)

rex (see **recks**)

reyns (see **rends**)

reys (see **raise**)

rhamn (see **ram**)

rhe (see **re**)

Rhea and **rhea** (see **rea**)

R(h)eims (see **reams**)

rhemes (see **reams**)

rhes (see **rees**)

rhesus a pale brown Indian monkey
risus laughter; mockery

rhetor (see **reader** and **redder**)

rheum a watery discharge from the mucous membranes of the eye or nose
room space; part of a building's interior
Rum a term originally applied by Moslems in medieval times to peoples of the Byzantine empire

<u>rum</u> a blue dye resembling indigo obtained from an East Indian shrub

rheumy affected with or subject to catarrh or rheumatism
roomy spacious; roommate
roumi a non–Muslim, often used disparagingly

Rhine a major river in western Germany
rine Russian hemp; a ditch

RHM a unit of gammaray source intensity
rhumb a line on the earth's surface making equal oblique angles with all meridians; a point on a mariner's compass
<u>rum</u> an alcoholic liquor prepared from fermented molasses

rhodeose an aldose sugar
roadeos a contest featuring events that test driving skills of professional truck drivers
rodeos public performances featuring such contests as bareback bronco riding, calf roping, and steer wrestling

Rhodes a person attending Oxford University who holds a (Cecil J.) Rhodes scholarship
roads passageways or highways for vehicles

Rhodester a person attending Oxford University who holds a (Cecil J.) Rhodes scholarship
roadster an open-bodied automobile having one cross seat and a rear luggage compartment or rumble seat

rhoding the journal bearing of a pump brake
roading highway construction and maintenance
roding the anchor line of a dory or similar small fishing boat

rhodite a native alloy of gold and rhodium
roadite a person addicted to driving (slang)

Rhoeo a monotypic genus of herbs, including the oyster plant

Rio Rio de Janeiro, a city on the southeast coast of Brazil

rhomb an equilateral parallelogram
rom a small computer memory that cannot be changed by the computer and that contains a special-purpose program (shortening of "read-only memory")

Rhône a major river flowing through southeastern France into the Mediterranean sea
roan a moderate reddish-brown; a roan-colored animal
rohun an East Indian tree having hard durable wood and tonic bark
rowan a Eurasian tree; an American mountain ash

rhos the 17th letter (plural) of the Greek alphabet
roes small European and Asiastic deer
Ros artificial languages intended to be international, such as esperanto
<u>rose</u> a flower; a perfume; a moderate purplish red color
<u>rows</u> propels a boat with oars; continuous lines or stripes

rhumb (see **RHM**)

Rhus a genus of shrubs and trees native to temperate and warm regions
ruse a stratagem or trick intended to deceive

rhyme identical or similar sounding words or lines of verse
rime granular ice tufts on the windward side of an exposed object
ryme the surface of water

ri (see **re**)

ria (see **rea**)

ribband a long narrow strip or bar used in shipbuilding; a single bendlet that surrounds outer heraldic bearings
ribbon a narrow band of material often used as adornment or trimming

rice (see **Rais** and **reis**)

rick a pile of cordwood, stave bolts, or other material split from short logs

rikk a small tambourine used in Egypt

wrick a strain or sprain of muscles

ridder a person that removes, clears off, or takes away

ritter a member of one of the lowest orders of German or Austrian nobility

ride to sit or be carried on the back of an animal or in a vehicle

wried twisted around

rider (see **reiter**)

riegel (see **regal**)

riel (see **real**)

riems (see **reams**)

rier (see **rear**)

riffed discharged from government service for reasons of economy

rift a fissure or split

rig (see **re**)

rigger a person who manipulates or fits ship riggings, or works on oil and gas well rigs

rigor severity, sternness, or exactness

right good or just; a privilege or prerogative; the position opposite to left

Rite the liturgy, especially an historical form of eucharistic service

rite a ceremonial act

wright a carpenter

write to produce symbols or words on paper

righter (see **reiter**)

rigor (see **rigger**)

rigs (see **rees**)

rikk (see **rick**)

rill (see **real**)

rime (see **rhyme**)

rimur (see **reamer**)

rine (see **Rhine**)

ring a circular or curved band

wring to compress by squeezing or twisting

ringer a game of marbles

wringer a machine or device for pressing out liquid or moisture

Rio (see **Rhoeo**)

riot a noise, uproar, or disturbance; persons acting in a turbulent and disorderly manner

ryot a peasant, in India

ripe ready for harvesting

rype the ptarmigan, a grouse of northern regions having completely feathered feet

rise to assume an upright or standing position; to get up from resting or sleeping

ryes hardy annual cereal grasses; whiskies distilled from rye; gypsy gentlemen

wrys twists around or wrings

rist to engrave, scratch, mark, or wound

wrist the joint or region of the joint between the human hand and the arm

risus (see **rhesus**)

ritard (see **retard**)

Rite and **rite** (see **right**)

ritter (see **ridder**)

ritz to snub or behave superciliously toward

writs written documents; legal instruments or mandatory processes

road a passageway or highway for vehicles

rode traveled by vehicle or animal

roed filled with fish eggs; mottled or streaked

rowed propelled a boat with oars

roadeos (see **rhodeose**)

roader a craft anchored in a roadstead or quasi-harbor; a stationary donkey engine for dragging

roter logs along a skid road; a person who repeats mechanically or by memory

rotor a part that rotates within a stationary part

roading (see **rhoding**)

roadite (see **rhodite**)

roads (see **Rhodes**)

roadster (see **Rhodester**)

roam to wander or rove
rom a male gypsy
Rome the capital of Italy; Roman Catholicism

roan (see **Rhône**)

roar (see **rawer**)

roar a full loud heavy prolonged sound; to utter such a sound
rower a person who uses oars to propel a boat

roaster a machine or contrivance for cooking by exposure to radiant heat
roster an itemized listing of a group or collection

rob (see **raab**)

roband a small piece of spun yarn or marline used to fasten the head of a sail to a spar (also **robbin**)
robin a large North American thrush; a small European thrush

rober a person who covers or invests with a robe
robur an English oak

robin (see **roband**)

robur (see **rober**)

roc a legendary bird of great size and strength
rock a large fixed stone; to move a child back and forth, as in a cradle
ROK a member of the armed forces of the *R*epublic *of S*outh *K*orea

roccellin a red monoazo dye
roccelline resembling plants of the genus Roccella

rock (see **roc**)

rocky (see **raki**)

rod (see **raad**)

rodd (see **raad**)

rodder a textile worker who folds double-width goods
rotter an unprincipled, lazy, or weak person

rode (see **road**)

rodeos (see **rhodeose**)

roding (see **rhoding**)

roed (see **road**)

roer a heavy long-barreled gun formerly used for hunting big game in southern Africa
Ruhr a mining and industrial region centered in western Germany

roes (see **rhos**)

roey having a mottled or streaked grain
roi the root stock of a fern roasted and eaten by the Maoris
rowy of uneven textue or appearance

rohun (see **Rhône**)

roi (see **roey**)

roil to make turbid by stirring up sediment or dregs
royal magnificent or regal; of kingly ancestry

ROK (see **roc**)

roke a seam or scratch filled with scale or slag on the surface of an ingot or bar
roque croquet played on a hardsurfaced court having a raised border to cushion bank shots

role a character assumed by a person
roll a list of names or items; to revolve by turning over and over

rom (see **rhomb** and **roam**)

Rome (see **rhomb** and **roam**)

rondeau a fixed form of verse

rondo a dance composition with a recurring movement theme

rondel a short peom of fixed form

rondelle a small disk of glass used as an ornament in a stained-glass window

rondo (see **rondeau**)

Rong a Mongolian people of Sikkim, India

wrong a principle, practice, or conduct contrary to justice, goodness, equity, or accepted law

rood a crucifix symbolizing the cross on which Christ died

rude lacking craftsmanship or artistic finish; raw, unpolished, coarse, or uncouth

rued regretted; repented

rookie a novice or beginner

rooky full of common Old World gregarious birds similar to the American crow

room (see **rheum**)

roomer a lodger

rumor a belief having no discernible foundation; heresay

roomy (see **rheumy**)

roos kangaroos

roux mixtures of flour and fat or butter used as thickening agents

rues regrets or repents

ruse a strategem or trick designed to deceive

root a portion of a plant growing underground; to dig in search of something; to fix or firmly attach

route a pathway, road, or highway

rooter a heavy plowing device for tearing up the ground surface, especially for a roadbed; an enthusiastic supporter

ruder more ill-mannered, discourteous, impolite, or uncivil

roque (see **roke**)

Ros (see **rhos**)

rosary a string of beads used in counting prayers

rosery a bed or bush of plants of the genus Rosa

rose (see **rhos**)

rosery (see **rosary**)

roset a dark reddish-orange color, often called brazil red

rosette an ornament or structure resembling a rose

ross (see **ras**)

roster (see **roaster**)

rosy characterized by or tending to promote optimism; having a rose-colored complexion

Rozi a Bantu-speaking people in Zambia known for their woodworking

rote a thing learned by memorizing; the mechanical repetition of a pattern

wrote produced symbols or words on paper

roter (see **roader**)

rotor (see **roader**)

rotter (see **rodder**)

rough coarse, shaggy, or harsh

ruff a fringe of long hair or feathers about a bird's or animal's neck

rougher a poultry dressr that pulls out tail and wing feathers only

ruffer a coarse type of flax hackle consisting of a board studded with long teeth

roughneck a crew member that builds and repairs oil wells; an uncouth person, especially one markedly inclined to violent, quarrelsome, or mischievous behavior

ruffneck a devotee of rap music

roumi (see **rheumy**)

rouse to awaken or stir

rows noisy disturbances; heated arguments

rout to expel by force or eject
route a road, highway, or pathway

route (see **root**)

roux (see **roos**)

rowan (see **Rhône**)

rowan a Eurasian tree; an American
mountain ash
rowen a stubble field left unplowed until
late autumn

rowed (see **road**)

rowen (see **rowan**)

rower (see **roar**)

rows (see **rhos** and **rouse**)

rowy (see **roey**)

royal (see **roil**)

Rozi (see **rosy**)

rubicand red bay, sorrel, or black with
flecks of white or gray, especially on the
flanks of horses
Rubicon a bounding or limiting line that
once crossed commits a person to an ir-
revocable change or decision
rubicon the winning of a card game before the loser has reached a certain prescribed score

rubiconed to defeat, as in bezique or piquet, with a score so low that it is added
to the winner's
rubicund inclining to redress

ruck horses that run in a group behind
those that set the pace
rukh a forest or jungle

rucks draws or works into wrinkles or
creases; large quantities indistinguish-
able from the aggregate
rux to worry; to play or sport (slang)

rud to redden
rudd a European freshwater cyprinid fish

rudder a ship's or airplane's steering
mechanism

rutter a plow for cutting ruts in a logging road for sled runners; a person
or animal that ruts; a set of sailing instructions used by ship captains and
pilots

ruddy having a reddish color associated
with the glow of good health or a
suffusion of blood
rutty full of tracks worn by a wheel or the
habitual passage of something

rude (see **rood**)

ruder (see **rooter**)

rued (see **rood**)

rues (see **roos**)

ruff (see **rough**)

ruffer (see **rougher**)

ruffneck (see **roughneck**)

Ruhr (see **roer**)

rukh (see **ruck**)

Rum (see **rheum**)

rum (see **rheum** and **RHM**)

Ruman a native or inhabitant of Romania
or Wallachia
rumen the large first compartment of a ruminant's stomach from which food is regurgitated

rumor (see **roomer**)

run (see **jen**)

rundown an item-by-item check, investi-
gation, or summary
run-down in poor health or physical condition

rung a ladder crosspiece; a stage in an ascent; sounded clearly as a bell
wrung compressed by squeezing or twisting

runover typeset matter that exceeds the
space estimated or allotted
run-over worn at one side

ruse (see **Rhus** and **roos**)

rusot an extract from the wood or roots of various shrubs of the genus Berberis that is mixed with opium and applied to infected eyelids

russet a reddish or yellowish brown or reddish gray color

russel a strong twilled woolen cloth

rustle to steal cattle; a quick succession of small clear sounds, like leaves in a breeze

russet (see **rusot**)

rustle (see **russel**)

rut (see **rath**)

rutter (see **rudder**)

rutty (see **ruddy**)

rux (see **rucks**)

rya (see **rea**)

ryes (see **rise**)

ryme (see **rhyme**)

ryot (see **riot**)

rype (see **ripe**)

Group I

ramulous - ramulus
reactance - reactants
recalcitrance - recalcitrants
recipience - recipients
recision - rescission
reclaim - re-claim
recount - re-count
recreance - recreants
recumbence - recumbents
recusance - recusants
reentrance - reentrants
reference - referents
reform - re-form
registerer - registrar
remanence - remanents
reminiscence - reminiscents

remonstrance - Remonstrants - remonstrants
repellence - repellents
residence - residents
resistance - resistants
resonance - resonants
respondence - respondents
responser - responsor
resurgence - resurgents
retardance - retardants
rumdum - rum-dum

Group I and II

ramose 'rā͵mōs
ramous 'rāməs

relic 'relik
relict 'relikt

Renaissance :renə:säns
renascence rə'nasᵊns

resin 'rezᵊn
rosin 'räzᵊn or 'rȯzᵊn

Group II

racy 'rāsē
recit rā'sē

radical 'radəkəl
radicel 'radəsel

rail 'rāl
rale 'ral

rainy 'rānē
ranny 'ranē

raisoné ͵rāzə'nā
raisonné ͵rāzō'nā

raki rə'kē or 'rakē or 'räkē
Reki 'rākē

rami 'rā͵mī
ramie 'rāmē

rapee 'rāpē
rappee ra'pē

ras   'räs or 'rəs
rasse   'ras

rath   'rä or 'räth
raw   'rȯ

raucous   'rȯkəs
Roccus   'räkəs

rawed   'rȯd
rod   'räd

recent   rēsᵊnt
resent   rē'zent

reclaim   re'klām
réclame   rā'klȧm

recognizer   'rekȯg,nīzər
recognizor   rȯ:kägnə:zȯr

recoverer   rȯ'kəvərər
recoveror   rə:kəvə:rȯr

registrar   'rejȯ,strär
registrer   'rejȯstrər

relais   ,re'lā
relay   'rē,lā

renin   'rēnȯn
rennin   'renȯn

resole   rē'sōl
rissole   'ri,sōl

rhesis   'rēsis
rhesus   'rēsəs

rhyton   'rī,tän
righten   'rītᵊn

rillet   'rilȯt
rillett(e)   rȯ'let

rival   'rīvəl
rivel   'rivəl

rocket   'räkȯt
roquette   rȯ'ket

roer   'rủər
ruer   'rüər

roily   'rȯilē
royally   'rȯiəlē

rot   'rät
wrought   'rȯt

royal   'rȯiəl
royale   'rȯi,al

rundale   'rən,dāl
rundle   'rəndᵊl

rupia   'rüpēə
Ruppia   'rəpēə

rushee   rə'shē
rushy   'rəshē

S

Saar (see **czar**)

saba fine textile from the fiber of the saba plant

sabha a public meeting in India

sabbat a midnight assembly of witches and sorcerers held in medieval and Renaissance times to renew allegiance to the devil

sabot a strap or wide band fitting across the instep in a shoe of the sandal type

sabe street smart; shrewdness

salvy resembling an unctuous adhesive composition in texture or oiliness

savvy expertness in a particular field

sabha (see **saba**)

sabot (see **sabbat**)

sabra a reddish prickly edible fruit of cacti growing on the coastal plains of Palestine; a prickly pear; a native-born Israeli

zabra a 16th and 17th century Spanish sailing vessel resembling a small frigate

Sacae an ancient people settled in eastern Iran

Sakai a forest people of Malaya

sockeye a small but very important Pacific salmon

saccharin a crystalline cyclic imide, remarkable for its sweetness and no food value

saccharine overly or affectedly pleasant; syrupy

sacci soft-walled cavities usually having a narrow opening or none at all

sake a Japanese alcoholic beverage made from fermented rice

saki any of several South American monkeys having a bushy non-prehensile tail

sachet a small bag or packet

sashay to strut about in a conspicuous manner

Sacs members of an Indian people of the Fox river valley and shores of Green Bay, Wisconsin

sacs pouches within an animal or plant

sacks plunders; large rectangular bags of coarse strong material

sacques baby jackets

sax a saxophone (by shortening)

Saxe a grayish blue color

sadder more unhappy or mournful

satyr a lecherous man; a hairy desert demon

saddest most unhappy or mournful

sadist a person who delights in physical or mental cruelty

sad(h)e the 18th letter of the Hebrew alphabet

soddy covered with or abounding in turf or sward

sadist (see **saddest**)

saeter a pasture high in the Norwegian or Swedish mountains

satyr a lecherous man; a hairy desert demon

Seder a Jewish ceremonial dinner held on the first evening of Passover

saeter a pasture high in the Norwegian or Swedish mountains

setter a large bird dog; a person that sets, as traps

safe secure from threat of danger; a receptacle to keep articles secure

seif a long narrow sand dune or chain of dunes

Sagai a group composed of the Beltir, Koibal, and other peoples on the Abakan river in south central Russia that speak a Turkic dialect

sagaie a Paleolithic bone javelin point

sail an expanse of fabric using wind to propel boats and ships

sale a transfer of property title for a consideration

sailable capable of being moved forward on water

sal(e)able marketable

sailer a sailing ship

sailor a member of a ship's crew

Sakai (see **Sacae**)

sake (see **sacci**)

saki (see **sacci**)

sal salt (in chemistry)

salle spoiled paper

sal an East Indian timber tree

Sol the sun

sol the sunny side or section of a bullfight arena; a fluid colloidal system; gold, as used in alchemy

salah a Muslim ritual prayer made five times daily

selah an exclamation used in the Psalms, possibly as a direction to temple musicians to play music or sing

sale (see **sail**)

sal(e)able (see **sailable**)

salle (see **sal**)

salon (see **Ceylon**)

saloop a hot drink made from sassafras, milk, and sugar or from dried tubers of various East Indian or European orchids

salop a widely distributed English breed of dark-faced hornless mutton-type sheep

salter (see **Psalter**)

saltery (see **psaltery**)

saltie an ocean-going sailor (slang)
salty engagingly provocative; experienced or sophisticated

salver a tray for serving food or beverages
salvor a person who engages in salvage

salvy (see **sabe**)

sama a snapper (fish) of the warmer parts of the western Atlantic; an eelpout
somma the rim of a volcanic crater or caldera

samara a dry indehiscent usually one-seeded winged fruit
samarra a Spanish Inquisition garment resembling a scapular

sambar a large Asiatic deer
somber gloomy, sullen, or melancholy in appearance or mood

same something identical with or similar to another
Sejm Poland's lower house of parliament

samite (see **psammite**)

sandhi modification of the sound of a morpheme conditioned by the context in which it is uttered, as in "dontcha" for "don't you"
sandy full of or resembling sand; an Australian swimming crab

sandhi modification of the sound of a morpheme conditioned by the context in which it is uttered, as in "dontcha" for "don't you"
sundae ice cream served with a topping of fruit, nuts, or syrup
Sunday the Christian sabbath; the first day of the week

sands small loose grain resulting from a rock's disintegration
sans without; deprived of

sandy (see **sandhi**)

sane mentally sound
Seine a major river in France that flows through Paris
seine a large net

saner more mentally sound
seiner a person or boat that fishes with a large net

sang produced musical tones with the voice
sangh an association whose goal is to unify different groups in Hinduism

sang a Persian harp of the middle ages
sangh an association whose goal is to unify different groups in Hinduism
Sung of, relating to, or having the characteristics of the period of the Sung dynasty (A.D. 960–1279)
sung produced musical tones with the voice

sangh (see both **sangs**)

sank (see **cinque**)

sann an East Indian plant the fiber of which closely resembles true hemp
son a male offspring
sun a star around which Earth revolves
sunn an East Indian plant, the fiber of which is used for rope and bags

sans (see **sands**)

Saracen (see **ceresin**)

sara(h) the painted trillium plant, a perennial herb of northeastern North America
sera the watery portion of animal fluids remaining after coagulation
serra a sawlike organ or part of a sawfish or sawfly

saran a tough flexible thermoplastic made of copolymerized vinylidene chloride
serein a mist or fine rain falling from an apparently clear sky
serin a small European finch related to the canary

sarcel a pinion feather of a hawk's wing

sarcelle any of the short-necked river ducks of America and Europe, such as the teal

sarcophagous carnivorous

sarcophagus a coffin made of stone

sarcophilous fond of flesh

Sarcophilus a genus of marsupials consisting of the Tasmanian devil

sardonics disdainful or skeptically humorous remarks

sardonyx onyx marked by parallel layers of sard and another colored mineral

sari a lightweight cloth garment worn by Hindu women

sorry feeling regret, penitence, or sorrow

sarsen a large loose residual mass of stone left after the erosion of a once continuous bed or layer

sarson an Indian cole resembling rape

sashay (see **sachet**)

sass back talk

sauce pert or insolent language or actions

sassy given to back talk; impertinent

saucy smart or trim, as a ship or automobile

satem constituting a part of the Indo-European language family in which palatal stops became palatal or alveolar fricatives

Sodom a place notorious for vice and corruption

satinay the wood of an Australian tree of the family Myrtaceae

satiné a timber tree of Brazil and the Guianas

satiric fond of or skilled at ironic or ridiculing comment

satyric related to a lecherous man or hairy desert demon

satyr (see **sadder** or **saeter**)

satyric (see **satiric**)

sauce (see **sass**)

saucy (see **sassy**)

sault a fall or rapid in a river

sew to become grounded, as a ship

Sioux a language stock of central and eastern North America; a group of peoples speaking Siouan languages

sou the smallest piece of money

sous of subordinate rank

su a mild, slightly sweet rice vinegar

sue to bring action against or prosecute judicially

saurel a horse mackerel (fish)

sorel a male fallow deer in its third year

sorrel a light bright chestnut horse

saury a slender long-beaked fish related to needle fish

sorry feeling regret, penitence, or sorrow

saver a person who economizes or hoards

savor to taste or smell with pleasure

savvy (see **sabe**)

sawder to flatter or praise excessively

solder a metallic alloy which, when melted, joins metallic surfaces; to unite with solder

sawer a person who cuts with a saw

soar to fly aloft; to rise

sore painful or tender; angered or vexed

sawt a group of lions

sought went in search of or looked for

sax (see **Sacs**)

Saxe (see **Sacs**)

say to express in words

se the seventh tone flatted of the diatonic scale

sei a widely distributed small white-spotted whalebone whale

sayyid an Islamic leader

side a direction or place with respect to the center; a surface that encloses or bounds space

sighed made a sound expressing weariness, relief, or grief

Sbrinz a hard cheese suitable for grating

sprintz runs or goes at top speed especially for a relatively short distance

scag heroin (slang)

skag a vessel's keel near the sternpost; a cigarette (slang)

scalar having an uninterrupted series of steps; a quantity in vector analysis having no direction, as time or mass

scaler a climber; a person who removes scale from metal or fish scales

scald to burn with steam or hot liquid

skald an ancient Scandinavian poet

scaler (see **scalar**)

scallop a marine bivalve mollusk whose shell is characteristically radially ribbed and the edge undulated

scolop the thickened distal tip of a vibration-sensitive organ in insects

scary frightening or alarming

skerry a rocky isle

scends heaves upward under the influence of a natural force

sends dispatches to a destination

sens Japanese monetary units each equal to 1/100 yen

scene a subdivision of a dramatic presentation; a display of passion or temper

seen perceived or verified by sight

<u>**sin**</u> the 21st letter of the Hebrew alphabet

scenery a picturesque view or landscape

senary consisting of six parts of things

scent (see **cent**)

scenter (see **center**)

scents (see **cense**)

scepter (see **cepter**)

(s)chappes (see **chaps**)

schapping a European method of fermenting and removing gum from silk wastes

shopping searching for, inspecting, or buying goods or services

schick (see **chic**)

schih dry grasslands of northern Africa

she a female person or animal

shea a rough-barked tropical African tree

sidhe an underground fort in which Gaelic fairies live

schilling the recent basic monetary unit of Austria

shilling a unit of value equal to 1/20 pound in many countries in or formerly in the British Commonwealth

skilling any of various old Scandanavian units of value equal to some small fraction of the Danish, Norwegian, or Swedish rix-dollars

schiz a schizophrenic or schizoid person

skits satirical or humorous stories or sketches often outwardly serious; parodies

skitz to go insane or crazy; to "flip out" (slang)

schout a Dutch sheriff

scout to explore an area to obtain information

schouw a light-draft open pleasure boat of the Netherlands

scow a large flat-bottomed boat for transporting materials; to fasten an anchor by its crown to the end of a cable

schuyt a bluff-bowed Dutch boat fitted with leeboards

skate a device worn on foot to glide on ice or roll over smooth ground; a ray (fish)

schwa an unstressed mid-central vowel that is the usual sound of the first and last vowels of "America"

Tswa a southeastern African people chiefly of northern Transvaal province and southern Mozambique

Scilla and **scilla** (see **Psylla**)

Scilly (see **cilly**)

(s)cion (see **cyan** and **Cyon**)

scirrhus (see **cerous**)

scissel metal clippings remaining after various mechanical operations
scissile able to be smoothly or easily split
Sicel a member of an ancient people occupying part of Sicily
sisal a strong durable white fiber used for cordage and twine
sisel a large short-tailed ground squirrel
syssel an Icelandic administrative district

scissel metal clippings remaining after various mechanical operations
scissile able to be smoothly or easily split
sizzle to burn up or sear with scorching heat or heated language

scissile (see both **scissel**s)

scold to utter a harsh reprimand or rebuke
skoaled drank an alcoholic beverage as a toast

scolop (see **scallop**)

scoot to go suddenly and swiftly
scute an external bony or horny plate

scoot to go suddenly and swiftly
skout a guillemot (bird)

scop an Old English poet
scope a general range of cognizance, activity, or influence

scout (see **schout**)

scow (see **schouw**)

scrapie a virus disease of sheep
scrapy sounding like harsh grating

screwee one of the partners engaged in sexual intercourse; a person being swindled or taken advantage of
screwy crazily absurd, eccentric, or unusual; winding or spiral

scrips paper currencies or tokens issued for special or temporary use in an emergency
scripts written texts of a stage play, screen play, or radio or television broadcast

scudder a leather worker who scrapes skins by hand or machine
scutter to move with a brisk rapidly alternating step; to damage severely or destroy completely

scuff to walk with a scraping movement without lifting the feet
squff to eat heavily (slang)

scull an oar used to propel a boat; a long narrow very light racing shell
skull the skeleton of a vetebrate's head

scur a small rounded portion of horn tissue attached to the skin of the horn pit of a polled animal
skirr a whirring, rasping, or roaring sound

scuse excuse (by shortening)
skews moves or turns aside

scute (see **scoot**)

scutter (see **scudder**)

scyes (see **psis**)

Scylla (see **Psylla**)

se (see **say**)

sea (see **C**)

sea-born originating in or rising from the sea
seaborne transported by ship

seafoam a brilliant to light green
sea-foam froth on the sea; a mineral (meerschaum) consisting of a hydrous magnesium silicate used for tobacco pipes

seal (see **ceil**)

sealer (see **coeler**)

seam a line of junction
seem to appear

seaman a person whose occupation is association with ships and the sea; a sailor
semen a viscid whitish fluid containing spermatozoa produced in a male's reproductive tract

seamer a person who fastens by stitches of thread or filament

seemer a pretender

sear (see **cere**)

seas (see **cees**)

season a period of time characterized by a particular feature or event

seisin a possession of land or chattels

seat (see **cete**)

seated situated or located

seeded sown; an area planted with seed

seater (see **cedar**)

seau a pottery pail used in typical 18th-century dinner service

sew to fasten with stitches of thread or filament

so in the manner indicated; conforming with actual fact(s); the fifth tone of the diatonic scale

sow to plant or scatter seed

sec a second (by shortening)

seck barren; unprofitable

secque a shoe similar to a sabotine, but lighter; a clog

Seckel (see **cycle**)

second to remove a person temporarily from one position for employment

seconde a parry or guard fencing position defending the lower outside right target

secque (see **sec**)

sects groups holding similar political, religious, or socio-economic views

sex one of two divisions of organisms designated as male or female; gender

sedent (see **cedent**)

Seder (see **saeter**)

seeded (see **seated**)

seeder (see **cedar**)

seedy abounding in seeds; shabby in dress or appearance

sidi an African Muslim holding a high position under a King of the Deccan

seek to search, look for, or hunt

sic intentionally so written

Sikh an adherent of the religion of Sikhism

seel (see **ceil**)

seem (see **seam**)

seemer (see **seamer**)

seen (see **scene**)

seep (see **cepe**)

seer (see **cere**)

seeress (see **cerous** and **cirrhus**)

sees (see **cees**)

sei (see **say**)

seidel a large beer glass or mug

sidle to move sideways

seif (see **safe**)

seignior a feudal lord of a manor (or **seigneur**)

senior an older person in age or service

Seine and **seine** (see **sane**)

seiner (see **saner**)

seisin (see **season**)

seize (see **cees**)

seizer (see **Caesar**)

seizor (see **Caesar**)

Sejm (see **same**)

sela rice that is heated before milling

selah an exclamation used in the Psalms, possibly as a direction to temple musicians to play or sing

selah (see **salah**)

sell (see **cell**)

sella (see **cella**)

sellar (see **cellar**)

seller (see **cellar**)

sematic serving as a warning of danger
somatic relating to or affecting the body of an organism

semen (see **seaman**)

semens viscid whitish fluids containing spermatozoa produced in the male reproductive tract
siemens the unit of electrical conductance equal to the reciprocal of the ohm

semi a trucking rig composed of a tractor and a semitrailer; a second-year student at some Scottish universities
semy in heraldry, having a pattern of small charges

semidouble having more than the normal number of petals or disk florets
semi-double a feast of the Roman Catholic church

semmel a bread roll with a crisp crust
semul a tree that produces silk cotton

semy (see **semi**)

senary (see **scenery**)

senate an assembly with legislative functions
senit a game of ancient Egyptian origin resembling backgammon
sen(n)et any of several barracuda fish
sennet a signal call on a trumpet or cornet for exit or entrance on the stage
sinnet a signal call on a trumpet or cornet for entrance or exit on a stage

sends (see **scends**)

senhorita an unmarried Portuguese or Brazilian woman
senorita a slender compressed cream and brown wrasse (fish)

senior (see **seignior**)

senit (see **senate**)

senn a herdsman of the Swiss Alps
Zen a Japanese school of Mahayana Buddhism

sen(n)et and **sennet** (see **senate**)

senorita (see **senhorita**)

sens (see **scends**)

sense (see **cense**)

senser (see **censer**)

senses (see **census**)

senso (see **censo**)

sensor (see **censer**)

sensorial (see **censorial**)

sensual (see **censual**)

sent (see **cent**)

sentry (see **centry**)

Seoul the capital of South Korea
sol the fifth tone of the diatonic scale
sole the undersurface of a foot or shoe; a flatfish
soul the immortal part of a person

seps a lizard of an Old World genus of the family Scincidae
septs branches of a family, members of which are believed to have descended from a single ancestor; partitions in a screen or railing that mark off an enclosed area set aside for a special purpose

sept (see **'cept**)

septime a parry or guard position in fencing
septum a dividing wall or membrane

septs (see **seps**)

septum (see **septime**)

sequence a continuous or connected series
sequents conclusions resulting from reason or argument

sera (see **sara[h]**)

seral (see **cirral**)

seraph a fiery six-winged angel guarding God's throne
serif a short line stemming from and at an angle to strokes of a letter

sere (see cere)

serein (see saran)

Seres (see ceres)

serf a person belonging to the lower class
  in various feudal systems
surf a sea swell that breaks on shore

serge a durable twilled fabric with a
  smooth clear face
surge to swell, roll, or sweep forward

serial (see cereal)

sericin (see ceresin)

series (see ceres)

series a group that has or admits an order
  of arrangement exhibiting progression
siris climbing (betel) peppers

serif (see seraph)

serin (see saran)

serious (see Cereus)

serous (see ceras and cerous)

serra (see sara[h])

serval a common African wildcat
servile related to or befitting a slave

service (see cervus)

servile (see serval)

session (see cession)

sessionary (see cessionary)

set to place with care or deliberate purpose
sett a Scottish tartan pattern; a small rectangular paving stone

setaceous (see cetaceous and psittaceous)

setal (see cetyl)

seton (see cetin)

sett (see set)

setter (see saeter)

settle (see cetyl)

settler a colonist; a person who establishes a residence or community
settlor a person who creates a trust of
  property

Sevillian (see civilian)

sew (see sault and seau)

sewer a person who fastens by stitches of
  thread or filament
soar to fly aloft; to rise
sore painful or tender; angered or vexed
sower a planter of seed

sewer a conduit to carry off waste material
soor a mycotic disease of the upper digestive tract in infants and young children;
  a purulent degenerative inflammation of
  the frog in a horse
suer a person who seeks justice from another by legal process

sewn fastened with stitches
son a folk song of Cuba, Mexico, and
  Central America; a Latin American ballroom dance
sone a subjective measure of loudness
sown planted or scattered seed

sex (see sects)

sexed having sexual instincts or sex appeal
sext the fourth of the seven canonical
  hours

sextan a fever characterized by parox-
  ysms that occur every six days
sexton a church custodian

sferics atmospherics; an electronic detec-
  tor of storms using devices for plotting
  electrical discharges
spherics spherical geometry or spherical
  trigonometry

sha (see pshaw)

Shah (see pshaw)

shake to undergo vibration; to quiver or
  tremble
sheik(h) a head of an Arab family, tribe,
  or village

sham (see **cham**)

shames the candle used to light the other candles in a Hanakkah menorah; the sexton of a synagogue
shamus a detective or police officer (slang)

shammy (see **chamois**)

shamus (see **shames**)

shanker (see **chancre**)

shant a large stein or pot
shan't a contraction of shall not

shanty (see **chant[e]y**)

sharki a southeasterly wind of the Persian gulf
shirky disposed to avoid a task because of laziness, lack of courage, or distaste

sharky (see **charque**)

sharpie (see **charpie**)

shaup a shell, pod, or husk
shop to search for, inspect, or buy goods or services

shay (see **chay**)

shays (see **chaise**)

she (see **schih**)

shea (see **chay** and **schih**)

shear to cut, clip, or sever something
sheer of very thin or transparent texture; absolute or pure
shire an administrative subdivision of land, as in colonial America

sheas (see **chaise**)

sheas rough-barked tropical African trees
she's the contraction of she is, she has, or she was

sheave (see **chive**)

sheen (see **'chine**)

sheer (see **shear**)

sheik(h) (see **chic** or **shake**)

sherd a brittle piece or fragment
shirred gathered cloth together along two or more parallel lines; baked until set, as of eggs

she's (see **sheas**)

shier more timid, bashful, or modest; a horse given to starting aside suddenly
shire an administrative subdivision of land, as in colonial America

shiever a double-crosser (slang)
shiver to tremble, quake, or vibrate, especially from an abnormally cold temperature

Shik (see **chic**)

shilling (see **schilling**)

shin (see **hsin**)

Shin and **shin** (see **'chine**)

shine to emit rays of light
sinh the hyperbolic sine

shinnery (see **chenier**)

shire (see **shear** and **shier**)

shirky (see **sharki**)

shirr to gather cloth together along two or more parallel lines; to bake until set, as of eggs
sure certain, positive, or reliable

shirred (see **sherd**)

shiv (see **chive**)

shive (see **chive**)

shiver (see **shiever**)

shivy (see **Chivey**)

shoal a sandbank or sandbar; a shallow place in a body of water
shole a plate placed beneath an object

shoddy inferior, vulgar, shabby, or disreputable
shotty hard and round, like a pellet of shot

shoe (see **chou**)

shoed put on or furnished with a shoe

shood rice husks used in adulterating linseed cake

shooed drove or sent away; dispelled

shoer a horseshoer
sure certain, positive, or reliable

shoes (see **chou**)

shofars (see **chauffeurs**)

shole (see **shoal**)

shone emitted light rays; gleamed
shown displayed or exhibited

shoo (see **chou**)

shood (see **shoed**)

shooed (see **shoed**)

shoos (see **choux**)

shoot (see **chute**)

shop (see **shaup**)

shopping (see **schapping**)

shor a salt lake, marsh, or pond
shore land bordering a large body of water

shore land bordering a large body of water
shower a person that exhibits or demonstrates

shortstop a workman at a rod mill who diverts the rod for winding in a coil
short-stop an acid rinse bath between a photograph developer and the fixing bath

shortswing a skiing technique developed for maximum speed
short-swing of or relating to capital assets held for less than six months

shot (see **chott**)

shott (see **chott**)

shotty (see **shoddy**)

shous (see **chose**)

shower (see **shore**)

shown (see **shone**)

shows (see **chose**)

shrewd marked by cleverness, discernment, or sagacity
shrewed treated with ill-tempered and intractable abuse

shu (see **chou**)

shudder to tremble or shake convulsively
shutter a movable cover or screen for a window or door

shute (see **chute**)

shutter (see **shudder**)

shy (see **Chi**)

si (see **C**)

sibyl (see **cibol**)

sic (see **seek**)

sic intentionally so written
sick diseased or unwell

Sicel (see **cycle** and **scissel**)

Sicilian (see **Caecilian**)

Sicily (see **cicely**)

sick (see **sic**)

sickle (see **cycle**)

sics incites or urges to attack, as a dog
sicks vomits
six the whole number between five and seven

Siddha one who has attained perfection, in Hinduism
siddha rice that is soaked in water and then boiled before milling
Sitta the type genus of Sittadae comprising various typical nuthatches

siddur a Jewish prayer book containing both Hebrew and Aramaic prayers
sitter a broody hen; a person who sits for a portrait or a bust

side (see **sayyid**)

sided (see **cited**)

sideliner a small pale-colored desert rattlesnake of the southwestern U.S.
side-liner a person who catches bass by forcing them to leap into the boat

sider (see **cider**)

siderous (see **Cidaris**)

sidhe (see **schih**)

sidi (see **seedy**)

sidle (see **seidel**)

siemens (see **semens**)

Siena a strong reddish brown color; a city in central Italy
sienna any of various earthy substances that are brownish yellow when raw

sig (see **cig**)

sighed (see **sayyid**)

sigher a person who makes a sound expressing weariness, relief, or grief
sire a male parent

sighs (see **psis**)

sight (see **cite**)

sighted (see **cited**)

sighter (see **cider**)

sign a signal, mark, or gesture
sine a trigonometric function
sinh the hyperbolic function analogous to the sine
tsine a wild ox of the Malay peninsula sometimes used for draft

signate (see **cygnet**)

signet (see **cygnet**)

sika (see **ceca**)

Sikh (see **seek**)

sil yellow ocher, a mixture of limonite usually with clay and silica used as a pigment
sild young herring canned as sardine
sill a horizontal member at the base of a door or window opening

Silicea (see **Cilicia**)

siliceous (see **cilicious**)

sliques (see **cylix**)

sill (see **sil**)

silly (see **cilly**)

sima (see **cyma**)

sin (see **scene**)

sin a transgression of religious law; a serious offense
syn characterized by certain atoms or groups on the same side of the molecule

sine (see **sign**)

sinewous marked by strong or prominent tendons
sinuous a serpentine or wavy form

single (see **cingle**)

single-seated a vehicle with one seat only, or seats suitable for one person to a seat
single-seeded a plant bearing fruit that contains one seed

singular (see **cingular**)

sinh (see **cinch** and **shine**)

sinical (see **cynical**)

Sinicism (see **cynicism**)

sink (see **cinque**)

sinnet (see **senate**)

sinter (see **cinter**)

sinuous (see **sinewous**)

Sion (see **cyan**)

Sioux (see **sault**)

sip (see **cyp**)

sipe (see **cepe**)

sir a respectful form of address
sur in law, on or upon

sire (see **sigher**)

Sirian resembling or relating to the star Sirius, a star in the constellation Canis Major and the brightest star in our sky

Syrian a native or inhabitant of Syria

siriasis (see **psoriasis**)

siris (see **cerise** and **series**)

Sirius (see **Cereus**)

sirred addressed as sir
surd lacking reason or rationale; in mathematics, an irrational radical with rational radicands

sis (see **cees** and **cis**)

sisal (see **scissel**)

sisel (see **scissel**)

siss (see **cis**)

sissed (see **cist**)

sistern (see **cistern**)

Sistine and **sistine** (see **cyst[e]in**)

sit (see **cit**)

site (see **cite**)

sitology (see **cytology**)

Sitta (see **Siddha**)

sitter (see **siddur**)

six (see **sics**)

sixte a parry or guard position in fencing
sixth the number six in a countable series

sixteen the whole number between fifteen and seventeen
Sixtine relating to any of the popes named Sixtus; relating to the Sistine chapel in the Vatican

sixth (see **sixte**)

Sixtine (see **sixteen**)

size (see **psis**)

sizer (see **cisor**)

sizzle (see **scissel**)

skag (see **scag**)

skald (see **scald**)

skarn (see **khan**)

skate (see **schuyt**)

skating gliding along on skates propelled by alternate action of the legs
skeyting a Scandinavian tribal ceremony used in making conveyances of land

skee whiskey (slang)
ski one of a pair of narrow strips of wood, metal, or plastic that are used to glide over snow

skeet trapshooting in which clay targets are thrown to simulate bird flight
skete a settlement of Eastern Orthodox monks inhabiting a group of small cottages around a church

skerry (see **scary**)

skete (see **skeet**)

skews (see **scuse**)

skeyting (see **skating**)

ski (see **skee**)

skidder a person or machine that skids or uses a skid, as with logs
skitter to pass or glide lightly or hurriedly

skiddles a game in which sticks are thrown at pins
skittles enjoyment or play

skiffed navigated in a small light sailing ship
skift a thin layer of snow or frost on the ground, or of ice on water; a wisp of clouds

skil a large elongated scorpaenid food fish of the Pacific coast from Alaska to southern California
skill a developed or acquired aptitude or ability

skilling (see **schilling**)

skirr (see **scur**)

skits (see **schiz**)

skitter (see **skidder**)

skittles (see **skiddles**)

skitz (see **schiz**)

skoaled (see **scold**)

skout (see **scoot**)

skull (see **scull**)

sky an expanse of space surrounding Earth
Skye a Skye terrier dog

slack not tight, tense, or taut; lacking in
firmness
slake to bring thirst to an end with re-
freshing drink

slade the sole of a plow
sleighed traveled over snow or ice in a
vehicle on runners
sleyed separated and arranged the warp
threads in a loom's reed

slain put to death violently
slane an L-shaped spade for cutting out
peat in blocks

slake (see **slack**)

slay to kill or slaughter
sleigh a vehicle on runners for transportation over snow or ice
sley to separate and arrange warp threads
in the reed of a loom

slambang exceptionally good or outstanding
slam-bang with violence and noise

slane (see **slain**)

sleave to separate into filaments
sleeve a part of a garment covering an arm

sleigh (see **slay**)

sleighed (see **slade**)

sleight cunning, trickery, or deftness
slight having a slim or delicate build;
scanty or meager

slew a large number or quantity; killed or
slaughtered
slough a marshy place

sley (see **slay**)

sleyed (see **slade**)

slide to go with a smooth continuous motion; to glide
slied moved shrewdly or with covert cunning

slider a person that coasts over a slippery
surface
slighter a person who disregards the
significance of

sliding going with a smooth continuous
motion; gliding
slighting characterized by disregard or
disrespect

slied (see **slide**)

slight (see **sleight**)

slighter (see **slider**)

slighting (see **sliding**)

slipe pulled wool removed from skins by
a lime process
slype a narrow passage

slipslop shallowness, or meaningless talk
or writing
slip-slop to move about in loose slippers

sloe a small dark-colored plum with astringent green flesh
slow mentally dull; lacking speed

slough (see **slew**)

slough something shed or cast off
sluff to discard a playing card; to eat
(slang)

slow (see **sloe**)

sluff (see **slough**)

slype (see **slipe**)

smellie a motion picture having odors
synchronized with the action
smelly malodorous

Smokey an officer or officers of the state
highway patrol (slang)
smoky emitting gaseous products of burning carbonaceous materials made visible

by the presence of small particles of carbon

snees cuts

sneeze a sudden violent audible spasmodic expiration through the nose and mouth

snide slyly disparaging or subtly derisive

snyed bent upward, especially the edge of a plank near a ship's bow or stern

snoek any of several vigorous active marine fishes, as the barracuda

snook a gesture of derision consisting of thumbing the nose

snoose snuff

snooze to take a nap or doze

snubbee a person that is checked or stopped with a cutting retort or remark

snubby having a snub-nose; blunt, stubby, or stumpy

snyed (see **snide**)

so (see **seau**)

soak to saturate

soke the specific territory or group of men included in a specific jurisdiction, in Anglo-Saxon law

soaper a serial drama performed usually on daytime radio or television (slang); a person that makes or deals in a cleansing agent made from fats and oils

sopor a profound or lethargic sleep

soar (see **sawer** and **sewer**)

soared flew aloft; rose

sord a group of mallards

sword a long-bladed weapon for cutting, slashing, and thrusting

soccer a game whose object is to manipulate a ball into a goal without using hands or arms

socker a hard puncher

sockeye (see **Sacae**)

socks hits or strikes forcefully

sox cloth foot coverings

sodded covered with the upper stratum of soil that is filled with roots of grass or other herbs

sotted wasted in drunkenness

soddy (see **sad(h)e**)

Sodom (see **satem**)

softs silly persons

sophs second-year students in a four-year high school or college (by shortening sophomore)

soja a widely distributed genus of trailing climbing herbs

soya an erect bushy hairy annual legume, the soybean

soke (see **soak**)

Sol and **sol** (see **sal**)

sol (see **Seoul**)

solace alleviation of grief or anxiety

solus without companions; in solitude

soulless lacking greatness or nobleness of mind or feeling

solan a large white gannet with black wing tips

Solen a genus of razor clams

solen a razor clam

solon a member of a legislative body

solar relating to the sun

soler a person who soles footwear

sold exchanged goods or services for money or the equivalent

soled put soles on footwear; having so-many soles, as "double-soled"

souled having a soul

solder (see **sawder**)

sole (see **Seoul**)

soled (see **sold**)

Solen and **solen** (see **solan**)

soler (see **solar**)

solon (see **solan**)

solus (see **solace**)

somatic (see **sematic**)

somber (see **sambar**)

some part of a number of things
sum a total or aggregate

somma (see **sama**)

son (see **sann** and **sewn**)

sone (see **sewn**)

sonny a young boy
sunny full of sunshine; optimistic

soogee clean rope yarns used to wash
with; to wash down, as the deck of a
ship
suji wheat granulated but not pulverized

soor (see **sewer**)

soot a black substance (chiefly carbon)
formed by combustion
suit a set of garments; cards in a pack of
playing cards bearing the same symbol,
as diamonds
suite a retinue or set; an instrumental musical form
sute a flock of mallards
tzut a brightly patterned square of cotton
used as a head cover

sooter a person who removes soot, as
from a boiler
suitor a person who courts a woman; a
pleader

sophs (see **softs**)

sopor (see **soaper**)

sora (see **psora**)

soras small short-billed North American
rails
sorus a cluster of reproductive bodies or
spores on a lower plant

sorbate a salt or ester of sorbic acid; a
substance taken up and held either by
absorption or adsorption
sorbet a sherbet made with a mixture of
fruits

sord (see **soared**)

sordid covered with filth; dirty; vile
sorted arranged according to some characteristics; classified
sworded armed, wounded, or killed with a
sword

sordor refuse or dregs
sorter a person or machine that classifies
or arranges things

sore (see **sawer** and **sewer**)

sorel (see **saurel**)

sorosis (see **cirrhosis**)

sorrel (see **saurel**)

sorry (see **sari** and **saury**)

sorted (see **sordid**)

sorter (see **sordor**)

sortes types of divination by lots
sorties sudden issuings of troops from a
defensive position to attack or harass the
enemy

sorus (see **psorous** and **soras**)

sotted (see **sodded**)

sou (see **sault**)

sough a moaning or sighing sound
sow an adult female swine

sought (see **sawt**)

soul (see **Seoul**)

souled (see **sold**)

soulless (see **solace**)

souma a disease of animals caused by insect vectors such as the tsetse and stable
flies
Suma a people or group of people of the
state of Chihuahua, Mexico
summa one or more treatises encompass-
ing an entire field of learning

soup a liquid food having meat, fish, or
vegetables as a base

<u>**sup**</u> in mathematics, a least upper bound
supe a supernumerary; a superintendent

souper a person who takes or distributes a broth of meat and/or vegetable(s)
super a person in a position of authority or superiority (by shortening superintendent); of great worth, value, or excellence

souple partially degummed silk
supple limber or lithe

sous (see **sault**)

<u>**sous**</u> the space outside the white ring of an archery target
souse to steep in a preservative; to pickle; to soak or submerge

sow (see **seau** or **sough**)

sower (see **sewer**)

sown (see **sewn**)

sox (see **socks**)

soya (see **soja**)

spade a tool for digging or turning soil; a card of one of the four suits in a deck of playing cards
spayed removed ovaries of a female animal

sparable a small headless nail used by cobblers to reduce wear on shoe soles
spareable that which can be relieved of the necessity of doing or undergoing

spatterdash a usually knee-high legging worn as protection from water and mud
spatter-dash a finish produced by scattering paint of a different color on a ground coat

spawn to produce or deposit eggs of an aquatic animal
spon money (slang)

spay to remove ovaries of a female animal
spet a small barracuda fish

spayed (see **spade**)

spear a long-shafted sharp-pointed throwing or thrusting weapon
<u>**spier**</u> a fixed and often architecturally treated screen

specks spots or stains; tiny bits
specs spectacles; specifications (or **spex**)

speel to climb
spiel to play music; to talk in a voluble often extravagant manner

speiss a mixture of impure metallic arsenides
spice any of various aromatic vegetable products used in cookery to season and flavor foods

spet (see **spay**)

spherics (see **sferics**)

Sphinx the type genus of Sphingidae moths
sphinx an enigmatic monster in ancient Greek mythology having a lion's body, wings, and the head and bust of a woman
Sphynx a hairless cat recognized as a breed in 1971

spicae spiral reverse plain or plaster bandages used to immobilize a limb or joint
spic(e)y somewhat scandalous, salacious, piquant, or racy; flavored with various aromatic vegetable products

spice (see **speiss**)

spic(e)y (see **spicae**)

spick spotlessly clean; quite new or fresh (spick-and-span, by shortening)
Spik Spanish American, especially Mexican (usually offensive)

spiel (see **speel**)

spier (see **spear**)

<u>**spier**</u> a person that watches in a furtive or stealthy manner
spire a steeply tapering roof surmounting a tower; a steeple

Spik (see **spick**)

spinner a person or machine that spins fibers

spinor in mathematics, a quantity that resembles a vector with complex components in a two- or four-dimensional space

spinous having spines, thorns, or prickles

Spinus a genus of small active often brightly colored finches

spiracle the blow-hole of a cetacian

spiricle one of the minute coiled threads in the coating of some seeds

spire (see **spier**)

spiricle (see **spiracle**)

spiritous impregnated with alcohol obtained by distillation; containing the nature of spirit

spiritus either of two marks used in writing Greek, the one to indicate aspiration, the other to indicate absence of aspiration

spits slender pointed metal rods for holding meat or other food while cooking; expectorates

spitz a dog native to northern areas, as a chow or pomeranian

spon (see **spawn**)

spoor a sign or mark left by an animal that has passed

spore a minute unicellular reproductive body

sprints (see **Sbrinz**)

sprite an elf, fairy, or goblin

spruit a sprout; young plant growth

sprits spars that cross a fore-and-aft sail diagonally from the mast

spritz a quick brief spray of liquid or rain

spruit (see **sprite**)

spudder a person that sets up and operates well-drilling machinery

sputter confused or excited speech; to

expel particles from the mouth with mildly explosive sounds

squadder a member of a police squad

squatter a person that settles on land without right or title

squaller a baby that cries excessively

squalor corruption; crassness; degradation

squatter (see **squadder**)

squff (see **scuff**)

squirl a curlicue or flourish

squirrel an arboreal rodent with a bushy tail

stabile not decomposing readily; resistant to chemical change

stable a building or part of a building in which domestic animals are lodged and fed

stade a stadium; a period of time represented by a glacial deposit

staid sober, sedate, or serious

stayed paused or remained; brought a ship about to the other tack

staff a long stick carried for support; personnel responsible for operating an organization

staph a staphylococcus bacteria (by shortening)

staggard a male red deer in its fourth year

staggered reeled from side to side; tottered; placed alternately on either side of a midline

staid (see **stade**)

stain a discoloration or blemish; a dye or pigment used to alter color or shade

steen a line with solid material to prevent soil caving in or washing away

stair a series of steps for moving from one level to another

stare to look fixedly

stere a metric measure of volume equal to one cubic meter

stake a pointed rod designed to be driven into the ground; a wager

steak a slice of meat cut from a fleshy part of a carcass

stamen the organ of the flower that gives rise to the male gamete

Stayman a variety of apples

staph (see **staff**)

star a self-luminous gaseous celestial body of great mass

starr a Jewish deed or bond releasing or discharging a debt

stare (see **stair**)

starlet a young movie actress who is being coached and publicized for starring roles; a little star

starlit lighted by the stars

starlight the light emitted by stars

starlite a blue zircon mineral

starlit (see **starlet**)

starlite (see **starlight**)

starr (see **star**)

stater an ancient gold or silver coin of the Greek city-states

stator a stationary part in a machine in or about which a rotor revolves

Statice a genus of low-growing usually coastal herbs

statice sea lavender or thrift, a tufted scapose herb of seacoasts and the mountains of the north temperate zone

status a comparative position of rank or condition

stationary immobile, stable, or static

stationery materials for writing or typing

stator (see **stater**)

status (see **Statice**)

stayed (see **stade**)

Stayman (see **stamen**)

steaded assisted or supported

stetted annotated with the word "stet" to nullify a previous direction to delete or amend

steak (see **stake**)

steal to take property of another illegally; to pilfer

steel commercial iron containing carbon; an instrument for sharpening knives

stele an arrow's shaft; the cylindrical central portion of a vascular plant

stealer a person that robs or steals

steeler a smith who steels edged tools; a person that inserts steels

stelar located in or resembling a stele

steel (see **steal**)

steeler (see **stealer**)

steelie the steelhead, a silvery rainbow trout that migrates to the sea before returning to spawn in fresh water

steely resembling or containing steel

stelae slabs or pillars of stone, usually carved or inscribed and used for commemorative purposes

stele the cylindrical central portion of the axis of a vascular plant

steen (see **stain**)

steer a bull castrated before sexual maturity; to guide or control

stere a metric measure of volume equal to one cubic meter

stelae (see **steelie**)

stelar (see **stealer**)

stele (see **steal** or **steelie**)

step a degree in a scale or range; a movement made by raising the foot and bringing it down in a different position

steppe arid land characterized by xerophilic vegetation

stere (see **stair** and **steer**)

sterling having a fixed standard of purity from admixture that is usually defined legally as represented by an alloy of 925 parts of silver with 75 parts of copper; conforming to the highest standard

Stirling an external-combustion engine in which heat from outside the cylinder causes air confined in the cylinder to expand and drive the pistons

stetted (see **steaded**)

stichs measured parts of something written in verse; tricks in various card games

sticks wood parts of a tree or shrub; twigs; pierces with something pointed; adheres to

Styx a river in Hades

stichtite a mineral consisting of a hydrous carbonate and hydroxide of chromium and magnesium

sticktight any plant of the genus Bidens; a bur(r) marigold

sticks (see **stichs**)

sticktight (see **stichtite**)

Stieng a people related to the Cambodians and inhabiting Thudaumot province, Vietnam

sting something that causes a keen pain or stimulation of the mind

stile a set of steps over a fence

style a manner, method, or mode

stilo in the style of, with reference to the calendar

stylo a stylographic pen (shortened)

sting (see **Stieng**)

Stirling (see **sterling**)

stoep a covered entrance to a building usually with separate roof

stoop to bend the body forward and downward; to lean or bow; a basin at the entrance of a Roman Catholic church containing holy water

stupe a cloth with hot water wrung out for external application

stolen obtained by theft

stollen a repeated section in a meistergesang; a rich, dried fruit-filled yeast bread often topped with icing and decorated with candied cherries

stolon a horizontal branch from a plant's base that produces new plants, as a runner

stoop (see **stoop**)

stooper a person who bends the body forward, or one who is bent forward

stupor numbness or stupefaction

store to accumulate; a business establishment where goods are kept for retail sale

stower a person who stores, especially a stevedore

straddle to stand, sit, or walk with the legs wide apart

stratal relating to a bed or layer

straight free from curves, bends, or angles; direct and uninterrupted; upright

strait a comparatively narrow passageway connecting two bodies of water; difficulty

straighten to alter from being crooked or bent to a straight form; to make correct

straiten to afflict physically or mentally; to continue in a narrow space

strait (see **straight**)

straiten (see **straighten**)

stratal (see **straddle**)

streak an irregular strip or line of contrasting color or texture; a narrow band of light

streek to stretch out

stricks bunches of hackled flax, jute, or hemp

Strix the type genus of the family Strigidae comprising owls that lack ear tufts

strix a fluting of a column

strider a person or animal that moves with long steps

stridor a harsh, shrill, or creaking noise

Strix and **strix** (see **stricks**)

studder a person who inserts hair springs into watches
stutter to speak with involuntary disruption or blocking of speech

stupe (see **stoep**)

stupor (see **stooper**)

stutter (see **studder**)

stylar leading to a seed plant's ovary; related to an elongated process
styler a person who designs, develops, or advises on fashions or styles

style (see **stile**)

styler (see **stylar**)

stylo (see **stilo**)

Styx (see **stichs**)

su (see **sault**)

subaural situated beneath the ear
suboral situated beneath the mouth

subbase another foundation below that which ordinarily forms the base
sub-base a mooring site or base for submarines
subbass a 16- or 32-foot pipe organ stop used in a pedal organ

subcast a secondary swarm of bees
subcaste a subdivision of an hereditary class in Hinduism

subhyalin beneath or under the opalescent substance resembling chiton which is the chief constituent of the wall of a hydatidcyst
subhyaline being somewhat less transparent than glass

suboral (see **subaural**)

subsequence a later or following event
subsequents streams that developed along a belt or belts of underlying weak rock

subsistence an irreducible minimum necessary to support life
subsistents abstract entities; things having existence

subtle delicate, refined, or skillful
suttle the weight remaining after the weight of a vehicle or container is deducted; net weight

subtler more delicate, refined, or skillful
sutler a provisioner to an army

succor help or assistance
sucker a person or device that draws something into itself by producing a partial vacuum; a shoot originating from roots or a lower part of a plant's stem

succubous leaves arranged so that the posterior margin of each over laps the anterior margin of the next older
succubus a demon assuming female form

sucker (see **succor**)

sudds floating vegetable matter composed of papyrus stems and aquatic grasses
suds froth or bubbles formed on a soapy water or beer

sue (see **sault**)

sued (see **pseud**)

suede leather finished by buffing the flesh side with an emery wheel
swayed moved in rhythmic back and forth oscillations; influenced a course of action or viewpoint

suer (see **sewer**)

suit (see **soot**)

suite (see **soot**)

suite a retinue or set; an instrumental musical form
sweet charming or nice; pleasing to the taste, as opposed to sour or bitter; sugary

suitor (see **sooter**)

suji (see **soogee**)

sulfinyl the bivalent group or radical SO occurring in sulfoxides, sulfinic acids, and derivatives of the acids

sulfonyl the bivalent group or radical SO_2 occurring in sulfones, sulfonic acids, and derivatives of the acids

Sullan of, pertaining to, or connected with the Roman dictator Lucius Cornelius Sulla

sullen gloomily or resentfully silent or repressed

sum (see **some**)

Suma (see **souma**)

sumac a shrub or tree of the genus Rhus

Sumak a smooth-faced pileless carpet from eastern Transcaucasia, woven in a peculiar form of tapestry weave with a herringbone effect

summa (see **souma**)

summarize present briefly, sum up, or recapitulate

summerize to make ready for summer use

summary a short restatement of the main points

summery relating to the season between spring and autumn

summerize (see **summarize**)

summery (see **summary**)

sun (see **sann**)

sundae (see **sandhi**)

Sunday (see **sandhi**)

sundri an East Indian tree with tannin-rich bark

sundry an indeterminate number

Sung and **sung** (see **sang**)

sunn (see **sann**)

sunny (see **sonny**)

sup (see **soup**)

supe (see **soup**)

super (see **souper**)

·superepic extraordinarily heroic

superepoch an extraordinary memorable event or date

supple (see **souple**)

sur (see **sir**)

sura the fermented juice of various East Indian palms

surra(h) a severe Old World febrile and hemorrhagic disease of animals transmitted by biting insects

surculus (see **circulus**)

surd (see **sirred**)

sure (see **shirr** and **shoer**)

surf (see **serf**)

surface one of the faces of a three dimensional object

Syrphus a genus of cyclorrhaphous dipterous flies

syrphus any of numerous active day-flying flies that feed on nectar; the hover-fly

surge (see **serge**)

surgency a personality factor characterized by quickness and cleverness

surgeoncy the office or position of a medical specialist who performs surgery

surplice a loose white ecclesiastical vestment

surplus the excess of receipts over disbursements; more than sufficient

surra(h) (see **sura**)

sute (see **soot**)

sutler (see **subtler**)

suttle (see **subtle**)

swallo a large holothurian, a worm-like aquatic animal

swallow to take through the esophagus into the stomach; to devour; to engulf; a small long-winged bird

swanneck an orchid of the genus Cyc-
noches

swan-neck a bend in a handrail of a stair
consisting of a ramp terminating in a
knee

swansdown a soft thick cloth of wool
mixed with rayon, silk, or cotton

swan's-down the fine soft feathers of the
swan

swath a stroke of a scythe

swathe to wrap or cover tightly in enveloping material

swatter a device to kill insects

swotter a student who studies hard and
constantly, especially for examinations
in Great Britain and New Zealand

swayed (see **suede**)

swayer a person that moves in usually
slow and rhythmic back and forth oscillations

swear to take an oath

Swedish related to Sweden

sweetish pleasing to the taste, as opposed
to sour or bitter; sugary

sweet (see **suite**)

sweetish (see **Swedish**)

sword (see **soared**)

sworded (see **sordid**)

swotter (see **swatter**)

sycosis (see **psychosis**)

syenite (see **cyanite**)

syke (see **cyke**)

sylvanite a telluride of gold and silver occurring in crystals or masses with luster

sylvinite an evaporite rock consisting of
halite and sylvite

symbol (see **cymbal**)

syn (see **sin**)

sync(h) (see **cinque**)

synechological pertaining to a continuum

synecological involving a branch of ecol-
ogy that deals with the structure, development, and distribution of ecological
communities in relation to the environment

sypher (see **cipher**)

Syria (see **ceria**)

Syrian (see **Sirian**)

Syrphus and **syrphus** (see **surface**)

syssel (see **scissel**)

Szis (see **cees**)

Group I

salience - salients
scaena - scena
scalenous - scalenus
schedular - scheduler
scirrhous - scirrhus
seer - see-er
semblance - semblants
semul - simal
senhor - senor - signor
senhora - senora - signora
sentience - sentients
septal - septil
serai - serail
shortchange - short-change
sibilance - sibilants
sibilous - sibilus
significance - significants
Silence - silence - silents
silvan - sylvan
slowpoke - slow-poke
somnolence - somnolents
sonance - sonants
sorceress - sorcerous
speluncar - spelunker
sphacelous - sphacelus
spondylous - spondylus
stabile - stable
stairstep - stair-step
steroptican - steropticon

stimulance - stimulants
stratous - stratus
strepsipteran - strepsipteron
subdominance - subdominants
subservience - subservients
subtile - subtle
subtiler - subtler
succulence - succulents
sugarloaf - sugar-loaf
superintendence - superintendents
suppliance - suppliants
surculous - surculus
surveillance - surveillants
susurrous - susurrus
syngnathous - Syngnathus

Group I and II

salon   sa:lōn
saloon   sə'lün

sclerose   'skli,rōs
sclerus   'sklirəs

sherif   shə'rēf
sheriff   'sher,əf

spinose   'spī,nōs
spinous   'spīnəs

squamose   'skwā,mōs
squamous   'skwāməs

stratose   'stra,tōs
stratus   'stratəs

Group II

Sa'an   'sän
sawn   'sȯn

sabaean   sə'bēən
sabian   'sābēən

sabal   'sā,bal
sable   'sābəl

sago   'sāgō
sego   'sēgō

salad   'saləd
salade   sə'lad

salleeman   'sālemən
sallyman   'salimən

samba   'sämbə
tsamba   'tsämbə

sapience   'sapēəns
sapiens   'sapē,enz

sappare   'sa,per
sapper   'sapər

sasin   'sāsᵊn
sasine   'sāsən

sauce   'sȯs
soss   'säs

Sauk   'sȯk
sock   'säk

sawed   'sȯd
sod   'säd

scion   'sīən
zion   'zīən

scissel   'sisəl
scissile   sisəl or sizəl
sessile   'sesəl
sistle   'sisl

scur   'skər
skyr   'skir

second   'sekənd
secund   'se,kənd

secret   'sēkrət
secrete   sə'krēt

seem   'sēm
xeme   'zēm

seesee   'sē,sē
tsetse   'sēsē

seigneury   'sānyərē
seignory   'sēnyərē

septenate   'septē,nat
septennate   'septə,nāt

serene   sə'rēn
serine   'se,rēn

serra   'serə
sirrah   'sirə

servant   'sərvənt
sirvente   sər'vent

shaikh   'shā͵kē
shaky   'shākē

shall   'shal
shell   'shel

sharki   'shərkē
sharky   'shärkē

shivaree   'shivə͵rē
shivery   'shivərē

silicon   'siləkən
silicone   'silə͵kōn

simbil   'simbil
symbol   'simbəl

similar   'similər
similor   'similōr

Sinapsis   sə'nāpsəs
synapsis   'sə͵napsəs

sing   'siŋ
singh   'siŋg

skeletin   'skelətin
skeleton   'skelət°n

slaughter   'slȯdər
slotter   'slädər

soared   'sȯrd
sward   'swȯrd

solan   'sōlən
so-lun   'sō͵lən

solely   'sōlē
soli   'sō͵lē

solemn   'säləm
solum   'sōləm

sori   'sȯr͵ī
sorry   'sȯrē

sot   'sät
sought   'sȯt

sowar   'sō'wär
sower   'sōər

spiritual   'spirəchəwəl
spirituel   :spirəl×chə:wel

stadic   'stātik
static   'statik

stalk   'stȯk
stock   'stäk

stamen   'stāmən
stamin   'stamən

stearic   'stē͵arik
steric   'sterik

sterile   'sterəl
sterol   'ste͵rȯl

stigma   'stigmə
stigme   'stigmē

stirrup   'stirəp
stir-up   'stir͵əp

stoop   'stüp
stupp   'stəp

succus   'səkəs
succuss   ͵sə'kəs

sudor   'südōr
suiter   'südər

summand   'sə͵mand
summoned   'səmənd

sunglo   'sùŋ'lō
sunglow   'sən͵glō

suni   'sünē
Sunni   'sùnē
sunny   'sənē

superaffluence   ͵süpər'aflüəns
supereffluence   ͵süpər'eflüəns

T

taar an Arabian tambourine

tahr a Himalayan beardless wild goat

tar a dark brown or black bituminous odorous viscid liquid obtained by the destructive distillation of organic materials

tabaret a stout upholstery silk with satin stripes

taboret a cylindrical seat or stool without arms or back

tachs tachometers, devices indicating speed of rotation (by shortening)

tacks attaches or joins; nail-like fastening devices; changes direction of a sailing vessel

tacts sensitive mental or aesthetic perceptions; diplomacies or delicacies

tax a pecuniary charge imposed by a public authority

tacit unspoken or implicit

tasset one of a series of overlapping plates in a suit of armor that forms a short skirt

tacked attached or joined; changed direction of a sailing vessel

tact diplomacy; considerateness; poise

tacks (see **tachs**)

Tacoma a city in west central Washington

Tecoma a genus of tropical American shrubs and trees having large showy flowers

tact (see **tacked**)

tacts (see **tachs**)

tahr (see **taar**)

tailer a person or animal that follows another

tailor a person who makes or alters wearing apparel

talar an ankle-length robe

tailles royal taxes in 15th century France; middle or tenor voices in early choral music

tails (plural) the part of a vertebrate's body that is posterior to the portion containing the body cavity

tales narratives of events

tailles middle or tenor voices in early choral music; royal taxes in 15th century France

Tais members of a widespread group of people in south China and southeast Asia associated ethnically with valley paddy-rice culture

tais Pacific porgy fish

Thais natives or inhabitants of Thailand

ties fastens, attaches, or brings together; equal scores in a contest

tyes chains or ropes, one end of each of which passes through the mast

Tyighs a Shahaptian people of west central Oregon

tailor (see **tailer**)

tails (see **tailles**)

taint to corrupt, defile, or stain

'taint the contraction of it ain't (substandard)

Tais and **tais** (see **tailles**)

tait a honey possum, a small chestnut-brown long-muzzled phalanger of western Australia

tête a high elaborately ornamented style of woman's hairdress or wig worn in the latter half of the 18th century

tet(h) the ninth letter of the Hebrew alphabet

takeout a bridge bid that takes a partner out of a bid

take-out designed for the sale of food that is not to be consumed on the premises

takt a beat or pulse in music

tocked made a sound similar to a tick, but

slightly lower and there fore more resonant, especially in a clock

talar (see **tailer**)

tales (see **tailles**)

talkee-talkee a broken or corrupted speech
talky-talky abounding in or containing
too much talk

talkie a sound motion picture
talky talkative
tawkee an arrow arum; an American
aquatic plant with a spadix of minute
yellow flowers

talky-talky (see **talkee-talkee**)

Tallin(n) the capital of Estonia
talon the claw of an animal, especially
that of a bird of prey

tamar relating to the last of four recognized ripening stages of the date
tammar a dama pademelon, a dark stocky
thick-coated wallaby of southern and
western Australia

tamarinds widely cultivated tropical trees
of the family *Leguminosae*
tamarins small South American marmosets of the genus *Leoutocebus*

tamber quality of tone that distinguishes
voices or instruments
tambor the red rockfish of the Pacific
coast

tamis a strainer made of worsted cloth in
a plain open weave
tammy a plain-woven often glazed cloth
of fine worsted or woolen and cotton

tammar (see **tamar**)

tammy (see **tamis**)

Tampan a native or resident of Tampa,
Florida
tampon a plug of cotton or other material
introduced into a body cavity to arrest
hemorrhage, absorb secretions, or fill a
defect

Tan (see **Dan**)

tang a sharp distinctive flavor; the extension of a knife blade that connects with
the handle
tangue any of numerous small often spiny
insectivorous mammals of the family
Tenrecidae of Madagascar

tangi a lamentation or dirge that accompanies a Maori funeral rite
tangy suggestive of a sharp distinctive
flavor that lingers on the tongue

tangue (see **tang**)

tangy (see **tangi**)

tank a unit of weight for pearls equal to
about .15 ounce
tonk a heavy unmusical clang; honky-
tonk (by shortening)

tanto much
Tonto one of various subgroups of the
Apache people

tao the unitary first principle in Taoism
from which all existence and change
spring; in Confucianism, the right way
of life
tau the 19th letter of the Greek alphabet; a
T-shaped mark or object

taos (see **daos**)

taper a slender wax candle; gradually nar-
rowing to a point; a person or device
that applies tape
tapir a large perissodactyl ungulate of
tropical America and southern Asia

tapet worked or figured cloth such as carpet, wall hanging, or tapestry
tappet a lever or projection moved by another device to cause a particular action,
as in some forms of an internal-combus-
tion engine

tapir (see **taper**)

tappet (see **tapet**)

tar (see **taar**)

tard a mentally challenged person; a retard (by shortening)

tarred covered with a dark brown or black bituminous odorous viscid liquid

tare a seed of vetch; the weight of a container or vehicle deducted from its gross weight to obtain the net weight of the cargo
<u>tear</u> to divide or separate forcibly

tariff a system of duties imposed by a government on imported or exported goods
teraph an image representing a primitive household god among ancient Jews and other Semitic peoples

taro an aroid of the Pacific islands grown for its edible starchy tuberous rootstalks
tarot any of 22 pictoral playing cards used for fortune-telling

tarred (see **tard**)

tarrier a person who lags behind, delays, or dawdles
terrier any of various usually small and rather low-built dogs kept chiefly as pets

<u>tarry</u> to linger, dawdle, or procrastinate
terry a loop forming the pile in uncut pile fabrics

Tartar a native or inhabitant of Tatary of Mongolic or Turkic origin; a person of irritable, violent, or intractable temper
tartar a reddish acidic compound found in the juice of grapes; an incrustation on teeth
tarter more acid, sharp, or piquant to the taste

tartarous containing or resembling cream of tartar
Tartarus the infernal regions of ancient mythology; hell

tarter (see **Tartar**)

Tass a Russian news-gathering agency
tasse one of a series of overlapping metal plates in a suit of armor that forms a short skirt covering just below the waist

Tass a Russian news-gathering agency
toss to throw around, heave, or tumble

tasse (see **Tass**)

tassel a pendent ornament used on clothing, curtains, and other articles
tosyl the para isomer of toluene sulfonyl

tasset (see **tacit**)

<u>tat</u> a coarse fabric especially as stretched on a frame and used for withering of tea leaves
tot small child or toddler

Tatar a member of one of the numerous chiefly Turkic peoples probably originating in Manchuria and Mongolia
totter to oscillate or lean dizzily; to move unsteadily

tau (see **tao**)

tau the 19th letter of the Greek alphabet; a T-shaped mark or object
<u>taw</u> a shooter used in the game of marbles; to convert skin into white leather; the 23rd letter of the Hebrew alphabet

taught instructed
taut tightly drawn

taupe a brownish gray color
tope a small shark; to drink intoxicating liquor to excess

Taurid any of a group of meteors appearing from 20–23 November
torrid giving off intense heat

taus T-shaped marks or objects; plural of the 19th letter of the Greek alphabet
touse to pull or handle roughly; dishevel

taut (see **taught**)

taw (see **tau**)

tawed prepared with alum, as animal skins for gloves
tod a mixture of alcoholic spirits and sweetened hot water, (toddy, by shortening)

tawkee (see **talkie**)

tax (see **tachs**)

taxer a person or authority that levies a tax

taxor a former officer at older British universities empowered to regulate the prices of student room and board

taxes manual restorations of displaced body parts, as reductions of a hernia; reflex movements by a freely motile and usually simple organism
taxi(e)s taxicabs, vehicles for hire (by shortening)

taxes pecuniary charges imposed by a public authority
taxis a manual restoration of displaced body parts, as the reduction of a hernia; a reflex movement by a freely motile and usually simple organism
Taxus a genus of trees and shrubs comprising yews

taxi(e)s (see **taxes**)

taxis (see **taxes**)

taxor (see **taxer**)

Taxus (see **taxes**)

tchus (see **chews**)

tea an aromatic beverage prepared from cured leaves of the shrub Camellia sinensis
tee a small artificial elevation from which a golf ball is struck; a short piece of T-shaped pipe
Ti an early Tatar people related to the Hsiung-Nu
ti the seventh tone of the diatonic scale; an Asiatic and Pacific tree

teach to direct, as an instructor
teache in sugar manufacturing, the last of the series of boilers or evaporating pans

teaer a person who drinks tea or attends tea parties
teer one who places the ball on a golf tee

teal a small short-necked river duck

teil a large European linden tree
til sesame, an East Indian annual erect herb

team a group of persons or animals associated in an activity
teem to abound or swarm; present in large quantity

teamer a person who drives a motor truck
teemer a worker who controls the rate at which stainless steel is poured into molds

tear (see **ptere** and **tare**)

tearable capable of being torn
terrible exiting extreme alarm

tearer a person who separates cloth from bolts
terrar a bursar of a religious house
terror intense fright or stark fear

teas aromatic beverages prepared from the cured leaves of the shrub Camellia sinensis
tease to disturb or annoy by persistent irritating action; to tantalize
tees small artificial elevations from which a golf ball is struck
tis seventh tones of the diatonic scale; Asiatic and Pacific trees

teat a protuberance through which milk is drawn from a mammal's breast
tit a titmouse; a small or inferior horse

tec a detective (by shortening)
tech technician or technology (by shortening)
TeX a highly sophisticated computer typesetting program
thèque an aggregation of nevocytes in the epidermis

technology the science of the application of knowledge to practical problems
tecnology the science and study of the life and development of children; soil science

Tecoma (see **Tacoma**)

tedder a machine for stirring and spreading hay to hasten drying and curing
tetter any of various vesicular skin diseases

tee (see **tea**)

teem (see **team**)

teemer (see **teamer**)

teen (see **ctene**)

teer (see **teaer**)

tees (see **teas**)

teeter to move unsteadily or waver precariously; to seesaw
titar a partridge of southern Asia
titer a point of temperature at which fatty acid that is liberated from fat solidifies

Teh(e)ran (see **pteron**)

teil (see **teal**)

telea (see **Ptelea**)

telestic mystical
telestich a poem in which consecutive final letters of lines spell a name

tellin a mollusk of the family Tellinidae; a sunset shell
telyn an old Celtic harp

Tempe a city in central Arizona
tempi rates of motion or activity, especially in musical passages

tempera a process of painting in which an albuminous or collodial medium is employed as the vehicle
tempora units of time in mensural music

tempi (see **Tempe**)

tempora (see **tempera**)

temps temporary employees (by shortening); temperatures (by shortening)
tempts entices to do wrong; seduces

tenace a combination of two high cards in a bridge hand separated in rank by the intervening card held by an opponent

tennis a game played with rackets and an elastic ball

tenant a person who rents or leases property from a landlord
tenent a projecting member of a piece of wood or other material for insertion into a mortise to make a joint; a tenon

tendance looking after someone or something
tendence tendency

tends cares for the wants of; directs toward a particular direction
TENS a self-operated portable device used to treat chronic pain by generating electrical impulses (*t*ranscutaneous *e*lectrical *n*erve *s*timulator)
tens ten-dollar bills

tenent (see **tenant**)

tenner a ten-dollar bill
tenor an intent or substance; the highest natural adult male voice

tennis (see **tenace**)

tenor (see **tenner**)

TENS and **tens** (see **tends**)

tense distinction in a verb form; taut or rigid; jittery
tenths musical intervals embracing an octave and a third; two or more of ten equal parts into which some thing is divisible
tents collapsible shelters of canvas or other material

tenser more rigid or jittery
tensor a generalized vector with more than three components

tenths (see **tense**)

tents (see **tense**)

tenuis an unaspirated voiceless stop
tenuous having little substance or strength; weak; vague

teraph (see **tariff**)

teras (see **Pteris**)

terce the third of the canonical hours
terse brief, concise, or devoid of superfluity

terek (see **pteric**)

termen the outer margin of a triangularly shaped insect wing
termine determine (by shortening)
termon church land exempt from secular taxation

termer a person serving a specific term, such as a prisoner
termor a person who has an estate for a specified period of years or life

termine (see **termen**)

termon (see **termen**)

termor (see **termer**)

tern a sea bird; something consisting of three items
terne sheet iron or steel coated with a lead-tin alloy
turn to move in a curved path; to change position

ternar a university student assigned to the third and lowest social rank and required to pay the lowest fees
turner a person that turns, or a device that is used in turning

ternary having three elements
ternery a place where flocks of terns breed
turnery fashioning material with a lathe

terne (see **tern**)

terneplate sheet iron or steel coated with a lead-tin alloy
turnplate a turntable; a flat steel plate used for turning railway cars from one line to another

ternery (see **ternary**)

ternes sheets of iron or steel coated with a lead-tin alloy
terns sea birds

turns a watchmaker's lathe

terp a large artificial mound in the Netherlands providing a site for a prehistoric settlement in a seasonally flooded area
turp turpentine (by shortening)

terrace (see **Pteris**)

terrain ground or a geographical area
terrane a rock formation or formations

terrar (see **tearer**)

terrene relating to this world or life; mundane
terrine an earthenware jar containing a table delicacy and sold with its contents
tureen a deep-footed serving dish

terrible (see **tearable**)

terrier (see **tarrier**)

terrine (see **terrene**)

terror (see **tearer**)

terry (see **tarry**)

terse (see **terce**)

testae the hard external coatings or integuments of a seed
teste the witnessing or concluding clause of a writ
testee a person who takes an examination

testar a West Indian clingfish
tester the frame on which the canopy of a bed rests; a person who checks the quality and conformance to predetermined specifications

teste the witnessing or concluding clause of a writ
testy easily annoyed or irritable

teste (see **testae**)

testee (see **testae**)

testees persons who take an examination
testes male reproductive glands; witnessing or concluding clauses of a writ

tester (see **testar**)

testes (see **testees**)

testy (see **teste**)

tête (see **tait**)

tet(h) (see **tait**)

tetrastichous arranged in four vertical rows
Tetrastichus a genus of minute chalcid flies comprising numerous hyperparasites

tetravalence in chemistry, having a valence of four
tetravalents quadruples, groups of four homologous chromosomes each of which is associate in synapsis

tetrazene either of two hypothetical isomeric hydrides of nitrogen
tetrazine an isomeric parent compound resembling benzene with four methylidyne groups replaced by nitrogen atoms

tetter (see **tedder**)

TeX (see **tec**)

Thais (see **tailles**)

thallic (see **phthalic**)

thalline (see **phthalin**)

thallous relating to or containing the metallic element thallium
thallus a plant body that is characteristic of the thallophytes

than a conjunction used with comparative adjectives and adverbs
then at that time

thaught a thwart on a boat
thought formed in the mind

the a definite article preceding a noun
thee a form of address; thou

their belonging to them
there in or at that place
there're the contraction of there are
they're the contraction of they are

theirs what belongs to them
there's the contraction of there is or there was

then (see **than**)

theocracy government by God's direction
theocrasy a fusion of different deities in the minds of worshipers

thèque (see **tec**)

there (see **their**)

therefor in return for that
therefore because of that

there're (see **their**)

there's (see **theirs**)

therm any of several units of quantity of heat
thurm to work a piece of wood with saw and chisel across the grain so as to produce patterns resembling those produced by turning

thermos a vacuum bottle or flask
Thermus a genus of gram-negative aerobic bacteria

they're (see **their**)

thiokol (see **phthiocol**)

thought (see **thaught**)

threw propelled through the air by the hand
through denoting penetration or passage

throes a condition of struggle, anguish, or disorder
throws propels through the air by the hand

thrombin a proteolytic enzyme that is formed from prothrombin
thrombon the entire body of blood platelets and their precursors that constitute a distinct organ of the body

throne a ceremonial seat
thrown propelled through the air by the hand

through (see **threw**)

thrown (see **throne**)

throws (see **throes**)

thruster a person who intrudes or pushes him or herself forward; a pusher
thrustor a combination oil pump and piston cylinder

Thule belonging to the Eskimo culture extending over arctic lands from Alaska to Greenland about A.D. 500–1400; a settlement in northwest Greenland
tule either of two large bulrushes growing abundantly on overflowed land in the southwestern U.S. and adjacent Mexico

thurm (see **therm**)

thyme a common garden herb
time a measured duration, period, or interval

thymene a liquid used for perfuming soap
thymine a crystalline compound obtained from fish spermatozoa

Ti and **ti** (see **tea**)

tiaras decorative bands or ornaments for the head
tiaris a tropical American finch

tiaras high and erect royal headdresses encircled with a diadem
tierras fine material of earth or rock mixed with quicksilver ore

tiaris (see **tiaras**)

tical the basic monetary unit of Thailand
tickle to excite amusement or merriment in

ticker something that ticks or produces a ticking sound, as a watch or the heart; a telegraphic instrument that prints stock quotations or news on a paper ribbon
tikor a starch or arrowroot made from the tubers of an East Indian herb

tickle (see **tical**)

ticks bloodsucking arachnids; light rhythmic tapping sounds
tics convulsive motions of muscles, especially facial
tix tickets (slang)

tidal related to the alternate rise and fall of oceans

title a descriptive or general heading; the distinguishing name of a book or production

tiddle to occupy oneself aimlessly; to putter about
tittle an extremely small or least possible amount; a point or small mark used in writing or printing

tide the alternate rise and fall of an ocean
tied fastened or attached; made an equal score in a contest

tier (see **ptere** and **tear**)

tier a person who fastens, closes openings, or binds articles
tire to become weary or exhausted; a continuous pneumatic rubber cushion encircling a wheel

tierras (see **tiaras**)

ties (see **tailles**)

tig the game of tag
tyg a large usually slip-decorated ceramic drinking cup with two or more handles

tighten to become tense or taut
titan a person gigantic in size or power

tighter more taught, tense, or dense
titer a point or temperature at which fatty acid that is liberated from fat solidifies

tigress a female tiger
Tigris a major river in Turkey and Iraq that joins the Euphrates

tikor (see **ticker**)

til (see **teal**)

til sesame, an East Indian annual erect herb
'til until
till up to a specified time; to work the soil

tilley seeds of the croton-oil plant
tilly composed of or having the character of clay

tiltup to incline or slant a camera

tilt-up of or relating to a method constructing concrete walls

timbal a kettledrum; a vibrating membrane in a cicada's shrilling organ

timbale a creamy mixture of food cooked in a mold or cup

timber trees or their wood

timbre the quality of sound depending chiefly on various overtones; the crest on a coat of arms

time (see **thyme**)

timpani a set of usually two or three kettledrums played by one person in a musical group

tympany a distention of the abdomen caused by accumulation of air or gas in the intestinal tract

tincal a mineral consisting of native borax

tinkle a series of short high ringing or clinking sounds

ting (see **ding**)

tinkle (see **tincal**)

Tinne an Athapaskan people occupying most of the interior of Alaska and northern Canada

tinny resembling, containing, or suggestive of tin

tip an end or extremity; a gratuity

typp a unit of yarn size

tiple a knd of guitar with ten strings tuned in four groups

tipple to indulge in intoxicating drinks habitually

tippet a shoulder cape, often with hanging ends

tippit the game of "up Jenkins"

tipple (see **tiple**)

tire (see **tier**)

tis (see **teas**)

tisane (see **ptisan**)

tit (see **teat**)

titan (see **tighten**)

titar (see **teeter**)

titer (see **teeter** or **tighter**)

title (see **tidal**)

tittle (see **tiddle**)

titty a teat or nipple on the breast of a female animal

tydie a small bird variously identified as a wren or the blue titmouse

tix (see **ticks**)

to a preposition indicating a spatial relationship or a relationship suggesting motion

too also or moreover

two the whole number between one and three

toa a tall usually spreading tree of northern Australia and the Pacific islands

Towa the language of the Jemez group of Pueblo Indians

toad a tailless leaping amphibian

tode a rude sled for hauling logs

toed reached with a foot's forepart

towed hauled or pulled

toady a person engaging in excessive deference through self-interest

tody a tiny non-passerine insectivorous West Indian bird

toat the handle of a joiner's plane

tote to transport from one place to another

tocked (see **takt**)

tocsin an alarm bell

toxin a poisonous substance produced by a living organism

tod (see **tawed**)

tode (see **toad**)

tody (see **toady**)

toed (see **toad**)

toey nervous, anxious, or worried

towhee any of numerous American finches

towie contract bridge for three to six players

tois plural of any of several Asiatic and Pacific trees or shrubs

toise an old French unit of length equal to 1.949 meters

toys things designed for play, amusement, or diversion

toke a puff on a marijuana cigarette (slang); a tip given by a gambler to a dealer in a casino

toque a soft hat with a very narrow brim and a full crown pleated into a snug headband worn in the 16th century

tol a Sanskrit school or college

tole decorative japanned or painted metal

toll a tax or fee paid for some liberty or privilege; to sound a bell as a signal or announcement

told narrated or recounted

toled enticed or allured; lured or decoyed game by arousing curiosity

tolled taxed; sounded, as a bell

tole (see **tol**)

toled (see **told**)

toll (see **tol**)

tolled (see **told**)

ton the prevailing fashion or mode

tone a vocal or musical sound; a color quality or value

ton a unit of U.S. weight equal to 2000 pounds

tonne a unit of mass equal to 1,000 kilograms, or 2,204.62 pounds

tun a large cask

tonal the force that acts on the mass of a ton to accelerate it equal to one foot per second squared

tunnel a covered passageway

tone (see **ton**)

tongue a fleshy process in most vertebrates' mouths

tung a Chinese tree grown for its seeds which yield tung oil

tonk (see **tank**)

tonne (see **ton**)

Tonto (see **tanto**)

too (see **to**)

toodle to make a continuous low sound, as in cooing or playing a small pipe

tootle to sound a short blast continuously or repeatedly on a wind instrument

tool an implement used in work

tulle sheer and often stiffened machine-made netting

tooling a gilt or blind impression stamped in intaglio on ornamental leatherwork

twoling a twin crystal

toon an East Indian and Australian tree; an animated drawing (cartoon shortened)

tune a musical composition

Toona a small genus of Old World trees closely related to a genus that includes the Spanish cedar

toona a Mexican tree that is a minor source of rubber

tuna any of numerous large vigorous scombroid fish; any of various flatjointed prickly pears

toot a short blast sounded on a wind instrument; a drinking bout or spreee

tout to proclaim loudly

tooter a person who sounds a short blast on a wind instrument

Tudor relating to the English royal family reigning from 1485 to 1603; marked by Tudor arches

tutor a person who instructs and guides

tootle (see **toodle**)

too-too to an affectedly or unpleasantly excessive degree; to produce a flat monotonous tootling sound

tutu a very short projecting skirt worn by a ballet dancer; an Hawaiian grandma or grandpa; any of several New Zealand shrubs or small trees

tope (see **taupe**)

topee a lightweight helmetlike hat often made of sola pith
topi a central African antelope

topline the outline on the top of an animal's body
top-line most featured or prominently advertised; top-level

topography the art or practice of detailed graphic delineation on maps or charts of the physical features of a place or region
typography the art of letterpress printing

topology a branch of mathematics that investigates the properties of a geometric configuration; the history of a region as indicated by its topography
typology a doctrine that things in the Christian dispensation are symbolized or prefigured by things in the Old Testament; a study based on types

toque (see **toke**)

tor a high craggy hill
tore divided or separated forcibly
torr a measure of pressure equal to 1333.2 bars

tora a large reddish hartebeest
Torah a scroll of the Pentateuch used in synagogues

torcel the larva of a South American botfly that lives beneath human skin
torsal of or pertaining to a surface generated by a straight line which constantly turns about some point in its length
torsel a piece of stone, iron, or wood supporting the end of a beam or joist

tore (see **tor**)

tore divided or separated forcibly; a torus, a doughnut-shaped surface
tower a person that smooths ceramic ware; a person or animal that pulls a barge or boat

tori large architectural moldings of convex profile commonly occurring as the lowest molding in the base of a column
Torrey a tall coniferous tree of California
Tory an American upholding the cause of the British Crown against supporters of the American Revolution
tory a person who emphasizes order, tradition, stability, or accepted canons of conduct

torous having the surface covered with rounded prominences; knobbed
torus in mathematics, the surface or solid formed by rotating a conic section about a straight line; an anchor ring

torr (see **tor**)

Torrey (see **tori**)

torrid (see **Taurid**)

torsal (see **torcel**)

torsel (see **torcel**)

tort a wrongful act
torte a cake or pastry of ground nuts or bread crumbs

torta a flat heap of moist crushed silver ore
torte a cake or pastry of ground nuts or bread crumbs

torte (see **tort**)

torulous somewhat knobbed
torulus the socket in which an insect's antenna articulates

torus (see **Taurus** and **torous**)

Tory and **tory** (see **tori**)

toss (see **Tass**)

tosyl (see **tassel**)

tot (see **tat**)

tote (see **toat**)

totter (see **Tatar**)

toughed endured
tuft a clump or cluster

toughs rowdy, surly persons
tuffs rocks composed of finer kinds of volcanic detritus
tufts clumps or clusters

tour a journey; a circular trip
tur a Caucasian wild goat

tourbillion something which whirls spirally, as a whirlwind
tourbillon a form of rotary carriage to carry the escapement so that the position errors are eliminated

tourn the circuit of en English sheriff to hold a court of record twice a year
turn to practice or perform gymnastic exercises

tournay a printed worsted upholstery fabric
tournee a game of skat

touse (see **taus**)

tout (see **toot**)

Towa (see **toa**)

towed (see **toad**)

tower (see **tore**)

towhee (see **toey**)

towie (see **toey**)

toxin (see **tocsin**)

toys (see **tois**)

trachycarpous rough-fruited
Trachycarpus a small genus of low East Asiatic fan palms, including the hemp palm

tracked pursued; traveled
tract a pamphlet or leaflet of exhortation or appeal; a land area

tracks trails or pathways
tracs tractors (by shortening)
tracts pamphlets or leaflets of exhortation or appeal; land areas

tract (see **tracked**)

tracts (see **tracks**)

trade to barter or buy and sell; a means of livelihood
trayed arranged on trays, as for drying fruit

trader a person who barters, buys, or sells
traitor a person who commits treason against his/her country, betrays another's trust, or is false to an obligation

trail to track game; to plod or trudge
treille in heraldry, a trellis or lattice

traitor (see **trader**)

tramp the succession of sounds made by the beating of the animal feet on a surface
tromp(e) an apparatus in which air is sucked through sloping holes in the upper end of a large vertical wooden tube and led to a furnace by a stream of falling water, as for a Catalan forge

trance a daze, stupor, or state of suspended animation
trans characterized by atoms on opposite sides of a molecule

transects sample areas of vegetation usually in the form of narrow continuous strips
transsex to assume the physical characteristics and gender role of the opposite sex

transladed transferred cargo, as in trans-shipping
translated converted into another language

transplantar lying across the sole of the foot
transplanter a person or machine that removes items from one location and introduces in another

transsex (see **transects**)

transverses lies or passes across
transversus a transveralis muscle

<u>**travail**</u> physical or mental exertion, especially of a painful or laborious nature (although usually treval)

travel to proceed on a trip or tour

trave a frame; to control an unruly horse or ox for shoeing

<u>**tref**</u> a homestead or hamlet acting as a single community

travel (see **travail**)

travois a primitive transportation device used by the Plains Indians of North American consisting of two trailing poles

travoy a small sled often made from the fork of a tree and used as an aid in skidding trees

tray a flat-bottomed low-rimmed open receptacle

trey a card or side of a die containing three spots or pips

trayed (see **trade**)

treatee a person who is entertained or treated to something

treaty a written agreement or convention between two or more political authorities

tref (see **trave**)

treille (see **trail**)

trews close-cut tartan short drawers worn under a Scottish kilt

trues brings to a desired mechanical accuracy

trey (see **tray**)

tri a dog having a coat of black, tan, and white

try to attempt or endeavor; to examine in a court of law

triaene an elongated sponge spicule with three divergent rays at one end

triene a chemical compound containing three double bonds

trichi a cigar made in India

tricky deceptively safe, easy, manageable, or orderly; intricate

tricorn an imaginary three-horned beast

tricorne a hat with brim turned up at three places

triene (see **triaene**)

trigon an ancient triangular harp; the cutting region of an upper molar's crown

trygon a stingray

triker a tricycle rider

trikir a three-branched candlestick used by bishops in the Eastern Orthodox Church

triol a chemical compound containing three hydroxyl groups

triole a group of three musical notes or tones performed in the time of two of the same value

trip to dance or skip with light quick steps; a journey

tryp a member of the genus Trypanosoma which comprises parasitic flagellate protozoans that as adults are elongated and somewhat spindle-shaped

triple a multiple of three; threefold

tripple a horse's gait resembling an amble

triptik a series of road maps

triptych a picture in three compartments side by side

tryptic relating to trypsin, a proteolytic enzyme present in the pancreatic juice, or to its action

triptych a picture in three compartments side by side

triptyque a customs pass for temporary importation of an automobile

triter more hackneyed, threadbare, or shopworn

tritor a grinding surface developed on the tooth

troche a medicinal lozenge or tablet

trochee a prosadic foot of two syllables, the first long and the second short

trollop an unkempt slovenly woman; a straggly mass

trollope a cry of protest against bad manners or boorish behavior, especially in a theater

tromp(e) (see **tramp**)

troolie one of the immense leaves of the bussu used for thatching

truli round stone buildings made with conical roofs and without mortar

truly truthfully; sincerely; realistically; accurately

troop a group or body of soliders; to move in an orderly manner

troupe a group of stage performers

trottie a small child; a toddler

trotty lively or brisk

trough any of various containers used for some domestic or industrial purpose, as in kneading

trow belief, faith, or covenant

troupe (see **troop**)

trousers outer garments extending from the waist to the ankle, covering each leg separately and worn chiefly by males

trowsers long drawers having an attached or detachable ruffle at the bottom of each leg

trousse a case for small instruments

truce a suspension of fighting; a respite

trow (see **trough**)

trowsers (see **trousers**)

truce (see **trousse**)

trues (see **trews**)

truli (see **troolie**)

truly (see **troolie**)

trussed secured closely; tied

trust confidence, reliance, or faith

truster a person who relies or believes

trustor a person creating a trust by transferral of property to a trustee

try (see **tri**)

trygon (see **trigon**)

tryp (see **trip**)

tryptic (see **triptik**)

tsine (see **sign**)

Tswa (see **schwa**)

tubar having the form of or consisting of a hollow cylinder

tuber a short fleshy, usually underground shoot or stem of a plant

tucks gathers in a fold; puts in a snug place

tux a tuxedo, a man's formal attire (by shortening)

Tudor (see **tooter**)

tuffs (see **toughs**)

tuft (see **toughed**)

tufts (see **toughs**)

tuille a hinged plate for the thigh in plate armor

tweel a closure of a glass furnace

tule (see **Thule**)

tulle (see **tool**)

tumtum a dog cart

tum-tum a reiterated strumming

tun (see **ton**)

tuna (see **Toona**)

tune (see **toon**)

tung (see **tongue**)

tunnel (see **tonal**)

tur (see **tour**)

turban a headdress

turbine a rotary engine

Turbit a breed of fancy pigeons

turbot a large European flatfish that is highly esteemed as a food fish

Turbo a genus of marine snails that usually have a heavy turbinate shell with a pearly lining

turbo turbosupercharger (by shortening)

turbot a large European flatfish that is highly esteemed as a food fish

turbot (see **Turbit**)

tureen (see **terrene**)

Turkey a country of southeast Europe and southwest Asia
turkey a large American bird
Turki relating to the peoples of Turkic speech; one of the Turki peoples

turn (see **tern** and **tourn**)

turner (see **ternar**)

turnery (see **ternary**)

turnip a biennial herb whose thick edible root is a vegetable
turnup a turned-up part of an article, as a pant cuff; a card turned face up

turnplate (see **terneplate**)

turns (see **ternes**)

turnup (see **turnip**)

turp (see **terp**)

turreted furnished with or as if with little towers
turritid a mollusk of the family Turritidae

tusch a flourish or fanfare of brass wind musical instruments and drums
Tush a member of a Georgian people north of Tiflis
tush buttocks (slang)

tussal relating to a cough
tussle a struggle or scuffle

tussic relating to a cough
tussock a small hummock of more solid ground in a marsh or bog

tussle (see **tussal**)

tussock (see **tussic**)

tutee a pupil
tutti a musical direction for voices or instruments to play together

tutor (see **tooter**)

tutti (see **tutee**)

tutu (see **too-too**)

tux (see **tucks**)

Twaddell according to a specific gravity reading of a Twaddell hydrometer
twaddle idle chatter; to babble

twee a thin or shrill piping note
Twi a dialect spoken by the Akwapim people of Ghana

tweel (see **tuille**)

twees thin or shrill piping notes
tweeze to extract, pluck, or remove with a small pincer-shaped tool

Twi (see **twee**)

twice-sold goods or services that are sold two times
twice-soled footwear that has been soled two times
twice-souled obtaining a soul on two occasions

twill a textile weave
'twill the contraction of it will or it shall

twister a person who wrings, wrenches, or wrests so as to dislocate or distort; a tornado
twistor a non-volatile computer memory element; consisting of a helix of magnetic wire wound under tension

two (see **to**)

twofold being twice as large, as great, or as many
two-fold two stage flats hinged together so that they fold face to face

twoling (see **tooling**)

two-seated a vehicle or machine equipped with two seats
two-seeded an area that is planted with two varieties of seeds

tydie (see **titty**)

tyes (see **tailles**)

tyg (see **tig**)

Tyighs (see **tailles**)

tympany (see **timpani**)

typography (see **topography**)

typology (see **topology**)

typp (see **tip**)

Tyr (see **ptere**)

tyrannis absolute rule, as by a dictator
Tyrannus the type genus of Tyrannidae
  comprising the kingbird

Tyre (see **ptere**)

tzut (see **soot**)

Group I

tablet - tablette
tamis - tamise - tammy
technic - technique
tele - telly
termer - termor
thrash - thresh
tinplate - tin-plate
topnotch - top-notch
toxin - toxon
traitoress - traitorous
transcendence - transcendents
transhumance - transhumants
transience - transients
trivalence - trivalents
tubulous - tubulus
tumulous - tumulus
Turkman - Turkmen
typhous - typhus
tyrannis - tryannous

Group I and II

thromboses thräm'bō₁sēz
thrombosis thräm'bōsəs

tickling 'tikliŋ
tikling tə'kliŋ

toilet 'tȯilət
toilette 'toi₁let

tortuous 'tȯrchəwəs
torturous 'tȯrchərəs

trustee :trə:stē
trusty 'trəstē

tuberculose tə'bərkyə₁lōs
tuberculous tə'bərkələs

Group II

tacet 'tä₁ket
tacit 'tasət
tassette 'tȯset

tache 'tach
tash 'täsh

tailleur tä'yər
tailloir ₁tä'ywər

taipo 'täē₁pō
type 'tīpō

takt 'täkt
talked 'tȯkt

talesman 'tālzmən
talisman 'tāləsmən

talk 'tȯk
tock 'täk

taller 'tȯlər
t(h)aler 'tälər

tambor 'tam₁bȯr
tambour 'tam₁bu̇r

tambourin 'tambərən
tombourine 'tambə₁rēn

tardy 'tärdē
tarte 'tärtē

tarpan tär:pan
tarpon 'tärpən

tatou tə'tü
tattoo 'ta₁tü

taught 'tȯt
tot 'tät

Tauri 'tȯ₁rī
tory 'tȯrē

Taurus 'tȯrəs
torose 'tōr₁ōs
torus 'tōrəs

tawed 'tȯd
tod 'täd

tear 'tir
teer 'tēər

techie 'tekē
techy 'techē

tempera 'tempərə
tempura ₁tempə'rä

tendence 'tendənts
tendenz ten'dents

terete tə'rēt
terret 'terət

testee 'te:stē
testy 'testē

tetanic te'tanik
titanic tī:tanik

tetragenous tə'träjənəs
tetragynous 'tetrə₁jīnəs

tetramine 'tetrə₁mən
tetrammine te'tramən

tetrapterous te'traptərəs
tetrapturus ₁te₁trap'tùrəs

thermal 'thərməl
thermel 'thər₁mel

thigh 'thī
thy '<u>th</u>ī

tippee ti'pē
tippy 'tipē

toastee tō'stē
toasty 'tōstē

tohi 'tōhē
towhee 'tō₁hē

tootsie 'tùtsē
Tutsi 'tütsē

torchere tȯr'sher
torture 'tȯrchər

torchon 'tȯr₁shän
torsion 'tȯrshən

tour 'tùr
turr 'tər

toured 'tùrd
turd 'tərd

tournay tür'nā
tourne(e) 'túrnē

tourneur tùr'nər
turner 'tùrnər

traiteur 'trä₁tər
traitor 'trātər

travail trə'väl
travale tra'val

treadle 'tredəl
tredille trə₁dil

treaties 'trēd•|ēz
treatise 'trēd•əs

triste 'trēst
tryst 'trist

troche 'trōkē
trochi 'trō₁kī

trophi 'trō₁fī
trophy 'trōfē

trotter 'trätər
trotteur trä'tər

tule 'tülē
tulle 'tül

turnip 'tərnəp
turnup 'tərn₁əp

Tyranni tə'ra₁nī
tyranny 'tirənē

U

uang a rhinoceros beetle

wang a member of the Chinese ruling class before and after the 3rd century B.C.

Uca a genus consisting of fiddler crabs

yuca any of several plants of the genus Manihot yieldig a nutritous starch; tapioca plant

Yucca a genus of American sometimes arborescent plants

yucca any plant of the genus Yucca

udder a large pendulous organ consisting of two or more mammary glands

utter to speak; remote; complete

ugh (see **a**)

ugli a hybrid between a tangerine or mandarin orange and either a grapefruit or a shaddock

ugly unpleasing, disagreeable, or loathsome in appearance

uhlan a lancer of the class of Tatarian origin introduced into European armies

yulan a Chinese magnolia with large white very fragrant flowers

ulmous resembling ulmin, a group of brown to black organic substances found in soil, peat, or coal

Ulmus a genus of trees comprising the elms

umbels (see **humbles**)

umber a grayling fish

umbre a dusky brown African wading bird

umbles (see **humbles**)

umbre (see **umber**)

unaccepted not having had responsibility for its maintenance received with consent by the government

unexcepted unalterable

unaffected free from affectation; genuine, sincere, or unpretentious; not acted upon or influenced

uneffected not accomplished, executed, or enforced

unaired without air or circulation

unheired having no inheritor(s)

unallowed not permitted; prohibited

unaloud not audible

unamendable not capable of reforming oneself

unemendable a literary work that is not subject to correction or editing

unassayed not analyzed or tested, as a mineral deposit

unessayed not made an effort to accomplish or perform

unbailed a boat that is not clear of water

unbaled an unbundled group of goods

unbaring stripping or uncovering

unbearing barren or infertile

unbilled not charged to a customer

unbuild to demolish

unborn not yet brought into life

unborne not endured or tolerated; not carried

unbreached not in violation of a standard or law

unbreeched not wearing short pants

unbuild (see **unbilled**)

uncal relating to a hook or claw; the anterior end of the hippocampal convolution

uncle the brother of either of one's parents

unceded not surrendered or relinquished

unseated having been removed or deposed from a political position; having been dislodged as a (horse) rider; not sitting

unseeded unsown, as a field; not selectively placed in the draw for a tournament

unchased not following or being followed rapidly and intently

unchaste not free from lewdness, obscenity, or indecency

uncited not brought to mind or called to attention

unsided without surfaces that enclose space

unsighted unable to see; unperceived; not aimed by means of a sighting device

uncle (see **uncal**)

uncomplementary not supplementing; mutually independent

uncomplimentary derogatory or unflattering

uncord to loosen or release from cords

uncored something from which the axial portion has not been removed, as an apple

undammed an unobstructed flow of water

undamned not condemned

underbilled charged less than the full amount

underbuild to build a supporting structure underneath; to build be low standard

underhold an encircling grip secured advantageously by a wrestler under an opponent's arm

underholed cut away the lower portion of or cut under a coal seam

undermade manufactured or prepared short of a required standard quality; incompletely made or finished

undermaid a domestic worker whose status is below a maidservant

undersold exchanged goods or services beneath the usual or competitive price

undersoled put a covering beneath the sole of the foot or shoe

underway no longer at rest, in port, or at anchor; moving

underweigh to fall short of a required or standard weight

undo (see **endue**)

undue (see **endue**)

uneffected (see **unaffected**)

unemendable (see **unamendable**)

unerupted not yet emerged through the gum, as a tooth not having emerged

unirrupted without sudden or violent invasion

unessayed (see **unassayed**)

unexcepted (see **unaccepted**)

unexercised untried or unpracticed

unexorcised not driven off or expelled

unfaded without loss of freshness, vigor, color, or health

unfated not controlled by destiny or fate

unfeted not celebrated or entertained

unfloured not sprinkled or coated with flour

unflowered not covered or decorated with flowers; without flowers

unfoaled (see **enfold**)

unfold (see **enfold**)

unfrees places in bondage; separates from freedom; coerces

unfreeze to thaw

ungild to remove gold or gilding from

ungilled not provided with gills; removed fish from a gill net

ungraded not classified according to ranks or grades; not assigned to a specific grade in school; not reduced to a gradual slope

ungrated not reduced to small bits by abrasion

unhealed not cured or restored to health

unheeled without the hind part of the foot or rear part of a shoe

unheard not perceived by the ear

unherd to disperse or separate from a herd of animals

unheated not warmed
unheeded disregarded or ignored

unheeled (see **unhealed**)

unheired (see **unaired**)

unherd (see **unheard**)

uniparous producing one egg or offspring at a time
uniporous having one spore

unirrupted (see **unerupted**)

unkeyed not provided with a key
unquayed not provided with a landing place or wharf beside water

unkilled not dead; alive
unkilned not cured, fired, or dried in a kiln

unkneaded unmixed or unblended, as bread
unneeded unnecessary; not needed

unknocked not struck or rapped
unnocked unnotched, as an arrow

unlade to unload
unlaid not placed or fixed

unlead to remove lead from, as between lines of type
unled lacking leadership or guidance

unlessened marked by constancy; not diminished
unlessoned lacking instruction

unlimbed dismembered
unlimned undelineated

unmassed not gathered or formed into a mass
unmast to remove or not furnish a mast

unmedaled not honored or rewarded with one or more medals
unmeddled not interferred with

unmissed not discovered or noticed the absence of
unmist to clear away haze, film, or mist

unneeded (see **unkneaded**)

unnocked (see **unknocked**)

unpadded not furnished with padding
unpatted not stroked or tapped with the hand

unpaired not matched or mated
unpared untrimmed or unpealed

unpatted (see **unpadded**)

unpealed unrung, as bells or chimes
unpeeled the outer layer not removed or stripped off

unpearled not set or adorned with pearls
unpurled not embroidered or edged with gold or silver thread

unpeddled not peddled, as a bicycle
unpetaled not covered with petals

unpeeled (see **unpealed**)

unpetaled (see **unpeddled**)

unplaited not woven into strands of yarn, fabric, or locks of hair; unbraided
unplated not overlaid with metal or other material

unplaited not woven into strands of yarn, fabric, or locks of hair; unbraided
unplatted not mapped

unplated (see **unplaited**)

unplatted (see **unplaited**)

unpoled not furnished with a pole or poles
unpolled not registered, cast, or counted at the voting polls

unpraying not addressing or seeking through prayer
unpreying not seizing and devouring

unpurled (see **unpearled**)

unquayed (see **unkeyed**)

unraided not victimized by hostile or predatory incursion
unrated not rated, scored, or evaluated

unraised not raised or elevated
unrazed not destroyed, or leveled to the ground; left standing

unrated (see **unraided**)

unrazed (see **unraised**)

unreal artificial or false
unreel to unwind

unreave to unravel
unreeve to withdraw rope from a ship's block or other opening

unrecked to be unconcerned; was of no interest
unwrecked not disabled or ruined

unreel (see **unreal**)

unreeve (see **unreave**)

unrested tired or exhausted
unwrested not forced or moved by violent wringing or twisting movements

unrhymed without identical sounding words or lines of verse
unrimed not covered with granular ice tufts

unright unjust or wrong; an injustice
unwrite to obliterate from writing; to expunge, erase, or rescind

unrimed (see **unrhymed**)

unrooted torn up or out by the roots
unrouted not routed or provided with an itinerary

unrung not having or wearing a ring; not pealed, as a bell or chime
unwrung not painfully affected; unmoved

unscent to deprive of scent or odor
unsent not dispatched or transmitted

unseated (see **unceded**)

unseeded (see **unceded**)

unsent (see **unscent**)

unsewn not stitched together
unsown not planted with seed

unsided (see **uncited**)

unsighted (see **uncited**)

unsold something that has not been exchanged for money or its equivalent

unsoled wearing apparel without soles
unsouled deprived of a soul or spirit

unsonned dispossessed of the character of a son
unsunned not exposed to sunlight

unsordid not covered with filth; not vile
unsorted not classified

unsouled (see **unsoled**)

unsown (see **unsewn**)

unstaid not demure, reserved, or well-ordered in behavior
unstayed not hindered, checked, supported, or upheld; not fastened with stays

unsunned (see **unsonned**)

unsure (see **ensure**)

untacks unfastens, loosens, or detaches by removing a tack or tacks
untax to remove from taxation; to take a tax from

unthrone to remove from a throne or ceremonial seat; to dethrone
unthrown not propelled through the air by hand

untold not related or revealed; not numbered or enumerated
untolled not having paid a toll or tax

unwaived not relinquished voluntarily
unwaved straight or not waved, as hair

unwanted not needed or desired; superfluous or unnecessary
unwonted unusual or unaccustomed; not made familiar by practice

unwaved (see **unwaived**)

unweaned not accustomed to the loss of a mother's milk; dependent on the mother for nourishment
unweened unbelieved; unimagined

unwedded not married
unwetted not suffused with tears
unwhetted unsharpened or dull

unweened (see **unweaned**)

unwetted (see **unwedded**)

unwhetted (see **unwedded**)

unwonted (see **unwanted**)

unwrapped (see **enrapt**)

unwrecked (see **unrecked**)

unwrested (see **unrested**)

unwrite (see **unright**)

unwrung (see **unrung**)

uranate a compound formed by reaction of a uranyl salt with a base
urinate to discharge liquid produced in or through the kidney(s)

Uranian of, pertaining to, or concerned with the heavens or the science of astronomy
uranion a keyboard instrument consisting of a series of pieces of wood, sounded by being pressed against a revolving wheel

uranous relating to or containing trivalent uranium
Uranus the plant seventh in order from the sun
urinous having the qualities or odor of urine

urb (see **herb**)

urd (see **erred**)

urea (see **Eurya**)

Uria (see **Eurya**)

urinate (see **uranate**)

urinous (see **uranous**)

urn (see **earn**)

use (see **ewes**)

use (see **ius**)

utter (see **udder**)

Group I

unctious - unctuous
unrepentance - unrepentants

Group I and II

umbellate　ˌem'belət
umbellet　'əmbelàt

Group II

uranyl　'yu̇rəˌnil
urinal　'yu̇rənᵊl

ursine　'ərˌsīn
urson　'ərˌsän

Uta　'yüdə
Utah　'yütä

V

---

vagrance a departure from an expected, normal, or logical order or course
vagrants insects or other small arthropods that produce no web, nest, gall, or other protective structure

vagus either of the tenth pair of cranial nerves supplying chiefly the viscera

'Vegas Las Vegas, the largest city in Nevada and a gambling mecca (by shortening)

Vai a Negro people of Liberia
vie to strive for superiority; to contend

vail to let fall; to lower, as a sign of respect or submission

vale a low-lying area usually containing a stream
veil to obscure; a curtain

vain fruitless or unsuccessful
vane a movable device to indicate wind direction
vein a blood vessel; a streak or stripe

vainest most fruitless or unsuccessful
Vanist a follower of Sir Henry Vane who as governor of the Massachusetts colony defended Anne Hutchinson on charges of antinomianism

vairé an heraldic vair consisting of tinctures other than argent and azure
vary to differ or diversify
very extremely

valance a pleated drapery or canopy often used for decoration or concealment
valence the degree of combining power of a chemical element or radical

vale (see **vail**)

valence (see **valance**)

valet a servant who performs personal services
valley an elongated depression of earth commonly situated between hills or mountains

vali a governor-general of a chief administrative division of Turkey
volley the simultaneous or nearly simultaneous discharge of a number of missile weapons

vallar a gold crown with palisades
valor bravery or courage

valley (see **valet**)

valor (see **vallar**)

valse a concert waltz
vaults burial chambers; arched masonry structures forming a ceiling; leaps or bounds

vane (see **vain**)

Vanist (see **vainest**)

variance the mean square of deviations from the arithmetic mean of a frequency distribution
variants cipher elements or code groups having the same significance as another and used to impede cryptoanalysis

varicose abnormally swollen or dilated
verrucose covered with wartlike elevations

varicosis the condition of being abnormally swollen or dilated
verrucosis a disease of citrus plants caused by an imperfect fungus

vary (see **vairé**)

vasal relating to an anatomical vessel
vassel a dependent, servant, or slave

vau a letter of the original Greek alphabet approximating the sound of the English w
vow a solemn promise, pledge, or oath

vault a burial chamber; an arched masonry structure forming a ceiling; to bound or leap
volte a gait in which a horse moves sideways and turns around a center

vaults (see **valse**)

vealer a calf suitable for veal, especially one less than three months old
velar relating to the soft palate

veer to change direction
vire an arrow used in a crossbow and feathered so as to acquire a rotary motion

'Vegas (see **vagus**)

veil (see **vail**)

vein (see **vain**)

vela membranes or membranous parts likened to a veil or curtain
vila a supernatural being or fairy of Slavonic lands

velar (see **vealer**)

veldt (see **felt**)

velocity quickness or motion
villosity a coating of long slender hairs

vena a blood vessel; a streak or stripe
vina a four-stringed musical instrument of India

venous characterized by veins
Venus a genus of marine bivalve mollusk; a beautiful and charming woman; the second planet from the sun

ventil a valve in various wind musical instruments
ventile in textiles, designed to exclude water while permitting free circulation of air

Venus (see **venous**)

veracious truthful or accurate
voracious greedy or ravenous

veracity conformity with truth or fact; accuracy
voracity a state of being greedy or ravenous

verdure greenness and freshness of growing vegetation
verger a church official who serves as usher

verrucose (see **varicose**)

verrucosis (see **varicosis**)

versed familiarized by close association, study, or experience; told or celebrated in metrical language or poetry
verst a Russian unit of distance equal to .6629 miles

verser a person who creates lines of metrical writing
versor in geometry, the turning factor of a quaternion

verses lines of metrical writing
versus in contrast to; against

versor (see **verser**)

verst (see **versed**)

versus (see **verses**)

very (see **vairé**)

vesical of or relating to a bladder
vesicle a blister or cyst; a small cavity in a mineral or rock

vew a yew tree
view the act of seeing or beholding

vial a small bottle
vile morally despicable, contemptible, or base
viol a bowed stringed musical instrument of the 16th and 17th centuries

vice evil conduct
vise a two-jawed tool for holding work

vie (see **Vai**)

view (see **vew**)

vila (see **vela**)

vile (see **vial**)

vilest of smallest worth; most morally despicable or abhorrent
violist a person who plays the viol, a bowed stringed musical instrument chiefly of the 16th and 17th centuries

villain a scoundrel or knave
villein a free commoner or peasant of a feudal class lower than a thane
villin an actin-binding protein that nucleates polymerization of actin filaments

villosity (see **velocity**)

villous having soft long hair
villus a small slender vascular process giving a velvety appearance to the surface of the small intestine's mucous membrane

vina (see **vena**)

vinal from wine
vinyl a univalent radical derived from ethylene

viol (see vial)

violet a plant of the genus Viola; a reddish blue hue

violette a viola d'amore, a tenor viol having usually seven gut strings

violin a bowed four-stringed musical instrument

violine a moderate to strong violet color

violist (see vilest)

vire (see veer)

viscous having a glutinous consistency and stickiness

viscus an internal body organ

vise (see vice)

viviparous producing living young (instead of eggs) from within the body

Viviparus a genus of freshwater snails

vlei (see fly)

vley (see flay)

voder an electronic device capable of producing a recogizable approximation of speech

voter a person who expresses an opinion or casts a ballot in an election

volant having the wings extended as if in fight, used of an heraldic bird

volent exercising volition

volé a ballet step that is executed with the greatest possible elevation

volet either folding side compartment or wing of a triptych

volent (see volant)

volet (see vole)

volley (see vali)

volt a unit of electrical potential and electromotive force

volte a gait in which a horse moves sideways and turns around a center

volte (see vault)

voracious (see veracious)

voracity (see veracity)

voter (see voder)

vow (see vau)

Group I

valiance - valiants
vesiculous - vesiculus
villainess - villainous
villous - villus
virous - virus
vitellin - vitelline
vomitous - vomitus

Group I and II

venose 'veˌnōs
venous 'vēnəs

Group II

vas 'vas
vase 'vās or 'väz or 'vås

Veda 'vādə
Vedda 'vedə

vellum 'veləm
velum 'vēləm

vervel 'vərvəl
vervelle 'vər'vəl

vicarious vī'karēəs
vicarius 'vīkäˌriəs

vila 'vēlə
villa 'vilə

virtu vər'tü
virtue 'vərchü

visit 'vizət
visite vē'zēt

vocal 'vōkəl
vocule 'väkül

volable   'välab^əl
voluble   'välyəbəl

voyager   'voijər
voyageur   :voii:jər

W

Wa a people in the northeastern states of Myanmar and adjoining parts of Yunnan province, China

wah an expression of anger, disgust, or grief; a long-tailed Himalayan carnivore related to and closely resembling the American raccoon

WAACS members of the *W*omen's *A*rmy *A*uxiliary *C*orps

wacks crackpots

WACS members of the *W*omen's *A*rmy *C*orps

wax to increase in size; a natural or synthetic substance resembling beeswax

whacks strikes with a smart or resounding blow; chops

wabble a botfly larva that destroys squirrel testes

wobble to move with an irregular rocking or staggering motion

wacks (see **WAACS**)

WACS (see **WAACS**)

wadder a person that inserts or crowds a small mass or bundle into something, such as a gun

water odorless tasteless liquid oxide of hydrogen (H_2O)

watter a light bulb or radio station having a specified wattage

waddle to walk with short steps swinging the forepart of the body from side to side, as a duck

wattle a fleshy process about the head or neck of an animal; a fabrication of interwoven rods, poles, or branches used in building construction

waddy a straight tapered throwing-stick used in hunting and war, especially by Australian aborigines

wadi a bed or valley of a stream in arid regions of southwestern Asia and northern Africa

wade to proceed slowly among things that hinder, as through water

wayed broke or trained a horse to the road

weighed determined the heaviness of an object; tested or balanced

waded proceeded slowly among hindrances

waited delayed or postponed until proper conditions occur

weighted made heavy; relatively adjusted

wader a person who steps in or through mediums that offer some resistance; a waterproof garment for wading

waiter a person who attends, serves, or waits on another; a tray on which something is carried

weighter a textile worker who increases the weight of yarns or fabrics by adding substances

wadi (see **waddy**)

WAFS members of the Women in the Air Force

wafts causes to move or goes lightly by or as if by the impulse of wind or waves

wah (see **Wa**)

wailer a person who laments or cries

waler a rather large rugged saddle horse of mixed ancestry exported from Australia to India

whaler a person or ship employed in whaling

wails laments, weeps, or cries
Wales the peninsula on the western part of Great Britain
wales streaks or ridges made on the skin; extra thick strong planks in the side of a wooden ship
whales the largest (aquatic) mammals

wain a wagon or cart
wane to decrease in size or extent

waist a small part of the body between the ribs and hips
waste wilderness; useless consumption or expenditure

waister a usually green or broken-down seaman stationed in the waist of the ship
waster a spendthrift or squanderer

waistless unshapely
wasteless incapable of being used up

waited (see **waded**)

waiter (see **wader**)

waive to relinquish voluntarily
WAVE a woman serving in the U.S. Navy, especially during World War II
wave to flutter in a breeze; to flap; an arm gesture

waiver the act of intentionally relinquishing or abandoning a known right, claim, or privilege
waver to vacillate irresolutey between options or attractions

waler (see **wailer**)

Wales and **wales** (see **wails**)

walk to move on foot
waulk to shrink and thicken woolen fabric by applying moisture, heat, friction, and pressure until the fibers become felt

wallah a person who holds an important position in an organization or particular situation
wallow to roll or move oneself about in an indolent ungainly manner

wands slender metal or wood rods or staffs

wans causes to appear pale or sickly
wons basic monetary units of South Korea since 1962

wane (see **wain**)

wang (see **uang**)

wans (see **wands**)

want to lack; to desire
wont accustomed to doing something

wants (see **once**)

war an armed hostile conflict
wore attached to the body or clothing

ward a large hospital room; an administrative division of a municipality; a person under protection
warred engaged in armed hostile conflict

ware a manufactured or crafted article or articles
wear to attach to the body or clothing
weigher a person that determines heaviness
weir an enclosure placed in a stream or inlet, often for capturing fish
wer the value set in Anglo-Saxon and Germanic law on the life of a person according to a fixed scale and paid as compensation to the kin of that person if slain
where at or in what place
where're the contraction of where are

wared took heed of or bewared of
weired placed an enclosure in a stream or inlet to capture fish
where'd the contraction of where had or where did

wares merchandise
where's the contraction of where is, where does, or where has

wari any of various twoperson games widely played in Africa and southern Asia with pebbles or stones
warree a white-lipped peccary

Warli a people of India inhabiting the region north of Bombay

whorly arranged or formed in coiled or spiral shapes

warn to put on guard or give notice
worn attached to the body or clothing; deteriorated by use

warred (see **ward**)

warree (see **wari**)

warren a place abounding in rabbits
warrin an Australian lorikeet

wart a horny projection on the skin
wort an infusion of malt fermented to form beer; a sweet edible European blueberry

wary keenly cautious or watchfully prudent
weri a composite structure that occurs in New Zealand that is made up of the mummified body of a caterpillar killed by a fungus
wherry a long light rowboat pointed at both ends

waste (see **waist**)

wasteless (see **waistless**)

waster (see **waister**)

water (see **wadder**)

watercourse a channel through which water flows
water-course a layer of defective or poor-quality concrete caused by the accumulation of excess mixing water

waterie any of numerous chiefly Old World birds related to the pipits, especially the water wagtail
watery consisting of or filled with water

wats Buddhist temples in Thailand
watts measurements of electrical power equal to one absolute joule per second
whats things meant or referred to
what's the contraction of what is, what has, or what does

watter (see **wadder**)

wattle (see **waddle**)

watts (see **wats**)

waulk (see **walk**)

WAVE and **wave** (see **waive**)

waver (see **waiver**)

wax (see **WAACS**)

way a path or road; a manner or style
Wei a Tatar dynasty in China during the 4th–6th centuries A.D.
weigh to determine heaviness; to test or balance
wey any of various old units of weight or capacity used locally in the British Isles
whey the watery part of milk separated from curd in making cheese

wayed (see **wade**)

wayman a railroad laborer employed in laying or keeping in repair the tracks
weighman a worker who weighs articles and goods

we (see **oui**)

weak deficient in strength
week a sequence of seven days

weaken to lessen the strength of
weakon a W or Z particle that is a carrier of the weak interaction (in physics)

weal a sound, healthy, or prosperous state
weel a wickerwork or slotted trap for eels
we'll the contraction of we will or we shall
wheal a steep-sided elevation characteristic of urticaria's lesions; a welt
wheel a circular frame attached to an axle on which it revolves

weald a heavily wooded area
w(h)ealed raised lines on the skin with a whip
wheeled revolved, rotated, or turned
wield to use an instrument with full power; to employ

wean to cause to cease to depend on the mother for nourishment
ween to believe, conceive, or imagine

weaner a device to prevent an animal from suckling

wiener a frankfurter

wear (see **ware**)

wearer a person who wears or carries something as a body covering

where're the contraction of where are

weasand the musculature associated with the gullet and windpipe; the throat

wizened dried up, withered, or shriveled

weaser the American merganser

wheezer a person who breathes with difficulty and with an audible sibilant or whistling sound

weather an atmospheric state at a specific time and place

wether a male sheep or goat castrated before sexual maturity

whether a conjunction indicating a choice between alternatives

weave to form by interlacing strands, as cloth with yarn or thread

we've the contraction of we have

weaver a person who interlaces strands of yarn or thread to make textiles

weever an edible marine fish with upward-looking eyes

we'd the contraction of we would or we had

weed a noxious plant

wedder a person who joins in marriage

wetter a worker who wets the work in various manufacturing processes; more damp, moist, or humid

wedding a marriage ceremony

wetting moistening or soaking with water or other liquid

whetting sharpening, as a tool or the appetite

wedgie a shoe having a heel extending from the back of the shoe to the front or the shank

wedgy resembling a device that tapes to a thin edge and is used to split wood or rock

wee (see **oui**)

weed (see **we'd**)

week (see **weak**)

weel (see **weal**)

ween (see **wean**)

weeny exceptionally tiny

wienie a frankfurter (slang)

weep to express deep sorrow by shedding tears

wheep the drawn-out shrill cry or whistle of certain birds, as the curlew or plover

weer very little

weir an enclosure placed in a stream or inlet, often for capturing fish

weet an exclamation simulative of a small bird's cry

wheat a cereal grain that yields a fine white flour

weetless unwitting

wheatless having no cereal grain that yields a fine white flour

weever (see **weaver**)

wee-wee (see **oui-oui**)

Wei (see **way**)

weigh (see **way**)

weighed (see **wade**)

weigher (see **ware**)

weighman (see **wayman**)

weighted (see **waded**)

weighter (see **wader**)

weir (see **ware** and **weer**)

weir an enclosure placed in a stream or inlet, often for capturing fish

wer the value set in Anglo-Saxon and German law upon the life of a man in accordance to a fixed scale; wergild (by shortening)

we're the contraction of we are

weird eerie, uncanny, unearthly, or mysterious

weired placed an enclosure or dam in a stream or inlet, often to capture fish

weired (see **wared**)

weld to join closely or inseparably, as in uniting metallic parts by heating their edges to a fluid state

welled rose to the surface in a copious stream; constructed with a well

we'll (see **weal**)

welled (see **weld**)

wells holes sunk in the earth to a depth sufficient to reach water supplies

wels very large elongated catfish of central and eastern European rivers

wen a sebaceous cyst

when at which or what time

wend to proceed or travel

when'd the contraction of when did

wends proceeds or travels

wens sebaceous cysts

when's the contraction of when is, when does, or when has

wer (see **ware**, **weer**, and **weir**)

wer wergild

were existed

whir(r) a continuous fluttering sound made by something in rapid motion

we're (see **weir**)

weri (see **wary**)

we's groups whose members consciously feel as a group

whees expresses delight or exuberance

wheeze a sibilant whistling sound caused by difficult or obstructed respiration

wet to soak or moisten with liquid

whet to hone, sharpen, or make keen

wether (see **weather**)

wetter (see **wedder**)

wetting (see **wedding**)

we've (see **weave**)

wey (see **way**)

whacks (see **WAACS**)

whaler (see **waler**)

whales (see **wails**)

whats (see **wats**)

what's (see **wats**)

whau a New Zealand tree of the family *Tiliaceae*

wow a sensational hit

wheal (see **weal**)

w(h)ealed (see **weald**)

wheat (see **weet**)

wheatless (see **weetless**)

whee (see **oui**)

wheel (see **weal**)

wheeled (see **weald**)

wheep (see **weep**)

whees (see **we's**)

wheeze (see **we's**)

wheezer (see **weaser**)

when (see **wen**)

when'd (see **wend**)

when's (see **wends**)

where (see **ware**)

where'd (see **wared**)

wherefor for which

wherefore for what reason; an answer or statement that provides an explanation

where're (see **ware** and **wearer**)

where's (see **wares**)

wherry (see **wary**)

whet (see **wet**)

whether (see **weather**)

whetting (see **wedding**)

whew (see **hew**)

whew to make a half-formed whistling sound; an expression of amazement, relief, or discomfort
whoo an expression of sudden excitement, relief, or astonishment
woo to seek to gain or bring about; to solicit in love
Wu a group of Chinese dialects spoken in the lower Yangtze valley

whey (see **juey** and **way**)

which a word introducing a relative clause; what one(s) out of a group
witch a woman practicing the black arts

whicker to neigh or whinny
wicker a rod for plaiting basketwork

whiff a quick puff or slight gust of air
wiff a wife (slang)

Whig an American favoring independence from Great Britain during the Revolution
wig artificial head hair; a toupee

Whiggery the principles, policies, and practices associated with Whigs
wiggery a business that deals in wigs

Whigling a petty Whig
wiggling tending to jiggle or oscillate; wriggly

whiled passed time without boredom or in a pleasant manner
wild not tamed or domesticated
wiled enticed; lured by a magic spell

whin a particularly hard rock
win to gain victory in a contest; prevail or succeed
wynn a type of timber truck or carriage

whines utters a high-pitched plaintive or distressed cry
winds twists, coils, or curls
wines provides with fermented juice of grapes

whing a sharp high-pitched ringing sound
wing an organ or manufactured structure that enables aerial flight

whinny to neigh, especially in a low or gentle fashion
Winnie any of several bronze statuettes awarded annually by a professional group for fashion design

whins particularly hards rocks; devices for raising ore or water from mines
winds natural air movements
wins gains victory in a contest
winze a steeply inclined opening connecting one mine with another at a lower level
wynns timber trucks or carriages

whiny whining, querulous, or habitually complaining
winy having the taste or qualities of wine

whirled moved quickly around an axis; became giddy or dizzy
whorled arranged in coiled or spiral shapes
world the earthly state of human existence; the planet Earth; a planet, especially one inhabited

whirley a crane free to rotate 360 degrees in picking up and depositing its load
whirly exhibiting a rotary or whirling motion; a small whirlwind
whorly arranged in coils or spirals
wurley the nest of the house-building rat of Australia; a native Australian hut

whir(r) (see **were**)

whirred moved rapidly with a vibrating sound
word a written character or characters representing a spoken sound

whirtle a perforated steel die through which steel wires or tubes are drawn
whortle a sweet edible European blueberry

whish a rushing sound
wish an unfulfilled desire or want

whist a card game
wist a unit of land area equal to about 16–18 acres

whit the smallest of particles
wit intellectual brilliance or astuteness of perception; humor; irony

white colorless; free from spot or blemish
wight a living creature
wite a penal fine for serious crimes

whiter more free from color; lighter or more palid in color
wider more extensive or broader

whither to what place; where
wither to shrivel up

whitish approaching being white or color-less
widish tending to be wide or broad

whitling a large sea trout
whittling cutting chips from wood with a knife
witling a person of little wit or under-standing

whittle to cut or shape wood with a knife
wittol a half-witted person

whittling (see **whitling**)

whiz to fly or move swiftly with a hissing or buzzing sound
wiz one endowed with exceptional skill or able to achieve something held to be im-possible; a wizard (by shortening)

whizbang one that speeds noisily to a cimax
whiz-bang excellent, expert, or notable

whizzled got by stealth or cunning
wizzled being wizened and shriveled

who (see **heugh**)

whoa (see **Ho**)

whoa a command to a draft animal to stop or stand still
wo a falconer's summons to a hawk or falcon
woe a miserable or sorrowful state

whoaed commanded a draft animal to stop
woad a European perennial herb formerly grown for the blue coloring matter yielded by its leaves

whole (see **hole**)

wholes (see **holds**)

whole-sail being a breeze or wind that permits the use of full or nearly full sail
wholesale relating to the sale of goods in quantity for resale; extensive or massive

wholly (see **holey**)

whom (see **hum**)

whomp a loud slap, crash, or crunch
womp an abrupt increase in the illumina-tion of a television screen resulting from an abrupt increase in signal strength

whoo (see **heugh** and **whew**)

whoof a deep full snorting sound
woof threads that cross the warp in woven fabric; the weft

whoop (see **hoop**)

whooper (see **hooper**)

whop to beat, strike, or thrash (seldom **wop**)
wop an Italian, used disparagingly

whore (see **hawer**)

whored (see **hoard**)

whoreson (see **hoarsen**)

whorled (see **whirled**)

whorly (see **Warli** and **whirley**)

whortle (see **whirtle**)

whos (see **hoos** and **oohs**)

who's (see **hoos** and **oohs**)

whose (see **hoos** and **oohs**)

whump a bang or thump
wump(h) a heavy sound caused especially by a falling object

whydah any of various African weaver-birds

widow a woman whose husband has died and has not since remarried

whys reasons or causes of something
wise sagacious or prudent
wyes things resembling the letter Y in shape; track arrangements with three switches and three legs for reversing the direction of an entire train

wicked evil, vicious, or vile
wicket a small gate or door; a grilled gate or window; a wire hoop used in croquet

wicker (see **whicker**)

wicket (see **wicked**)

wider (see **whiter**)

widish (see **whitish**)

widow (see **whydah**)

wield (see **weald**)

wiener (see **weaner**)

wienie (see **weeny**)

wiff (see **whiff**)

wig (see **Whig**)

wiggery (see **Whiggery**)

wiggling (see **Whigling**)

wight (see **white**)

wild (see **whiled**)

wiled (see **whiled**)

wilkeite a mineral consisting of an hydroxylapatite
Willkieite an adherent of Wendell Lewis Willkie, 1940 Republican candidate for the U.S. presidency

willeys textile machines with a revolving spike drum that opens and cleans cotton or wool
willies waybills for a loaded railroad car; a fit of nervousness or acute mental discomfort

Willkieite (see **wilkeite**)

win (see **whin**)

windlass any of various machines for hoisting or hauling
windless marked by the absence of wind

windroad a pass for a current of air, often underground as in a mine
windrode a moored vessel riding with the force of the wind
windrowed raked hay into rows for drying before being rolled or baled

winds (see **whines** and **whins**)

wines (see **whines**)

wing (see **whing**)

Winnie (see **whinny**)

wins (see **whins**)

winy (see **whiny**)

winze (see **whins**)

wise (see **whys**)

wish (see **whish**)

wist (see **whist**)

wistaria a pale purple or light violet color
Wisteria a genus of chiefly Asiatic mostly woody vines

wit (see **whit**)

witch (see **which**)

wite (see **white**)

with a word to indicate connection, association, or relationship
withe a band consisting of a twisted twig

wither (see **whither**)

witling (see **whitling**)

wittol (see **whittle**)

wiz (see **whiz**)

wizened (see **weasand**)

wizzled (see **whizzled**)

wo (see **whoa**)

woad (see **whoaed**)

wobble (see **wabble**)

woe (see **whoa**)

womp (see **whomp**)

won (see **one**)

wons (see **wands**)

wont (see **want**)

wont accustomed to doing something
won't the contraction of will not

wonts (see **once**)

woo (see **whew**)

wood a hard fibrous substance making up
the greater part of trees and shrubs
would used to express a wish, desire, or
intent

woof (see **whoof**)

wop (see **whop**)

word (see **whirred**)

wore (see **war**)

workout an exercise designed to test or
increase one's fitness
work-out a market not characterized by
firm bids and offers

world (see **whirled**)

worm any of numerous relatively small,
elongated, usually naked and soft-bod-
ied animals resembling an earthworm
Würm the fourth and last stage of glacia-
tion in Europe

worn (see **warn**)

worst most unfavorable, unpleasant, or
reprehensible
wurst a sausage

wort (see **wart**)

would (see **wood**)

wow (see **whau**)

wrack (see **rack**)

wraith an apparition of a living person in
his/her exact likeness seen usually just
prior to the person's death

wraithe an expansible reed or comb for
beaming and warping, in weaving

wrangle (see **rangle**)

wrapped (see **rapped**)

wrasse (see **rasse**)

wrath (see **rath**)

wreak (see **reek**)

wreathes things twisted or intertwined into
an approximately circular or spiral shape
wreaths causes to writh, twist, or contort

wreck (see **rec**)

wrecked (see **rect**)

wrecks (see **recks**)

wren (see **jen**)

wrens (see **rends**)

wrest (see **rest**)

wretch (see **retch**)

wrick (see **rick**)

wried (see **ride**)

wright (see **right**)

wring (see **ring**)

wringer (see **ringer**)

wrist (see **rist**)

write (see **right**)

writer (see **reiter**)

writs (see **ritz**)

wrong (see **Rong**)

wrote (see **rote**)

wroth (see **rath**)

wrung (see **rung**)

wrys (see **rise**)

Wu (see **whew**)

wump(h) (see **whump**)

wurley (see **whirley**)

Würm (see **worm**)

wurst (see **worst**)

wyes (see **whys**)

wynn (see **whin**)

wynns (see **whins**)

Group I

waistcoat - **weskit**
wedgie - **wedgy**
whirtle - **wordle**
windthrow - **wind-throw**
winterkill - **winter-kill**
wreathes - **wreaths**

Group I and II

warrantee 'wärən:tē
warranty 'wärəntē

Group II

wacke 'wakē
whack 'wak

wah 'wä
waw 'väv

wakan wä'kän
walkon 'wȯk₁än

walk 'wȯk
wok 'wäk

wallet 'wȯlət
wallette wȯ'let

warehous 'wärə:haȯz
warehouse 'war₁haȯs

warren 'wȯrən
warrin 'wȯrin

weakened 'wēkənd
weekend 'wē:kend

wherry 'werē
worry 'wȯrē

wolffish 'wȯlf₁fish
wolfish 'wȯlfish

woold 'wüld
wooled 'wüld

X

x (see **ex**)

xanthene an isomeric compound that is the parent of the colored forms of xanthene dyes
xanthine a feebly basic crystalline nitrogenous compound that is found in animal tissue and plants

xanthin a carotenoid pigment that is soluble in alcohol
xanthine a feebly basic crystalline nitrogenous compound that is found in animal tissue and plants

xanthine (see **xanthene**)

xanthous yellowish
Xanthus an ancient city of Lycia near the mouth of the Xanthus river in southwestern Asia

xat (see **cat**)

xenia the effect of genes introduced by a male nucleus on structures other than the embryo; presents given by ancient Greeks and Romans to a guest or stranger
zinnia a tropical American herb having showy flower heads

xeric (see ceric)

Xiphias a genus of large scombroid fishes comprising the common swordfish

Ziphius a genus of nearly cosmopolitan beaked whales

xiphioid resembling or related to the genus Xiphias, a genus of large scombroid fishes comprising the common swordfish

ziphioid relating to the Ziphiidae, a family of toothed whales

xis (see psis)

xurel (see jurel)

Group I and II

xenodocheum zenədə'kēəm
xenodochium zenənədə'kīəm

Y

yabbi a Tasmanian wolf
yabby a small burrowing crayfish

yacca any of several West Indian podocarps
yakka work or labor

yager (see jaeger)

yahoo an uncouth or rowdy person
yahu a scholarly transliteration of the Hebrew tetragrammaton that constitues a divine proper name, such as Jehovah

yak a laugh, joke, or gag; a large ox of Tibet and central Asia
yogh a letter used in Middle English to represent a palatal fricative

yakka (see yacca)

y'all you-all, a direct address indicating two or more persons
yawl a fore-and-aft rigged sailboat

Yap one of the Caroline Islands in the west Pacific Ocean
yap to bark snappishly; to scold; to chatter
yapp a bookbinding style often used for Bibles and hymnbooks

yar characterized by speed and agility; nimble
yarr corn spurrey, a small European weed

yawed deviated radically from a course; gaped or yawned
yod the voice glide or spirant sound that is the first sound of yes; the tenth letter of the Hebrew alphabet (also yodh)

yawl (see y'all)

yawn a deep intake of breath through a wide open mouth usually as an involuntary reaction to fatigue or boredom
yon yonder; an Indian tree yielding very strong wood

ye a second person pronoun still used in selected religious faiths
yi in Chinese ethical philosophy, the faithful performance of one's specified duties to society

yew (see ewe)

yews (see ewes)

yi (see ye)

yippee an expression of exuberant delight or triumph
Yippie Youth International Party (by shortening), a group of radical political active hippies
yippie a member of the Yippie group

yo (see ewe)

yock to laugh in a boisterous or unrestrained manner

yuck an expression of rejection or disgust

yod (see yawed)

yogh (see yak)

yogh a letter used in Middle English to represent a palatal fricative
yoke a framework joining two draft animals at their necks for working together
yolk a yellow sperhoidal mass of the egg of a bird or reptile (seldom yoke)

yon (see yawn)

yore a time long since past
your belonging to you

you (see ewe)

you'll the contraction of you will or you shall
yule Christmas

your (see ewer and yore)

you're (see ewer)

youse (see ewes and ius)

yu (see ewe)

yuca (see Uca)

Yucca and yucca (see Uca)

yuck (see yock)

yulan (see uhlan)

yule (see you'll)

Yuman (see human)

Group II

Yankee   'yaŋkē
Yanqui   'yäŋkē

Z

zabra (see sabra)

zacs Caucasian ibexes
zax a tool used for trimming and puncturing roofing slates

zax (see zacs)

zayin the seventh letter of the Hebrew alphabet
Zion the Jewish homeland that is symbolic of Jewish national aspiration

Zea the genus of large grasses having broad ribbon-shaped leaves
zea the fresh styles and stigmas of Indian corn formerly used as a diuretic
Zia a Keres people occupying a pueblo in northwestern New Mexico

Zen (see senn)

Zia (see Zea)

Zilla a genus of thorny plants of northern Africa
zillah a district or administrative division in India

zinc a bluish white crystalline bivalent metallic element
zink a Renaissance woodwind instrument used especially with church chorale music

zinnia (see xenia)

Zion (see zayin)

ziphioid (see xiphioid)

Ziphius (see Xiphias)

zoo a collection of animals
Zu an evil storm-god, represented as a black bird

Group I

zephyrous - zephyrus

Group II

zebras ˈzēbrəz
zebrass ˈzēˌbras

Homographs

A

a \\'ā\\ someone or something arbitrarily or conveniently designated as the first in order or in a class

a \\ə\\ used to replace have or of, as kinda for kind of

Ab \\äb\\ the 11th month of the civil year and the 5th month of ecclesiastical year in the Jewish calendars

Ab \\'ab\\ the spirit of the physical heart and the seat of the will and intentions

aba \\a'bä\\ a loose sleeveless Arabian outer garment

aba \\'abə\\ a telescopic instrument

abaisse \\ə'bäsä\\ a thin undercrust of pastry

abaissé \\ə'bäs\\ in heraldry, turned downward, as a bird's wingtips

abate \\ə'bāt\\ to diminish

abate \\'äbä,tä\\ a title of respect for any ecclesiastic without other distinguishing title

ablative \\'ablətiv\\ in grammar, expressing typically the relation of separation and source, cause, time, place, or accordance

ablative \\a'blātiv\\ tending to carry away, or remove by cutting, erosion, melting, or evaporation

absent \\'absənt\\ not present or not attending

absent \\ab'sent\\ to keep away

acedia \\,asə'dēə\\ an Atlantic ocean flatfish

acedia \\ə'sēdēə\\ sloth or apathy

acerous \\'asərəs\\ needle-shaped, as pine leaves

acerous \\,ā'sērəs\\ having no antennae or horns

Acoma \\äkə mō\\ a Keresan pueblo people of New Mexica

acoma \\ə kōmə\\ a tree of Florida and the West Indies used in shipbuilding

actus \\'aktəs\\ the right to drive a beast or a vehicle over another's land

actus \\'äk,tůs\\ a mental or spiritual act done

adage \\'adij\\ a saying usually embodying a common experience

adage \\ädáazh\\ an easy graceful manner; in music, adagio

adduct \\a'dəkt\\ to draw toward or past the median axis of the body

adduct \\'a,dəkt\\ the cyclic product of the addition reaction of a diene with another unsaturated compound

Aedes \\ā'ēdēz\\ a large cosmopolitan genus of mosquitoes

aedes \\'ēdēz\\ a building for worship in Roman antiquity not formally consecrated by the Augurs

Afar \\'ä,fär\\ an Hamitic people of northeast Ethiopia

afar \\ə'fär\\ from or at a great distance

affricate \\'afrəkət\\ a stop or explosive, followed by a slow separation of the articulating organs, in phonetics

affricate \\ə'frikāt\\ to rub out or grate on

Agama \\ə'gämə\\ a genus of Old World terrestrial lizards

agama \\ə'gämə\\ a lizard of the genus Agama

agama \\'ägəmə\\ a class of tantric treatises accepted as scripture in Hinduism and Buddhism

agape \\ə'gāp\\ wide open

agape \\ä'gä,pä\\ spontaneous self-giving love

aged \\ājd\\ showed the effects of or underwent change with the passage of time

aged \\ājəd\\ well advanced toward reduction to base level (used in topographic features)

agnostic \\ag'nästik\\ a person who doubts the existence of a god

agnostic \\ag:nōstik\\ an inability to recognize familiar objects by eye, ear, or touch

akela \ə'kālə\ a shrub or climber of Hawaii

akela \ə'kēlə\ a leader of a cub scout pack

ala \'ālə\ a winglike process

ala \'älä\ a large Sumerian drum

Alans \'ālanz\ a Scythian people in pre–Slavic Russia and the Black Sea regions

alans \'alanz\ in heraldry, short-eared dogs

Alas \'ä,läs\ an Indonesian people of northern Sumatra

alas \ə'las\ an expression of sorrow, pity, or concern

alba \'älbə\ a Provençal lyric dealing with lovers parting at dawn

alba \'albə\ the white matter of the brain and spinal cord

alegrias \alə'grēəz\ certain herbs of the genus *Amaranthus*

alegrias \'älə'greəs\ a solo flamenco dance performed by a woman

alem \'ä,lem\ a shrub yielding medicinal fruit

alem \'al,em\ the imperial standard of the Ottoman empire

allege \ə'lej\ to assert without proof

allège \a'lezh\ a thinned part of a wall

allongé \:a,lōⁿzhā\ a ballet movement with both arms and one leg extended to form a long line

allonge \a'lōⁿzh\ paper attached to a bill of exchange for additional endorsements

allure \ə'lür\ to lure, sway, or entice with some tempting appeal

allure \'al,ūr\ a passagewalk, as the walk along one side of a cloister

ally \'a,lī\ someone or something associated with another, as a helper or supporter

ally \'alē\ a superior playing marble

Aloe \'alə,wē\ a genus of succulent chiefly southern African plants

aloe \'alō\ a pale green color

alp \'alp\ a very high mountain

alp \'älp\ a demon or tomenting witch, in Teutonic folklore

alum \'aləm\ a double sulfate of aluminum having a sweetsour astringent taste

alum \ə'ləm\ a graduate or former student of an educational institution (by shortening **alumna** or **alumnus**)

alvar \'al,vär\ southern Indian Vaishnara saints of the 7th and 9th centuries

alvar \'äl,vär\ mosses growing on overlying Scandinavian limestone

ambientes \,ambē 'en,tēz\ thigh muscles of certain birds that allow the knees to bend and the feet to clasp the perch on which the bird sits

ambientes \'aam byentēs\ atmospheres or environments

ambos \'äm,bōz\ large pulpits or reading desks in early churches and in contemporary Greek and Balkan churches

ambos \'am,bäs\ the middle of a chain of three small bones (the anvil) in the ear of mammals

Ament \ə'ment\ a Thebian goddess usually represented by a sheep's head, in Egyptian religion

ament \'amənt\ a mentally deficient person; a racemose influorescence

amental \'āməntᵊl\ resembling an indeterminate spicate inflorescence bearing scaly bracts and apetalous unisexual flowers

amental \'ā,mentᵊl\ devoid of mind

Anas \'anəs\ the type genus of *Anatidae* comprising a large number of widely distributed freshwater ducks

anas \'ānəz\ collections of anecdotes or interesting curious information

anathema \,anə'thēmə\ a thing set aside or consecrated for a diety

anathema \ə'nathəmə\ any object of intense dislike or loathing

anay \ä'nī\ a white ant or termite

anay \a'nī\ a Guatemalan fruit resembling the avocado

ancone \'aŋkōn\ a bracket, elbow, or console used as an architectural support

ancone \'aŋ kōnē\ a domestic fowl of a breed resembling Leghorns

Angers \än'zhä\ of or from the city of Angers, France

angers \'aŋgərz\ strong feelings of displeasure and usually antagonism

ani \ä'nē\ any of several black cuckoos with arched laterally compressed bills found from tropical America to the southern U.S.

ani \'anī\ the posterior openings of alimentary canals

anon \ə'nän\ at another time

anon \ä'nōn\ the sweet pulpy fruit of the sweetsop

Anti \'äntē\ an Arawakan people of the upper valley of the Ucayali river in eastern Peru

anti \'an‚tē\ one who is opposed

Apache \ə'pachē\ an Athapaskan people of Arizona, New Mexico, and northern Mexico

Apache \ə'pash\ a member of a gang of criminals, especially in Paris, noted for their violent crimes

ape \'āp\ a monkey; to imitate

ape \'äpā\ an herbaceous ornamental plant of Hawaii

aper \'āpər\ a person that imitates or mimics

aper \'äpər\ a European wild boar

Apios \'āpē äs\ a widely distributed genus of trailing or climbing herbs

apios \'äpē ōz\ tropical American perennial herbs related to carrots

apolysis \ä'pólē‚sēs\ a concluding prayer in the Eastern Church

apolysis \ə'päləsəs\ the shedding of segments in the neck area of a tape worm

appropriate \ə'prōprē‚āt\ to take possession of; to take without permission or consent

appropriate \ə'prōprēət\ suitable of fitting for a particular purpose

Ara \'ärə\ a constellation south of the tail of the Scorpion

Ara \'ärə\ a genus of macaws containing the great blue-and-yellow macaw

ara \'ärə\ a macaw; a textile screw pine

arête \a'rāt\ a sharp crested mountain ridge

arete \‚arə'tā\ good qualities that make character

aria \ärēə\ an elaborate melody sung in an opera or oratorio

aria \ə'rēə\ a European ornamental tree with corymbose white flowers and red fruits

Arkansas \'ärkən‚só\ a state in south central U.S.

Arkansas \‚är'kanzəs\ a river flowing through east and southeast Kansas, Oklahoma, Arkansas, and into the Mississippi River

arras \'arəs\ a wall hanging or hanging screen of tapestry

arras \'ä‚räs\ a gift made by a husband to his wife upon marriage in Spanish cultures

arrive \:arē:vä\ a person who has risen rapidly to success, power, or fame

arrive \ə'rīv\ to reach a destination

arses \'ärsəs\ the bottom end of wooden pulley blocks in which are the score for the rope straps

arses \'är sēz\ the weak or unaccented parts of musical measures

As \'äs\ in music, Aflat

as \'äs\ a Persian card game resembling poker

As \'as\ a chief god of pagan Scandinavia

as \az\ like

asana \\'äsənə\\ a manner of sitting in the practice of yoga

asana \\ˌäsə'nä\\ any of several timber trees of the genus Pterocarpus

ascon \\ȧskōⁿ\\ an Haitian voodoo fetish

ascon \\'aˌskän\\ a sponge

aspirate \\'aspəˌrāt\\ to draw or withdraw by suction; to pronounce with an h-sound as the initial element

aspirate \\'aspərȧt\\ silent but not preceded by liaison or elision

aspire \\ə'spīr\\ to seek to attain or accomplish something

aspiré \\ˌaspə'rā\\ initial in the orthography of a word before which elision and liaison do not occur (without respect to **h** in French)

assai \\ä'sī\\ in music, very

assai \\ˌäsä:ē\\ a slender pinnate-leaved palm

assemblé \\ˌȧsäⁿblā\\ a ballet movement

assemble \\ə'sembəl\\ to bring together

assis \\a'sē\\ sitting down (of animals in heraldry)

assis \\'asēz\\ any of several shrubs or trees of the genus *Ilex*; a holly of the southern U.S.

Asterias \\a'stirēəs\\ a genus of echinoderms that includes certain typical starfishes

asterias \\a'stirēəz\\ gem stones cut so as to show star-shaped figures

ate \\'āt\\ consumed food

ate \\'äd•ē\\ a blind impulse or reckless ambition

ates \\'āˌtēz\\ blind impulses, reckless ambitions, or excessive follies that drive people to ruin

ates \\'äˌtes\\ the sweet pulpy fruits of a tropical American tree

Atis \\'ädēz\\ members of the predominantly pagan Negritoid people of Panay, Philippines

atis \\ə'tēs\\ a monkshood found in the Hi-

malayas; any of several trees including the sweetsop

Atta \\'adə\\ a New World genus of leaf-cutting chiefly tropical ants often very destructive to crops

atta \\'äˌtä\\ unsorted wheat flour or meal, in India

attaches \\ə'tachəz\\ makes fast or joins; binds, fastens, or ties

attaches \\'atəˌshäz\\ experts on duty with the country's diplomatic representative at a foreign capital

attention \\ə'tenchən\\ an act of civility or courtesy; care for the wishes, comfort, or pleasure of others

attention \\əˌten'chän\\ a position assumed by military personnel with heels together at a 45° angle, body erect, and eyes to the front

attribute \\'atrəˌbyüt\\ a quality or characteristic belonging to a thing or person

attribute \\ə'tribyüt\\ to explain as caused or brought about by

August \\'ȯgəst\\ the eighth month of the Gregorian calendar

august \\ȯ:gəst\\ marked by majestic dignity

august \\'aůˌgůst\\ a clown, typically one suggesting in appearance or action an awkward waiter

aval \\a'val\\ a written engagement by one not a drawer, acceptor, or endorser of a note or bill of exchange that it will be paid at maturity

aval \\'āval\\ pertaining to a grandparent or grandparents

ave \\'ävā\\ salutation of greeting or leave-taking

ave \\'av\\ avenue (by shortening)

Aves \\'āvāz\\ Ave Marias or salutations to the Virgin Mary

aves \\'ävāz\\ salutations of greeting or leave-taking

Aves \\'āvēz\\ a class of Vertebrata including all fossil and recent birds

awa \'äwä\ a large active silvery herbivorous food fish widely distributed in the warm parts of the Pacific and Indian oceans

awa \'ävə\ an Australasian shrubby pepper from whose crushed roots an intoxicating beverage is made

awing \'óiŋ\ frightening or terrifying
awing \ə'wiŋ\ flying

<u>**axes**</u> \'aksəs\ cutting tools
axes \'ak₁sēz\ straight lines around which things rotate

ayah \'äyə\ a native nursemaid or lady's maid
ayah \'äyä\ a sign; a divine portent

<u>**aye**</u> \'ī\ an affirmative vote
aye \'ā\ for an indefinite time

acerbate
acuminate
address
adiposes
affectionate
affix
agglomerate
agglutinate
alternate
alveolites
ammonites
ananas
anastomoses
ankyloses
antipodes
approximate
arithmetic
arsenic
ascomycetes

Group I

abstract
abuse

B

bakkie \'bä₁ki\ excrement
bakkie \'bäki\ anything filthy or distasteful, as spoiled soup or rancid butter

balance \bə:län:sā\ a ballet movement
balance \'baləns\ a measuring device; equilibrium; to maintain a state of equipoise

Balanites \balə'nidēz\ a genus of Old World tropical trees
balanites \'balə₁nitēz\ fossil balanoid shells

<u>**ballet(t)**</u> \'balət\ a partsong often in stanzas with a refrain
ballet \'ba₁lā\ artistic dancing

<u>**ban**</u> \'ban\ to prohibit
<u>**ban**</u> \'bän\ a provincial-military governor

of former times in Hungary, Croatia, or Slavonia

banal \'bānəl\ lacking originality or freshness
banal \'bänəl\ relating to a provincial governor in Hungary with military powers during war

banga \'baŋgə\ an Australian cycad, the seeds of which are baked and eaten
banga \'baŋ'ä\ a large spherical water jar made of baked clay

banged \'baŋd\ struck against or bumped
banged \'banjd\ lounged about or loafed

BAR \'bē₁ā'är\ a Browning automatic rifle
<u>**bar**</u> \'bär\ a straight piece of metal or wood; to confine or shut out

Baré \'bä͵rā\ an Arawkan people in northern Brazil and Venezuela

bare \'bar\ exposed to view

Baris \'bärēz\ members of a Nilotic Negro people in the Sudan

baris \'bärəs\ a Balinese spear or warrior's dance

barrage \bə'rä|zh\ a massive concentrated and continuous discharge or shower of weaponry, speech, or writing

barrage \'bärij\ an artificial dam to increase water depth or direct it into a channel

barre \'bär\ a handrail for ballet dancers during exercises

barré \bä'rā\ a striped pattern in fabrics; all strings on an instrument stopped by the forefinger laid across them

bases \'bā͵sēz\ foundations or principal components; the actual yields on bonds; original costs of property used in computing capital gains or losses for income tax purposes

bases \'bāsəz\ compounds capable of reacting with an acid to form salts; the corner bags, including home plate, in baseball

basis \'bāsəs\ a fundamental ingredient or essence

basis \'bä͵sēz\ fermented Philippine beverages

bass \'bās\ a person or instrument able to create the lowest pitched sounds

bass \'bas\ an edible spiny-finned fish

Batak \'bə'täk\ a small predominantly pagan native group inhabiting northern Palawan, Philippines

Batak \'bä͵täk\ an Indonesian ethnic group inhabiting the highlands of Sumatra

Baule \͵bäü'lā\ a people of the Ivory Coast region of West Africa renowned for their carved wooden statuary

baule \'bȯl\ or \'bōl\ the theoretical amount of nitrogren or a mineral necessary to produce one-half the maximum possible crop yield

begum \'bāgəm\ a high-ranking Muslim woman, especially a widow

begum \bə'gəm\ to smear, soil, or clog with a gummy substance

Bel \'bāl\ the god of Earth, in Babylonian religion

bel \'bel\ a thorny tree of India with aromatic orangelike fruit

bend \'bend\ to turn from a straight line

bend \'bē:end\ the end of a railway car on which the handbrake is located

bene \'bēnē\ well

bene \'bene\ a wild hog of New Guinea

benet \'bēnet\ to ensnare or capture with a net

benet \'benet\ the third of the four minor orders in the Roman Catholic Church; an exorcist who ranks just below an acolyte

Beni \'benē\ a Negro people of southern Nigeria

beni \'beni\ sesame oil used primarily for making soap

berg \'bərg\ an iceberg

berg \'berk\ a mountain

Bern(e) \'bərn\ the capital of Switzerland

berne \'bernə\ a botfly that attacks mammals in warm parts of the Americas

Beta \'bētä\ a small genus of glabrous succulent herbs, including chard and the beet

beta \'betä\ the second letter of the Greek alphabet

betises \'bēdəsəz\ Philippine trees the fruits of which yield an illuminating oil

bêtises \bā'tēzəz\ acts of foolishness or stupidity

beurre \'bər\ buttered, as "peas au buerre"

beurré \'bü͵ri\ any of many varieties of pear having soft and melting flesh

bin \'bēn\ a four-stringed musical instrument of India with a long bamboo fingerboard

bin \'bin\ a box or crib used for storage

bind \'bīnd\ to make secure by tying

bind \'bind\ a twining stem or flexible shoot

binger \'binjər\ a person who goes on a spree, or who engages in food extravaganzas

binger \'biŋˌər\ a homerun, in baseball

binocle \'binəˌkəl\ binoculars

binocle \'bīnəkˌəl\ a card game of the bezique family

bios \'bīōz\ biographies (by shortening)

bios \'bīˌäs\ a mixture of vitamins of the B complex; organic nature

bioses \'bīˌäsəz\ organic natures; mixtures of vitamins of the B complex

bioses \'bīˌōsəz\ any of a class of sugars that yield on hydrolysis two monosaccharide molecules

birling \'bərliŋ\ the sport of logrolling

birling \'birliŋ\ a chieftain's barge used in the Hebrides

bis \'bis\ in music, to direct repetition of a passage or to request an encore

bis \'bīz\ bisexual persons (slang)

blessed \'blest\ praised or glorified

blessed \'blesəd\ a person beatified by the Roman Catholic Church

blither \'blīthər\ more light-minded, casual, or heedless

blither \'blithər\ to talk foolishly or nonsensically

blond \'bländ\ flaxen, golden, light auburn, or pale yellow hair; pale white or rosy white skin

blond \'blȯn\ a concentrated meat juice or stock added to a sauce to strengthen or color it

BO \'bē'ō\ body odor

bo \'bō\ a hobo; a fig tree of India

bola \'bōlə\ a weapon consisting of two or more heavy balls or stones attached to the ends of a cord that is hurled at an animal and entangles it

bola \'bōlä\ either of two malvaceous tropical trees

bole \'bōl\ any cylindrically shaped object or mass

bole \'bōˌlē\ a unit of momentum equal to one gram moving at one centimeter per second

Bologna \bə'lōnyə\ Italy's fifth largest city

bologna \bə'lōnē\ a large moist sausage; pretentious nonsense (often baloney, but seldom belonye)

bombard \'bämˌbärd\ a piece of heavy ordnance formerly used to throwing stones and other missiles

bombard \ˌbäm'bärd\ to stuff, as a fillet of veal; to croquet a ball so that it displaces another ball

bombé \bam:bā\ having an outward swelling curve in furniture

bombe \'bäm\ a frozen molded dessert

Bon \'bȯn\ a pre–Buddhist animist religion of Tibet; a popular Japanese festival

bon \'bän\ the broad or kidney bean; the stiff dried hand-cleaned but not completely degummed fiber of ramie

bootee \'büd•ē\ an infant's sock of knitted or crocheted wool

bootee \'bü:tē\ a boot with a short leg

bore \'bōr\ to pierce or drill a hole

bore \'bōˌrē\ a lively old French dance tune in duple meter

borism \'bōrˌizm\ boring qualities or behavior; ennui

borism \'bōˌrizm\ poisoning caused by the continued use of borax

borne \'bȯrn\ endured or tolerated

borné \bȯr:nā\ lacking scope or variety

bouché \bü:shā\ stopped with the hand, as in French horn playing

bouche \'büsh\ a slit in the edge of a medieval shield; a bushing made of metal or other material

bought \'baút\ a twist or turn in the grain of a bowstave

bought \'bȯt\ purchased

boule \'bül\ a game similar to roulette; a pear-shaped mass of some substance formed synthetically in a Verneuil furnace

boule \'bülē\ a legislative council of ancient Greece

bourgeois \'búrzh,wä\ a middle-class person

bourgeois \bər'jȯis\ an old size of approximately 9-point type

bow \'baú\ to bend down; the forward part of a ship or boat

bow \'bō\ a weapon used to propel an arrow; an implement used to play a stringed musical instrument

bower \'baúər\ a covered place in a garden made with tree boughs or intertwined vines

bower \'bōər\ a musician who performs with a bow on a stringed instrument

bowman \'bōmən\ an archer

bowman \'baúmən\ a boatman, oarsman, or paddler stationed at the front of the boat or canoe

Brahman \'brämən\ a member of the highest or sacerdotal class among Hindus

Brahman \'brāmən\ any of several breeds of Indian cattle

branchier \'bräⁿshyä\ a showy American duck which nests in hollow trees, (a wood duck)

branchier \'branchēər\ more covered or overgrown with stems growing from the trunk or limbs of a tree

Brava \'brävə\ a descendant of immigrants from the Cape Verde islands, resident especially on Cape Cod and around New Bedford, Massachusetts,

brava \'brävä\ a shout of approval or approbation in applauding a woman

breathed \'brēthd\ drew air into and expelled it from the lungs

breathed \'bretht\ uttered without voice, or voiceless

broché \brō:shä\ woven with a raised figure

broche \'brōsh\ a shuttle used in handweaving tapestry

bromide \'brōməd\ a binary compound of bromine and usually a more electropositive element

bromide \'brō,mīd\ a conventional and commonplace or tiresome person

bruit \'brüē\ any of several generally abnormal sounds heard on auscultation

bruit \'brüt\ to publicize or tout

Brut \'brüt\ a medieval chronicle of Britain

brut \'brüt\ very dry, as of champagne

buffet \'bəfət\ a blow; the vibration of an airplane

buffet \:bə:fā\ a counter for refreshments and food

bund \'bənd\ an embanked thoroughfare along a river or the sea used for business or as an esplanade

bund \'búnt\ a grouping for some evil purpose (slang)

Bunter \'búntər\ relating to the lowest division of the European Triassic

bunter \'bəntər\ a gripping device for a planing machine; a baseball player who bats or taps the ball lightly into the infield

bure \'bürä\ a large house in the Fiji Islands

bure \'byúr\ a moderate yellowish brown color

buri \'bürē\ a Fijian tree which yields a plumlike fruit

buri \bü'rē\ a talipot palm, the fiber of which is used in making straw hats

buro \'byürō\ the policy-forming committee of the Communist party of the former U.S.S.R.

buro \'bürō\ a Philippine dish of fish prepared with boiled rice and spicy seasonings

bustier \'bəstēər\ having larger breasts
bustier \'büst͡ēyā\ a long-line usually strapless brassiere or foundation garment that uplifts the bosom

---

Group I
bacchanal
baculites

bamboo
batatas
baton
beloved
bezantee
blessed
Boshas

C

---

cabriole \'kabrē͵ōl\ a form of furniture leg common in Queen Anne and Chippendale furniture
cabriole \'kȧbrēȯl\ a ballet leap in which one leg is extended in mid-air and the other struck against it

cache \'kask\ a hiding place
cache \kä'shā\ an early device used as an applicator in radio-therapy

caïque \kä'ēk\ a Levantine sailing vessel
caique \kä'ēkä\ any of various small stocky often brightly colored parrots

Cajun \'kājən\ one of a people of mixed white, Indian, and Negro ancestry in Alabama and adjoining sections of Mississippi
cajun \kə'hün\ a West Indian fiber plant

cala \'kalə\ a picnic ham, a shoulder of pork with much of the butt removed commonly smoked and often boned
cala \kə'lä\ a Creole fried cake made mainly of rice

Caliana \kal'yänə\ an Indian people of Venezuela
calianá \:kalyə:nä\ a Tupi-Guaranian people of northeastern Brazil

calk \'kȯk\ a tapered wedge of iron or steel projecting downward on the shoe of a draft animal to prevent slipping
calk \'kalk\ to copy, by rubbing a sheet of

paper with colored chalk, then placing a clean sheet between the first sheet and the object to be copied and passing a blunt style over the two sheets

calver \'kavər\ a pregnant cow
calver \'kal͵vər\ to prepare meat a certain way in cooking

Canada \'kanədə\ a country in North America
canada \'kanədə\ the Jerusalem artichoke
canada \kən'yädə\ a small canyon or creek

canal \kə'nal\ an artificial waterway designed for navigation, irrigation, or drainage
canal \kə'näl\ a waterspout or eaves trough

canard \kə'närd\ a fabricated report
canard \kȧnȧr\ the flesh of a duck used as food

Canarian \kə'nerēən\ a native or inhabitant of the Canary Islands
Canarian \͵kä'nyäriən\ pertaining to a minor linguistic family of South American Indians, comprising the extinct Canaris

canon \'kanən\ an ecclesiastical law or rule of doctrine or discipline enacted by a council
canon \kä'nōn\ the zither, a musical in-

strument consisting of a shallow sound-board overlaid with 30 to 40 strings

Canton \'kantᵊn\ a city in Ohio

Canton \'kanˌtän\ a Chinese city

canton \'kantᵊn\ to divide into parts

cape \'kāˌpē\ a judicial writ, now abolished, relative to a plea of lands or tenements

cape \'kāp\ an extension of land jutting out into the water; a sleeveless outer garment

capo \'kāpō\ a bar or movable nut attached to the fingerboard of a guitar or other fretted instrument to uniformly raise the pitch of all the strings

capo \'kapˌō\ or \'käˌpō\ the chief of a branch of the Mafia

Cara \'kärə\ an ancient Indian people of northern Ecuador

cará \kə'rä\ a tropical American yam with small yellow-skinned edible tubers

caraipi \kə'rīpē\ a Brazilian tree of the family *Rosaceae* the burnt bark of which is pulverized for mixing with pottery clay

caraipi \:karə:pē\ any of several Brazilian trees of the genus *Catalpa*

Carandas \kə'randəs\ a large genus of spiny shrubs

carandas \kə'randəs\ any plant of the genus *Carissa*

carandas \'karənˌdäz\ tropical palms that yield a wax similar to carnauba

carbon \'kärˌbən\ a nonmetallic chiefly tetravalent element

carbon \kär'bōn\ a Guatemalan timber tree with reddish wood

casal \'käsəl\ of or pertaining to grammatical case

casal \kə'säl\ a hamlet

Cassia \'kasēə\ a genus of herbs, shrubs, and trees native to warm regions

cassia \'kashə\ any of the coarser varieties of cinnamon bark

Cassis \'kasə̇s\ a genus of mollusks comprising forms with a very large body whorl

cassis \ka'sēs\ a syrupy liquor of low alcoholic strength made from black currants

cat \'kät\ a shrub cultivated by the Arabs for its leaves which act as a stimulant narcotic when chewed or used in tea

cat \'kat\ a member of the family Felidae

catchup \'kechəp\ a yellowish moderate red

catch-up \'kaˌchəp or 'keˌchəp\ an activity or move intended to close a gap and attain a theoretical norm

catted \'kad•ə̇d\ built up or bonded with clay

catted \'kadə̇d\ flogged with a cat-o'-nine-tails; searched for a sexual mate

cave \'kav\ the sum which each player puts on the table at the beginning of play in such card games as brelan and bouillote

cave \'kāv\ a hollowed-out chamber in the earth

cay \'kē\ a small low island or emergent reef

cay \'kī\ a monkey of the genus Cebus

cello \'chelō\ a stringed instrument

cello \'selō\ made of cellophane

cénacle \sānȧkl\ a philosophical, literary, or artistic group

cenacle \'senə̇kəl\ a retreat house

central \'sen•trəl\ basic, essential, principal, or dominant

central \sen'träl\ a mill for making raw sugar from cane

centum \'sentəm\ a hundred

centum \'kentəm\ belonging to the Indo-European language family

Ceres \'sirēz\ a moderate orange color

ceres \'sirz\ protuberances or tumid areas at the base of a bird's bill

Cete \'sē͵tē\ an order of aquatic mammals, including whales

cete \'sēt\ a group of badgers

Cha-Cha \'shä͵shä\ one of a group of poor whites of French ancestry in the Virgin Islands

cha-cha \'chä͵chä\ a fast rhythmic ballroom dance of Latin-American origin

Cham \'chäm\ a people in central coastal Annam linguistically related to the Cambodians

cham \'kam\ a local chieftan, especially in Afghanistan, Iran, and some areas of central Asia

cham \'sham\ champagne (by shortening)

Chama \'kāmə\ a genus of eulamellibranchiate bivalve mollusks of warm and tropical seas

Chama \'chämə\ a Panoan people of northeastern Peru

Chamar \chə'mär\ a member of a low Indian caste whose occupation is leatherworking

chamar \'chəmər\ a fan typically made of a yak's tail or peacock feathers

chap \'chap\ a fellow; sore roughening of the skin

chap \'chäp\ a jaw; (not usually 'chap) or the fleshy covering of a jaw

charas \'karəs\ plants of the genus *Chara*

charas \'chärəs\ a narcotic and intoxicating resin that exudes from the flower heads of hemp

chargé \shär:zhā\ a chargé d'affaires

charge \'chärj\ an instruction; an accusation; an expenditure

chassé \sha:sā\ a dance or figure skating step

chasse \'shäs\ a saint's shrine

chay \'chī\ the root of an East Indian herb that yields a red dye

chay \'shā\ a light carraige or pleasure cart

chebac \chē'bek\ a xebec, a Mediterranean sailing ship with a long overhanging bow and stern

chebac \shə'bek\ the least flycatcher

chela \'kēlə\ a claw, as on a crab or lobster

chela \'chälä\ a disciple

Chi \'shī\ Chicago (by shortening)

chi \'kī\ the 22nd letter of the Greek alphabet

chi \'chē\ the vital life force in the body supposedly regulated by acupuncture

chil \'chil\ an Indian kite (a bird)

chil \'chēl\ the cheer pine

chimer \'chimər\ a loose sleeveless robe worn by some bishops of the Anglican Communion

chimer \'chīmər\ a person who plays a set of musically tuned bells

chimere \shə'mir\ a loose sleeveless robe

chimere \kī'mir\ a fabrication of the mind

China \'kēnə\ a large genus of trees native to the Andean region of northwestern South America

China \'chīnə\ a country in Asia

china \'chīnə\ vitreous porcelain wares

chiné \shə'nā\ having a mottled pattern of supposed Chinese fashion

chine \'chīn\ cut through the backbone

Choco \chə'kō\ a people of northwestern Colombia and Panama

choco \'chäkō\ an Australian conscript in World War II

Chol \'chōl\ an Indian people of northern Chiapas, Mexico

chol \'chäl\ a desolate plain, in central Asia

chose \'shōz\ a piece of personal property

chose \'chōz\ selected

Chosen \:chō͵sen\ the former official name of Korea

chosen \'chōzᵊn\ marked to receive special favor

choux \'shüz\ soft cabbage-shaped ornaments or rosettes of fabric used in women's wear

choux \'shü\ darlings, used as a term of endearment

chunked \'chəŋkd\ removed heavy pieces of wood from a skid road

chunked \'chəŋkəd\ having or characterized by a stout solid body

citrine \'sī,trēn\ resembling citron or lemon

citrine \si'trēn\ a semiprecious yellow stone resembling topaz but actually black quartz

civet \'sivət\ a substance found in a pouch of a true civet cat

civet \sēvā\ a highly seasoned game stew

civil \'sivəl\ involving the relations of citizens with one another or with the body politic

civil \,sē'vēl\ a coarse strong bask fiber derived from a Mexican shrub

classes \'klasəs\ social ranks; denominations

classes \'kla,sēz\ ecclesiastical governing bodies of a district

claves \'klävāz\ small cylindrical wooden sticks used as percussion instruments by being struck together

claves \'klā,vēz\ keys or glossaries serving as aids to interpretation

close \'klōz\ to shut or terminate
close \'klōs\ near; compact

closer \'klōsər\ nearer; more compact

closer \'klōzər\ a sewing-machine operator who sews the final seams; the last stone completing a horizontal course

clothing \'klōthiŋ\ covering for the human body, or garments in general

clothing \'klȯthiŋ\ material consisting of leather or cloth in which teeth are set that is used for wrapping the cylinders of carding machines

coachee \kō'chē\ an American carriage shaped like a coach but longer and open in front

coachee \'kōchē\ a horse used or adapted for drawing a coach

Coalite \'kō,līt\ a smokeless fuel made by heating bituminous coal in a retort

coalite \'kōə,līt\ to unite or associate

coax \'kōks\ to persuade or influence

coax \kō:aks\ a coaxial transmission line in which one conductor is centered inside and insulated from an outer metal tube that serves as a second conductor

Cocos \'kō,käs\ a genus of pinnate-leaved palms

cocos \'kōkōz\ any of several aggressively woody sedges

coif \'kwäf\ a manner of arranging the hair

coif \'kȯif\ a cap covering the sides of the head like a small hood

colla \'kälə\ necks or necklike parts or processes

colla \'kōlyə\ a period of rainy windy weather from the southwest in the Philippines

collect \kə'lekt\ to bring together

collect \'kälikt\ a short prayer during church service

collegiate \kə'lējət\ marked by power or authority vested equally in each of a number of colleagues; a British or Canadian secondary school

collegiate \kə'lējēāt\ to constitute or organized as a college or a collegiate church

colleter \kə'lēdər\ one of the mucilage-secreting hairs that clothes many plant surfaces

colleter \'kälədər\ a worker who attaches the inner coil of a watch hairspring to a collet for assembly to the balance wheel

colon \kə'lōn\ a colonial farmer, planter, or plantation owner

colon \'kōlən\ part of the large intestine

that extends from the cecum to the rectum; the punctuation mark ":"

comal \'kōməl\ in botany, having or being an assemblage of branches forming a leafy crown

comal \kō'mäl\ a griddle of earthenware, metal, or a flat slab of sandstone

comate \'kōmāt\ a companion

comate \'kō,māt\ covered with hair or filaments

combine \kəm'bīn\ to unite

combine \'käm,bīn\ a harvesting machine

<u>**come**</u> \'kōm\ or \'kùm\ the dried rootlets produced in malting grain

come \'kəm\ to move toward something or advance

comes \'kəmz\ moves toward something

comes \'kō,mēz\ a Roman Catholic service book; the answer in a fugue

comes \'kōmz\ dried rootlets produced in malting grain

<u>**commit**</u> \'kämət\ a card game

commit \kə,mit\ to obligate to take some action

commune \kə'myün\ to receive Communion by partaking of the Eucharist

commune \'kä,myün\ a small group of people living together

complicate \'kämplə,kāt\ to make complex, involved, or difficult

complicate \'kämpləkət\ folded longitudinally one or more times, as of insects' wings

comport \kəm'pōrt\ conduct or behavior

comport \'käm,pōrt\ a bowl-shaped dish

compose \kəm'pōz\ to calm, settle, or tranquilize; to create by mental or artistic labor

composé \'kòn,pōzā\ combining harmonious colors or tones

compress \kəm'pres\ to reduce the size, duration, or degree of concentration by pressure

compress \'käm,pres\ a covering of folded cloth applied and held firmly by a bandage over a wound

compromises \'kämprə:mēz\ agreements in Roman civil law between private persons referring a dispute between them to a designated third party for decision

compromises \kämprə:mīzēz\ puts in jeopardy

concha \'käŋkə\ the plain semidome of an apse

concha \'känchə\ a metal disk, usually shell-shaped and silver, used as decoration on clothing and harness

concinnate \'känsə,nāt\ adjust or trim; arrange in good order

concinnate \kən'sinət\ put together with neat propriety, as of speech or writing

Concord \'käŋkərd\ the capital of New Hampshire

concord \'kän,kòrd\ or \'käŋ,kòrd\ a state of agreement

concord \kən'kòrd\ to act together

conduct \'kändəkt\ a standard of personal behavior

conduct \kən'dəkt\ to manage, control, or direct

confect \kən'fekt\ to put together; to prepare

confect \'kän,fekt\ a confection consisting of a solid center that is coated with layers of sugar

conglomerate \kən'glämərət\ in zoology, irregularly grouped in spots, such as eyes

conglomerate \kən'glämə,rāt\ to form into a mass or coherent whole

conjure \'känjər\ to call forth or send away by magic arts

conjure \kən'jùr\ to entreat earnestly or solemnly; to beseech

conjuror \'känjərər\ a person who practices magic arts, legerdemain, and illusion

conjuror \ˌkän'jərər\ a person bound by a common oath with others; a coswearer

<u>connex</u> \'käniks\ constituting one syntactical unit

<u>connex</u> \'käneks\ the infinity of points and lines in mathematics

conserve \kən'sərv\ to keep in a sound or safe state

conserve \'kän,sərv\ a candied fruit preserve

console \kən'sōl\ to comfort

console \'kän,sōl\ a cabinet or panel

consort \'kän,sȯrt\ a group of musicians entertaining by voice or instrument, or the entertainment they afford

consort \kən'sȯrt\ to be or come into accord

consummate \känsəmət\ extremely skilled and accomplished

consummate \'känsə,māt\ to complete marital union by the first act of sexual intercourse after marriage

conte \'kōnt\ a short tale, especially of adventure

conté \'kōn:tā\ a hard crayon made of graphite and clay

content \kən'tent\ pleased or gratified

content \'kän,tent\ substance or subject matter

contest \kən'test\ to make the subject of litigation

contest \'kän,test\ an earnest struggle for superiority or victory

contract \'kän,trakt\ to enter into with mutual obligations; an agreement or covenant

contract \kən'trakt\ to shorten or draw together

converse \kən'vers\ to engage in conversation

converse \'kän,vərs\ a thing or idea that is opposite another

convert \kən'vərt\ to exchange property or money for a specified equivalent

convert \'kän,vərt\ a person that is persuaded or converted to a religious faith or to a particular belief, attitude of mind, or principle

convict \kən'vikt\ to find or declare guilty of an offense or crime

convict \'kän,vikt\ any of various striped or barred fishes

cooper \'küpər\ a person that makes or repairs wooden casks or tubs

cooper \'kōpər\ a vessel equipped to supply liquor and tobacco to deepsea fishers in the North Sea

cooperage \'küpərij\ casks for draft beer or bulk wine

cooperage \'kōpərij\ the business for which a trading vessel (a cooper) is employed

<u>coops</u> \'küps\ small enclosures for small animals

<u>coops</u> \'kō,äps\ groups working for mutual benefit; cooperatives (by shortening)

Coos \'küs\ a Kusan people of Oregon

<u>coos</u> \'küz\ soft low cries, as of a dove or pigeon

Coronilla \ˌkȯrə'nilə\ a genus of Old World often woody herbs

coronilla \ˌkȯrə'nēyə\ a valuable timber tree of Argentina

corselet \'kȯrslət\ the hard prothorax of a beetle

corselet \:kȯrsə:let\ a foundation garment combining girdle and brassiere

couch \'kau̇ch\ an article of furniture for sitting or reclining

<u>couch</u> \'küch\ a board covered with flannel on which sheets of handmade paper are pressed

counterchange \'kau̇ntər,chānj\ the contrast of a dark area against a light ground with a light area against a dark ground in a painting

counterchange \:kau̇ntər,chānj\ to cause to change places or characteristics

countercheck \'kaúntər,chek\ a constraint or restraint

countercheck \:kaúntər,chek\ to check a second time for verification

countryman \'kəntrēmən\ an inhabitant or native of a specified nation, province, or district

countryman \'kəntrē,man\ a person living in a rural area; a farmer

<u>**coupe**</u> \'küp\ a dessert; a closed two-door automobile with one seating compartment

<u>**coupe**</u> \kü'pā\ a ballet step

<u>**couped**</u> \'küpt\ in heraldry, cut off short at the ends so as not to extend to the edges of the field

<u>**couped**</u> \'küd\ executed a bridge coup in playing a hand

cover \'kəvər\ something that protects, shelters, or guards

cover \'kōvər\ a person who lives in a small sheltered inlet or bay

coze \'kəz\ a cousin (by shortening)

coze \'kōz\ to shat or gossip

crabbed \'krabd\ moved sideways or in a diagonal manner

crabbed \krabəd\ difficult to understand or read

crochet \krō'shā\ needlework consisting of interlocked looped stitches

crochet \'krächet\ one of three secondary folds of the crests of lophodont molar teeth

crooked \'krúkt\ turned or bent from a straight line, as a crooked neck

crooked \'krúkəd\ fraudulent or dishonest

<u>**crotal**</u> \'krōdᵊl\ a small spherical rattle on a harness

<u>**crotal**</u> \'krädᵊl\ a reddish brown color

<u>**crus**</u> \'krüz\ French vineyards that produce wine grapes

crus \'krüs\ the part of the hind limb between the thigh and ankle

cube \'kyüb\ a regular solid having six equal square sides

cube \'kyü,bā\ any of several tropical American shrubs or climbers used as fish poisons

Cuclus \'kükələs\ the type genus of Cuculidae comprising the typical cuckoos

cuculus \kyü'kələs\ the anterior dorsal shield of the cephalothorax in pseudoscorpions

<u>**cumal**</u> \'küəl\ a standard of value in ancient Ireland, most often equal to from 3–10 cows

cumal \'kümal\ the bivalent radical $C_3H_7C_6H_4CH$

curé \kyə'rā\ a parish priest

cure \'kyúr\ to heal; to age or ripen

cussed \'kəst\ cursed

cussed \'kəsəd\ obstinate or cantankerous

custodes \kü'stōdēz\ building superintendents; agencies that monitor and take care of securities and assets

custodes \kü'stō,däs\ a superior of a Franciscan province

cuter \'kyütər\ more attractive or pretty

cuter \'kyüd•ər\ a 25-cent piece

cutin \'kət,in\ something inserted

cutin \'kyütᵊn\ the insoluble water-impermeable complex aggregate of waxes, soaps, and higher alcohols

cyanoses \,sīə'nō,sēz\ a dusky bluish or purplish discoloration of skin or mucous membranes due to deficient oxygenation of the blood

cyanoses \'sīə,nōsez\ minerals consisting of copper sulfate

Group I

calamites
certificate
chassis
chromides
cicerone

cleanly
combat
comex
commiserate
commune
compassionate
concatenate
concrete
confederate
confine
congest
congress
conscript
construct
contrary
convoy
cordon
corporate

counterbore
counterbrace
countercharge
countercurrent
counteretch
countermarch
countermark
countermine
countermure
countersink
counterstain
counterstamp
counterweight
counterwork
curate
cursed
curtail
cyclostomes

D

Dago \'dägō\ a member of a Negro tribe formerly the most powerful in Darfur

dago \'dāgō\ a person of Italian or Spanish birth or descent, usually considered offensive

dah \'dä\ a large Burmese knife; a dash in radio and telegraphic code

dah \'da\ a Negro nurse

dancetté \dan:sed•ā\ in heraldry, having usually three large indentations

dancette \dan'set\ a zigzag patterned architectural molding

das \'das (sometimes 'däs)\ a hyrax of southern Africa

das \'däs\ a Hindu slave or servant

das \'däz\ valuable fiber plants of the East Indies

dauphiné \:dȯfə:nā\ mashed potatoes shaped into balls and fried

dauphine \dȯ'fēn\ a dauphin's wife

decameter \də'kamədər\ a poetic line of ten feet

decameter \'dekə,mēdər\ a metric unit of length equal to ten meters

decanal \də'kanəl\ relating to a dean

decanal \'dekə,nal\ a high-boiling liquid aldehyde

degrade \də'grād\ to postpone entering the examination for a degree in honors at Cambridge University beyond the usual or required time

degrade \'dē,grād\ lumber or a log found to be below quality

denier \də'nīər\ a person who disavows or contradicts

denier \'denyər\ a unit of fineness for silk, rayon, or nylon yarn

desert \də'zər|t\ a reward or punishment deserved or earned

desert \'dezert\ a relatively barren tract

determinate \də'tərmənət\ being, having the form of, or derived from an inflorescence in which the main and secondary axes always terminate in a single flower

determinate \də'tərmən₁āt\ to fix the identity of

devise \də'vīz\ to develop a plan
Devise \dā'vēzə\ foreign exchange in readily available form

devote \də'vōt\ to attach the attention or center the activities wholly on a specific object
dévote \dē'vȯt\ a woman who is an ardent follower or supporter of a cause

diastases \'dīə₁stāsēz\ mixtures of amylases obtained usually as yellowish white powders
diastases \dī'astə₁sēz\ in medicine, abnormal separations of parts normally joined together

diffuse \də'fyüz\ to spread out
diffuse \də'fyüs\ wordy; unconcentrated or scattered

digest \'dī₁jəst\ a short summation of or the compressed kernel of a body of information
digest \də'jest\ to change the nature of a substance by various means

Diné \də'nā\ an Athapaskan people of northern New Mexico and Arizona (also called Navaho)
dine \'dīn\ to eat a meal

dinged \'diŋd\ invoked damnation upon; made a ringing sound
dinged \'dinjd\ made a depression in

dingy \'diŋē\ crazy; groggy or dazed
dingy \'dinjē\ shabby, mean, or squalid

dire \'dīər\ exciting horror or terror
dire \'dērə\ a fine, whether large or small, in Irish Brehon law

Dis \'dis\ an underworld god in Roman religion, identical with Greek god Pluto
dis \'dēs\ any of several superhuman female beings in Norse mythology; the lowest trump in some card games, like pinochle

dit \'dit\ a dot in telegraphic code

dit \'dē\ a short usually didactic poem in French literature

dive \'dīv\ to plunge into water head first; to fall precipitously
dive \'dē₁vä\ prima donnas

divers \'dī₁vərs\ more than one but indefinite in number
divers \'divərz\ persons who plunge into water, or descend or fall precipitously

Dives \'dī₁vēz\ a rich man
dives \'dīvz\ plunges into water head first; falls precipitously; nightspots, often disreputable

do \'dü\ to perform
do \'dō\ the first tone of the diatonic scale

does \'dōz\ adult females of various mammals, as deer and rabbits
does \'dəz\ performs or acts

dogged \'dägd\ hunted or tracked like a hound; loafed on the job
dogged \'dȯgəd\ obstinately determined

dogman \'dȯgmən\ a person who takes care of kennels
dogman \'däg₁man\ a fancier or specialist of members of the family *Canidae*

Dom \'dōm\ a member of a Hindu caste of untouchables
dom \'dōm\ the doom palm, a large African fan palm important as a soil stabilizer in desert regions
dom \'däm\ an address of a dignitary of certain monastic orders

dos \'dōz\ the first tones of the diatonic scale
dos \'dōs\ property settled by a husband on his spouse at the time of marriage

doublé \dü:blä\ a bookbinding made with ornamental lining
double \'dəbəl\ having a twofold character or relation

dove \'dōv\ plunged into water head first; fell precipitously
dove \'dəv\ a bird

drawer \'dròr\ a sliding box or receptacle

drawer \'dróǝr\ a person that draws, as a draftsman or wire-former

duces \'düˌchāz\ dictators

duces \'dyüˌsēz\ military commanders stationed in a province of the later Roman Empire

dulce \'dülsā\ a sweet Spanish wine; sweetmeat or candy

dulce \'dǝls\ any of several coarse red seaweeds found principally in northern latitudes and used as a food condiment

<u>**dun**</u> \'dǝn\ dark or gloomy; to ask repeatedly for an overdue payment

<u>**dun**</u> \'dün\ a fortified residence in Scotland and Ireland

dural \'dyu̇rǝl\ of or relating to the dura mater, the tough fibrous membrane enveloping the brain

dural \'dyu̇ˌral\ an alloy of aluminum, copper, manganese, and magnesium

Durban \'du̇rbǝn\ a Mongol people in the western part of the Mongolian plateau

Durban \'dǝrbǝn\ a city in the Union of South Africa

Group I

debris
decode
degenerate
degras
deliberate
depauperate
desolate
desperate
diagnoses
differentiate
digest
dimidiate
disconcert
discorporate
discriminate
divaricate
divorce
docent
dona
doña

E

effacé \ːefǝːsā\ a ballet movement

efface \ǝ'fās\ to cause to disappear

effuse \e'fyüz\ to flow out

effuse \eːfyüs\ lips of certain shells being separated by a gap

eject \ǝ'jekt\ to drive out, especially by physical force

eject \'ēˌjekt\ the act of perceiving a mental object as spatially and sensibly objective, or of objectifying what is primarily subjective

elaborate \ǝlabǝrǝt\ marked by complexity or ornateness; intricate

elaborate \ǝlabǝˌrāt\ to alter the chemical makeup of a foodstuff to that which is more suited to bodily needs

Elater \'elǝdǝr\ the type genus of Elateridae, comprising the beetles

elater \'elǝdǝr\ any beetle of the family Elateridae

elater \ē'lādǝr\ a person who raises the spirits of or inspires

elegant \'elǝgǝnt\ in pharmacy, pleasant in taste, attractive in appearance, and free from objectionable order

elegant \ālāgä^n\ a fashionable man; a dandy

Empire \'ämˌpiǝr\ the color cadmium green; furniture characterized by classic and oriental motives; clothing characteristic of the French Directoire style

empire \'emˌpīǝr\ extended territory usually comprising a group of nations, states, or people under the domination of a single sovereign power

engage \ən'gāj\ to come in contact with or interlock

engagé \ˌäŋgä'zhä\ committed to or supportive of a cause

ensign \'ensən\ the most junior commissioned naval officer ranking just below a lieutenant junior grade and above a chief warrant officer-5

ensign \ən'sīn\ to distinguish by a mark or ornament

Entrance \'entrəns\ a solemn procession, in the Eastern Church's liturgy, through the body of the church to the altar, bisop's throne, and clergy stalls

entrance \'entrəns\ the bow or entire forepart of a ship below the waterline; a place or passage for admission or penetration

entrance \ən•'trans\ to put in a trance; to carry away with emotion

epicrisis \ːepē:krīsəs\ a secondary crisis

epicrisis \ə'pikrəsəs\ an analytical summary of a medical case history

erg \'ərg\ an absolute unit of work in the centimeter-gram-second system (seldom 'erg)

erg \'erg\ a desert region of shifting sand

ergotism \'ergəˌtizəm\ logical or sophisticated reasoning

ergotism \'ərgədˌizəm\ a toxic condition produced by eating grain products or grasses infected with ergot fungus

erythroses \'erəˌthrōsəz\ syrupy aldose sugars

erythroses \ˌerə'thrōˌsēz\ red or purplish colors of the skin resulting from vascular congestion

escort \əˌskȯrt\ to take or lead by force

escort \'eˌskȯrt\ a male who goes on a date with a female

esses \'esəs\ things resembling the 19th letter of the alphabet

esses \'esēz\ actual beings or essential natures

Eta \'äˌtä\ an outcast class formerly segregated in Japan

eta \'ādə\ the seventh letter of the Greek alphabet

eve \'ēv\ evening (by shortening)

Eve \'āˌvä\ a Negro people of Ghana, Togo, and border regions of Dahomey

Even \'āˌwən\ a member of a Siberian people living in northeast Russia

even \'ēvən\ flat or level; truly or indeed

even \'ēvᵊm\ in knitting, without change by increasing or decreasing

evening \'ēvniŋ\ the latter part and close of the day, and the early part of darkness and night

evening \'ēvəniŋ\ making a surface smooth or uniform

excuse \ek'skyüz\ to free from an obligation or duty

excuse \ek'skyüs\ an inferior example or instance of a kind

extract \ek'trakt\ to draw forth or pull out

extract \'ekˌstrakt\ a certified copy of a document

Ewe \'āˌwä\ a Negro people of Ghana, Togo, and Dahomey

ewe \'yü\ a female sheep, goat, or smaller antelope

Group I

eclipses
effeminate
elegant
ellipses
enervate
exenterate
expose
extrados

F

fade \'fād\ insipid, vapid, or trite

fade \'fād\ to recede into indistinctness and lack of clarity of outline and detail

fakir \'fākər\ a swindler

fakir \'fəkir\ a Muslim mendicant or ascetic; a pale orange yellow color

file \'fīl\ a hardened steel smoothing tool; to arrange in a particular order

filé \fə'lā\ powdered young sassafras leaves

fine \'fīn\ a monetary penalty; superior in character; minute

fine \'fēnā\ the finish or end

fine \fēn\ an ordinary French brandy

flageolet \:flajə:let\ or \:flajə:lāt\ a small flute resembling a treble recorder

flageolet \flázhólā\ a green kidney bean of France

fleer \'flēər\ a person who runs away

fleer \'fliər\ to laugh at contemptuously

flower \'flaùər\ the part of a seed plant that normally bears reproductive organs

flower \'flōər\ a river, stream, or other flowing body of liquid

fob \'föb\ a small pocket just below the front waistband of men's trousers

FOB \'ef'ō'bē\ without charge for delivery at a specified place, free on board

folia \'fōlēə\ processes or parts resembling plates of the cerebellar cortex

folia \fō'lēə\ a noisy carnival dance of Portuguese origin

footer \'fúd•ər\ a pedestrian; a hawk that seizes prey with the talons

footer \'fúd•ə4\ to talk or act foolishly

forearm \'fōr'ärm\ to arm in advance for attack or resistance

forearm \'fōr,ärm\ the part of the arm or forelimb between the elbow and the wrist in primates

forerun \fōr'rən\ to announce or introduce as a harbinger

forerun \'fōr,rən\ the most volatile portion of a distilland

foreset \fōr'set\ to arrange beforehand

foreset \'fōr,set\ relating to or forming the steeper slope on the outer margin of a delta

forestall \'fōr,stól\ an offense under old English law of feloniously waylaying on the highway; a plate of armor attached to a horse's bridle with holes for the eyes and nostrils

forestall \fōr'stól\ to exclude, hinder, or prevent by prior occupation or by measures taken in advance

forget \fər'get\ to lose the remembrance of

forget \'fōrjət\ the strip or shaved piece used for the sides of the fingers of a glove

formal \'fórməl\ following or in accord with established custom, rule, or form

formal \fór'mal\ any acetal derived from formaldehyde and an alcohol

forme \'fórm\ a pattern for the upper part of a shoe; a low bench on which shoemakers formerly sat when working

formé \'fōr,mā\ arms of a cross being narrow at the center and expanding toward the ends, as a maltese cross

forte \'fōrt\ a person's strong point

forte \'fòr|d•ā\ in music, loudly

fortes \'fōrtz\ a person's strong points; the parts of swords nearest the hilt

fortes \'fōr,tāz\ musical tones or passages played loudly

fortes \'fōr,tēz\ consonants produced with stronger expiration and greater articulatory tenseness

fourchette \'fůr‚shet\ a small fold of membrane connecting the labia minora in the posterior part of the vulva

fourchette \'fȯr‚shet\ the shaped piece used for the sides of the fingers of a glove

fourchette \:fůrshə:tā\ in heraldry, having the end of each arm divided so as to terminate in a V

frappe \'frap\ an iced and flavored semi-liquid mixture served in glasses

frappe \fra'pā\ a ballet movement in which the free foot beats against the ankle of the supporting foot

fray \'frī\ a clerical title in various religious orders in Spanish countries

fray \'frā\ commotion; to wear off by rubbing

frette \'fret\ a hoop of wrought iron or steel shrunk on a cast-iron gun to strengthen it

frette \'fre‚tā\ in heraldry, covered with narrow interlacing bands

fronton \‚frəⁿ•'tōⁿ\ a pediment over a door or window

fronton \'frän•‚tän\ a court or building for the game of jai alai

fundi \'fəndē\ a tropical African grass cultivated for its seed that resembles millet

fundi \'fən‚dī\ the lower back parts of bladders

Fur \'fůr\ a Nilotic-Negro people in Darfur province, western Sudan

fur \'fər\ the fine soft thick hairy covering of mammals

fusee \'fyü‚zē\ a conical spirally grooved pulley in a timepiece; a wooden match with a bulbous head not easily blown out when ignited; a red signal flare

fusee \‚fü'zā\ in music, an arbitrary ornament for the performer

Group I

federate
ferment
fimbriate
finales
forefeel
foreshadow
foretaste
foretoken
fragment

G

gab \'gab\ to talk in an idle, rapid, or thoughtless manner

gab \'gȯb\ an East Indian persimmon tree

galet \'gālət\ the fossa, a slender lithe mammal that is the largest carnivore of Madagascar

galet \'galət\ a chip of stone

gallant \gə'lant\ notably marked by courtesy and attentiveness to women especially in a spirited, dashing, or elaborate way

gallant \'galənt\ splendid or stately

gally \'galē\ to put to flight by frightening

gally \'gȯlē\ marked by bare spots

ganged \'gaŋd\ assembled or operated simultaneously as a group of persons or pieces of equipment

ganged \'ganjd\ protected by winding, as the part of the line next to a fishhook

gaufre \'gōfər\ or \'gȯfər\ a very thin wafer baked with a wafer iron

gaufre \'gȯ‚frā\ crimped, plaited, or fluted linen or lace by means of a heated iron

Ge \\'gā\ Gaia, the earth goddess in Greek mythology

Ge \\'zhā\ pertaining to or designating an important linguisitic family of South American Indians, the Tapuyan

gee \\'jē\ a command to make a horse turn to the right; an expression of surprise, excitement, enthusiasm, or disappointment

gee \\'gi\ a man or guy; gum opium prepared for smoking

gems \\'jemz\ precious or sometimes semi-precious stones cut and polished for ornament

gems \\'gems\ a small agile goatlike antelope of Europe and the Caucacus

gender \\'jendər\ sex; any of two or more subclasses within a grammatical class of a language

gender \\'genˌdər\ a Javanese percussion instrument like a xylophone

gene \\'jēn\ a complex protein molecule that transmits hereditary characteristics

gene \\'zhen\ embarrassment or uneasiness

genet \\'jenət\ a small European carnivorous mammal related to the civet

genet \zhə'nā\ woodwaxen, a yellow-flowered Eurasian shrub

genial \\'jēnyəl\ diffusing good cheer and warmth

genial \jə'nīl\ relating to the chin

ger \\'gər\ a circular domed tent consisting of skins or felt stretched over a collapsible lattice framework and used by the Kirghiz and Mongols

ger \\'ger\ an alien resident in Hebrew territory protected from oppression by a native patron in accordance with early Hebrew law

gib \\'gib\ a castrated male cat; a removable machined plate of metal or other material that holds other mechanical parts in place

gib \\'jib\ a prison (slang)

gibber \\'jibər\ a rapid, inarticulate, and often foolish utterance

gibber \\'gibər\ a desert stone polished or sculptured by sandblast

gig \\'jig\ a gigolo (by shortening)

gig \\'gig\ a musical engagement for a single evening

gill \\'jil\ a U.S. liquid measure equal to ¼ pint

gill \\'gil\ an organ in fish for obtaining oxygen from water

gimel \\'gimel\ the third letter of the Hebrew alphabet

gimel \\'jiməl\ vocal part writing in medieval music in which the voices usually progress in parallel thirds

glacé \gla:sā\ having a lustrous surface

glace \\'glas\ a frozen dessert

glower \\'glau̇ər\ to stare with sullen brooding annoyance or anger

glower \\'glōər\ the luminous element in a Nernst lamp

Glycine \\'glisᵊnˌē\ a widely distributed genus of trailing or climbing herbs having tuberous roots, as the groundnut

glycine \\'glīˌsēn\ a poisonous compound used in photography as a fine-grain developer; a sweet crystalline amino acid usually made by the reaction of chloroacetic acid with ammonia

Gogo \\'gōgō\ a Bantu people of the highlands in Tanganyika

gogo \gō'gō\ a vine found in the Philippines the bark of which produces a soap substitute

gone \\'gȯn\ past

gone \\'gōn\ a germ cell

goût \\'gü\ artistic or literary good taste

gout \\'gau̇t\ a painful inflammatory disease of the joints

granite \\'granət\ a natural igneous rock formation of visible crystalline texture

granite \grä͵ni'tā\ a frozen dessert of coarse-grained sherbet

<u>**grave**</u> \'gräv\ an accent mark indicating a vowel is pronounced with a fall in pitch

grave \'grāv\ a burial place; a dignified appearance; to practice engraving

grave \'grävā\ in music, slowly and solemnly

<u>**Graves**</u> \'gräv(z)\ red or white table wine(s)

graves \'grāvz\ burial places

grille \'gril\ a grating or openwork barrier usually with a decorative metal design

grille \'grē͵yā\ having an ornamental bar or grate pattern across open areas of a lace motif

grind \'grīnd\ to reduce to powder by friction

<u>**grind**</u> \'grind\ any of several small toothed whales related to the dolphins

grouser \'graůsər\ an habitual complainer

grouser \'graůzər\ a set of cleats on a tractor wheel

Grues \'grüēz\ a suborder of *Gaviformes* consisting of the cranes and trumpeters

grues \'grüz\ fits of shivering

gruntling \'grəntᵊliŋ\ putting in good humor

gruntling \'grəntliŋ\ a young pig

Guaná \gwə'nä\ an Arawakan people of Mato Grosso, Brazil and the Chaco region of Paraguay

guana \'gwänə\ either of two malvaceous tropical trees, the balibago and the blue mahoe

Guara \'gwarə\ a genus of ibises containing the New World white and scarlet ibises

guara \gwə'rä\ any of several South American wild dogs; a South American crab-eating raccoon

guara \'gwärə\ a tropical American tree of the genus Cupania

gungy \'gəŋgē\ ultrazealous in carrying out instructions or enforcement of regulations

gungy \'gənjē\ dirty, grimy, or sticky

gurges \'gərjəz\ surges or swirls; turbulent fountains

gurges \'gər͵jēz\ an heraldic charge consisting of a spiral

gyro \'jī͵rō\ a gyroscope or gyrocompass

gyro \'zhēr'ō\ or \jēr͵ō\ a sandwich of lamb, tomato, and onion on pita bread

---

Group I

graduate
granulate
guesstimate

H

---

habitant \'habədənt\ a resident or inhabitant

habitant \:habē:tä\ relating to, characteristic of, or produced by the French farmers of Canada

<u>**hache**</u> \'hash\ a hatchet or axe

hache \hä'shä\ minced or hashed

Hades \'hā͵dēz\ the abode or state of the dead; hell

hades \'hādz\ deviates from the vertical, as a vein, fault, or lode

hakim \hə'kēm\ a Muslim physician

hakim \'hä͵kēm\ a Muslim ruler

<u>**hale**</u> \'hāl\ sound or healthy; to haul, pull, or draw

hale \'hälä\ an Hawaiian house

<u>**halo**</u> \'halō\ containing halogen (by shortening)

halo \\'hālō\\ a circle of light surrounding a luminous body

halter \\'hȯltər\\ a rope or strap for leading or tying a horse or other animal

halter \\'haltər\\ one of the modified second pair of insect wings that serve to maintain balance in flight

Hamburg \\'häm,bůrg\\ a city in northern Germany

Hamburg \\'ham,bərg\\ a European breed of rather small domestic fowls

hamburg \\'ham,bərg\\ a hamburger (by shortening)

Hamites \\'ha,mītz\\ a group of African peoples including the Berbers, Tuaregs, and Tibbu

Hamites \\hə'mīdez\\ a genus of extinct Cretaceous ammonoids

hartal \\här'täl\\ concerted cessation of work and business as a protest against a political situation or an act of government

hartal \\hȧr'tȯl\\ an orange to yellow mineral consisting of arsenic trisulfide

has \\'häz\\ utters an expression of surprise, joy, or grief

has \\'haz\\ holds, keeps, or retains

he \\'hē\\ a male person or animal

he \\'hā\\ the fifth letter of the Hebrew alphabet

headman \\'hed:man\\ overseer, foreman, or chief

headman \\'hed,mən\\ an executioner or worker who severs heads

headward \\'hedwərd\\ in the direction of the head

headward \\'hed,wȯrd\\ a feudal service consisting of acting as a guard to the lord

heavy \\'hevē\\ having great weight

heavy \\'hēvē\\ affected with heaves, as a horse

Hebe \\'hēb\\ an offensive term for a Jew

Hebe \\'hēbē\\ a genus comprising the shrubby evergreen venonicas of the southern hemisphere

hebe \\'hēbē\\ any veronica of the genus Hebe

heigh-ho \\'hī'hō\\ used typically to express boredom, weariness, or sadness

heigh-ho \\'hī,hō\\ a yellow-shafted flicker

helios \\'hēlē,ōz\\ a telescope adapted for viewing the sun

helios \\'hēlē,äs\\ the luminous intensity of a surface in a given direction per unit of projected area

helioses \\'hēlē,äsez\\ luminous intensities of surfaces in a given direction per unit of projected area

helioses \\'hēlēō,sēz\\ exposures to the sun

here \\'he,re\\ an invading army in Anglo-Saxon times

here \\'hir\\ at this point in space

heres \\'hirz\\ at these points in space

heres \\'hā,rās\\ the universal successor of a deceased person; an heir

heres \\'he,rez\\ armies of invasion

hermitage \\'hərməd•ij\\ a hermit's residence

Hermitage \\:hermē:täzh\\ a red Rhône Valley wine

hinder \\'hindər\\ to interfere with activity

hinder \\'hīndər\\ situated behind

hires \\'hīərz\\ employs for wages

hires \\'hī,rez\\ high resolution (by shortening)

his \\'hiz\\ something that belongs to him

his \\'hīz\\ expressions of greetings or to attract attention

horned \\'hȯrnd\\ having bony processes, usually paired, that arise from the upper part of the head of many ungulate mammals

horned \\'hȯrnəd\\ made a man a cuckhold

house \\'haůs\\ a business organiation, management of a gambling establishment, or a body of persons forming a deliberative or consultative assembly

house \'haůz\ to encase, enclose, or shelter

housewife \'haů‚swīf\ a married woman in charge of a household

housewife \'həzəf\ a pocket-sized container for carrying small articles

hum \'həm\ to make a low prolonged sound like that of an insect

hum \'hüm\ an isolated residual hill or mass of limestone

Huron \'hyůrən\ an Iroquoian people of the St. Lawrence valley, Ontario, and midwestern U.S.; the second largest of the five Great Lakes in North America in water surface area

huron \'hyůrən\ a largemouth black bass

huron \ü'rōn\ the weasellike South American grison

hypostases \'hīpō‚stāsəz\ disks of liquified tissue formed at the base of an ovule in certain orders of plants

hypostases \hī'pästə‚sēz\ sediments or deposits

Group I

hautbois
heretic
hui
hyphomycetes

I

ID \'ī'dē\ identification (by shortening)

id \'id\ the primitive undifferentiated part of the psychic apparatus that reacts blindly on a pleasure-pain level

impair \im'per\ to diminish in quantity, value, excellence, or strength

impair \'im‚par\ the odd numbers in roulette when a bet is made on them

impropriate \ǝm‚prōprē‚āt\ to take over and make one's own

impropriate \ǝm‚prōprē‚ǝt\ lay as distinguished from clerical

incense \'in‚sens\ material used to produce a fragrant odor when burned

incense \in:sens\ to arouse the wrath or indignation of

incept \in'sept\ to take in or ingest; to receive as a member

incept \'in‚sept\ the first accumulation of cells in an embryo recognizable as the start of a developing part or organ

ingenerate \in'jenə‚rāt\ to cause

ingenerate \in'jenərǝt\ inborn or innate; not generated

inscriber \ǝnz'krībər\ a person that writes, engraves, or prints

inscriber \'inz'krībər\ a device for transferring data from a punched tape onto a medium for use in an electronic computer

instar \in'stär\ to adorn with stars

instar \'inz‚tär\ an insect between two successive molts

interchange \intər'chānj\ to put each of two or more things in place of the other; to give and take mutually

interchange \'intər‚chānj\ a junction of two or more highways without the crossing at grade of traffic systems; a traffic cloverleaf

intermediate \intər'mēdə‚āt\ to come between, or intervene; to mediate

intermediate \:intər:mēdēət\ lying or being in the middle place or degree; between extremes or limits

intimate \'intə‚māt\ to give notice of

intimate \'intə‚mǝt\ very close contact

intricate \'in•trəkət\ showing complex involvement of detailed considerations requiring precise analysis; difficult to analyze or solve

intricate \'in•trə,kāt\ to intermesh or interlock

invalid \in:valəd\ without foundation

invalid \'invələd\ sickly or disabled

invert \ən'vərt\ to turn inside out or upside down

invert \'in,vərt\ the lowest point in the internal cross section of an artificial channel; a postage stamp having an overprint

inward \'inwərd\ toward the inside

inward \'in,wórd\ a king's bodyguard

irony \'īərnē\ made or consisting of iron

irony \'īrənē\ humor, ridicule, or light sarcasm that adopts a mode of speech the intended implication of which is opposite the literal sense of the words (seldom 'īərnē)

Group I

impact
impersonate

implant
impound
impregnate
importunate
imprint
inarch
incarcerate
incipit
inclined
incorporate
incurve
indurate
infatuate
infuriate
inroad
insert
insult
insurge
intercept
interlayer
interleaf
intersect
intrados
intricate
inwall

J

Jacana \'jakənə\ the type genus of *Jacanidae* comprising the New World jacanas

jacana \'jakənə\ a coastal freshwater wading bird

jacana \'häkənə\ a West Indian timber tree

jackal \'jakəl\ any of several wild dogs of the Old World

jackal \'hə,käl\ a crude house or hut in Mexico and southwestern U.S.

jaeger \'yāgər\ a large spirited rapacious bird that inhabits northern seas

jaeger \'yägər\ a high quality diamond of bluish white grade

jagged \'jagd\ drunk (slang)

jagged \'jagəd\ having a sharply uneven edge or surface

jam \'jam\ to press into a tight or close position; a product made by boiling fruit and sugar to a thick consistency

jam \'jäm\ the ruler in some northwest Indian states

Jambos \'jam,bäs\ a genus of woody plants with leathery leaves

jambos \'jambōz\ any of several tropical plants or their fruits; rose apples

Job \'jōb\ a person who sustains patiently a life of poverty and affliction
job \'jäb\ a piece of work or performance

jog \'jäg\ to go at a low leisurely pace; to push or shake by prodding
jog \'jōg\ yoga

jube \'yü‚bā\ a gallery above a screen that separates the church chancel from the nave, or the screen itself
jube \'jüb\ a lozenge like a jujube

Jubilate \‚yübə'lätā\ the third Sunday after Easter
jubilate \'jübə‚lāt\ to utter sounds or make demonstrations of joy and exultation

Junker \'yünkər\ a member of the Prussian landed aristocracy
junker \'jəŋkər\ an automobile ready for scrapping

junkman \'jəŋkmən\ a crew-member of a junk
junkman \'jəŋk‚man\ a person dealing in resalable junk

Jura \'jŭrə\ the Jurassic geological period, or the rocks belonging to it
jura \'yŭrə\ legal principles, rights, or powers

jus \'yüs\ or \'jəs\ a legal principle, right, or power
jus \'jüs\ or \'zhüs\ juice or gravy

K

Ka \'kä\ a people of Negal of mixed Mongoloid and Indo-Aryan blood
Ka \'kə\ the unknown god, in Hinduism
ka \'kä\ the personality double believed in ancient Egypt to be born with an individual

Kachin \kə'chin\ a Tibeto-Burman ethnic group inhabiting upper Myanmar
kachin \'kachən\ pyrocatechol used as a photographic developer

kaki \'käkē\ a Japanese persimmon
kaki \kä'kē\ a blackish stilt of New Zealand

kas \'käz\ the personality doubles believed in ancient Egypt to be born with individuals
kas \'käs\ a Dutch cupboard or wardrobe common in the late 17th and the 18th centuries

Kasha \'kashə\ a soft napped twilled fabric of fine wool and hair

kasha \'kashə\ a mush made from coarse cracked buckwheat or other grains

Kate \'kätə\ a people of the Huon peninsula in New Guinea
kate \'kāt\ a pileated woodpecker

ketoses \'kē‚tōsəs\ sugars containing one ketone group per molecule
ketoses \kē'tōs‚sēz\ nutritional diseases of cattle and sometimes sheep, goats, or swine

khanda \'kəndä\ a double-edged sword
khanda \'kəndä\ the impermanent elements (in Hinduism and Buddhism), which enter into man's constitution, assumed in incarnation

Kin \'jin\ a Tatar people that founded an 11th century dynasty in China
kin \'kin\ one's immediate family or related group

kiri \'kērē\ a paulownia tree

kiri \'kē,ri\ a short wooden club with a heavy round knob at one end that may be thrown or used in close combat

ki-yi \kī:yī\ an expression of exultation; a bark or yelp of a dog; a small brush used in the U.S. Navy for scrubbing clothing or canvas

ki-yi \'kē,yē\ a small lake herring abundant in deep water in the Great Lakes

Kora \'kōrä\ the almost extinct Hottentot dialect of the Korana in South Africa

kora \'kōrə\ a large gallinule of south eastern Asia and the East Indies

Kuba \'kübə\ a Bantu-speaking people of the central Congo

kuba \kü'bä\ an eastern Caucasian carpet of coarse but firm weave

Group I

Kanaka

L

labor \'lābər\ to work or toil
labor \lə'bōr\ an old Texas unit of land measure equal to about 177 acres

lacet \läs'et\ pertaining to a kind of braid of various widths and patterns
lacet \'lāset\ a bootlace

Lais \'līz\ a Mongoloid people of the Chin Hills in Myanmar
lais \'lāz\ medieval short tales of lyric poems in French literature

Lak(h)s \'läks\ members of a division of the Lezghian people in southern Russia on the western shore of the Caspian Sea
laks \'laks\ performances of the male capercaillie (the largest European grouse) during courtship

lamé \la:mā\ a brocaded clothing fabric
lame \'lām\ physically disabled

lamed \'lāmd\ made lame or crippled
lamed \'lä,med\ the twelfth letter of the Hebrew alphabet

lances \'lan,səs\ weapons of war consisting of long shafts with sharp steel heads
lances \'lan,sēz\ or \'läŋ,kās\ an ancient Roman platter, usually of metal

land \'land\ ground or soil; to catch and bring to shore

land \'länt\ a governmental unit in Germany

landsman \'lanzmən\ an inexperienced sailor below an ordinary seaman
landsman \'läntsmən\ a fellow Jew, especially from eastern Europe

Lari \'lä,rī\ a suborder of the Charadriiformes that includes gulls, terns, jaegers, and skimmers
lari \'lä,rī\ money consisting of silver wire doubled, either twisted to form a fishhook or straight

laser \'lā,zər\ a device that uses natural oscillations of atoms to amplify or generate electromagnetic waves
laser \'lä,sər\ a drastic purgative gum resin obtained from laserwort

lat \'lät\ a separate column or pillar in some Buddhist buildings in India, similar to the Greek stela
lat \'lat\ a broad flat superficial muscle on each side of the lower back (latissimus dorsi, shortened)

latex \'lā,teks\ any of various emulsions in water of a synthetic rubber or plastic obtained by polymerization and used chiefly in paint and other coatings and adhesives

LaTeX \'lā,tek\ a typesetting system, especially used in scientific and mathematical books

lather \'lathər\ foam or froth

lather \'lathər\ a person who puts up or makes lathing

lather \'lāthər\ a person who works with a lathe

laud \'lȯd\ to praise; public acclaim

laud \lä'üd\ a lute or cittern

lax \'lax\ not stringent; easygoing

lax \'läx\ salmon

Laze \'läzə\ a Muslim Kartvelian Sunnite people of Caucasia found along both sides of the Turkish-Soviet frontier

laze \'lāz\ to pass in idleness or relaxation

lead \'led\ a heavy metallic element

lead \'lēd\ to guide or precede

leadman \'ledmən\ a person who uses a sounding lead to determine water-depth

leadman \'lēdmən\ a skilled employee who supervises one or more groups of workers

leadsman \'ledzmən\ a person who uses a sounding lead to determine water-depth

leadsman \'lēdzmən\ the player who throws the jack and bowls first in lawn bowling, or who throws the first stone in curling

lech \'lech\ to practice inordinate indulgence in sexual activity (by shortening **lechery**)

lech \'lēk\ a prehistoric monument stone

led \'led\ guided or marked the way

LED \,elē'dē\ a semiconductor diode that emits light

legate \'legȧt\ an emissary or deputy

legate \lȧ'gāt\ to bequeath

legged \'legd\ bestirred oneself for someone or something

legged \:legȧd\ having (such or so many) appendages that are used for walking

lied \'līd\ conveyed an untruth

lied \'lēt\ a German folksong

Liege \lē'āzh\ a city in Belgium

liege \'lēj\ bound by obligations resembling those existing between a feudal lord and his vassals

lien \'lēn\ a charge on real property in satisfaction of a debt

lien \'līən\ a spleen

liken \'līkən\ to be or become similar or identical

liken \'lē'kēn\ a former Chinese tax at inland stations on imports or articles in transit

Lima \'lēmə\ the capital of Peru

lima \'līmə\ a bean; a bivalve mollusk

limbers \'limərz\ loggers who trim limbs from felled trees

limbers \'limbərz\ conduits on each side of ship keels that provide passages for water to the pump well; horse-drawn two-wheel vehicles to which guns may be attached; makes flexible or pliant

limes \'līmz\ small globose citrus fruit of the lime tree; whitewashes with a solution of lime and water

limes \'lī,mēz\ a fortified frontier of the ancient Roman Empire

limon \lē'mōⁿ\ an unstratified deposit of loam ranging from clay to fine sand (loess)

limon \'līmən\ a hybrid fruit from crossing a lemon and lime

lineage \'līnij\ the number of lines of printed or written matter

lineage \'linēij\ descent in a line from a common ancestor

lira \'līrə\ a ridge on some shells resembling a fine thread or hair

lira \'lērə\ also \'lirə\ a bowed stringed musical instrument; the recent basic monetary unit of Italy

lis \'lēs\ a fleur-de-lis

lis \'lisz\ an ancient Irish fortification or storage place enclosed by a circular mound and or trench

lisses \'lēsəz\ silk gauzes used for dresses and trimmings

lisses \'lisəz\ ancient Irish fortifications or storage places

litre \'lētər\ a metric unit of capacity equal to 1.057 liquid parts

litre \'lētra\ a poisonous Chilean shrub whose hardwood is used in cabinetry

live \'līv\ charged with fissionable material or explosives

live \'liv\ to maintain oneself; to outlast strorm or danger

liver \'livər\ a large vascular glandular organ of vertebrates

liver \'līvər\ more alive

loa \'lōə\ an African filarial worm

loa \lə'wä\ a Haitian voodoo cult deity

lores \'lōrz\ things that are learned

lores \'lō,rez\ low resolution (by shortening)

lower \'lōər\ situated further below or under; to bring down; to reduce

lower \'laůər\ to look sullen; a dark, gloomy, or sullen look

Luger \'lügər\ a 9 mm German pistol

luger \'lüzhər\ a person who rides on a small sled (a luge)

lung \'ləŋ\ one of the usually two compound saccular organs that constitute the basic respiratory organ of air-breathing vertebrates

lung \'lüŋ\ a beneficent supernatural creature in Chinese mythology connected with rain and floods

lunged \:lənd\ having one or more respiratory organs common to air-breathing vertebrates

lunged \'ləjd\ made a forceful forward movement, as a thrust or pass with a foil

lunger \'lənjər\ a person who moves forward forcefully

lunger \'ləŋər\ a person suffering from a lung disease; a glob of sputum, phlegm, or other expectorant

lupine \'lü,pīn\ wolfish; ravenous

lupine \'lüpən\ a plant of the genus Lupinus

lure \'lůr\ to entice, tempt, or seduce

lure \'lü,rə\ a long curved trumpet for calling cattle

lyrist \'līrəst\ a player of the lyre

lyrist \'lirəst\ a writer of lyrics

Group I

landwards
laureate
learned
leeward
legitimate
lip-read
litnites
lyses

M

Macon \mā'kən\ a city in central Georgia

Macon \mä'kōⁿ\ a still Burgundy French wine in both red and white varieties

Madrilene \'madrə,lēn\ of or from Madrid, Spain

madrilene \:madrə:len\ a consommé flavored with tomato and served hot or cold

maja \\'mäjä\\ a lower class Spanish belle

Maja \\'mäjə\\ a nearly cosmopolitan genus of crabs

majo \\'mähō\\ a Spanish dandy of the lower class

majo \\'mäjō\\ a tropical American shrub or tree, the bark of which yields a tonic infusion

mala \\'mälə\\ offenses against right or the law

mala \\'mälə\\ the grinding surface of an insect's mandible

Male \\'mälä\\ a member of a Dravidian animistic people of Bengal; the capital of the Maldive Islands

Male \\'mälē\\ the capital of the Maldive Islands (an alternate pronunciation to that immediately above)

male \\'mäl\\ the sex that usually performs the fertilizing function in generation

Mam \\'mäm\\ an Indian people of southwestern Guatemala

mam \\'mam\\ madam

mamma \\'mämə\\ mother

mamma \\'mamə\\ a mammary gland or teat

manas \\'mänəz\\ impersonal supernatural forces or powers that may be concentrated in persons or objects

manas \\'mänəs\\ the faculty of mental perception that receives impressions from the senses and transmits them to the atman, according to Hinduism

mane \\'mān\\ neck hair

mane \\'mänä\\ in pharmacy, in the morning

manes \\'mānz\\ neck hairs

manes \\'mä,näs\\ ancestral spirits worshipped as gods

Mangue \\'mäŋgä\\ a Chorotegan people of southwestern Nicaragua

mangue \\'maŋ\\ a small dark brown burrowing carnivorous mammal related to the mongoose

Manil(l)a \\mə'nilə\\ the capital city of the Philippines; made from Manilla hemp

manilla \\mə'nēlyə\\ a piece of metal shaped like a horseshoe used by some peoples of western Africa for ornamental purposes and as a medium of exchange

Manis \\'mānəs\\ the type genus comprising the pangolins

manis \\'mänēs\\ peanuts

Mano \\'mänō\\ a Negro people inhabiting the northern tip of the central province of Liberia and adjacent Ivory Coast

mano \\'mänō\\ a handstone used as the upper millstone for grinding grains

mano \\mə'nō\\ any of several large sharks

manqué \\'mäⁿ,kā\\ short of fulfilling one's aspirations

manque \\'mäⁿk\\ in roulette, numbers 1–18 when a bet is placed on them

Manus \\'mä,nüs\\ a people inhabiting Manus Island, north of New Guinea

manus \\'mänəs\\ the distal segment of a vertebrate's forelimb including the carpus and forefoot or hand

maquis \\'mäkēz\\ Chilean shrubs of the family *Elaeocarpaceae*

Maquis \\mä'kē\\ a member of an underground movement or organization

maquis \\mä'kē\\ thick scrubby underbrush profuse along Mediterranean shores

Mara \\'marə\\ of or from Maracaibo, Venezuela

mara \\mə'rä\\ a long-legged long-eared rodent closely related to the cavies

mare \\'maər\\ a female horse

mare \\'mä|rä\\ a dark expanse on the moon or Mars

margarita \\,märgə'rītə\\ the vessel in which the consecrated Host is preserved, in the Eastern Church

margarita \\,märgə'rētə\\ a low poisonous shrub of the southwestern U.S. and Mexico

Margarites \ˌmärgəˈrīˈdēz\ a genus of minute top shells

margarites \ˈmärgəˌritz\ primary forms of rock crystallization in which globules are arranged linearly like beads

maria \məˈrēə\ any of several shrubs and trees of tropical America

maria \ˈmärēə\ dark areas of considerable extent on the surface of the moon or Mars

Marseilles \ˈmärˌsā\ of or from the city of Marseilles in southeast France on the Mediterranean sea

Marseilles \märˈsālz\ a firm reversible cotton fabric that usually has small fancy designs and is used for vests or trimmings

mate \ˈmāt\ one customarily associated with another; to checkmate in chess; a deck officer

maté \ˈmätä\ an aromatic South American beverage

math \ˈmath\ the relationship and symbolism of numbers and magnitudes (by shortening **mathematics**)

math \ˈmoth\ a Hindu monastery

matie \ˈmad•ē\ a young fat herring with roe

matie \ˈmād•ē\ a shipmate or comrade (slang)

matte \ˈmat\ a mixture of sulfides formed in smelting sulfide ores of metals

matte \ˈmätä\ an aromatic South American beverage

mayoral \ːmäkyəːräl\ an overseer in Spain

mayoral \ˈmärərəl\ of or relating to a chief magistrate of a city or that office

me \ˈmē\ myself

me \ˈmā\ a sol-fal syllable in the chromatic scale

Medic \ˈmēdik\ the Iranian language of ancient Media

medic \ˈmedik\ a plant of the genus Medicago; a person engaged in medical work

melange \ˌmeˈlänzh\ to print colors on top of woolen yarn

melange \ˈmāˌlänzh\ a mixture or medley

melanoses \ˈmeləˌnōsēz\ diseases of grapevines caused by a fungus

melanoses \ˌmeləˈnōˌsēz\ conditions characterized by abnormal disposition of melanins in body tissues

Meles \ˈmēlēz\ a genus of mustelid mammals comprising the typical Old World badgers

meles \ˈmālāz\ Hawaiian songs or chants

Melo \ˈmēˌlō\ a genus of marine shells comprising the melon shells (also ˈmelō)

melo \ˈmelō\ melodrama (by shortening)

melon \ˈmeˌlän\ a yellow powder formed on heating various cyanogen compounds

melon \ˈmelən\ a soft-fleshed sweet-flavored fruit with a hard rind such as muskmelon or watermelon; a small reddish or chestnut brown wallaby extensively distributed in Australia and New Guinea

melos \ˈmelōz\ melodramas (by shortening)

melos \ˈmēˌläs\ characteristic tone succession considered apart from rhythm

Mensa \ˈmensə\ the Table constellation located at about 75° south declination

mensa \ˈmensə\ the central slab on which the eucharistic elements are placed

mensa \ˈmensē\ or \ˈmenˌsī\ the grinding surface of a tooth

mere \ˈmir\ exclusive of anything else

mere \ˈmerē\ a Maori war club

meringue \məˈraŋ\ a mixture of beaten egg whites and powdered sugar baked at low temperature and used as a topping

méringue \māˈraŋ\ a popular Dominican and Haitian ballroom dance with a limping step

meros \ˈmärōz\ any of several large groupers of jewfishes of warm seas

meros \ˈmēˌräs\ the plain surface between

the channels of an architectural ornament in the frieze of the Doric order

mescal \me'skal\ a small cactus; a usually
colorless Mexican liquor

mescal \'me͵skäl\ a Mexican elm

Meshed \mə'shed\ Iran's fourth largest city

meshed \'mesht\ resembling a network;
interlaced

meta \'metə\ characterized by or being
two positions in the benzene ring separated by one carbon atom

meta \'mētə\ a column or post, in ancient
Rome, placed at each end of a racetrack
to mark the turning places

metra \'mētrə\ a uterus, the organ in female mammals that contains and usually
nourishes the young during development
prior to birth

metra \'me͵trə\ the minimal unit of measure in classical Greek verse

micrometer \'mīkrō͵mēdər\ a unit of
length equal to one millionth of a meter

micrometer \mī'krämədər\ a caliper having a spindle moved by a finely machined
screw and used with a telescope or mi-
croscope to make precise measurements

mignon \'min͵yän\ a moderate purple
color

mignon \mēn'yōⁿ\ filet mignon (by shortening), a fillet of beef cut from the thick
end of a beef tenderloin

millet \'milət\ an annual cereal and forage
grass

millet \mə'let\ a non–Muslim group in
Turkey

mina \'mēnä\ a member of a low caste or
watchmen

mina \'mīnə\ an Asiatic starling that is
often tamed and taught to pronounce
words

mind \'mīnd\ the intellect or brain; to
obey; to take care of

mind \'min\ a thin gold ornamental plate
used by ancient Celts

minute \'minət\ a unit of time and angular measurement

minute \mī:nyüt\ of very small size or
importance

minutely \mī'nyütlē\ with precision or
exactly

minutely \'minətlē\ from minute to
minute, or happening every minute

mire \'mēr\ a fixed mark due north or
south of a meridian

mire \'mīr\ wet spongy earth; a bog or
marsh

mises \'misəz\ dried dung used as fuel

mises \'mēzəz\ issues in a legal proceeding upon a writ of right

Mobile \mō'bēl\ a large city in south
western Alabama

mobile \'mōbəl\ movable

mobile \'mäbəlē\ the lower classes of a
community; the masses

Mod \'mōd\ a meeting to study and perform Gaellic arts

mod \'mäd\ modern (by shortening)

moderate \'mädərət\ limited in scope or
affect; not severe in effect

moderate \'mädə͵rāt\ to preside over or
act as chairperson

Moi \'mōē\ a group of Veddoid or Indo-
Australoid people living in the mountain
uplands of Annam, Vietnam

moi \'mō'ē\ an Hawaiian ruling chief or
sovereign

Mojo \'mō͵hō\ an Arawakan people of
northern Bolivia

mojo \'mōjō\ a voodoo spell or amulet

Mole \'mō͵lä\ a people of the west central
Sudan

mole \'mōl\ a congenital mark or discoloration on the skin; a burrowing mammal

mole \'mōlē\ a highly spiced meat sauce

Moline \'mōlēn\ a city in northwest Illinois

moline \'mōlən\ a cross having the end of each arm forked and recurved

molle \'mälē\ in music, lower by a half step; flat

molle \'mȯˌya\ a Peruvian evergreen tree; a small shrubby New Zealand tree

moly \'mälē\ molybdenum, a fusible polyvalent metallic element

moly \'mōlē\ a European wild garlic

Mon \'mōn\ the dominant native people of Pegu in Myanmar

mon \'män\ the usually circular badge of a Japanese family; a usually large plank boat resembling a canoe common in Melanesia

Monas \'mōˌnas\ a genus of small aquatic flagellates

monas \'mōˌnas\ a flagellate protozoan; metaphysical entities

monas \'mōnəz\ small West African guenon monkeys

Montana \män'tanə\ a state in north western U.S.; a sheep bred or raised in Montana

montaña \män'tanyə\ a forested region of the eastern slopes of the Andes

montes \'mänˌtez\ body parts or areas raised above or demarcated from surrounding structures

montes \'mantēz\ card games resembling monte bank

moped \'mōˌped\ a lightweight lowpowered motorbike that can be pedaled

moped \'mōpd\ acted in a brooding, dull, or dejected manner

Mora \'mōrə\ a small genus of tall half-evergreen forest trees of northern South America

mora \'mōrə\ the minimal unit of quantitative measure in temporal prosodic systems

mora \mō'rä\ low wicker stool or footstool

mora \'mȯrə\ delay in the performance of an obligation; an Italian game in which a player extends a number of fingers of her/his hand in an attempt to match the number of fingers simultaneously extended by the opponent

Moré \mə'rä\ a people of the west central Sudan

more \'mōr\ of larger size or extent

morel \mə'rel\ any of various nightshades, especialy the poisonous black nightshade

morel \'mȯrel\ an edible fungus of the genus Morchella

Mores \mə'räz\ a people of west cental Sudan

mores \'mȯräz\ the fixed customs or folkways of a particular social group

mores \'mōrz\ additional numbers, amounts, or lengths of time

morné \mȯr:nä\ in heraldry, a lion without teeth, tongue, or claws

morne \'mȯrn\ gloomy or dismal

mot \'mō\ a pithy or witty saying; an epigram

mot \'mät\ a grove or clump of trees, especially in open prairie country

mother \'məthər\ a woman who gives birth to a child

mother \'mȯthər\ a collector or specialist in identifying any of the various insects that constitute a major division of the order *Lepidoptera*

mouth \'maúth\ an opening through which food passes into an organism

mouth \'maúth\ to swage the top of a metal can to receive the cover

mow \'mō\ to cut down or off

mow \'maú\ a stack of hay or straw; a contortion of the face or lips especially so as to produce a mocking or derisive expression

mug \'məg\ a drinking cup

mug \'müg\ the pulse (edible seed) or mung bean of India

multiply \'məltəˌplī\ composed of several or multiple layers of folds

multiply \'məltə‚pli\ to make more numerous; to add quantity to; to calculate the product of two or more numbers

Mura \'mürə\ an Indian people of northwestern Brazil
mura \'mürə\ a rural community in Japan

murid \'mü'rēd\ a Sufi disciple in Islam
murid \'myûrəd\ relating to a very large family of relatively small rodents including the house mouse and common rats

Mus \'məs\ a genus of rodents including the common house mouse
mus \'myüz\ bridging groups that join central atoms or ions; the plural of the 12th letter of the Greek alphabet

musar \'myü‚zär\ a 12th century ballad singer of Provence

musar \'mü‚sär\ a 19th century Jewish religious-ethical movement

Muter \mü'ter\ a nomadic Bedouin people in Arabia
muter \'myüdər\ more unable to utter articulate sounds; less able to speak

Group I

macerate
maculate
mediate
medicament
mislead
misread
misuse

N

nadir \'nādər\ the lowest point
nadir \'nä‚dir\ a Malayan light-draft fishing boat

nag \'nag\ to engage in persistent petty fault finding, scolding, or urging
nag \'näg\ any of several very venomous Asiatic and African elapid snakes, as a cobra

Nair \'nīər\ a people of the Malabar coast of India
nair \'nīər\ a member of the Nayar people
nair \'nä‚ir\ a large percoid fish of river mouths and brackish waters; the common Indian otter

Nama \'nämə\ one of a Hottentot people of southwestern Africa
Nama \'nämə\ a genus of blue-flowered perennial herbs

nana \'nanə\ a child's nurse or nursemaid
nana \'nə'nä\ a pineapple; mint

nana \'nänə\ dwarfish, especially of genetic variants of economic plants

nance \'nänsä\ a type of tree of the genus Brysonima, or its fruit
nance \'nans\ an effeminate male

naos \'naûz\ medium-sized sailing ships of the late middle ages
naos \'nä‚äs\ an ancient temple or shrine

Nasi \'näsē\ the chief presiding officer of the Sanhedrin, according to the rabbinical tradition
nasi \'näsē\ one of the Scriptural fathers of the human race or of the Hebrew people
nasi \'nē‚sī\ prolongations on the front of the head of a crane fly or of various termites

Natal \nə'tal\ a province in the eastern part of the Republic of South Africa
natal \'nādəl\ relating to birth; relating to the buttocks

nature \\'nāchər\\ the essential character or constitution of something

nature \\nə'tûr\\ very dry, usually containing less than 1.5% sugar by volume (brut)

Nice \\'nēs\\ a seaport city on the southeast coast of France; a grayish-blue color (also called Quimper)

nice \\'nīs\\ refined, cultured, pleasant, or satisfying

nightman \\'nītmən\\ a person who empties privies between dusk and dawn

nightman \\'nīt,man\\ a watchman on duty between dusk and dawn

none \\'nən\\ not any

None \\'nōn\\ the canonical ninth hour

nudge \\'nəj\\ to touch or push gently; to prod lightly

nudge \\'nüj\\ to annoy with persistent complaints, criticism, or nagging; a pest

number \\'nəmbər\\ a numeral, digit, or integer

number \\'nəmər\\ more devoid of sensation

nun \\'nən\\ a woman belonging to a religious order, especially under vows of poverty, chastity, and obedience

nun \\'nün\\ the 14th letter of the Hebrew alphabet

Nut \\'nüt\\ in Egyptian religion, the goddess of the sky

nut \\'nət\\ a hardshelled dry fruit or seed; a perforated block of metal with an internal screw thread for attachment to a bolt

Group I

necroses

O

object \\'äbjikt\\ something visible or tangible

object \\əb'jekt\\ to oppose or protest

odal \\'ōdəl\\ an estate owned by Scandanavian individuals or families

odal \\'ädəl\\ an East Indian woody vine, the seeds of which yield an oil used as a cure for rheumatism

officiate \\ə'fishē,āt\\ to perform a prescribed or traditional ceremony

officiate \\ə'fishēət\\ a body of officials

oke \\'ōk\\ any of three units of weight varying around 2.8 pounds and used in Bulgaria, Egypt, Greece, and Turkey

oke \\'ōkā\\ an alcoholic liquor distilled from ti or taro root

Olive \\'ō'lēvā\\ an Indian people of northeastern Mexico

olive \\'älēv\\ or \\'äləv\\ a plant of the genus Olea, or its oblong drupaceous fruit

ombre \\'ämbər\\ a European grayling; a three-handed game played in Spain

ombre \\äm:brā\\ shaded, especially in fabrics with a dyed or woven design

one \\'wən\\ being a single unit or entire being or thing and no more

one \\wən\\ an individual of a particular kind

oner \\'ōnər\\ a heavy blow with a fist (slang)

oner \\'wənər\\ one of a kind

ore \\'ōr\\ a natural usually unrefined mineral that can often be mined

öre \\'ər•ə\\ a Danish and Norwegian unit of value equal to ¹⁄₁₀₀ krone; a Swedish monetary unit equal to ¹⁄₁₀₀ krona

Oriental \:ōrē:ent°l\ relating or situated in the Far East

Oriental \ōre,en'täl\ a native or inhabitant of Uruguay

os \'äs\ a bone; a mouth

<u>os</u> \'ōs\ an esker, a long narrow often sinuous ridge of debris deposited between ice walls by a stream flowing within a stagnant glacier

outman \'aůtmən\ one living or working outside the limits of a medieval English town

outman \,aut'man\ outnumber

outward \'aůtwərd\ toward the outside

outward \'aůt,wȯrd\ a detached hospital ward; a ward outside the original bounds of a borough

overage \:ōvər:āj\ too old

overage \'ōverij\ excess or surplus

overuse \'ōvəryüz\ to make familiar by excessive repitition or continued practice

overuse \'ōvəryüs\ excessively accustomed or overly unusual procedure

Group I

obdurate
obliterate
obstinate
orbed
osmoses
overweight

P

---

pace \'pās\ a rate of motion or performance

pace \'pāsē\ with all due respect

Pala \'pä,la\ a language mentioned in the Boghazkeui inscriptions

pala \pä'lä\ an ivory tree affording an inferior quality of indigo

pala \'palə\ an impala

<u>Pali</u> \'pälē\ an Indic language found in the Buddhist canon

<u>pali</u> \'pälē\ a steep slope in Hawaii; an Indian timber tree

pali \'pä,lī\ upright slender calcareous processes surrounding the central part of the calyculus of some corals

Palladian \pə'lādēən\ relating to wisdom or learning

Palladian \pə'lädeən\ relating to the classic architectural style based on Andrea Palladio's work

pallas \'paləz\ loose outergarments worn by women of ancient Rome

pallas \'päyəs\ Incan princesses

palled \'pald\ acted as a pal to someone

palled \'pȯld\ covered with a shroud; lost strength

palling \'pȯliŋ\ failing in vigor or effectiveness

palling \'paliŋ\ keepng company; behaving as an intimate with someone

palsy \'pȯlzē\ a condition characterized by uncontrollable tremoring of the body or one or more of its parts

palsy \'palzē\ having or giving the appearance of having a high degree of intimacy

Palus \,pa'lüs\ wines from vineyards planted in the rich alluvial soil of southwest France

palus \'pāləs\ any of several upright slender calcareous processes surrounding the central part of the calyculus of some corals

Pan \\'pan\\ a genus of anthropoid apes containing the chimpanzee

<u>**pan**</u> \\'pan\\ a shallow container; to rotate a camera in any direction; to wash earth deposits in search of precious metal

<u>**pan**</u> \\'pän\\ a betal palm leaf; a card game resembling rummy

panaché \\:panə:shā\\ comprised of several foods

panache \\pə'nash\\ an ornamental tuft or tufts on a helmet; an heroic flourish of manner

<u>**pane**</u> \\'pān\\ a window or door section

pané \\ˌpa'nä\\ food prepared with bread crumbs; breaded

papa \\'päpə\\ a father; a potato; a bluish New Zealand clay used for whitening fireplaces

papa \\pə'pä\\ a parish priest of the Eastern Orthodox Church

papa \\'pāˌpa\\ a baboon; a king vulture

papa \\'päpȯ\\ any of several American shrubs or trees of the genus Asiminia

Papio \\'pāpēˌō\\ a genus of typical baboons

papio \\'päpyō\\ a young food fish of Hawaiian waters

parade \\pə'rād\\ a pompous show or formal display

parade \\pə'räd\\ a defensive action made to deflect a thrust or blow from an opponent

parados \\pə'rädōz\\ boastful swaggering airs

<u>**parados**</u> \\'parəˌdäs\\ a bank of earth behind a fortification trench

parison \\'parəˌsän\\ even balance between members of a sentence

parison \\'parəsən\\ a gob of glass partially shaped into an object

Passé \\ˌpä'sā\\ a member of an Arawakan tribe of northwestern Brazil

<u>**passé**</u> \\pa'sā\\ past one's prime; no longer fashionable; a ballet movement in which one leg passes behind or in front of the other

passe \\'päs\\ in roulette, the numbers 19–36 when a bet is made on them

passes \\pa'saz\\ ballet movements in which the leg passes from one position to another

passes \\'päsəz\\ groups of high numbers in roulette when a bet is made on them

passes \\'pasəz\\ moves on or proceeds

pastel \\ˌpa'stel\\ pale and light in color; delicate

pastel \\'pastel\\ a woad plant, of the mustard family

<u>**pasty**</u> \\'pastē\\ a pie consisting of a meat and vegetable or fruit mixture

pasty \\'pāstē\\ pallid and unhealthy in appearance; sickly

pata \\'pətä\\ a land grant engraved on metal; a gold plate tied on the forehead in ceremonies of investiture

pata \\'pətä\\ a long straight gauntlet-hilted two-edged sword

<u>**pate**</u> \\'pāt\\ the top of the head

pâte \\'pät\\ plastic material for pottery

paté \\pə'tā\\ a cross with arms narrow at the center and expanding toward the ends

pâté \\pä'tā\\ a spread of finely mashed seasoned and spiced meat

pathoses \\'pāˌthäsēz\\ elements in experience or in artistic representation evoking pity or compassion

pathoses \\pə'thōˌsēz\\ diseased states or abnormal conditions

patron \\'pāˌtrən\\ a person who is a customer, client, or paying guest

patron \\pä'trȯn\\ a boss or employer

<u>**patte**</u> \\'pat\\ a decorative band, strap, or belt to fasten garments

patté \\ˌpa'tā\\ in heraldry, having arms of a cross narrow at the center and expanding toward the ends

<u>**pau**</u> \\'paú\\ in Hawaii, completed or consumed

pa'u \'pä͵ü\ an Hawaiian sarong formerly made of tapa and now of silk and worn by women

pave \'pāv\ to cover with material making a firm level surface for travel

pave \͵pə'vā\ in jewelry, a setting of stones placed close together so as to show no metal between them

peaked \'pēkt\ pointed

peaked \'pēkəd\ looked pale, wan, or sickly

Peba \'päbä\ a member of the Peban tribe of northeastern Peru

peba \'pebə\ a small armadillo having nine moveable bands of scutes and ranging from Texas to Paraguay

peer \'pir\ a person of equal standing; a member of one of the five ranks of the English peerage

peer \'pēər\ a urinator

pension \'penchən\ a fixed sum paid regularly to a person, usually following retirement from service

pension \pän^s:yȯⁿ\ or \:pän^sē:ōn\ a payment for room and board; to receive board and lodging at a fixed rate

peon \'pēən\ a person in a position of subordination or servility; an unskilled laborer

peon \pā'ōn\ a bullfighter's attendant

peppier \'pepēər\ more full of energy or initiative; more alert or lively

peppier \͵pep^ē͵yā\ a waiter who asks diners if they desire freshly ground pepper on their foodstuffs

perfect \'pərfikt\ constituting a form of the verb that expresses an action or state completed at the time of speaking or at a time spoken of; relating to a note in mensural notation equaling three rather than two of the next lower denomination

perfect \pər'fekt\ to bring to a state of supreme excellence (seldom 'pərfikt)

permit \'pər͵mit\ a large up to three feet long blue and silver pompano (fish)

permit \pər'mit\ to make possible; to give an oppoertunity

perpend \pər'pend\ to reflect on or ponder

perpend \'pərpənd\ a brick or large stone reaching through a wall and acting as a binder

pes \'päz\ the 17th letter of the Hebrew alphabet

pes \'pēz\ the distal segment of the hind limb of a vertebrate including the tarsus and foot

phalanges \fə'lan͵jēz\ bodies of heavily armed infantry in ancient Greece

phalanges \fä'lanj͵ēz\ segments of an insect's tarsus

pia \'pīə\ the delicate and highly vascular membrane of connective tissue investing the brain and spinal cord (**pia** mater, by shortening)

pia \'pēə\ a perennial herb of East India, Australasia, and Polynesia cultivated for its large starch-yielding root

piano \pē'änō\ in music, softly or quietly

piano \pē'anō\ a stringed percussion instrument

piazza \pē'azə\ a portico or single colonnade before a building

piazza \pē'atzə\ a town square or open market

pic \'pik\ a motion picture or photograph (slang)

pic \'pēk\ the top of a hill or mountain; in piquet, the scoring of thirty points before one's opponent scores a point

Pila \'pīlə\ the type genus of the family Pilidae comprising the apple snails and dextral shells

pila \'pīlə\ heavy javelins of a Roman foot soldier

pila \'pēlə\ a communal fountain

pili \pē'lē\ a nut of any of various trees of the genus Canarium

pili \\'pēlē\ a perennial grass of worldwide distribution that is used as forage in southwestern U.S.

pili \\'pī͵lī\ a hair or a structure resembling a hair

pin \\'pin\ a usually cylindrical piece of wood or metal used for fastening separate articles together

pin \\'pēn\ to flatten or shape by hammering

pinches \\'pēnchāz\ South American marmosets having tufted heads

pinches \\'pinchəz\ presses hard between the ends of the finger and thumb

pinite \\'pē͵nīt\ a compact mineral that is essentially muscovite

pinite \\'pī͵nīt\ fossil wood

piqué \\'pēkā\ a durable ribbed cotton, rayon, or silk clothing fabric; inlaid, as a knife handle; a glove seam; a ballet movement

pique \\'pēk\ to stimulate by wounding pride or inciting jealousy or rivalry

pirr \\'pir\ a gust of wind or a flurry

pirr \\'pər\ to blow with a whiz; to speed along

piscine \\pə'sēn\ a stone basin with a drain located near the church altar for disposing of water from liturgical ablutions

piscine \\'pi͵sīn\ having the characteristics of a fish

pita \\'pēdə\ the century plant; the yucca

pita \\'pētä\ any of several small South American deer

placer \\'plāsər\ a person that places something

placer \\'plasər\ a deposit containing a valuable mineral

Planes \\'plā͵nēz\ a genus of small pelagic crabs

planes \\'plānz\ makes smooth or even; trees of the genus Platanus; soars on wings or skims across water

plaque \\'plak\ an ornamental brooch; an inscribed identification tablet; a film of bacteria-harboring mucus on a tooth

plaqué \\pla:kā\ a seal fixed directly to the face of a document

plat \\'plat\ a detailed plan of an area; a small tract of land

plat \\'plä\ a dish of food

platy \\'pläd•ē\ consisting of plates or flaky layers

platy \\'plad•ē\ a small stockily built fish native to southern Mexico

plebes \\'plēbz\ firstyear cadets at a military or naval academy

plebes \\'plē͵bēz\ common peoples of ancient Rome

plies \\'plīz\ folds or layers of material

plies \\͵plē'āz\ bendings of the knees by a ballet dancer with the back held straight

poise \\'pȯiz\ easy composure or manner marked especially by assurance and gracious dignity

poise \\'pwäz\ an absolute measure of viscosity

policize \\'pälə͵sīz\ to act in a politic, diplomatic, or crafty manner

policize \\͵pō'lēsīz\ to govern by means of police

Polish \\'pōlēsh\ of, relating to, or characteristic of Poland

polish \\'pōlēsh\ a lace shoe

polish \\'pälish\ to make smooth and glossy by a mechanical process; to burnish

poll \\'pōl\ voting at an election; to cut off the head, horns, or treetops

poll \\'päl\ a college or university degree without honors

polos \\'pōlōz\ games played by teams of players mounted on horseback, on bicycles, or swimming, the object of which is to drive a ball through goalposts

polos \\'pä͵läs\ a high crown or headdress of cylindrical shape

pone \'pōnē\ an original writ now su-
perceded by the writ of certiori; a player
on the dealer's right who cuts the cards

pone \'pōn\ a cake of stiff cornmeal

pose \'pōz\ to put or set in place or in a
given position

posé \'pōzā\ a ballet movement in which
the dancer steps from one foot to the
other with a straight knee

potty \'päd•ē\ a small child's pot for
voiding

potty \'päti\ haughty or supercilious in
bearing or speech

pram \'präm\ a small lightweight nearly
flatbottomed boat usually with a
squared-off bow

pram \'pram\ a baby carriage; a milk carrier's handcart

prayer \'prāər\ a supplicant

prayer \'preər\ a slight or minimal
chance, say to succeed or survive

Precis \'prēsəs\ a widely distributed genus
of chiefly tropical nymphalid butterflies

précis \prā'sē\ a brief summary of essential points, statements, or facts

predicament \'predēkəmənt\ the character, status, or classification assigned by
an affirmation or assertion

predicament \prē'dikəmənt\ a difficult,
perplexing, or trying situation

predicate \'predəkət\ the part of a sentence or clause that expresses what is
said of the subject

predicate \'predə,kāt\ to affirm, declare,
or proclaim

present \prē'zent\ to make a gift or dona-
tion

present \'prezᵊnt\ existent; now

prima \'prēmə\ the first or leading person
or item

prima \'prīmə\ the word at which reading is to be resumed after an interrup-
tion

primer \'primər\ an elementary instruction book

primer \'prīmər\ a device to ignite an explosive charge

Principes \'priŋkə,pās\ *Palmales*, a large
order of chiefly tropical monocotyledo-
nous plants

principes \'prīnsə,pēz\ the head of the
state under the Roman Empire

principes \'prēnsē,pāz\ eldest sons of
Spanish or Portuguese kings

prion \'prēän\ an infectious agent about
100 times smaller than a normal virus

prion \'prī,än\ any of several petrels of
the southern hemisphere

proceeds \prō'sēdz\ moves forward from
a point

proceeds \'prō,sēdz\ a total amount
brought in

process \'prō,ses\ to subject to a particular
method, system, or technique

process \prō'ses\ to move along; to go

produce \prō'dyüs\ to bring forth; to give
being, form, or shape to

produce \'prō,düs\ agricultural products
and goods

product \'prädəkt\ something produced

product \prədəkt\ to lengthen out

project \'prä,jekt\ a devised or proposed
plan

project \prō'jekt\ to throw or cast forward; to put or set forth

promoter \prō'mō,tər\ a Scottish university officer who presents university students for degrees

promoter \prə'mōtər\ a person or thing
that encourages or furthers

prosthesis \'prästhəsəs\ the addition of a
sound or syllable to a word, especially
by prefixing

prosthesis \präs'thēsəs\ an artificial device to replace a missing part of the
body

pud \\'pəd\\ an animal's paw or child's hand

pud \\'pu̇d\\ a penis

pugh \\'pü\\ an expression of disgust or disdain

pugh \\'pyü\\ a long-handled hooked prong for pitching fish

pulvini \\ˌpəl'vē ˌnī\\ clearly defined blocks resting on the capitals of columns in Byzantine and Romanesque architecture

pulvini \\ˌpəl'vīnˌnī\\ cushionlike enlargements of the base of a petiole or petiolule

punto \\'pən•tō\\ to hit, in fencing

punto \\'püntō\\ the ace of trumps, as in ombre

Pus \\'pu̇s\\ a month of the Hindu year

pus \\'pəs\\ thick opaque usually yellowish white fluid matter formed in connection with an inflammation

pussy \\'pu̇sē\\ a catkin of the pussy willow; a cat

pussy \\'pəsē\\ full of or like pus

put \\'pət\\ a blockhead or dolt; to hit a golf ball

put \\'pu̇t\\ to place

putter \\'pu̇d•ər\\ a person who puts or places something

putter \\'pəd•ər\\ a golf club

putting \\'pu̇tiŋ\\ placing in a specified position

putting \\'pətiŋ\\ making a golf stroke on or near the green to cause the ball to roll near or into the cup

putz \\'pu̇ts\\ a Nativity scene, especially one placed beneath a Christmas tree

putz \\'pəts\\ to fool, mess, or putter around or about

Group I

paramedic
paraphrases
passement
periphrases
pignorate
ponderate
precedent
predominate
preponderate
progress
proofread
proportionate
proximate
purport

Q

quart(e) \\'kär|t\\ a fencer's parry or guard position; a sequence of four playing cards of the same suit

quart \\'kwȯr|t\\ a U.S. liquid measure equal to two pints or ¼ gallon

Quiche \\'kēˌchä\\ an Indian people of south central Guatemala

quiche \\'kēsh\\ a baked custard pie

quinate \\'kwiˌnāt\\ composed of sets of five

quinate \\'kwīˌnāt\\ a salt or ester of quinic acid

quite \\'kwīt\\ to a considerable extent

quite \\'kētä\\ a series of passes made by a matador to attract the bull away from a horse or fallen picador

Group I

quintuplicate

R

Rabat \rə'bät\ the capital of Morocco

rabat \'rabət\ a polishing material made from potter's clay

rabat \'rabē\ a short cloth breast-piece worn by clergymen

rabat \rə'bat\ to rotate a plane about a trace into coincidence with another plane

rabbi \'raˌbī\ a Jew qualified by study of Jewish civil and religious law to expound and apply it

rabbi \'rabē\ a short cloth breast-piece worn by clergymen

ragged \'ragəd\ roughly unkempt

ragged \'ragd\ persecuted in petty ways

Rainier \ˌrə'nēr\ the highest mountain in Washington state (14,410 feet), and fifth highest mountain in the 48 contiguous United States

rainier \'rānēər\ wetter or more showery

Raja \'rājə\ a genus of skates

Raja \'räjə\ an Indian prince or king

raja \'räjə\ a silk clothing fabric with a rough surface

Rama \'rämə\ a Chibchan people of southeastern Nicaragua

Rama \'räˌma\ either the sixth, seventh (the most famous), or the eighth incarnation of Vishnu

rams \'ramz\ male sheep; strikes with violence

rams \'rämz\ a card game similar to loo

Rana \'rānə\ a nearly cosmopolitan genus of frogs

rana \'ränə\ an Indian prince

rape \'rāp\ an annual herb of European origin; illicit sexual intercourse without the consent of the victim; an outrageous violation

rape \rä'pā\ a highly seasoned hash used in the Middle Ages

rath \'räth\ a hill residence fortified with an earthen wall

rath \'rət\ a car or chariot, especially one used to carry an image of a god

raven \'rāvən\ a large glossy black bird

raven \'ravən\ to devour eagerly or greedily

rayon \'rāˌän\ a synthetic textile fiber made from modified cellulose

rayon \rā:ōⁿ\ a ray or beam; a radius

read \'rēd\ the fourth or true digestive stomach of a rumiinant

read \'red\ interpreted and performed, such as a musical passage

Reading \'rediŋ\ a city in southeast Pennsylvania

reading \'rēdiŋ\ mentally formulating written words or sentences

real \rē'äl\ a former monetary unit of several Spanish American countries and Spain

real \'rēl\ actual, true, or objective

reason \'rezᵊn\ a horizontal timber over a row of posts supporting a beam

reason \'rēzᵊn\ an explanation or justification; to think; the power of comprehending

rebel \ˌrebəl\ opposing or taking arms against the government or ruler of a country

rebel \rē'bel\ to feel or exhibit anger or revulsion

recollect \ˌrekə'lekt\ to recall or remember something

recollect \:rē•kə'lekt\ to gather together again

record \rē'körd\ to make an account or note of

record \'rēkərd\ an officially, or sometimes nonnofficially, attested top performance or achievement

recreate \'rekrē͵āt\ to refresh after toil

recreate \:rē:krē:āt\ to form anew or again

redial \͵rē'dī(ə)l\ to remanipulate a dial, as on a telephone or television

redial \'rēdēəl\ pertaining to a larva produced within the sporocyst of many trematodes

refuse \rə'fyüz\ to decline to accept; to replace a fuse in; to remelt

refuse \'re͵fyüs\ a useless part of something

regale \rə'gāl\ to entertain

regale \rə'gālē\ a royal prerogative; symbols indicative of royal status

reis \'rīs\ a Muslim ruler, chief, or ship captain

reis \'rās\ or \'rāz\ a former basic monetary unit of Spain and Spanish-America

relent \rə'lent\ to become less severe; to slacken

relent \'rē͵lent\ loaned money again to a borrower

relict \'relikt\ a widow

relict \rə'likt\ left behind in the process of change

relievo \rē'lēvō\ a mode of sculpture in which forms and figures are distinguished from the surrounding plane surface

relievo \rə'lēvō\ a game in which members of one team are given time to hide, then are sought by those of the other team

repent \rə'pent\ to feel regret or contrition

repent \'rēpənt\ creeping

repetition \͵repə'tishən\ the act of repeating something that has already been said or done

repetition \:rē͵pə'tishən\ to again make a request for something

repress \rə'pres\ to restrain

repress \'rē:pres\ to press again

reprise \rə'prīz\ an annual deduction or charge to be made out of a manor or estate

reprise \rə'prēz\ to repeat the performance

res \'rās\ in law, a particular thing

res \'rāz\ second notes in the diatonic scale

resaca \rə'sakə\ the dry channel or the former often marshy course of a stream

resaca \rə'zäkə\ a rebounding billow

resent \rē'zent\ or \rə'zent\ to feel, express, or exhibit indignant displeasure

resent \rē'sent\ transmitted by means of a repeater; sent again

reserve \rē'zərv\ to keep in store for future or special use

reserve \'rē͵sərv\ to furnish or supply again or anew

reside \rə'zīd\ to have one's residence or abode

reside \rē'sīd\ to install new or different siding on a structure

resole \'rē͵sōl\ to put a new sole on a shoe

resole \'re͵zōl\ a fusible resin soluble in alkali and alcohol

resoluble \rə'zälyəbəl\ able to be resolved

resoluble \rē:sälyəbəl\ able to be dissolved into solution again

resound \rə'zaůnd\ to become filled with sound; to become renown

resound \re:saůnd\ to sound again

résumé \:re͵z|ə:mä\ a condensed statement

resume \rə'züm\ to begin again

retail \rə'tāl\ to relate in detail or to one person after another

retail \'rē͵tāl\ the sale of commodities or goods in small quantities to ultimate consumers

retiré \rə:tē:rā\ a ballet movement

retire \rə'tīr\ to withdraw from activity

rheum \'rüm\ a watery discharge from mucous membranes of the eye or nose

Rheum \'rēəm\ a genus of Asiatic herbs with large leaves

rig \'rē\ an ancient Irish king

rig \'rig\ to furnish with apparatus or gear; to equip

rima \'rīmə\ a long narrow aperture; a cleft or fissure

rima \'rēmä\ a breadfruit

rissole \rə'sōl\ minced meat or fish covered with pastry and fried in deep fat

rissolé \'risəlē\ browned by frying in deep fat

Rite \'rīt\ the liturgy, especially an historical form of eucharistic service

rite \'rīt\ a ceremonial act

rite \'rīd•ē\ undistinguished achievement in academic requirements for graduation

river \'rivər\ a watercourse

river \'rīvər\ a person who splits blocks of wood

robin \'räbən\ a large North American thrush; a small European thrush

robin \'rōbən\ a toxalbumin similar to the toxic abrin and ricin

Rochet \'rōshā\ a fourth growth red wine from Medoc, France

rochet \'rächət\ a European gunard (fish) that is chiefly red; a closefitting white ecclesiastical vestment resembling a surplice

rom \'räm\ a small computer program that cannot be changed by the computer and that contains a special-purpose program (by shortening read-only memory)

rom \'rōm\ a male gypsy

rose \'rōz\ a flower; a perfume; a moderate purplish red color

rosé \rō:zā\ a table wine made from red grapes

rouge \'rüzh\ a powdery cosmetic

rouge \'rüj\ scrimmage in an English type of football

rower \'rōər\ a person who rows a boat

rower \'raùər\ a person who naps cloth by hand

rows \'rōz\ propels a boat with oars; continuous lines or strips

rows \'raùz\ noisy disturbances; heated arguments

rugged \'rəgd\ covered with a blanket or rug

rugged \'rəgəd\ hardy, robust, vigorous

Rum \'rüm\ a term originally applied by Moslems in medieval times to peoples of the Byzantine empire

rum \'rüm\ a blue dye resembling indigo obtained from an East Indian shrub

rum \'rəm\ an alcoholic liquor prepared from fermented molasses

rural \'r̵urəl\ living in the country or farmland areas

rural \ˌrü'räl\ a municipal police officer

Group I

rearward
recast
regenerate
regress
reiterate
replicate
reset
rissole

S

Sabia \'sābēə\ a genus of tropical Asiatic shrubs

sabia \səb'yä\ a Brazilian thrush

Sabine \'sābīn\ a member of an ancient people inhabiting chiefly the Apennines

sabine \'sabin\ a red cedar in North America

sabot \sa'bō\ a wooden work shoe worn in various European countries

sabot \'sabət\ a shoe having a wide band fitting across the instep

saga \'sägə\ a prose narrative sometimes of legendary content

saga \'sägə\ square or rectangular cloaks made of coarse wool

said \'sed\ expressed in words

said \'säid\ an Islamic chief or leader

sake \'säkē\ a Japanese alcoholic beverage made from fermented rice

sake \'sāk\ enhancement of an object or group

sal \'säl\ an East Indian timber tree

sal \'sal\ salt

saline \sə'lēn\ a spring of salt water

saline \'sälən\ a crude potash obtained from beet residues

Saliva \'säləvə\ a people of the Orinoco valley, Venezuela

saliva \sə'līvə\ a viscid secretion in the mouth

saltier \'sól₁tēər\ more engagingly provocative

saltier \'sal₁tīr\ in heraldry, an ordinary consisting of a bend dexter and a bend sinister crossing in the center of the field

salve \'sav\ a healing ointment

salve \'salv\ to save from destruction

salve \'sal₁vē\ an exclamation of greeting; hail

salver \'savər\ a person who salves or cures

salver \'salvər\ a tray for serving food and beverages

Same \'sämē\ sometimes \'saami\ a member of a people of northern Scandanavia, Finland, and the Kola peninsula of northern Russia who are typically nomadic herders of reindeer, fishermen, and hunters of sea mammals (preferable to "Laplander")

same \'sām\ resembling in every way

San \'sän\ a race of nomadic hunters of southern Africa now chiefly confined to the Kalahari dessert

san \'san\ a sanatorium (by shortening)

sancho \'saŋkō\ a primitive guitar with fiber strings

sancho \'sanchō\ the nine of trumps in sancho pedro

sang \'saŋ\ produced musical tones with the voice

sang \'səŋ\ a Persian harp of the Middle Ages

Santal \₁sən'täl\ a member of a Kolarian people in southeastern Bihar and adjacent Bengal

santal \'santəl\ a crystalline compound derived from flavone and obtained from red sandalwood and cam wood

santon \'santən\ a saint in Muslim countries

santon \sänₜōⁿ\ a small clay image usually of a saint

sapo \'sä₁pō\ a toadfish

sapo \'sä₁pō\ a sodium soap, such as castile soap

Sara \sə'ró\ a people of the Carolinas tentatively assigned to the Siouan language family

Sara \'särə\ a people of the Shari river in central Africa

sardine \sär₁dēn\ any of several small or immature clupeid fishes

sardine \'sär₁dīn\ a deep orange-red variety of chalcedony

sat \'sat\ rested in a position in which the body is essentially vertical and supported chiefly on the buttocks

sat \'sət\ eternal and immutable existence, in Hinduism

sate \'sāt\ to cloy with overabundance

sate \₁sä'tä\ an Indonesian and Malaysian dish of marinated, bite-sized pieces of meat

satiné \'sat∂n₁ā\ a timber tree of Brazil and the Guianas

satine \'sa₁tēn\ a smooth durable lustrous fabric usually made of cotton

saucier \'sȯs₁ēər\ more impudent

saucier \'sȯs₁yā\ an assistant chef who specializes in preparing sauces and soups

saucy \'sasē\ smart or trim, as a ship or automobile

saucy \'saasē\ marked by impertinent boldness or forwardness

scamper \'skampər\ to run away or flee

scamper \'skamp₁ər\ a person who performs in a hasty, neglectful, or imperfect manner

scena \'shänə\ a scene or accompanied dramatic recitative in an opera

scena \'sēnə\ the structure of an ancient Greek theater behind the orchestra facing the cavea

scragged \'skragd\ executed by hanging or garrotting

scragged \'skrag∂d\ lean or scrawny

second \sə'känd\ to remove a person temporarily from one position for employment elsewhere; to lend someone temporarily to another organization

second \'sekənd\ next to the first in value or degree

secreta \sə'krätä\ a prayer said in a low or inaudible voice by the celebrant just before the preface in the mass

secreta \sə'krēdə\ private seals

secrete \sə'krēt\ to produce or generate in the manner of a gland

secrète \sə'kret\ a 17th century steel skullcap worn under a soft hat

seer \'sēər\ a person who sees

seer \'sir\ a person who predicts events or developments; a prophet

semis \'semēz\ semifinished metal; trucking rigs

semis \sə'mē\ a scattering repetition of small design motifs to produce an overall pattern

Separate \'sepərət\ a member of a group favoring revivalism and emotionalism in religion

separate \'sepə₁rāt\ to divide, sever, or detach

Sere \'särä\ one of a Negroid people in eastern Sudan

sere \'särä\ in Hebrew, a vowel point written below its consonant

sere \'sir\ dried up or withered

Serer \sə'rer\ a Negro of a people who dwell about Cape Vert, Senegal

serer \'sirər\ more dried up or withered

Seres \'sīrēz\ a people of eastern Asia mentioned by Greeks and Romans as making silk fabrics

seres \'sirz\ periods of dryness

seton \'sēt∂n\ one or more threads or horsehairs, or a strip of linen introduced beneath the skin

seton \'set₁∂n\ the place or way in which a thing is set on

severer \sə'viər\ or \sē'viər\ more strict or uncompromising in judgment or discipline

severer \'sevər₁er\ a person who divides or breaks up into parts

sew \'sō\ to fasten with stitches of thread or filament

sew \'sü\ to become grounded, as a ship

sewer \'sōər\ a person who fastens by stitches of thread or filament

sewer \'süər\ a conduit to carry off waste material

shames \'shäməs\ the sexton of a synagogue; the candle used to light the other candles in a Hanukkah menorah

shames \'shāmz\ covers with contempt; dishonors or disgraces

shaves \'shavz\ the two long pieces of wood between which a horse is hitched to a vehicle

shaves \'shāvz\ removes a thin layer from

Shin \'shēn\ a major Japanese Buddhist sect growing out of Jodo

shin \'shēn\ the 22nd letter of the Hebrew alphabet

shin \'shin\ the front part of a leg below the knee

shove \'shəv\ to cause to go by the application of force

shove \'shōv\ a thin wooden bung for casks or a thin flat cork for stopping a widemouthed bottle

shower \'shōr\ a person who exhibits or demonstrates

shower \'shaủ̇ər\ a rainfall of short duration; a party given by friends to present a person with gifts

sika \'sēkə\ any of several deers of the eastern Asiatic mainland closely related to the Japanese deer

sika \'sikə\ a flea which is common in the West Indies and South America

simile \'siməlē\ a figure of speech comparing two unlike things, as "a heart as cold as stone"

simile \'sēmə‚lā\ a musical direction to continue whatever has been previously directed

sin \'sin\ a transgression of religious law; a serious offense

sin \'sēn\ the 21st letter of the Hebrew alphabet

singer \'siŋər\ a person who produces musical tones with the voice

singer \'sinjər\ a person who singes, as a textile worker with cloth

siris \'sirēz\ climbing peppers whose leaves are wrapped around or mixed with a whole betel nut

siris \sə'rēs\ an Asiatic tree having flowers with long silky stamens, or a silk tree

sis \'sēz\ plural of the seventh tone of the diatonic scale

sis \'sis\ sister (by shortening)

Siva \'sevä\ one of the supreme deities of Hinduism

siva \'sēvə\ a western Polynesian gesture dance with vocal accompaniment

skean \'skān\ a loosely coiled length of yarn or thread

skean \'skēn\ a bronze double-edged dagger used in Ireland

skene \'skēnē\ the structure of an ancient Greek theater behind the orchestra facing the cavea

skene \'skēn\ a bronze doubleedged dagger used in Ireland

skied \'skēd\ glided over snow or water on skis

skied \'skīd\ hit a ball high in the air; rose precipitously

skiver \'skivər\ to skewer or impale

skiver \'skīvər\ a thin soft leather made of the grain side of a split sheepskin

slaver \'slāvər\ a person engaged in the trade of persons held in servitude

slaver \'slavər\ or \'slävər\ to let saliva dribble from the mouth (rarely 'slāver)

sliver \'slivər\ a splinter or fragment

sliver \'slīvər\ a loose soft untwisted strand of textile fiber produced by a carding machine and ready for drawing or roving

slouch \'slaủ̇ch\ a person devoid of energy; to stoop one's head and shoulders

slouch \'slüch\ a pipe through which an engine takes up water

slough \'slü\ a marshy place
slough \'sləf\ something shed or cast off
slough \'slaü\ to strike heavily

SOB \:e₁sō'bē\ a son-of-a-bitch
sob \'säb\ to cry or weep; a noise made while weeping

Sol \'säl\ the sun
sol \'säl\ gold as used in alchemy; a fluid colloidal system; the sunny side or section of a bullfight arena
sol \'sōl\ the fifth tone of the diatonic scale in solmization

sola \'sōlä\ an East Indian shrubby herb the pith of which is used to make hats and toys
sola \'sōlə\ an unduplicated bill of exchange

Solea \'sōlēə\ the type genus of Soleidae, a family of flatfishes comprising the typical soles
solea \sō'leə\ a raised part of the floor in front of the inner sanctuary in an Eastern Orthodox Church

son \'sən\ the male offspring of human beings
son \'sōn\ a folk song of Cuba, Mexico, and Central America; a Latin American ballroom dance

sonar \sō'när\ a member of a Hindu artisan caste of goldsmiths and silversmiths
sonar \'sō₁när\ a device that detects the presence of and location of a submerged object by means of sonic and ultrasonic waves

sones \'sōnäs\ folk songs of Central America, Cuba, and Mexico
sones \'sōnz\ subjective units of loudness for a given listener

sorites \'sōr₁ītz\ indifferent commonly amoeboid interstitial cells
sorites \sə'rīdēz\ an abridged form of stating a series of syllogisms in a series of propositions

sortie \'sȯrdē\ the sudden issuing of troops from a defensive position to attack or harass the enemy
sortie \sȯr'tē\ an entry aria in opera

soufflé \su:flä\ an entree or dessert made with white sauce and eggs
souffle \'süfəl\ a blowing sound heard when monitoring internal body parts

sous \'sü\ of subordinate rank
sous \'saüs\ the space outside the white ring of an archery target
sous \'süs\ the smallest pieces of money

sow \'sō\ to plant or scatter seed
sow \'saü\ an adult female swine

spathose \'spa₁thōs\ composed of or arranged in a thin plate or plates
spathose \'spā₁thōs\ having a sheathing bract or pair of bracts subtending or enclosing an inflorescence, in plants

spier \'spīᵊrē\ a person that watches in a furtive or stealthy manner
spier \'spīrē\ a fixed and often architecturally treated screen

spiry \'spīər\ rising in a slender tapering form to a point
spiry \'spiər\ curving or coiling in spirals

springer \'spriŋər\ a person or animal that moves by leaps or bounds
springer \'sprinjər\ a person who sets a trap or ensnarement

Squalid \'skwäləd\ relating to the Squalidae, a family of sharks having a spine in each dorsal fin
squalid \'skwäləd\ marked by filthiness and degradation, usually from neglect (seldom 'skwāləd)

stark \'stärk\ lacking in flexibility or suppleness; rigid
stark \'shtärk\ loudly or forte, in music

statist \'stātəst\ an advocate of concentrating all economic controls and planning in the hands of a highly centralized government

statist \\'statəst\ a person who collects statistics

steinbock \\'stēn,bäk\ any small antelope of the plains of southern and eastern Africa

steinbock \\'stīn,bäk\ one of several wild goats living in the Alps

stingy \\'stinjē\ reluctant to part with something

stingy \\'stiŋē\ having a sting

stipes \\'stīps\ short stalks or supports

stipes \\'stī,pēz\ the second basal segment of a maxilla of an insect or crustacean

stipulate \\'stipyə,lāt\ to specify as a condition or requirement of an agreement or offer

stipulate \\'stipyələt\ furnished with stipules, the leaflike or membranous appendages that arise at the base of a leaf

subject \\'səbjəkt\ something that forms an underlying theme or topic

subject \\səb'jekt\ to bring under control or domination; to reduce to submission

Sung \\'sůŋ\ relating to, or having the characteristics of the period of the Sung dynasty of China

sung \\'səŋ\ to produce musical tones by means of the voice

<u>**sup**</u> \\'süp\ in mathematics, a least upper bound

sup \\'səp\ to eat supper or the evening meal

suppliance \\'səplēəns\ a supplication or entreaty

suppliance \\sə'plīəns\ the act or process of supplying

supply \\sə'plī\ to provide or furnish

supply \\'səplē\ in a limber or compliant manner

sures \\'shůrz\ certainties

sures \\'sü,rās\ southerly winds on the coasts of Chile and Peru

swinger \\'swiŋər\ a person or thing that sways to and fro

swinger \\'swinjər\ a person that singes or scorches the pinfeathers off, as of poultry

syringes \\sə'rinjəz\ devices used to inject fluids into or withdraw them from the body or its cavities

syringes \\sə'rin,jēz\ vocal organs of birds that are a special modification of the lower part of the trachea and/or the bronchi

---

Group I

satiate
saturate
says
scleroses
segment
snagged
stark
stenoses
subordinate
subsequence
suspect
syndicate

T

---

tain \\'tān\ thin tin plates

tain \\'thȯn\ one of a class of Irish epic tales, the central theme of which is a marauding expedition for cattle

<u>**tales**</u> \\'tālz\ narratives of events

tales \\'tālēz\ persons added to a jury from those in a courthouse

tali \'tā͵lī\ ankles, especially of human beings

tali \'tälē\ a gold piece tied about a bride's neck by the bridegroom in India that is worn during his life

tally \'tȯlī\ in a tall manner

tally \'talī\ a reckoning or recorded account of something

tallyho \͵talē'hō\ a dark grayish yellowish brown color; a four-in-hand coach

tallyho \'talē͵hō\ to utter the cry sounded by hunters upon sighting the fox

Tampan \'tampən\ a native or resident of Tampa, Florida

tampan \'tam͵pan\ any of various argasid ticks, especially the chicken tick

Tan \'dän\ a boat-dwelling people whose boats form compact colonies in the river, especially at Canton and Foochow, China

tan \'tan\ to covert skin into leather; a brownish color

Tana \'tänə\ a small genus of Bornean and Sumatran tree shrews

Tana \'tänä\ one of the rabbis of Palestine during the first two centuries A.D.

tana \'thȯnə\ Irish epic tales the central theme of which is a marauding expedition for cattle

Tang \'täŋ\ having characteristics of the Tang dynasty in China

tang \'taŋ\ a sharp distinctive flavor; the extension of a knife blade that connects with the handle

tangi \'taŋē\ a lamentation or dirge that accompanies a Maori funeral rite

tangi \'tän͵gē\ a narrow gorge

Tangier \tan'jir\ a major Moroccan seaport near the Strait of Gibraltar; a strong orange color

tangier \'taŋēər\ having a sharper or more distinctive flavor

tank \'täŋk\ a unit of weight for pearls equal to about .15 ounce

tank \'tank\ a usually large artificial receptacle used for holding, storing, or transporting liquor

Tanka \'dän'gä\ a boat-dwelling people whose boats form compact colonies in the river, especially at Canton and Foochow, China

tanka \'täŋkə\ a Japanese fixed form of verse of five lines; a Tibetan religious painting

Taos \'taús\ a Taoan people occupying a pueblo in New Mexico

taos \'daúz\ paths of virtuous conduct, in Confucionism

tap \'tap\ a light usually audible blow or rap

tap \'təp\ malarial fever

tapa \'täpə\ a coarse cloth made in the Pacific islands from pounded bark of a variety of plants

tapa \'täpä\ a snack or appetizer

Tapé \͵tä'pā\ an Indian of a former Tupian tribe dwelling on the headwaters of the Uruguay River

tape \'tāp\ a narrow limp or flexible strip or band

Tara \'tärä\ a savior goddess, in Buddhism

tara \'tärä\ a fern or brake, the thickened rootstalk of which is eaten

tara \'tärə\ a book palm

tarry \'tarē\ to linger, dawdle, or procrastinate

tarry \'tärē\ covered with tar

Tat \'tät\ an agricultural people living in scattered groups throughout Transcaucasia

tat \'tät\ a coarse fabric stretched on a frame and used for withering tea leaves

tat \'tat\ to make delicate handmade lace

tattoo \ta'tü\ to mark the skin by pricking in coloring matter; a call or signal sounded shortly before taps

tattoo \'tatü\ a native-bred pony of India

Tatu \\'tätü\\ a genus of armadillos

Tatu \\'tätü\\ an Indian people of the Eel river valley in northwestern California

taw \\'tȯ\\ a marble used as a shooter; to convert skin into white leather

taw \\'täf\\ the 23rd letter of the Hebrew alphabet

taxes \\'taksəs\\ pecuniary charges imposed by a public authority

taxes \\'tak،sēz\\ manual restorations of displaced body parts, as reductions or a hernia; reflex movements by a freely motile and usually simple organism

taxis \\'taksəs\\ a manual restoration of displaced body parts, as the reduction of a hernia; a reflex movement by a freely motile and usually simple organism

taxi(e)s \\'taxēs\\ chauffeur-driven automobiles available on call to transport passengers usually within a city for a fare (by shortening)

tear \\'tir\\ a drop of fluid secreted by the lacrimal gland near the eye

tear \\'tar\\ to divide or separate forcibly

teer \\'tēər\\ a golfer who places the ball on the tee

teer \\'ter\\ to stir up, as colors in block calico printing

temps \\'temps\\ temperatures, tempos, or temporary employees (by shortening)

temps \\'tän\\ a part of a ballet step without change of weight

tenues \\tənue\\ modes of dress; bearings or deportments

tenues \\'tenyə،wēz\\ unaspirated voiceless stops

terminate \\'tərmə،nāt\\ to bring to an ending or cessation in time, sequence, or continuity

terminate \\'tərmənət\\ indicating an action as a whole

terrace \\'terəs\\ a raised embankment with the top leveled; a gallery or portico

terrace \\tə'ras\\ a light-colored volcanic tuff resembling pozzolana

tested \\'testəd\\ determined the attributes or performance characteristics of

tested \\'testēd\\ having the witnessing or concluding clause of a writ attached

Thais \\'tīz\\ natives or inhabitants of Thailand

Thais \\'thāəs\\ a widely distributed genus comprising marine shells with a rough thick shell

theoric \\thē'ȯrik\\ relating to an ancient Greek public spectacle

theoric \\'thēərik\\ an early astronomical device for calculating positions of celestial bodies

thou \\'thaù\\ the person being addressed

thou \\'thaù\\ a thousand of anything

Thule \\'tülē\\ belonging to the Eskimo culture extending over arctic lands from Alaska to Greenland about A.D. 500–1400; a settlement in northwest Greenland

Thule \\'thülē\\ the northernmost part of the habitable world

thus \\'thəs\\ in this or that manner or way

thus \\'thəs\\ the oleoresin that hardens on a tree and is scraped off

tier \\'tir\\ a row, rank, or layer of articles

tier \\'tīər\\ a person who fastens, closes openings, or binds articles

tierce \\'tirs\\ any of various units of liquid capacity, especially one equal to 42 wine gallons; the tone two octaves and a major third above a given tone

tiercé \\'tir:sā\\ in heraldry, divided into three parts of different tinctures or bearing different coats of arms

till \\təl\\ used as a fuction word indicating position before a clock hour

till \\'til\\ to turn or stir and prepare for seed; a money drawer

ting \\'tiŋ\\ a high-pitched sound, as made by a small bell

ting \\'diŋ\\ an ancient Chinese ceremonial vessel

tinged \\'tinjd\\ slightly shaded or discolored

tinged \'tiŋd\ made a high-pitched sound, as made by a small bell

titi \'tī͵tī\ a tree found in the southern U.S.
titi \tə'tē\ a small South American monkey
titi \'tē͵tē\ a New Zealand blue-footed petrel

toilé \twä:lā\ a closely worked solid pattern in lace making that is contrasted with a net ground
toile \'twäl\ a cloth consisting of various fibers

ton \'tən\ a unit of U.S. weight equal to 2,000 pounds
ton \'tōⁿ\ the prevailing fashion or mode

tonal \'tənᵊl\ the force that acts on the mass of a ton to accelerate it equal to one foot per second squared
tonal \'tōnᵊl\ relating to the principle of organizing musical chords and notes in recognition of key relationships

tone \'tōn\ a vocal or musical sound; a color quality or value
tone \'dōnē\ a fishing or coastwise trading boat of India

tonite \'tō͵nīt\ a blasting explosive consisting of pulverized gun cotton impregnated with barium nitrate
tonite \tə'nīt\ on this present night or the night following this present day (simplified spelling of tonight)

toots \'tüts\ sounds a note or call suggesting the short blast of a wind instrument
toots \'tu̇ts\ a woman or girl (slang)

topi \tō'pē\ a lightweight helmet-like hat with a curved brim
topi \'tōpē\ an antelope of eastern Central Asia

touches \'təchəz\ perceives or experiences through the tactile sense; handles
touchés \tü'shāz\ used to acknowledge hits in fencing, successes of arguments, or accuracies of accusations

tout \'tau̇t\ to solicit patronage or canvass for customers

tout \'tüt\ winning in a game every thing in sight; to proclaim loudly

tower \'tōər\ a person or animal that pulls a barge or boat; a person who smoothes ceramic ware
tower \'tau̇ər\ a high vertical structure

traject \'tra͵jekt\ a place for passing across; a crossing route
traject \trə'jekt\ to transmit light through space or a medium

transect \tran'sekt\ to cut across or transversely
transect \'tran͵sekt\ a sample area of vegetation usually in the form of a narrow continuous strip

transform \tranz'fȯrm\ to change completely or essentially in composition or structure
transform \'tranz͵fȯrm\ the substitution of one configuration for or the alternation of a mathematical expression into another in accord with a mathematical rule

travail \trə'vāl\ physical or mental exertion, especially of a painful or laborious nature
travail \trə'vī\ a primitive vehicle used by the Plains Indians of North America

tref \'trāv\ a homestead or hamlet acting as a single community
tref \'trāf\ ritually unclean according to Jewish law

Triodia \trī'ōdēə\ a genus of American perennial grasses
triodia \trī'ōdēə\ any grass of the genus *Triodia*
triodia \trē'ȯthyȧ\ a liturgical book of the Eastern church

trite \'trīt\ stale or hackneyed
trite \'trī͵tē\ a notation in ancient Greek music

Triton \'trītᵊn\ one of a class of minor sea divinities or partly human monsters, as the mermaid
triton \'trītᵊn\ any of the very large marine gastropod mollusks

triton \'trī͵tän\ the nucleus of the tritium atom; *tri*nitro*to*luene (TNT or dynamite)

Troglodytes \͵trägləˈdī͵tēz\ a genus of typical wrens

troglodytes \'tragə͵dītz\ members of primitive people dwelling in caves or pits

tropical \'trōpəkəl\ rhetorically changed from its exact original sense

tropical \'träpəkəl\ a lightweight suiting of various fibers

trough \'trō\ any various bowls, tanks, or basins in which something is prepared or processed by kneading, in baking

trough \'tròf\ a conduit for water or liquid

tuberose \'tü͵brōz\ a Mexican bulbous herb commonly cultivated for its spike of fragrant white flowers

tuberose \'tübə͵rōs\ resembling a short thickened fleshy stem or root

tun \'tən\ a large cask

tun \'tùn\ a period of 360 days used as the basis of the Mayan calendar

turbines \'tərbənz\ rotary engines actuated by the reaction and/or impulse of a current of fluid subject to pressure

turbines \'tərbə͵nēz\ any of numerous marine snails with thick spiral nacreous shell

Tush \'tùsh\ a member of the Georgian people north of Tiflis

tush \'tùsh\ buttocks (slang)

tush \'təsh\ a long pointed tooth; a tusk

Group I

thromboses
topgallant
transgress
transplant
transport
treen
trefle
triturate

U

Ulva \'əlvə\ a genus of green seaweeds

Ulva \'ülvä\ a people of Nicaragua and Honduras

um \'əm\ a murmured interjection expressing hesitation or inarticulateness

um \'üm\ a mantra in Hinduism representing the triple constitution of the cosmos

umbones \͵əmˈbōnēz\ the bosses of shields sometimes having sharp spikes

umbones \'əm͵bōnz\ the lateral prominences just above the hinge of a bivalve shell

umph \'həmf\ an expression of skepticism or disgust

umph \'ùmf\ personal charm or magnetism, spirit, or sex appeal

unanimate \ənˈanəmāt\ not enlivened; dull

unanimate \yüˈnanəmāt\ to make unanimous

uncrooked \:ənˈkrùkt\ not turned or bent from a straight line

uncrooked \:ənˈkrùkəd\ honest or reliable

underage \'əndərˈaj\ less than mature or legal age

underage \'əndərij\ a shortage or deficit

underair \'əndər͵er\ the lowest stratum of the atmosphere

underair \͵əndərˈer\ to give insufficient ventilation

undercast \'əndər͵kast\ a passsage for air carried under a road or floor

undercast \ˌəndər'kast\ to carry underneath or on the lower side of

underdrive \'əndərˌdrīv\ a transmission gear which transmits to the drive shaft a speed less than engine speed or less than the speed provided by the normal gear set

underdrive \ˌəndər'drīv\ to impart forward from beneath

underlayer \'əndərˌlāər\ a substratum

underlayer \ˌəndər'lāər\ a cobbler

underman \'əndərˌman\ a person who is subordinate or inferior to another in some way

underman \ˌəndərˌman\ to furnish with an inadequate personnel force or leave short-handed

unionize \'yünyəˌnīz\ to form into a labor union

unionize \ːən'īəˌnīz\ to cancel or destroy an equivalent number of oppositely charged ions

unPolish \ːən'pōlish\ not characteristic of Poland or its people

unpolish \ːən'pälish\ to make dull; to remove or deprive of polish

unwind \ːən'wīnd\ to uncoil, disentangle, or straighten out

unwind \ːən'wind\ to deflate or remove the wind from

upset \'əpˌset\ a physical disorder or slight illness

upset \ˌəp'set\ to defeat unexpectedly

upwind \ːəp'wīnd\ to roll or coil upward

upwind \ːəp'wind\ in a position toward the direction from which the wind is blowing

use \'yüs\ a part of a sermon in which a doctrine is applied to life; a rough block of iron or steel suitable for working up into small forgings or for welding in making larger ones

use \'yüz\ to spend time in some occupation, interest, or activity

used \'yüzd\ employed in accomplishing something

used \'yüst\ accustomed; experienced

user \'yüzər\ a person who uses alcoholic beverages or drugs

user \'üˌzər\ the exercise of a right to the enjoyment of property

Uta \'yüd•ə\ a large genus of iguanid lizards

uta \'üd•ə\ a skin infection occurring in Central and South America

utas \'ütuz\ Japanese songs of any kind, generally applied to verses, especially the tanka

utas \'ütəs\ the octave (eighth day) of a church feast or festival

Uvea \ü'vāə\ the Polynesian language of the Wallis islands

uvea \'yüvēə\ the posterior pigmented layer of the iris and eye

Group I

ultimate
unable
uncleanly
underdose
underlet
underlie
underreach
underset
unlearned

V

vale \'vāl\ a low-lying area usually containing a stream

vale \'v|älä\ a salutation on leave-taking

vat \'vat\ a large vessel, tub, or barrel

vat \'vät\ a temple or other religious monument

veer \'vir\ to shift from one direction or position to another

veer \'vēər\ a smith who hammers blocks of metal or wood that are used as wedges, shims, or lever fulcrums

vice \'vīs\ evil conduct

vice \'vīsē\ in place of

vide \'vīdē\ see (to direct a reader to another item)

vide \'vēd\ a musical direction indicating a passage to be omitted

Viola \vī'ōlə\ a genus of leafy stemmed herbs or undershrubs, including the pansy and violet

viola \vē'ōlə\ a musical instrument of the violin family (seldom vī'ōlə)

violet \'vīələt\ a plant of the genus Viola; a reddish blue color

violet \'vīə,let\ a tenor viol having usually seven strings

violist \'vīələst\ a person who plays the viol

violist \vē'ōləst\ a person who plays the viola

vise \'vīs\ a two-jawed tool for holding work

visé \'vē,zā\ a visa

visto \'vē,stō\ in music, very quick

visto \'vis,tō\ a vista

viva \'vēvə\ an expression of good will or approval

viva \'vīvə\ an oral examination

vole \'vōl\ a rodent closely related to lemmings and muskrats

volé \vō'lā\ a ballet step that is executed with the greatest possible elevation

volet \vō'let\ a short flowing veil worn by women in the Middle Ages

volet \vō'lā\ either of the folding side compartments or wings of a triptych

volte \'valt\ or \'vōlt\ a gait in which the horse moves sideways and turns around a center

volte \'vōltä\ an early French dance with pivots and high springs

volva \'välvə\ a membranous bulbous sac or cup surrounding the base of the stipe in many gill fungi

volva \'välvä\ a wise woman or seeress in Norse mythology

Group I

vitiate

W

Wagnerite \'vägnə,rīt\ an adherent of Wagner's theory of operatic composition

wagnerite \'vägnə,rit\ magnesium fluorophosphate

wall \'wȯl\ the external layer of structural material surrounding an object

wall \'wəl\ to roll the eyes so as to show the white

whoo \'wü\ an expression of sudden excitement, astonishment, or relief

whoo \'hü\ the cry of an owl

wicked \'wikəd\ of evil character

wicked \:wikt\ having a wick, as a lamp

winder \'wīndər\ a worker or machine that winds yarn or thread

winder \'windər\ something that takes the breath away, as a hard blow with the fist or a fast run

winds \'wīndz\ twists, coils, or curls

winds \'windz\ natural air movements

won \'wən\ gained victory in a contest

won \'wän\ the basic monetary unit of South Korea since 1962

woodward \'wu̇ˌdwərd\ toward a wood

woodward \'wu̇ˌdwȯrd\ an officer charged with guarding a forest

wound \'wünd\ an injury to the body

wound \'waund\ encircled

Group I

winged

Y

ya \'ya\ an expression of disgust, contempt, defiance, or derision

ya \'yä\ scholarly transliteration of the Hebrew tetragrammatron that constitutes a divine proper name, such as Jehovah

yang \'yäŋ\ the masculine and positive principle in Chinese cosmology that interacts with its opposite yin; a Siamese gurjun balsam tree

yang \'yaŋ\ a cry of the wild goose

Yonkers \'yäŋkərz\ a large suburb of New York City

yonkers \'yəŋkərz\ young men

yungas \'yüngəz\ densely wooded valleys or slopes in South America

yungas \'yüngəs\ a Peruvian rice rat

Z

Zemi \'zämē\ a Naga people found chiefly in the Barail area of the Assam-Myanmar frontier region

zemi \zə'mē\ an object believed to be the dwelling place of a spirit and to possess magical potency

Zonites \zō'nīdēz\ the type genus of the family *Zonitidae* snails

zonites \'zōˌnītz\ body segments of a diplopod

Appendix: Unusual Groupings

Homophones

Five or more 1-syllable words

ai - ay - aye - eye - I/i
air - are - e'er - ere - err - eyre - heir

Baal/baal - bael - bail - bale
bait - bate - Bete/bete - beth
baos - boughs - bouse - bouws - bows
baule - bole - boll - Bolle - bowl
beau - beaux - bo - boh - boo - bow
beurre - birr - buhr - bur - bur(r)
bharal - birl - birle - burl - burral - burrel
bi - buy - by - bye - 'bye
braes - braise - brays - braze - breys
   - brys

calf - calve - coff - cough - Kaf - kaph -
   koff
calk - Cauc - cauk - caulk - cawk
cart - carte - kart - quart - quart(e)
cat - cot - cotte - Kot - xat
cay - k - qua - quai - quay
cees - C's - psis - seas - sees - seize - sis
   - Szis
chou - shoux - shoe - shoo - shu
crews - cruise - crus - cruse - krewes -
   Krus
croes - Cros/cros - Crows/crows - croze

Dan/dan - dawn - don - Tan
daos - dauws - dhows - dows - dowse
   - taos

gnu - knew - new - Nu/nu

hays - haze - he(h)s -heighs - heis - heys
heugh - hoo - Hu - who - whoo
hoos - hoose - whos - who's - whose
Ho/ho - hoe - Hoh - whoa

knot - nat - naught - naut - not

lacks - lacs - Lak(h)s - laks - lax
lais - lase - lays - laze - leas - leis - les -
   leys
Lak(h)s - lax - lochs - locks - lox
leachy - lichi - Litchi/litchi
leud - lewd - lood - looed - lowed - lude
lieu - loo - Loup/loup - Lu

meuse - mews - mus - Muse/muse
mhos - mohs - mos - mots - mows
mohr - moire - Moor/moor - mor - more
mohr - Moor/moor - more - mower

oohs - ooze - whos - who's - whose

packs - PACS/pacs - pacts - Paks - Pax/
   pax
peer - pier - Pierre - pir - pirr - pyr
picks - pics - Picts - pix - pyx
plait - plat - Platt - Platte/platte
psis - scyes - sighs - size - xis
ptere - tear - tier - Tyr - Tyre

raise - rase - rays - raze - rehs - reis - res
   - reys
re - Ree/ree - rhe - ri - rig
reams - reems - rhemes - R(h)eims - riems
rhos - roes - Ros - rose - rows
right - Rite/rite - wright - write

Sacs/sacs - sacks - sacques - sax - Saxe
sault - sew - Sioux - sou - sous - su
   - sue
soot - suit - suite - sute - tzut

tailles - Tais/tais - Thais - ties - tyes -
   Tyighs

351

WAACS- wacks - WACS - wax - whacks
ware - wear - weigher - weir - wer
  - where - where're

way - Wei - weigh - wey - whey
weal - weel - we'll - wheal - wheel
whins - winds - wins - winze - wynns

Four or more 2-syllable words

aerie - aery - airy - arrhae - arrie - Eire
aerie - eerie - Eire - Erie
aire - Ara/ara - arrah - arrha - Erie
antae - ante - anti - auntie
Aster/aster - Astur/astur
axal - Axel - axil - axle

Baatan - bataan - Batan - baton
baetyl - beadle - beetle - betel - bietle
bai-u - bayou - bio - byo
beanie - beany - beenie - bene
Beni - ben(n)e - Benny/benny

caama - cama - comma - kaama - Kama/
  kama
caapi - copje - copy - kappie - kopje
cala - Calla/calla - callow
capa - cappa - coppa - kappa
carat - caret - carrot - karat
caries - carries - Carys - karris
carol - carrel - Karel - kerril - keryl
carry - Cary - karri - kerrie - Kerry
catarrh - Kitah - Kuttar - Qatar
caucus - coccous - Coccus/coccus
cedar - ceder - cedor - cedre - seater
  - seeder
censer - censor - senser - sensor
cerous - cirrus - scirrhus - seeress
  - serous
Champagne/champagne - champaign -
  champain
Chermes - Kermes/kermes - kermis
cider - citer - sider - sighter
cocci - cocky - kaki - khaki
coco - cocoa - Koko/koko
Conches/conches - conch(e)s - conscious
coolie - cool(l)y - coulee - Kulli
Cora/cora - corah - kora
cyan - Cyon - (s)cion - Sion
cycle - Seckel - Sicel - sickle
cypress - Cypris/cypris - Cyprus

deasil - decile - decyl - desyl
decan - Deccan - decken - dekan

Dewar - dewer - doer - dour - dur
dooley - doolie - dooly - duly

enfold - infold - unfoaled - unfold

gala - Gal(l)a - galla - gallow
galley - Galli - gallie - gally
gaufre - gofer - goffer - gopher

hallo - hallow - halo - hello - hollo
holey - Holi - holy - wholly

leaver - lever - levir - liefer - livre
lewder - looter - loutre - luter

Mahri - Maori - Mari - marri
Male - Mali - mal(l)ie - maulie - molle -
  molly - moly
marischal - Marshall - marshal(l) - martial
marquees - Marquis/marquis - marquise
masi - Mossi - mossie - mossy
Mason/mason - maysin - meson
medal - meddle - metal - mettle
Merlin/merlin - merlon - murlin
Moho/moho - Mojo/mojo

nodus - nodus - notice - Notus

palate - palette - pallet - pallette
pallae - pally - polly - poly
patens - patents - pattens - Pattons
Psylla/psylla - Scilla/scilla - Scylla

rabat - rabbet - rabbit - rabot
raiser - raser - razer - razor
rea - Rhea/rhea - ria - rya
reiter - rider - righter - writer

scissel - scissile - Sicel - sisal - sisel -
  syssel
senate - senit - sen(n)et - sennet - sinnet
solan - Solen/solen - solon
steelie - steely - stelae - stele

tori - Torrey - Tory/tory

whirley - whirly - whorly - wurley

Three or more 3-syllable words

accidence - accidens - accidents
acetic - ascetic - Ossetic
aerial - areal - ariel

alcanna - Alkanna/alkanna
alfonsin - alphonsin - Alphonsine
allision - elision - Elysian

alluded - eluded - eluted - illuded
allusion - elusion - illusion
Ammanite - Ammonite/ammonite
area - aria - eria
Austria - Ostrea - ostria - Ostrya

Barbary - barberry - barbery
barrier - berrier - burier

caatinga - Cotinga/cotinga
cadalene - Catalan - Catalin
calabar - calabur - califer
ceresin - Saracen - sericin
Cereus - serious - Sirius
chorea - Correa/correa - keriah - Korea
Cidaris/cidaris - siderous
cirrhosis - psorosis - sorosis
confidant - confidante - confident - confitent
Cyclamen - cyclamin - cyclamine

deviser - devisor - divisor

Entrance/entrance - entrants
Eurya - urea - Uria

filander - Philander/philander
manacan - manakin - manikin - mannequin - mannikin
Mandarin/mandarin - mandarine
marabou - Marabout/marabout

parasite - Parisite/parisite
Paridae - parity - parody - parroty
pertinence - pertinents - purtenance
populace - populous - Populus

receded - receipted - reseated - reseeded
reciting - residing - resighting - re-siting
rhodeose - roadeos - rodeos
rubicand - Rubicon/rubicon

ternary - ternery - turnery

unceded - unseated - unseeded
uncited - unsided - unsighted
unfaded - unfated - unfeted
unsold - unsoled - unsouled
unwedded - unwetted - unwhetted
uranous - Uranus - urinous

All 4, 5, and 6-syllable words

Acacian - acaciin
Acadian - Akkadian
acclamation - acclimation
acephalous - acephalus
Aceria - Assyria
Achillean - achilleine
acrogenous - acrogynous
Adelea - Adelia
adventuress - adventurous
agaricin - agaricine
Alectrion - Alectryon
allegation - alligation
allegator - Alligator/alligator
alliterate - illiterate
aluminate - illuminate
amaretto - amoretto
Ambassadeur - ambassador
America - Amerika
amphibalus - amphibolus
amphibian - amphibion
amygdalin - amygdaline
androgenous - androgynous - androgynus
annunciate - enunciate
antecedence - antecedents
aplanatism - aplanetism
apophasis - apophysis
Appalachian - appellation
appositive - oppositive
araneous - Araneus
Arianism - Aryanism

aureolin - aureoline
autonomous - autonymous

bacillary - basilary
basilican - basilicon
Bougainvillaea - Bougainvillia

Caecilian - Sicilian
caliginous - kaligenous
calumniation - columniation
Camptosaurus - Camptosorus
Carinthian - Corinthian
censorial - sensorial
cerulean - c(o)erulein
cessionary - sessionary
Chamaeleon - chameleon
chlorogenin - chlorogenine
Chrysochloris - chrysochlorous
Cilicia - Silicea
Colombia - Columbia
Colombian - Columbian
comedia - commedia
commissariat - commissariot
compellation - compilation
complementary - complimentary
concubitous - concubitus
confectionary - confectionery
confirmation - conformation
consensual - consental
continuance - continuants

conventical - conventicle
corydalis - Corydalus
covariance - covariants
Crioceras - Crioceris
cyanidin - cyandine
cynicism - Sinicism
cynocephalous - Cynocephalus/cynocephalus
Cysticercus - cystocercous
cytology - sitology

delegation - deligation
deprevation - deprivation
diaphane - diaphony
dissipater - dissipator
distributer - distributor
divertisement - divertissement

ectocarpous - Ectocarpus
enterocele - enterocoele
enumerable - innumerable
ephemeris - ephemerous
escaladed - escalated
euonymous - Euonymus/euonymus
ex-patriate - expatriot

Filipena - philopena

geophilous - Geophilus

heterogenous - heterogynous
heteronomous - heteronymous
hypogenous - hypogynous

ideogram - idiogram
ideograph - idiograph
impartable - impartible
impassable - impassible
infirmation - information
installation - instillation
intercession - intersession
interdental - interdentile
interosseous - interosseus
interpellate - interpolate

Jacobean - Jacobian

leptocephalous - Leptocephalus
leptodactylous - Leptodactylus
lysigenic - lysogenic

macrocephalous - Macrocephalus
menology - monology
micropterous - Micropterus
miliary - milliary
millenary - millinary
monogeneous - monogynous
myatonia - myotonia

noncereal - nonserial

orinthorhynchous - Orinthorhynchus/
   orinthorhynchus
overflour - overflower

overhigher - overhire
overmeddled - overmettled

papagallo - papagayo
paragnathous - paragnathus
Parthenopean - Parthenopian
pentamerous - Pentamerus
periodic - periotic
perpetuance - perpetuants
phenology - phonoloy
philogeny - philogyny
physocarpous - Physocarpus
pluripotence - pluripotents
pneumatophorous - Pneumatophorus
polydactylous - Polydactylus
polygenist - polygynist
polygenous - polygynous
polymathy - polymythy
positivest - positivist
precedential - presidential
precipitance - precipitants
projicience - projicients
propodeum - propodium
psoriasis - siriasis
pterocarpous - Pterocarpus

sarcophagous - sarcophagus
sarcophilous - Sarcophilus
semidouble - semi-double
senhorita - senorita
single-seated - single-seeded
stationary - stationery
subhyalin - subhyaline
superepic - superepoch
synechological - synecological

talkee-talkee - talky-talky
technology - tecnology
tetrastichous - Tetrastichus
tetravalence - tetravalents
theocracy - theocrasy
topography - typography
topology - typology
trachycarpous - Trachycarpus

unaccepted - unexcepted
unaffected - uneffected
unamendable - unemendable
uncomplementary - uncomplimentary
unerupted - unirrupted
unexercised - unexorcised
uniparous - uniporous
Uranian - uranion

varicosis - verrucosis
velocity - villosity
veracity - voracity
viviparous - Viviparus

wistaria - Wisteria

Homographs

Please refer to the appropriate word grouping in the Homograph section for the pronunciation and meaning of each word.

Three or more words each with a different pronunciation

As/as
August/august
Cham/cham
Chi/chi
comes
Concord/concord
das
Even/even
fine
fortes
fourchette
grave
Guara/guara
heres
lather
Male/male
Maquis/maquis
Mobile/mobile

Mole/mole
Mora/mora
Mores/mores
nana
Pala/pala
papa
Passe/passé/passe
passes
pate/pâte/paté/pâté
pili
Principes/principes
Rabat/rabat
salve
slough
sous
Tana/tana
titi

Homophones and Homographs

The following words are both homophones and homographs. Pronunciation of each word is reflected in the Homograph section.

aba	benet	cala	colon
abaisse	Beni	cape	come
aloe	berg	Cassia	commit
anti	Bern(e)	cassia	connex
arête	beurre	cat	connex
Arkansas	bin	cave	coops
arras	bo	cay	coops
As	bole	cay	coos
aspirate	bombard	cete	couch
ate	bombé	cham	coupe
ate	bombe	cham	coupe
atta	Bon	chamar	couped
axes	bon	chap	crotal
aye	bootee	chap	crotal
	bore	chela	crus
ballet(t)	borne	Chi/chi	cumal
ban	bouché	chi	
ban	bought	chil	dah
bar	boule	chose	desert
bare	bow	choux	dine
barre	bow	choux	dingy
bases	bruit	classes	dis
basis	Brut	close	dit
bass	buffet	coax	dit
baule	buro	coax	do
bene		coif	do

does
Dom
dom
dos
dos
dun
dun

Entrance/entrance
eta
eve
ewe

fakir
file
filé
flageolet
flower
formal
forme
forte
forte
frappe
fray
frette
fur

gallant
gally
gaufre
Ge
gene
genet
ger
gig
gill
gill
gimel
glace
goût
grave
Graves
grind

hache
hale
halo
Hamburg
has
headward
here
hires
hum

kaki
Kasha
kate
Kin

Lais
lais

Lak(h)s
laks
laser
lat
lax
laze
lead
lech
led
lied
lied
lien
lien
liken
limbers
lira
lis
lisses
live
lores
lower

Male
male
Mam
mane
Maquis
maquis
mare
maria
matte
Melo
melo
mere
mere
mind
mire
Mod
Mojo
mole
mole
molle
moly
moly
Mon
more
mores
mores
morné
morne
mot
mow
mow
multiply
Mus
mus

nance
naos

Nice
nice
None
none
nun
nun
Nut
nut

oke
oke
ombre
oner
ore
os

Pali/pali
pan
pan
pane
parados
passé
pasty
pate
pâte
patte
pau
peer
peon
Pila/pila
piqué
pique
pirr
pirr
piscine
planes
plat
poise
poll
poll
pone
pram
prayer
present
primer
prion
put
putting
putz

quart(e)
quiche
quite

rabat
rath
rath
Reading
reading
real

reason
refuse
reis
reis
res
res
rheum
rig
Rite/rite
robin
rom
rom
rose
rows
rows
Rum/rum
rum

sake
sal
sal
salver
sang
sang
satiné
saucy
second
seer
sere
sew
sew
sewer
sewer
shames
Shin/shin
shin
shower
sin
sin
siris
siris
sis
sis
slough
slough
Sol/sol
son
son
sous
sous
sow
sow
spier
spier
sup

tales
Tampan
tang

tangi	teer	travail	whoo
tank	terrace	tref	whoo
tarry	Thais	tun	winds
tat	Thule	Tush/tush	winds
taw	tier		won
taxes	tier	vale	won
taxes	ton	vice	
taxi(e)s	ton	vise	
taxis	tonal	volé	
tear	tone	volte	
tear	tower		

Annotated Bibliography

The following books and articles were consulted in preparing this volume. The terms **homophone** (bona fide, Group I, and Group II), **homograph** (bona fide and Group I), and **homonym** used in these annotations are defined in the table on page 4 and the text on pages 3 and 5 of this dictionary.

Anderson, James G. *Le Mot Juste: A Dictionary of English and French Homonyms* (revised by L. C. Harmer). New York: Dutton, 1938. A listing of French and English words that are similar in spelling, meaning, and or pronunciation, such as **abscond** (English)/**abscondre** (French). 383 pp.

Bailey, Mildred Hart. *Spelling Steps, Part 3*, revised. Austin, TX: Steck-Vaughn, 1984. 144 pp. Thirty bonafide homophones are included in this children's book.

Baillairge, Charles P. Florent. *Vocabulary of English Homonyms*. Quebec: C. Darveavy, 1891. A mixture of homonyms, homophones (bona fide, Group I, and Group II), and homographs without segregation. Proper names, places, rivers, and words such as **a loft/aloft** are included. 190 pp.

Barnhart, Robert W. *Hammond Barnhart Dictionary of Science* (Sol Steinmetz, managing editor). Maplewood, NJ: Hammond Inc., 1986. 740 pp. + xxiv pp. Encompasses the disciplines of astronomy, biology, chemistry, forestry, geography, geology, mathematics, meteorology, mineralogy, physics, and associated fields.

Barrett, Bryon S. *Book of Homonyms: With Copious Exercises on Homogenous and Homophonous Words*. New York: Pitman, 1908. The book is written from a "practical rather than a theoretical viewpoint," and contains compound and hyphenated words, uses of the apostrophe and figures, and rules for spelling, formation of plurals, and contractions. Approximately 600 words are included, reflecting a mixture without segregation of "homophonous" words (words pronounced alike but spelled differently) and "homogenous" words (words somewhat alike in pronunciation or spelling, with different or similar meanings, such as **affect, effect, effects, in effect,** and **effective**). Numerous proper names are included. 192 pp.

Bartlett's Roget's Thesaurus. Boston: Little, Brown & Co., 1996. A comprehensive volume providing information about an idea, as opposed to merely providing synonyms and definitions of a word. The index includes approximately 113,050 entries. 1,415 pp.

Basil, Cynthia. *How Ships Play Cards*. New York: Morrow, 1980. An illustrated children's book containing 13 homonyms. 32 pp.

_____. *Nailheads and Potato Eyes: A Beginning Word Book*. New York: Morrow, 1976. An illustrated children's book containing several homonyms. 32 pp.

Bechtel, John H. *135,000 Words Spelled and Pronounced Together with ... List of Homophones*. Philadelphia: George W. Jacobs & Co., 1904. A considerable number of bonafide homophones is reflected on pp. 617–670. 670 pp.

Beech, Linda Ward. *Analogies: Grades 6–8*. New York: Scholastic Professional Books, 2002. 48 pp. A children's instruction book that includes 139 bonafide homophones.

Behler, Violet E. *Homonyms: A Selective Dictionary Including ... Heteronyms*. Houston: Houston Public Library, 1967. A list of bonafide homophones (mislabeled homonyms) plus several bonafide homographs (termed heteronyms). 74 pp.

Behrens, June. *What Is a Seal?* LaPuente, CA: Jay Alden, 1975. An illustrated children's book of homonyms. 32 pp.

Bey, A. F. Inglott. *A Dictionary of English Homophones: Pronouncing and Explanatory*. London: Kegan Paul, Trench, Trübner & Co., 1899. A collection of many bonafide homophones plus assorted "confusables" like: **bacon, baking, beacon,** and **beckon**; or **bend, bent, pend,** and **pent**. 184 pp.

Bilucaglia, Marino. *Gli Omonimi nella Lingua Inglese (The Homonyms in the English Language)*. Milan: Istituto Editoriale Cisalpino, ca. 1968. A book of English homonyms translated into Italian. 159 pp.

Bolander, Alyce, and Donald O. Bolander (editors). *The New Webster's Medical Dictionary*. Hartford, CT: Lewtan Corp., 1992. 289 pp.

Boning, Richard A. *Reading Homonyms*. Baldwin, NY: Dexter and Westbrook, Ltd., 1974. A series of 37 booklets containing numerous bonafide homophones (mislabeled homonyms) for grade levels 1–9.

_____. *Reading Homographs*. 2nd edition. Baldwin, NY: Dexter & Westbrook, 1975, 23 pp. Each of ten key words in this illustrated children's book are homonyms misclassified as homographs.

Bossom, Naomi. *A Scale Full of Fish and Other Turnabouts*. New York: Greenwillow Books (Division of Wm. Morrow & Co.), 1979. An illustrated children's book containing 20 homonyms. 24 pp.

Bostick, Charles W. "Homophones Pairs," *Word Ways*. Vol. 10, No. 1, Feb. 1977, p. 26.

Brandreth, Gyles. *More Joy of Lex: An Amazing and Amusing Z to A and A to Z of Words*. New York: Morrow & Co., 1982. An assemblage of oddities, puns, and word amusements in the English language. 287 pp.

Bridges, Sir Robert Sheldon. *On English Homophones*. (Society for Pure English Tract No. II.) Oxford, England: Clarendon Press, 1919. England's poet laureate from 1913 to 1930 makes a broadside indictment of Daniel Jones' system of phonetic spelling and pronunciation. Sir Robert's arguments are: (1) Homophones are a nuisance and are mischievous; (2) They are exceptionally frequent in the English language; (3) They are self-destructive and tend to become obsolete (although he admitted that this argument was difficult to prove); (4) Nonetheless, their loss impoverishes the language; and (5) This impoverishment is proceeding at an accelerated pace due to the general prevalence of the Southern English standard of speech encouraged by Mr. Jones' theory of fanatic phoneticism which is causing "the mauling of words." 48 pp.

Burch, Marilyn Myers. *Instant File-Folder Games for Reading*. New York: Scholastic Professional Books, 2001. 64 pp. Several homophones are included, plus antonyms, synonyms, nouns, verbs, etc.

Carruth, Gorton, David H. Scott, and Beverly J. Yerge. *The Transcriber's Handbook: With the Dictionary of Sound-Alike Words*. New York: Wiley, 1984. Numerous bona fide homophones and homographs, Group I and Group II homophones, and often confused words such as **laboratory/lavatory** are contained in the Dictionary section, pp. 22–274. 519 pp.

Cerutti, Bruno Augusto. *Dizionario degli Omofoni Englesi (Dictionary of English Homophones)*. Milan: Casa Editrice Ceschina, 1967. English homophones are translated into Italian and incorporated into illustrative English sentences. 1,277 pp.

Chapman, Robert L. (editor). *Dictionary of American Slang*, 3rd edit. New York: Harper-Collins Publishers, 1995. 617pp + xxiipp.

Cherington, Janelle. *See the Sea*. New York: Scholastic, 1997. 16 pp. An illustrated children's book containing four bonafide homophones.

Cook, Jean. *Word Study Fun: Homophones, Homographs, and Compound Words, Grades 2–3*. Elizabethtown, NJ: Continental Press, 1989. 26 pp. Several bonafide homophones are incuded in this illustrated children's book. However, all words classified as homographs are homonyms.

Cook, Olive Marie. *Sparks for Sparkle: A Book of Homonyms and Double-Duty Words*. Upland, IN: A. D. Freese & Sons, 1963. The intended audience for this book includes persons who enter advertising jingle contests and complete such phrases as "Brand X peanut butter is great because..." 129 pp.

Crabtree, James William. *The Crabtree Speller: The 5000 Troublesome Words Classified and Graded, Including ... Homonyms*. Chicago: The University Publishing Co., 1915. Included are about 238 bonafide homophones and ten homographs. 83 pp.

Cronk, Brian Christopher. *Semantic and Repetition Priming with Homophones*. Milwaukee: University of Wisconsin–Milwaukee, 1993. 94 pp. A doctoral dissertation that encompasses fifty pairs of bonafide homophones.

Daniel, Claire. *Possessives, Contractions, Compound Words, and Homophones*. New York: Scholastic Professional Books, 1997. 32 pp. A children's illustrated instruction book that includes 24 bonafide homophones.

Devine, Felice Primeau. *Goof-Proof Spelling*. New York: Learning Express, 2002. 98 pp. + xvi pp. An instruction book that includes 51 bonafide homophones.

Dictionary of American Regional English. Volume I, Introduction and A–C. (Frederic G. Cassidy, chief editor.) Cambridge, MA: Belknap Press of Harvard University Press, 1985. 903 pp. + clvi pp.

_____. *Volume II, D–H.* (Frederic G. Cassidy, chief editor.) Cambridge, MA: Belknap Press of Harvard University Press, 1991. 1175 pp. + xv pp.

_____. *Volume III, I–O.* (Frederic G. Cassidy, chief editor.) Cambridge, MA: Belknap Press of Harvard University Press, 1996. 927 pp. + xv pp.

_____. *Volume IV, P–Sk.* (Joan Houston Hall, chief editor.) Cambridge, MA: Belknap Press of Harvard University Press, 2002. 1014 pp. + xix pp.

Dilworth, Thomas. *A New Guide to the English Tongue (1793)*. Delmar, NY: Scholar's Facsimiles & Reprints, 1978. A section on homophones is reflected on pp. 80–89.

Disch, Thomas M. *A Children's Garden of Grammar*. Hanover, NH: University Press of New England, 1997. 88 pp. + vi pp. Six bonafide homophones are included in this illustrated children's book.

Downes, John, and Jordan E. Goodman (editors). *Dictionary of Finance and Investment Terms*, 5th edit. Hauppauge, NY: Barron's Educational Series, 1998. 730 pp + vi pp.

Downing, Douglas A., Michael A. Covington, et al. *Dictionary of Computer and Internet Terms, 8th edition*. Hauppage, NY: Barron's Educational Series, 2003. 572 pp. + iv pp.

Duggan, Norman E. *A Lexicon of Homophones*. West Bath, ME: N. E. Duggan, 1992. A short collection of bonafide homophones, including several archaic and obsolete words. 15 pp.

Durso, Mary Wilkes. *Mastering Confusing Words: A Basic Approach to Meaning and Spelling*. New York: Wiley, 1965. Several bona fide and Group II homophones and confusing words such as **defer/differ**. 245 pp.

Ellyson, Louise Withers. *A Dictionary of Homonyms: New World Patterns*. Mattituck, NY: Banner Books (Amereon Ltd.), 1977. This volume claims to be the first serious and complete dictionary of English language homonyms. Homonyms, homophones (bona fide and Group I), and homographs are intermixed, such as **sew, so, sow** (to plant), and **sow** (a female pig). Numerous proper names are included. "Bruisers" (near-homonyms or words that are so much alike as to be easily confused, such as **accidence/accidents, adieu/ado, assay/essay, bauble/bubble,** and **bellow/below**) are included in a separate section. 166 pp.

Espy, Willard R. *An Almanac of Words at Play*. New York: Clarkson N. Potter, 1975. Several bona fide homophones are on pp. 15, 131–132, and 315–316. 360 pp.

_____. *The Game of Words*. New York: Grosset & Dunlap, 1972. Several bona fide homophones are reflected on pp. 126–132, plus numerous homonyms (mislabeled homophones), puns, oxymorons, palindromes, tongue-twisters, clichés, rebuses, and anagrams. 279 pp.

_____. *Say It My Way*. Garden City, NY: Doubleday & Co., 1980. A few bona fide homophones are included on p. 87. 219 pp.

Fallows, Samuel. *A Complete Dictionary of Synonyms and Antonyms, ... with an Appendix Embracing ... Homophonous Words ... Printing*. New York: Fleming H. Revell, 1886. A short list of homophonous words is reflected on pp. 392–404. 512 pp.

Fischer, Walter. *Englische Homophone*. Munich: Max Hueber Verlag, 1961. A paperback compendium of about 1,000 English homophones translated into German. 88 pp.

Fleming, John, and Hugh Honour. *Dictionary of the Decorative Arts*. New York: Harper and Row, 1977. 896 pp.

Franklyn, Julian. *Which Witch? Being a Grouping of Phonetically Compatible Words*. Boston: Houghton Mifflin, 1966. Homophones (bona fide, Group I, and Group II) are intermixed with homographs. Numerous proper names are included. Groups of homophonic words are arranged in illustrative sentences or paragraphs, such as "skill with the adze adds virtue to the man." 198 pp.

Games. Published monthly at PO Box 10145, Des Moines, IA 50340, often provides several homophones and homographs. The publisher is PSC Games Ltd. Partnership, 810 Seventh Avenue, New York, NY 10019 (212-246-4640).

Gartman, Linda Martinson. *Masked Versus Distributed Repetition of Homographs: A Test of the Differ-*

ential Encoding Hypothesis. Columbus: Ohio State University, 1971. 63 pp. Since the examples used throughout this master's thesis are homonyms, the title should better read *homonyms* rather than *homographs*.

Gentry, Larry. *Relative Frequency of Homophones in Children's Writing*, Technical Note 2-82721. Los Alamitos, CA: Southwest Regional Laboratory for Educational Research & Development, 1982. 9 pp. A composite listing of the 99 most commonly used bonafide homophones in grades 2–8 is provided.

Gilliéron, Jules, and Mario Roques. *Études de Géographie Linguistique: L'Atlas Linguistique de la France (Studies of Linguistic Geography: According to the Linguistic Atlas of France)*. Paris: Honoré Champion, 1912. In this work, Gilliéron introduces the doctrine that two words of different origin which become homonyms by regular sound changes may interfere (due to ambiguity and confusion) with one another to such as extent that one is ultimately excluded from the vocabulary of a particular dialect. 155 pp. plus maps.

Gilman, Mary Louise. *6,000 Soundalikes, Look-Alikes, and Other Words Often Confused*. Vienna, VA: National Court Reporters Association, 1992. The most numerous category in this volume is words often confused, with a minority being bonafide homophones, plus a few homographs. 200 pp.

_____. *3000 Sound-Alikes and Look-Alikes*. Vienna, VA: National Shorthand Reporters' Association, 1986. The volume contains bona fide homophones, homonyms, and confusing words like **abduct/adduct.** 60 pp.

Godard, Russell H. *Homophones and Homographs*. Corvallis, OR: Franklin, 1999. 310 pp. An extensive collection of bonafide homophones and bonafide homographs. However, several Group I homographs are misclassified as bonafide homographs. The narrative contains many of the author's (often idiosyncratic) rules, procedures, and criteria for identifying homophones and homographs.

Gonzales, Joseph Ralph. *A Resource Guide to Teach Homophones and Pure False Cognates to Spanish Speakers Learning English as a Second Language*. Sacramento: California State University at Sacramento, 1984. 123 pp. A master's thesis that incorporates 206 bonafide homophones in the discussion.

Gordon, Jo Ann. *Vocabulary Buiding with Antonyms, Synonyms, Homophones, and Homographs*. Superduper Pubs., 1999. 189 pp. + vi pp. A children's instruction book containing 124 bonafide homophones. However, sixty homonyms are misclassified as homographs.

Gross, Barbara J. *Retrieval of Divergent Lexical Definitions of Homographs in Young, Mature, and Elderly Adults*. Omaha: University of Nebraska at Omaha, 1985. 48 pp. The ten stimulus words cited in Appendix A that are used throughout the experiment are homonyms, rather than homographs.

Gwyne, Fred. *A Chocolate Moose for Dinner*. New York: Windmill Books/ Simon and Schuster, 1976. An illustrated children's book of several bona fide homophones and homonyms. 47 pp.

_____. *The King Who Rained*. New York: Windmill Books and E. P. Dutton, 1970. An illustrated children's book of 19 homonyms and homophones. 40 pp.

_____. *A Little Pigeon Toad*. New York: Simon and Schuster Books for Young Readers, 1988. An illustrated children's book of thirteen bona fide homophones and seven homonyms. 47 pp.

_____. *The Sixteen Hand Horse*. New York: Windmill/Wanderer Books, 1988. An illustrated children's book containing six bona fide homophones and sixteen homonyms. 47 pp.

Hagan, S. F. *Which Is Which? A Manual of Homophones*. London: Macmillan Press. 1982. A dictionary containing several bonafide homophones, homographs, and numerous homonyms, Group I homophones, and Group I homographs. 128 pp.

Hambright, Peggy W. *Vocabulary and Spelling Mind Builders: Grades 4–6*. Greensboro, NC: The Education Center, 2001. 48 pp. Several bonafide homophones are included in this children's instruction book, plus antonyms, snyonyms, etc.

Hanlon, Emily. *How a Horse Grew Hoarse on the Site Where He Sighted a Bare Bear: A Tale of Homonyms*. New York: Delacorte Press, 1976. An illustrated children's book containing several bona fide homophones. 32 pp.

Hanna, Paul R., Jean S. Hanna, et al. *Power to Spell: Textbook-Notebook* edition. Boston: Houghton-Mifflin, 1970. 152 pp. A classroom instruction book containing about sixty bonafide homophones, misclassified as homonyms.

Hanson, Joan. *Homographic Homophones: Fly and Fly and Other Words That Sound the Same but Are as Different in Meaning as Bat and Bat*. Minneapolis: Lerner, 1973. An illustrated children's book of 26 homophones. 32 pp.

_____. *Homographs: Bow and Bow and Other Words That Look the Same but Sound as Different as*

Sow and Sow. Minneapolis: Lerner, 1972. An illustrated children's book of homographs (bona fide and Group I). 32 pp.

_____. *Homonyms: Hair and Hare and Other Words That Sound the Same but Look as Different as Bear and Bare.* Minneapolis: Lerner, 1972. An illustrated children's book of 26 homophones. 26 pp.

_____. *More Homonyms: Steak and Stake and Other Words That Sound the Same but Look as Different as Chili and Chilly.* Minneapolis: Lerner, 1973. An illustrated children's book of 26 homophones. 32 pp.

_____. *Still More Homonyms: Night and Knight and Other Words That Sound the Same but Look as Different as Ball and Bawl.* Minneapolis: Lerner, 1976. An illustrated children's book of 26 homophones. 32 pp.

Harder, Keith C. "The Relative Efficiency of the 'Separate' and 'Together' Methods of Teaching Homonyms." *Journal of Experimental Education,* Sept., 1937, pp. 7–23. An abstract of Harder's doctoral dissertation at Iowa State University in which he tested two methods of teaching the spelling of homonyms (actually homophones): (1) presenting each pair of words (such as **dear** and **deer**) together simultaneously; and (2) presenting the words separately with a three- to four-day interval between exposure to each word. He concluded that pupils learned to spell by either method and the range of differences in learning between the two was small.

Harrison, Jim. *Confusion Reigns: A Quick and Easy Guide to the Most Easily Mixed-Up Words.* New York: St. Martin's Press, 1987. This volume contains a mix of bona fide homophones, homonyms, and easily confused words like **ablution/absolution** and **flounder/founder**. 119 pp.

Herbst, Sharon Tyler. *The New Food Lover's Companion,* 3rd edit. Hauppauge, NY: Barron's Educational Series, Inc., 2001. Comprehensive definitions of nearly 6,000 food, drink, and culinary terms. 772 pp.

Hobbs, James B. *Homophones and Homographs: An American Dictionary.* Jefferson, NC: McFarland, 1986. This first edition of the present volume contains 3,625 bona fide homophones, 602 bona fide homographs, numerous Group I homophones and homographs, Groups I and II homophones, unusual groupings, and an annotated bibliography. 264 pp.

_____. *Homophones and Homographs: An American Dictionary.* 2nd edition. Jefferson, NC: McFarland, 1993. The second edition of this volume contains 7,149 bonafide homophones, 1,469 bonafide homographs, and all the other features of the first edition. 302 pp.

_____. *Homophones and Homographs: An American Dictionary.* 3rd edition. Jefferson, NC: McFarland, 1999. This edition contains 7,786 bona fide homophones, 1,552 bona fide homographs, plus other features of the first and second editions. 318 pp.

Hodges, Richard. *A Special Help to Orthographie or the True-Writing of English.* Ann Arbor: Edwards Bros., 1932. A mixture of bona fide homophones and confusing words like **beholden/beholding, valley/value** are included. 27 pp.

Homographs & Heteronyms: Grades 4–6. Scottsdale, AZ: Remedia Pubs. (undated). 28 pp. + ii pp. A basic skills booklet that includes 18 bonafide homographs (called heteronyms) and 89 homonyms that are misclassified as homographs.

Houston, Thomas Rappe, Jr. *Comparable Common Factors in English Homophone Recognition.* Technical report #163. Madison: Wisconsin Research & Development Center for Cognitive Learning, University of Wisconsin, 1971. Appendix A (pp. 90–162) is an extensive list of English homophones. 168 pp.

Hunt, Bernice Kohn. *Your Ant Is a Which: Fun with Homophones.* New York: Harcourt Brace Jovanovich, 1975. An illustrated children's book containing several bona fide homophones. 32 pp.

Jarman, Patricia L. *The Source of Null Phonemic Masking Effects with Homophones: The Role of Phonological Competition and List Structure.* Boca Raton: Florida Atlantic University, 1985. 52 pp. Ninety bonafide homophones are identified in Appendices A and B, although three bonafide homophones in Appendix A are misidentified as pseudo-homophones. Twenty bonafide homophones in Appendix C are misidentified as non-homophones.

Jones, Sandra Suzanne. *The Influence of Subliminal Stimulation on the Attribution of Meaning to Homographs.* San Angelo, TX: Angelo State University, 1987. 59 pp. A master's thesis in which only two of the eight words that are identified as homographs for examination in Appendices 1, 4, and 5 are bonafide homographs—close and wind. The remaining six are homonyms.

Kilduff, Edward Jones. *Words the Secretary Must Watch; Homophones, Semi-Homophones, and Homophonic Sequences.* New York: F. S. Crofts, 1940. Section I contains several homophones; and a few bonafide homophones are interspersed in Section II. 67 pp.

Kilpatrick, James Jackson. *The Ear Is Human: A Handbook of Homophones and Other Confusions.*

Kansas City, KS: Andrews, McMeel & Parker, 1985. A mix of bona fide homophones and confusing words like **appraise/apprise** are included. 119 pp.

Kirtland, Elizabeth. *Write Is Right: A Handbook of Homonyms*. New York: Golden Press, 1968. Contains 1,650 homonyms and homophones (bona fide and Group I, such as **mucous/mucus**). Numerous obsolete and archaic words, proper names, and suffix-extended words such as **dyeing/dying** are included, plus a homonym quiz containing 108 exercises. 128 pp.

Klasky, Charles. *Rugs Have Naps (But Never Take Them)*. Chicago: Children's Press, 1984. An illustrated children's book containing several homonyms. 31 pp.

Klepinger, Lawrence. *Write English Right: An ESL Homonym Workbook*. New York: Barron's Educational Series, 1993. An instruction book offering English-as-a-second-language students a method to unravel complexities surrounding numerous English homophones. 160 pp.

Kokeritz, Helge. *Two Sets of Shakespearean Homophones*. The Review of English Studies, Vol. 19, No. 76, Oct. 1943, pp. 357–365. A linguistic archaeologist examines two pairs of homophones that appear in Shakespeare's works—hour/whore and told/tolled.

Kreivsky, Joseph, and Jordan L. Linfield. *The Bad Speller's Dictionary*. New York: Random House, 1987. A large listing of frequently misspelled and often confused words, including numerous "look-alikes," almost "look-alikes," "sound-alikes," and almost "sound-alikes." 186 pp.

_____, and _____. *Word Traps: A Dictionary of the 7,000 Most Confusing Sound-Alike and Look-Alike Words*. New York: Collier Books–Macmillan Publishing Co., 1993. A compendium of about 2,000 bona fide homophones, ten homographs, several Type II homophones, and numerous other confusing words, such as *haircut* and *haricot*. 319 pp.

Kruger, Gustav. *Synonymik un Wortgebrauch der Englischen Sprache (Synonyms and Word Usage of the English Language)*. Dresden and Leipzig: C. A. Koch, 1897. Contains mostly English synonyms (such as **tall, large, great, big,** and **huge**) translated into German. 1,528 pp.

Kudrna, Charlene Imbior. *Two-Way Words*. Nashville: Abingdon, 1980. An illustrated children's book of twelve pairs of bona fide homophones and twelve pairs of homonyms. 32 pp.

Langer, Margaret, and Edward Fry. *Homophones Workbook A: Grades 3–6*. Laguna Beach, CA: Laguna Beach Education Books, 1997. 44 pp. A children's instruction containing 89 bonafide homophones, plus one proper name.

_____. *Homophones Workbook B: Grades 3–6*. Laguna Beach, CA: Laguna Beach Education Books, 1997. 44 pp. A children's instruction book containing 86 bonafide homophones.

Laurita, Raymond E. *1001 Homonyms and Their Meaning ... with Defining Sentences*. Camden, ME: Leonardo Press. 1992. Numerous bonafide homophones are listed and defined. 138 pp.

Lecky, Prescott. *The Playbook of Words*. New York: F. A. Stokes, 1933. An illustrated children's book of homonyms. 36 pp.

Lederer, Richard. *Get Thee to a Punnery*. NY: Dell Pub. Co. (Dell Books), 1988. Two hundred bonafide homophones, plus 65 homonyms misclassified as homographs. 149 pp.

Lesch, Mary F. *Differential Effects of Exposure Duration on Semantic Priming from Homophones: Evidence for Van Ordens (1987) verification model*. Amherst: University of Massachusetts at Amherst, 1990. 76 pp. Thirty-two pairs of bonafide homophones are used to support argumention in this master's thesis.

Lessie, Pat. *How to Spell Homophones*. Westminster, CA: Teacher Created Materials, 1999. 48 pp. About 700 bonafide homophones are presented in this children's instruction book, plus a few Group I and Group II homophones, a dozen proper names, and about 15 non-homophones of any type.

Lincoln, Nancy H. *Visual Priming of Homophones in an Implicit Memory Task*. Gainesville, FL: University of Florida, 1998. 51 pp. Thirty-eight bonafide homophones are presented on p. 17 of this master's thesis.

The Lincoln Library of Essential Information, 18th edition, Vol. I. Buffalo, NY: Frontier Press, 1949. Several bona fide homophones are reflected on pp. 67–69.

Linfield, Jordan L., and Joseph Krevisky. *Word Traps: A Dictionary of the 5,000 Most Confusing Sound-Alike and Look-Alike Words*. New York: Collier Books, 1993. A substantial list of bonafide homophones, Type I & II homophones, plus numerous words that appear to look or sound like another (such as **billion** and **bullion**). 374 pp.

Lipton, James. *An Exaltation of Larks: Or the Veneral Game, 2nd Edition*. New York: Penguin Books, 1977. 138 pp. Compilation of group titles for various animal species, birds, etc. dating from 1450 and 1486 to date.

Longman, Harold S. *Would You Put Your Money in a Sand Bank? (Fun with Words)*. Chicago: Rand

McNally, 1966. An illustrated children's book containing several bona fide homophones and homonyms. 46 pp.

Maestro, Giulio. *Riddle Roundup: A Wild Bunch to Beef Up Your Word Power*. New York: Clarion Books, 1989. A fun-and-pun illustrated children's book with eight bonafide homophones interwoven. 64pp.

_____. *What's a Frank Frank? Tasty Homograph Riddles*. New York: Clarion Books, 1984. An illustrated children's book containing several bonafide homophones. 64pp.

_____. *What's Mite Might: Homophone Riddles to Boost Your Word Power*. New York: Clarion Books, 1986. An illustrated children's book containing 123 bonafide homophones. 64pp.

Malkiel, Yakov. "A cluster of four homophones in Ibero-Romance." University of California: *Hispanic Review*, Vol. XXI, 1953. pp. 20–36. A heavily footnoted scholarly article regarding issues associated with Jules Gilliéron's thesis of phonological drift leading to convergence.

Manchester, Richard B. *The Mammoth Book of Word Games*. New York: Hart Publishing, 1976. Several homophones are reflected on pp. 38–39, 88–89, 449, 456, and 458. 510 pp.

Manus, Gerald I., and Muriel R. Manus. *Phonic Follers: A Creative Arts Dictionary of Homophones*. Berkely, CA: Creative Arts Books Co., 1998. A collection of about 2,700 bonafide homophones and a few Group I homophones. Liberal use of plurals and suffixes augments the collection. 231 pp. + x pp.

McGraw-Hill Dictionary of Scientific and Technical Terms (Sybil P. Parker, editor). 3rd edition. New York: McGraw-Hill, 1984. A reference work containing 98,500 scientific and technical terms. 1,781 pp.

McLenighan, Valjean. *One Whole Doughnut, One Doughnut Hole*. Chicago: Children's Press, 1982. An illustrated children's book of fifteen pairs of bona fide homophones. 30 pp.

Meister, Barbara. *The Pear-Pair Tree*. New York: Vantage Press, 1972. An illustrated collection of bonafide homophones for children. 90 pp.

Menner, Robert J. "The Conflicts of Homophones in English." *Language* 12 (1936), pp. 229–44. Professor Menner critiques and refines the doctrine (advanced by Jules Gilliéron from 1902 to 1921) that two words of different origin which become homonyms by regular sound changes may interfere (due to ambiguity and confusion) with one another to such an extent that one is ultimately excluded from the vocabulary of a particular dialect.

Molter, Carey. *Bass Cannot Play Bass*. Edina, MN: Abdo Publications Co. (Sand Castle), 2002. 24 pp. Seven pairs of bonafide homographs are included in this illustrated children's book.

_____. *Fruit Trees Produce Produce*. Edina, MN: Abdo Publications Co. (Sand Castle), 2002. 24 pp. Eight pairs of bonafide homographs are presented in this illustrated children's book.

_____. *Live Lions Live on Land*. Edina, MN: Abdo Publications Co. (Sand Castle), 2002. 24 pp. An illustrated children's book containing seven pairs of bonafide homographs.

_____. *Pete Presents the Presents*. Edina, MN: Abdo Publications Co. (Sand Castle), 2002. 24 pp. Eight pairs of bonafide homographs are contained in this illustrated children's book.

Murdoch, John. *The Dictionary of Distinctions in Three Alphabets*. London: 1811. The book consists of three sections called "alphabets": (1) "Words the same in sound, but of different spelling and signification; with which are classed such as have any similarity in sound, proper names are not excepted." This section includes homophones (bona fide and Group I), near-homophones (such as **adapt/adept/adopt** and **clef/cliff**), obsolete and archaic words, dialects (such as dropping an *h* to make homophones like **eddy/heady** or **hitch/itch**), and names of cities and countries; (2) "Showing how one orthography has a plurality of pronunciations, and varies in sound or meaning according to the circumstances of accentuation or connection" (such as **a vast/avast**); and (3) "Which points out the various changes, in sound and sense, produced by the addition of the letter *e*, whether final or medial" (such as **bar/bare**, or **bar/bear**).

Muschia, Gary Robert. *The Writing Teacher's Book of Lists: With Ready-to-Use Activities and Worksheets*. Englewood Cliffs, NJ: Prentice-Hall, 1991. 264 pp. + xxi pp. Numerous bonafide homophones are included, plus eight pairs of bonafide homographs, and many homonyms misclassified as homographs.

Nader, Jouar C. *Prentice Hall's Illustrated Dictionary of Computing, 3rd edition*. NY: Prentice-Hall, 1998. 777 pp.

Newhouse, Dora. *The Encyclopedia of Homonyms: 'Sound-Alikes.'* Hollywood, CA: Newhouse Press, 1976. Contains homophones (bona fide, Group I, and Group II), archaic and obsolete words, dialects, proper names, and places. 238 pp.

_____. *Homonyms: Sound-Alikes—Homonimos: A Bilingual Reference Guide to the Most Mispronounced, Misspelled, and Confusing Words in the English Language*. Los Angeles: Newhouse

Press, 1978. This volume is an updated and expanded version of Newhouse's *Encyclopedia of Homonyms* containing about 3,500 English words that are translated into Spanish. Includes homophones (bona fide, Group I, and Group II), homonyms, obsolete and archaic words, dialects, foreign coins and measures, geographic locations, and suffixes. 247 pp.

The Official Scrabble Players Dictionary. Springfield, MA: G & C Merriam Co., 1978. 662 pp. + viii pp. Maximum length of words is eight letters. Includes many British, archaic, and dialectic words.

Ogata, Hideo, and Roger Julius Inglott. *A Dictionary of English Homonyms: Pronouncing and Explanatory.* Tokyo: 1942. Approximately 2,900 English words are translated into Japanese, including homophones (bona fide, Group I, and Group II), obsolete and archaic words, dialects, proper names, countries and nationalities, foreign coins and weights, and suffixes. 271 pp.

O'Harra, Nancy. *Before Reading: A Language Comprehension Program; Synonyms, Definitions, Homonyms, Homophones, Homographs, and Antonyms.* Tigard, OR: C.C. Publications, 1985. 105 pp. An illustrated children's instruction book containing 65 bonafide homophones and 20 bonafide homographs.

Olness, Gloria Steit. *The Influence of Pictorial Context on Lexical-Semantic Processing of Ambiguous Auditory Homophones: A Cross-Modal Lexical Priming Experiment.* Eugene: University of Oregon, 1993. 98 pp. Eighteen bonafide homophones are identified in Appendices A–C. An additional 31 words are presented as homonyms, although 18 are bonafide homophones.

Osmond, Anne Erickson. *An Analysis of Spelling Errors of Common Homographs Among Children at Different Reading Levels.* Sacramento: California State University at Sacramento, 1971. 143 pp. Twenty-five bonafide homographs are used to demonstrate this master's thesis argument.

Ours, Nicole. *Word Study Fun: Homophones, Homographs, Prefixes, and Suffixes, Grades 4–6.* Elizabethtown, PA: Continental Press, 1988. A word study book containing several bonafide homophones, plus numerous homonyms mislabeled homographs. 25 pp.

The Oxford English Dictionary, 2nd edition. J. A. Simpson and E. S. Weiner, compilers. Oxford: Clarendon Press, 1989. Volumes I–XX. This classic reference was a useful arbiter in deciding several technical issues that arose during the compilation of each edition of this book. 21,475 pp. + ccxx pp.

Paxson, William C. *The New American Dictionary of Confusing Words.* New York: Signet, 1990. A dictionary of approximately 2,000 commonly confused words and terms, such as **ectomorph, endomorph,** and **mesomorph.** A few bona fide homophones are included. 311 pp.

Phythian, B. A. *A Concise Dictionary of Confusables: All Those Impossible Words You Never Get Right.* New York: John Wiley & Sons, 1990. A dictionary of frequently confused words, such as insidious/invidious, maladroit/malapropos, perpetrate/perpetuate, and repairable/reparable. A few bona fide homophones are included. 198 pp.

Pop-up Sound Alikes: A Hilarious Collection of Homonyms. NY: Random House, 1973. An illustrated children's pop-up book containing 27 homophones. 18 pp.

Powell, David. *Look-Alike, Sound-Alike, Not-Alike Words: An Index of Confusables.* Washington, DC: University Press of America, 1962. A particularly useful source of bona fide homophones and homographs (plus confusing words). 185 pp.

Presson, Leslie. *A Dictionary of Homophones.* Hauppage, NY: Barron's, 1997. 136 pp. + vi pp. A collection of bonafide homophones, interspersed with cartoons.

_____. *What in the World Is a Homophone?* Hauppauge, NY: Barron's, 1996. An illustrated children's book of numerous bonafide homophones, a few Type I Homophones, and a few Type II homophones. 1,992 pp.

Raith, Josef von. *Englische Dictate mit Homophonen (English Dictation with Homophones).* Stuttgart: Ernst Klett, 1970. Contains about 375 homophones with numerous illustrative sentences, paragraphs, exercises, and examination questions. 61 pp.

The Random House Dictionary of the English Language. 2nd edition, unabridged (Stuart B. Flexner, editor in chief). New York: Random House, 1987. 2478 pp. + xlii + 32 pp. of maps.

Random House Historical Dictionary of American Slang, Volume 1, A-G (J. E. Lighter, editor). New York: Random House, 1994. 1,006 pp.

Random House Historical Dictionary of American Slang, Volume II, H–O (Jonathan Evan Lighter, editor). New York: Random House, 1997. 736 pp. + xxviii pp.

Raymond, Eric S. (ed.) *The Hacker's Dictionary.* Boston: MIT Press, 1991. A comprehensive compendium of computer terminology and slang, illuminating many aspects of hacker tradition, folklore, and humor. 433 pp.

Rendon, Clara, et al. *Learning Achievement Packages: Language Arts–English Grammar.* Austin, TX:

Dissemination and Assessment Center for Bilingual Education, 1976. An instruction book containing exercises and answer keys for use in elementary through high school grades. The second segment contains 97 bonafide homophones (mislabeled homonyms) in nine exercises with accompanying answer keys. 127 pp.

Rockey, Denyse. *Phonetic Lexicon of Monosyllabic and Some Diasyllabic Words, with Homophones, Arranged According to Their Phonetic Structure*. London: Heyden & Son, 1973. Developed from material compiled during Rockey's years of professional work in speech and hearing clinics, this volume has a practical clinical orientation. Seventy-nine tables, each in a matrix format of 19 columns and 40 lines (monosyllabic and disyllabic only), contain 7,754 words positioned according to their initial, medial, and final sound. Approximately 3,500 homophones are listed, including proper names, letters of the alphabet, colloquialisms and slang, common abbreviations, contractions, acronyms, foreign words adopted by English, obsolete and archaic words, dialect, and technical words. 250 pp.

Roets, Lois F. *Word Searches: Synonyms, Antonyms, Homonyms*. Compton, CA: Educational Insights, 1981. An instruction book of spirit masters containing 7 pp. of bonafide homophones, mislabeled homonyms. 19 pp.

Rondeau, Amanda. *Bella Blew Blue Bubbles*. Edina, MN: Abdo Publications Co. (Sand Castle), 2002. 24 pp. An illustrated children's book containing nine pairs of bonafide homophones.

_____. *Can You Hear from Here*? Edina, MN: Abdo Publications Co. (Sand Castle), 2002. 24 pp. This illustrated children's book presents variations on the bonafide homophone pair **hear, here**.

_____. *Do We By, Buy, or Bye Tickets*? Edina, MN: Abdo Publications Co. (Sand Castle), 2002. 24 pp. Variations on the bonafide homophone triplet **buy, by, bye** are contained in this illustrated children's book.

_____. *The Prince Left His Prints*. Edina, MN: Abdo Publications Co. (Sand Castle), 2002. 24 pp. Nine pairs of bonafide homophones are contained in this illustrated children's book.

_____. *Sue Threw the Goop Through the Hoop*. Edina, MN: Abdo Publications Co. (Sand Castle), 2002. 24 pp. Eight pairs of bonafide homophones are contained in this illustrated children's book.

_____. *We Have a Wee Whale*. Edina, MN: Abdo Publications Co. (Sand Castle), 2002. 24 pp. An illustrated children's book containing eight pairs of bonafide homophones and one pair of Group II homophones: **walk, wok**.

Sage, Michael. *If You Talked to a Boar*. Philadelphia: Lippincott, 1960. An illustrated children's book of 24 homophones. 31 pp.

Salzman, Mary Elizabeth. *My Deer Is Dear*. Edina, MN: Abdo Publications Co. (Sand Castle), 2002. 24 pp. An illustrated children's book containing eight pairs of bonafide homophones.

_____. *The Knight Waits at Night*. Edina, MN: Abdo Publications Co. (Sand Castle), 2002. 24 pp. Eight pairs of bonafide homophones, and one pair of homophones using a proper name, **knicks, Nicks,** are included in this illustrated children's book.

_____. *They're There in Their Boat*. Edina, MN: Abdo Publications Co. (Sand Castle), 2002. 24 pp. An illustrated children's book containing variations on the homophone triplet **their, there, they're**.

_____. *Where Do I Wear Water Wings?* Edina, MN: Abdo Publications Co. (Sand Castle), 2002. 24 pp. An illustrated children's book containing variations on the single pair of homophones **wear, where**.

_____. *Who's on Whose Spot?* Edina, MN: Abdo Publications Co. (Sand Castle), 2002. 24 pp. An illustrated children's book presenting the single pair of homophones **who's, whose**.

_____. *You're on Your Phone*. Edina, MN: Abdo Publications Co. (Sand Castle), 2002. 24 pp. The single pair of homophones **your, you're** are the subject of this illustrated children's book.

Schaphorst, William F. and Mabel G. Schaphorst. *A Compilation of Homophones*. Atlantic Highlands, NJ; 1976. 3 pp. Private unpublished assortment of numerous bonafide and Group I homophones.

Scheunemann, Pam. *Flour Does Not Flower*. Edina, MN: Abdo Publications Co. (Sand Castle), 2002, 24 pp. Nine pairs of homophones are contained in this illustrated children's book.

_____. *Fred Read the Red Book*. Edina, MN: Abdo Publications Co. (Sand Castle), 2002. 24 pp. An illustrated children's book containing eight pairs of homophones.

_____. *Harry Is Not Hairy*. Edina, MN: Abdo Publications Co. (Sand Castle), 2002. 24 pp. Eight pairs of homophones are contained in this illustrated children's book.

_____. *The Moose in the Mousse*. Edina, MN: Abdo Publications Co. (Sand Castle), 2002. 24 pp. An illustrated book presenting eight pairs of homophones.

_____. *Sam Has a Sundae on Sunday*. Edina, MN: Abdo Publications Co. (Sand Castle), 2002. 24 pp. Nine pairs of homophones are presented in this illustrated children's book.

_____. *Two Kids to Go Too*. Edina, MN: Abdo Publications Co. (Sand Castle), 2002. 24 pp. An illustrated children's book containing variations on the homophone triplet—to, too, two.

Schindler, M. M. *An Index of over 2,500 Homophones*. Pittsburgh: Dorrance Publishing Co., 1994. A collection of bonafide, Type I, and Type II homophones—many included by adding **ing, ed, es**, and other suffixes. 31 pp.

Schmidt, Jacob Edward. *English Speech for Foreign Physicians, Scientists, and Students.* Springfield, IL: Chas. C. Thomas, 1972. This book was designed "to knock down the barricades and widen the bottlenecks of communication between visitors and natives of the United States." A 78-page section includes approximately 890 words containing a mixture of homonyms, homophones (bona fide and Group I), homographs, and other closely associated but confusing words like **exalt/ extol/exult**. 237 pp.

Scholastic Dictionary of Synonyms, Antonyms, Homonyms. New York: Scholastic Inc., 1965. About 24 pp. of bonafide homophones (mislabeled homonyms) are reflected on pp. 197–220. 220 pp.

Scinto, Joyce. *Homonex.* Woburn, MA: Curriculum Associates, 1977. A compilation of numerous bonafide, Type I, and Type II homophones, plus several confusing words such as **candid** and **candied**. 72 pp.

Settle, Anita V. *Cued Forgetting in the False Recognition of Homophones.* Columbia: University of Missouri at Columbia, 1973. 50 pp. Two dozen bonafide homophones support the argument in this master's thesis.

Shipley, Joseph Twadell. *Playing with Words.* Englewood Cliffs, NJ: Prentice-Hall. Several homophones are reflected on pp. 73–75 and 119. 186 pp.

Sieron, Martha. *Dictionary of Confusing Words.* Miami: M. Sieron, 1986. A mixture of bonafide homophones and homographs, plus confusing words like **ablate/oblate** and **accrue/ecrue**. 431 pp.

Simpson, Carol. *Daily Writing Prompts.* Parsippany, NJ: Good Year Books, 2000. 382 pp. A children's instruction book that includes twelve bonafide homophones.

Sinclair, John (editor). *Collins COBUILD English Guides 6: Homophones.* London: Harper-Collins, 1995. 240 pp. + xv pp. A dictionary containing about 690 bonafide homophones, plus some words that are unique to Great Britain.

Sitton, Rebecca, and Robert Forest. *The Quick-Word Handbook for Practical Writing.* North Billerica, MA: Curriculum Associates, 1994. 30 pp. A children's instruction pamphlet containing 232 bonafide homophones.

Smith, Carl Bernard. *Building a Strong Vocabulary: A 12-week Plan for Students.* Bloomington, IN: EDINFO Press (ERIC—Educational Resources Information Center), 1997. 189 pp. + ix pp. Included are several bonafide homophones, together with synonyms, antonyms, suffixes, prefixes, etc.

Snow, Emma. "My List of Homophonenous [sic] Words." *The Association Review.* American Association to Promote the Teaching of Speech to the Deaf: 1903. Contains a list of homophonous words that cause frequent confusion among lip-readers, being relatively difficult to distinguish visually, such as **back, bank, bag, bang,** and **pack.**

Sommer, Elyse. *The Words You Confuse.* Holbrook, MA: Bob Adams, Inc., 1992. Includes about 16 bonafide homophones. 167 pp.

Soohoo, Irene. *Homophones: An Illustrated Dictionary.* Whittier, CA: Peacock Enterprises. An illustrated compilation of about 800 homophones, including numerous archaic, obsolete, Scottish, and English dialectic words. 176 pp.

Steadman's Medical Dictionary, 26th edition (Marjory Spraycar, editor). Baltimore: Williams and Wilkins, 1995. 2030+ pp. + xli pp.

Steere, Fran H. *Sound-Alike Words: Fun Activities with Homonyms, Homographs, and Homophones.* Englewood Cliffs, NJ: Prentice-Hall, 1977. 62 pp. A children's illustrated instruction book containing 101 bonafide homophones, but neither homographs nor homonyms.

Stephan, Gary. *Book of Nine.* New York: Museum of Modern Art, 1983. 40 pp. A beautifully although enigmatically illustrated booklet containing nine bonafide homographs.

Synonyms, Antonyms, Homophones. St. Louis, MO: McDonald Publishing, 1993. 20 pp. A children's illustrated booklet intermixing several bonafide homophones with antonyms and synonyms.

Terban, Marvin. *The Dove Dove: Funny Homophone Riddles.* New York: Clarion Books, 1988. An illustrated children's book containing several bona fide homographs. 64 pp.

_____. *Eight Ate: A Feast of Homonym Riddles.* New York: Clarion Books, 1982. An illustrated children's book containing several homonyms. 32 pp.

_____. *Funny You Should Ask: How to Make Up Jokes and Riddles with Wordplay.* New York: Clarion Books of Houghton Mifflin Co., 1992. An illustrated book of several homophones, "almost homophones," and homonyms (which are misidentified as homographs). 64 pp.

_____. *Hey, Hay! A Wagonful of Funny Homonym Riddles.* Boston: Clarion Books of Houghton Mifflin Co., 1991. An illustrated book of 214 homophones, including several proper names. 64 pp.

Tester, Sylvia Root. *Never Monkey with a Monkey: A Book of Homographic Homophones.* Elgin, IL: Child's World, 1977. An illustrated children's book containing several homonyms. 32 pp.

_____. *What Did You Say? A Book of Homophones.* Elgin, IL: Child's World, 1977. An illustrated children's book of 32 homophones. 30 pp.

Thomas, Jonathan. *English as She Is Fraught.* London: Wolfe, 1976. A collection of numerous homonyms, homophones, and double entendres—many of which are off-color or have sexual overtones. Illustrated. 95 pp.

Townsend, William Cameron. *A Handbook of Homophones of General American English.* Waxhaw, NC: International Friendship, 1975. Numerous bona fide homophones and homographs, plus closely associated words like **abase/a base**. 121 pp.

Truby, Henry Mayer. *The Homoneme: Research Paper RJ-312.* San Jose, CA: IBM San Jose Research Laboratory, 30 JUL 1964. A brief introduction to the then-current and still-remaining problem of distinguishing audibly between any two bonafide homophones, such as **hour** and **our**, other than by contextual association. 22 pp.

Tune, Newell W. *Homophones, Homographs, and Heterographs: The Deceitful Words of English.* North Hollywood, CA: Spelling Progress Bulletin, prior to 1975. 16 pp. A pamphlet containing numerous bonafide homophones and homographs, interspersed with archaic, Scottish, and British verbiage.

Valind, Brigitte, and Lars Valind. *Effects of Subliminal Stimulation on Homographs.* Lund, Sweden: Lund University, Psychological Research Bulletin, Vol. 8, No. 8, 1968. 9 pp. Seven Swedish homonyms and three English homonyms, all misclassified as homographs, are the examples used in this study.

Tyschler, Iosif Solomonovich. *Slovar' Omonimov Sovremennogo Iazya Angliiskogo (Dictionary of Contemporary English Homonyms).* Saratov, U.S.S.R.: Saratov University Press, 1963. Contains English homophones and homonyms translated into Russian. 231 pp.

Van Gelder, Rosalind. *Monkeys Have Tails.* New York: David McKay Co., 1966. An illustrated children's book containing several bona fide homophones and homonyms. 48 pp.

Waite, C. B. *Homophonic Vocabulary: Containing More Than 2,000 Words.* Chicago: C . V. Waite, 1904. Over 2,000 words that are common to nearly all Indo-European languages are included. For example **alcohol** (English, Spanish, Dutch); **alkohol** (Danish, German, Norwegian, Swedish); **alkogol'** (Russian—the **g** is a guttural **h**); and **alcool** (French, Italian, Portuguese). 162 pp.

_____, and C. V. Waite. *Homophonic Conversations: In English, German, French, and Italian.* Chicago: C. V. Waite, 1903. The principal words of almost every sentence and phrase in this book have a similar sound and meaning in at least three of the four languages selected. For example: **At what hour** (English); **À quelle heure** (French); **A che ora** (Italian); **um wieviel Uhr** (German). 137 pp.

Wallace, Viola. *Wordwise.* New York: Vantage Press, 1968. Contains approximately 1,670 "homophones," 140 "heteronyms," 730 "homographs," and 290 "accent shifts." 262 pp.

Webster's Computer Terms Dictionary ,with Guide to Office Economics, New revised edition. Hartford, CT: Lewtan Book Line, 1994. 254 pp.

Webster's Encyclopedia of Dictionaries: Twelve Complete Dictionaries in One. (John G. Allee, editor). Baltimore: Ottenheimer Publishers, 1978. A considerable number of bonafide homophones and several homonyms are reflected in the "Homonyms" section on pp. 507–514. 1246 + pp.

Webster's New International Dictionary of the English Language. Second edition unabridged. (William A. Neilson, Thomas A. Knott, and Paul W. Carhart, editors.) Springfield, MA: G & C Merriam Co., 1949. 3,210 pp.

Webster's Third New International Dictionary of the English Language Unabridged. (Philip B. Gove, editor in chief.) Springfield, MA: G & C Merriam Co., 1981. 2,765 pp.

Webster's Treasury of Synonyms, Antonyms, and Homonyms. NY: Avenel Books, 1962. A dictionary that includes numerous bonafide homophones (mislabled homonyms) on pp. 173–192. 192 pp.

Welch, Patrick E. *Mini Veri Tech Reading Lab, 1: Book 7—Homonyms, Homographs, etc.* Montreal, Canada: Brault & Bouthillier, 1978. 29 pp. An instruction booklet that contains either explicit or implicity 168 bonafide homophones, which are misclassifed as homonyms. Among the homographs are 22 bonafide homographs, four Group I homographs, and a few homonyms.

Wentworth, Harold, and Stuart Berg Flexner. *Dictionary of American Slang, 2nd Supplemented Edition*. New York: Thomas Y. Crowell Publishing, 1975. 766 pp.

White, Mary Sue. *Word Twins*. New York: Abingdon Press, 1962. An illustrated children's book of 30 homophones. 32 pp.

Whitford, Harold Crandall. *A Dictionary of American Homophones and Homographs*. New York: Teachers College Press, 1966. Contains over 800 homophones (bonafide and Group I) and approximately 220 homographs (bona fide and Group I), including proper names, foreign countries, suffixes, and 40 oral and written exercises. 83 pp.

Williams, Edna Rees. *The Conflict of Homonyms in English*. New Haven, CT: Yale University Press, 1944. Professor Williams' 1936 Yale doctoral dissertation deals with the loss or change in form or status of certain words due to their being homonyms. 127 pp. and seven maps.

Williams, Stephen N. *The Concise Dictionary of British and American Homophones*. Japan: Kenkyusha Shuyppan, 1988. 164 pp. A collection of numerous bonafide homophones, plus several words which by dropping the *r* become homophones.

_____. *The Dictionary of British and American Homophones*. London: Brookside Press, 1987. A particularly useful volume containing numerous bona fide homophones and a few homographs. 503 pp.

Wolpow, Edward R. "Humorous humerus." *Word Ways*. Vol. 14, No. 1, Feb. 1981, pp. 55 and 64.

Word Ways: Journal of Recreational Linguistics. Published quarterly at Spring Valley Road, Morristown, NJ 07960, (A. Ross Eckler, editor and publisher, 201-538-4584). This periodical frequently provides several homophones and homographs.

Zambrano, Nahora Edith Bryan. *Modern Bilingual Dictionary: Synonyms, Antonyms, and Homophones*. Colombia: Casa del Diccionario Impresores, 1995. 944 pp. An English-Spanish, Spanish-English dictionary containing numerous bonafide homophones, some rather advanced for a basic bilingual compendium.

Zorfass, Judith M. *Aspects of the Reading Process in Deaf Sign Language Users: An Example of Word Recognition and Comprehension Through the Use of Homographs*. Cambridge, MA: Graduate School of Education, Harvard University, 1983. 247 pp. Several homonyms (*not homographs*) are used to support the major thesis of this doctoral dissertation.

_____. *Knowledge and Use of Multiple Meanings for Printed Homographs by Deaf Readers*. Cambridge, MA: Graduate School of Education, Harvard University, 1981. 78 pp. The 35 homographs used throughout this qualifying paper are homonyms, *not homographs*.

Zviadadze, Givi. *Dictionary of Contemporary American English Contrasted with British English*. Atlantic Highlands, NJ: Humanities Press, 1983. Contains several bonafide homophones and homographs. 460 pp.